DISCUSSING BILINGUALISM IN DEAF CHILDREN

This collection unites expert scholars in a comprehensive survey of critical topics in bilingual deaf education. Drawing on the work of Dr. Robert Hoffmeister, chapters explore the concept that a strong first language is critical to later learning and literacy development. In thought-provoking essays, authors discuss the theoretical underpinnings of bilingual deaf education, teaching strategies for deaf students, and the unique challenges of signed language assessment. Essential for anyone looking to expand their understanding of bilingualism and deafness, this volume reflects Dr. Hoffmeister's impact on the field while demonstrating the ultimate resilience of human language and literacy systems.

Charlotte Enns is Professor in the Department of Educational Administration, Foundations and Psychology at University of Manitoba, Canada.

Jonathan Henner is Assistant Professor in the School of Education at University of North Carolina Greensboro, USA.

Lynn McQuarrie is Professor in the Department of Education Psychology at University of Alberta, Canada.

DISCUSSING BILINGUALISM IN DEAF CHILDREN

Essays in Honor of Robert Hoffmeister

Edited by Charlotte Enns, Jonathan Henner, and Lynn McQuarrie

NEW YORK AND LONDON

First published 2021
by Routledge
52 Vanderbilt Avenue, New York, NY 10017

and by Routledge
2 Park Square, Milton Park, Abingdon, Oxon, OX14 4RN

Routledge is an imprint of the Taylor & Francis Group, an informa business

© 2021 Taylor & Francis

The right of Charlotte Enns, Jonathan Henner, and Lynn McQuarrie to be
identified as the authors of the editorial material, and of the authors for
their individual chapters, has been asserted in accordance with sections 77
and 78 of the Copyright, Designs and Patents Act 1988.

All rights reserved. No part of this book may be reprinted or reproduced or
utilised in any form or by any electronic, mechanical, or other means, now
known or hereafter invented, including photocopying and recording, or in
any information storage or retrieval system, without permission in writing
from the publishers.

Trademark notice: Product or corporate names may be trademarks or
registered trademarks, and are used only for identification and explanation
without intent to infringe.

Library of Congress Cataloging-in-Publication Data
A catalog record for this title has been requested

ISBN: 978-0-367-37376-4 (hbk)
ISBN: 978-0-367-40719-3 (pbk)
ISBN: 978-0-367-80868-6 (ebk)

Typeset in Bembo
by MPS Limited, Dehradun

CONTENTS

List of contributors	*viii*
Foreword	*x*
Rachel I. Mayberry	
Preface	*xx*
Charlotte Enns, Jonathan Henner, and Lynn McQuarrie	

PART I
Seaworthy Construction: Theoretical Underpinnings
of Bilingual Deaf Education   **1**

1 Two Centuries of Deaf Education and Deaf Agency in the
United States   3
Brian H. Greenwald

2 Sign Language Acquisition in Context   17
Jenny L. Singleton and Richard P. Meier

3 Iconicity: A Threat to ASL Recognition or a Window
into Human Language Acquisition?   35
Naomi Caselli, Amy Lieberman, and Jennie Pyers

4 The Acquisition of Motion Events in Verbs of Motion   48
Frances Conlin

vi Contents

5 Sustained Visual Attention in Deaf Children: A
Deafcentric Perspective 60
Matthew Dye and Brennan Terhune-Cotter

6 Theoretical Underpinnings of Acquiring English via Print 73
Catherine L. Caldwell-Harris

PART II
Launching the Voyage: Bilingual Teaching Strategies
for Deaf Students 97

7 Revisiting Rethinking Literacy 99
Marlon Kuntze and Debbie Golos

8 How Can You Talk About Bilingual Education of the
Deaf If You Do Not Teach Sign Language as a First
Language? 113
Vassilis Kourbetis and Spyridoula Karipi

9 The Bedrock Literacy Curriculum 132
Kristin A. Di Perri

10 Crossing the Divide: The Bilingual Grammar Curriculum 150
Todd Czubek

11 The Relationship between ASL Fluency and English
Literacy 171
Jessica Scott

12 Using ASL to Navigate the Semantic Circuit in the
Bilingual Mathematics Classroom 187
Claudia M. Pagliaro and Christopher Kurz

PART III
Sailing into the Wind: Challenges of Signed
Language Assessment 197

13 Building the ASL Assessment Instrument 199
Patrick J. Costello

14 Assessing ASL Vocabulary Development 208
Rama Novogrodsky

Contents **vii**

15 Assessing ASL: Comprehension, Narrative, and
Phonological Awareness 217
Lynn McQuarrie and Charlotte Enns

16 The Legacy of Robert Hoffmeister: On the Importance of
Supporting Deaf Scholars 229
Jonathan Henner, Patrick Rosenberg, and Rachel Benedict

Index *241*

CONTRIBUTORS

Rachel Benedict, Teacher, Rocky Mountain School for the Deaf, Denver, CO

Catherine L. Caldwell-Harris, Associate Professor, Psychology and Brain Sciences, Boston University

Naomi Caselli, Assistant Professor, Programs in Deaf Studies and Deaf Education, Boston University

Frances Conlin, Instructor, Northern Essex Community College, Haverhill, MA

Patrick J. Costello, Former Director of Deaf Cultural Center, The Learning Center for the Deaf, Framingham, MA

Todd Czubek, Lecturer, Programs in Deaf Studies and Deaf Education, Boston University

Kristin A. Di Perri, Independent Literacy Consultant and Instructor, Deaf Studies, Boston University

Matthew Dye, Associate Professor, National Technical Institute for the Deaf, Sensory Perceptual and Cognitive Ecology Center, Rochester Institute of Technology

Charlotte Enns, Professor, Faculty of Education, University of Manitoba

Debbie Golos, Associate Professor, Educational Psychology, University of Minnesota

Brian H. Greenwald, Professor and Director of Schuchman Deaf Documentary Center, Gallaudet University

Contributors **ix**

Jonathan Henner, Assistant Professor, School of Education, University of North Carolina at Greensboro

Spyridoula Karipi, Head of Special Kindergarten for the Deaf & Hard-of-Hearing of Argyroupoli and University of Western Macedonia, Greece

Vassilis Kourbetis, Senior Counselor of Special Education, Ministry of Education, Greece

Marlon Kuntze, Professor, Government and Public Affairs, Gallaudet University

Christopher Kurz, Professor, National Technical Institute for the Deaf, Rochester Institute of Technology

Amy Lieberman, Assistant Professor, Programs in Deaf Studies and Deaf Education, Boston University

Rachel I. Mayberry, Professor, Department of Linguistics, University of California San Diego

Lynn McQuarrie, Professor, Faculty of Education, University of Alberta

Richard P. Meier, Professor, Department of Linguistics, University of Texas at Austin

Rama Novogrodsky, Senior Lecturer, University of Haifa

Claudia M. Pagliaro, Professor, School of Education, University of North Carolina at Greensboro

Jennie Pyers, Professor, Psychology, Wellesley College

Patrick Rosenberg, Teacher and Adjunct, Heathlands School for the Deaf and Northeastern University, London, UK

Jessica Scott, Assistant Professor, Program Coordinator Deaf Education, College of Education and Human Development, Georgia State University

Jenny L. Singleton, Professor, Department of Linguistics, University of Texas at Austin

Brennan Terhune-Cotter, Joint Doctoral Program in Language and Communication Disorders, San Diego State University and University of California, San Diego

FOREWORD: THE RADICAL IDEA THAT ASL IS LANGUAGE

The Linguistic Bulwark of Professor Robert Hoffmeister's Vision

Rachel I. Mayberry

The Boston University Conference on Child Language Development (BUCLD) has been my go-to research meeting since the beginning of my career because sign language research of some sort is always being presented and discussed there. This was true long before the topic appeared at other conferences, aside from the Linguistics Society of America, and long before it became a hot topic in the evolution of language (Evolang13, 2019). I am deeply grateful to BUCLD for organizing their annual research forum over the years. I am also grateful to BUCLD for introducing me to Professor Robert Hoffmeister. When we first met, I knew his name and something of his reputation. I even called him up out of the blue one day (this was before email) to seek his advice when a sudden fork appeared in the path of my career. The man standing at the back of the room quizzing me about a positive correlation between ASL and reading comprehension didn't look familiar. I could see that he was tall, but I couldn't quite make out his face from the podium because my contact lenses were underpowered that year. I don't remember the specific questions he asked at my talk, but I do remember that our discussion afterward lasted so long that I missed the following session entirely. I also remember that his initial questioning of my research had the air of deep skepticism, the thought-provoking kind.

Once we figured out that we were on the same theoretical page, our sporadic conversations have remained on the longish side over the years. That might be due to the fact that we were both exposed early in our careers to the destructive educational ideology that language comes only out of the mouth and into the ears. One psychology text explained that if children couldn't hear, that this one missing sense led to disordered thinking because intelligent thought was possible only with language, which required auditory functioning to clear the path for speech. Knock out hearing and intelligent thought comes tumbling down like a house of cards (Myklebust, 1964). There was a less popular theory that sign language was not language, for heaven sakes, but no worries. Deaf school children can perform well on Piagetian tasks. The interpretation was obvious. Deaf children can reason and, hey, they don't even need language to do it (Furth, 1966). All that hand waving going on in classrooms was deaf children trying to get their teachers' attention. Bob was one of the few people who listened and acted. But to appreciate his vast array of accomplishments, it's important to understand what the educational zeitgeist was when Bob started his career.

When Bob began graduate school, the educational practice of actively discouraging sign language from making the slightest appearance in classrooms for deaf children was in full display. Over the course of Bob's trailblazing career, the theoretical and clinical rationales for barring ASL from the classrooms of deaf children have shifted in waves gnashing against his boat docked in the safe harbor of home. What is most remarkable about Professor Robert Hoffmeister's academic career is that he was so prescient in his radical idea that ASL is language, an idea he grasped the implications of well before the day he first stepped foot in a classroom to teach deaf children.

Bob was originally an engineering major. Fortunately for us all these decades later, he ran out of money. This forced him to take a job teaching sign language to a group of 80 intellectually disabled institutionalized individuals from the ages of 7 to 65. While engineering didn't exactly prepare him for a job teaching sign language, being the son of two deaf teachers of deaf children probably made him the most qualified of the applicants on the University of Connecticut campus. It was here that he took an undergraduate course called *Thinking* that changed his life. Reading Chomsky (1965), Bob encountered the radical idea that all children possess the propensity to learn language. Why would this be such a radical idea, and for Bob of all people? The background for this idea arose from the many times Bob over-heard and over-saw heated arguments about classroom language and employment equity. The arguments were about the policy that deaf children only prosper when not allowed to see or use sign language when young. The people making these arguments were the educated deaf staff of a residential school for deaf children, most of whom were not allowed to teach academic subjects to the younger students because they either couldn't or preferred not to speak. Navigating a childhood with one foot in the Deaf community of a residential campus overflowing with righteous indignation that ASL was banned from many classrooms and the other foot in the hearing English community surrounding the campus is a fascinating story, one that is Bob's to tell.

When I interviewed him for this foreword, he said I could mention that during his first year of graduate studies at the University of Minnesota, his advisor sent him to the American School for the Deaf[1] to teach for a year with his dad. Bob, being the hearing teacher, was assigned to teach social studies to the elementary students using "simcom" because the classroom was in a school that embraced a "Total Communication" policy. Bob had to speak in English at all times while

xii Foreword

simultaneously signing and trying to teach the little ones social science. His dad, the deaf teacher, taught math in ASL on the third floor to the middle school students. For most of his tenure at the school, Bob's father was relegated to the teaching of printing skills in the vocational courses for the high school boys not headed to college event though he had an advanced math degree. There is an irony to the historical fact that the male graduates of residential schools for deaf children manned the printing presses of many major newspapers across the country. The irony is that these deaf high school graduates worked with written words all day long when one motivation for the educational policy of withholding sign language from them when they were young was to ensure that the sensory form of the words in their heads was of the right kind. Hold that thought because it will be important later.

The language that Bob and his dad were mandated to use in their classrooms embodied the educational zeitgeist of the time. First, there was the age dimension: younger children were spoken to in English with some version of sign support, while the older school children were signed to in ASL. Then there is the hearing/deaf dimension. The younger children got the hearing speaking teacher while older children got the deaf signing one. This set up only works if the younger children successfully develop spoken English because they certainly wouldn't have been able to understand much of the ASL math lessons when they were older if they hadn't developed functional language by the time they'd aged into middle-schoolers (Mayberry & Kluender, 2018). The attempt to steer the early language environment away from ASL when deaf children are young but let it drift back when they are older is what language policy in classrooms for deaf children looked like when Bob decided to step into the fray. The following quote from a special committee report to the US Department of Education memorializes this policy:

> This Committee, recognizing that it cannot resolve a question that has been a lively one for the past hundred years in this country ... has therefore arrived at this consensus: A clear difference is recognized between primary reliance on a restrictive means of communication in the educational process and such reliance in later life. It is generally agreed that primary emphasis should be placed on teaching speech and speechreading to young deaf children. The Committee does not rule out the employment of finger spelling as an adjunct to oral methods in language teaching if the combination proves more effective, since the symbol system of the spoken and written language is retained. In order to encourage keeping open as wide a range of subsequent choices as possible for deaf young people, the Committee urges that educators of the deaf continue to place emphasis on oral methods, but that manual methods be employed in individual cases when it is clear beyond a reasonable doubt that success by oral methods is unlikely (Babbidge, 1965, pp. xxvii–iii).

The fields of deaf education and sign language research owe Professor Hoffmeister an enormous debt of gratitude for his tenaciously faithful promulgation of his radical idea: ASL is language. This linguistic bulwark undergirds his logical framework of how language in deaf children's classrooms affects their development. Bob came to this framework in several ways. One avenue came from his erudite upbringing, with Deaf adults discussing ASL in his family living room where the deaf staff of the school would often congregate. Another route to his framework came from seeing how quickly deaf students could learn scouting through ASL. Bob concluded that the work of the classroom needs to be done in real language. Real language is the most efficient vehicle for learning. ASL is language. This was and is Bob's logical framework.

Around the time he decided to attend graduate school, psychiatrists and psychologists were openly questioning the wisdom of banishing sign language from the classroom (Mindel, 1974; Vernon & Koh, 1971). Bob's initial approach was to study ASL acquisition in natural circumstances, recording and analyzing the ASL of young deaf children of deaf parents (Hoffmeister, 1977; Hoffmeister & Moores, 1975; Hoffmeister & Wilbur, 1980). Asked to establish an ASL program at Temple University, Bob created the first such program to be fully staffed by Deaf ASL teachers. When Bob moved to Boston University to establish the first undergraduate and graduate programs in Deaf Studies, he collaborated with his colleagues the late Harlan Lane and former student Ben Bahan to write *A Journey in the Deaf World* (1996), describing American Deaf culture from multiple vantage points, the Deaf adult, the CODA, and the researcher. Portions of this book were required reading in a large linguistics undergraduate course when I arrived at UCSD.

The popularity of Total Communication (TC) as an educational policy where teachers speak while signing could be seen as a positive step in a transition to bring ASL into the classrooms for deaf students by helping hearing teachers become comfortable with the concept and act of signing and helping them gain proficiency by hooking signing into their knowledge of English. This would seem to satisfy both the guidelines to present spoken English to young children and to add lexical cues from ASL to supplement English meaning for those students who need it. But Bob saw the situation differently from his logical framework. He believes that a menu of communicative options, such as a little bit of speechreading, mixed with some gesture and ASL signs and a bit of fingerspelling sprinkled on top, impedes language development. This mashup is not language in his view. Each natural language has its own internal logic, known as its grammar, but all languages also share large swaths of semantic and syntactic, mental and neural networks that are developed in early childhood. This is how language creates the vehicle necessary for so much of the learning that takes place in the classroom.

To Bob, the TC craze marked a time when educators were wandering in the dark. There was no systematic study of the sign language of deaf students, and

xiv Foreword

sign language research was just getting off the ground. He tells the story of teachers of deaf students pointing to a particular student's communicative attempt and labeling it as being ASL. They didn't understand it, so it must be ASL. But Bob could easily see that what the student was saying was gibberish. He believes that you can only help students with gaps in their language if you know and use the language to figure out what those gaps are and how to mend them. I too have had the experience of being asked to look at the sign language of a student. Her teachers and parents assumed they couldn't understand her because she was "using ASL." But her signing was non-sensical and actually aphasic as later confirmed by brain scans showing damage to the language network. But trained professionals in deaf education thought she was using ASL because they couldn't understand her. No one concerned with the education and welfare of children born deaf can think that this lack of understanding of deaf children's language is okay, Bob certainly didn't.

To be sure, the ability to analyze the language of deaf children requires an appreciation of the linguistic structure of ASL. Fortunately, an explosion of research into the structure of sign languages burst onto the scene just in time to help Bob come up with some linguistic tools to train teachers on how to use ASL in the classroom. The accumulating discoveries that ASL signs had sublexical structure (Liddell, 1984; Stokoe, Casterline, & Croneberg, 1976/1965); ASL utterances had syntax and morphology (Klima & Bellugi, 1979); the brain language system does not distinguish signed from spoken language (Poizner, Klima, & Bellugi, 1987); and that the ASL mental lexicon is organized like the spoken one (Mayberry & Wille, 2021). All these discoveries help explain why the attempt to yank signs out of ASL utterances and shove them into signed ones with spoken English was as misguided as it was well intentioned (Marmor & Petitto, 1979).

The pieces, or structures, of language grammar are intricately interwoven. Knowing a language means knowing how to create new words, phrases, and sentences; what comes next; and how to know that you've missed something or don't understand. Bob was convinced that successful classrooms for deaf children needed to be grounded in their teachers' ASL proficiency and the meta-linguistic understanding that comes from learning and studying a language. Bob fought with the university administration to establish an ASL language program staffed by ASL signers who were deaf. This move allowed him to create a systematic curriculum for undergraduate and graduate students, where they could learn ASL as a second language while, in other courses, they studied the structure of ASL and its development. ASL programs are now widely populated on college campuses across the nation, but, for Bob, this represented just the first step in his curricular vision for teacher education. The second step was creating a graduate program curriculum to train teachers to be able to implement the use of two natural languages in the classroom, ASL and English, based on curricula created for hearing students' learning of two languages through dual language instruction

(Hoffmeister, 2004; Humphries, 2013; Kourbetis, Hoffmeister, & Simpsa, 2004; Nover & Andrews, 1999).[2] Over 300 undergraduate and graduate students have gone through Bob's programs. Talk about the successful real-world implementation of a radical idea!

The policy arguments against ASL in the classroom have swayed over time from total banishment to asking how a language with morpho-syntax not identical to that of English could help deaf children learn to read. As Bob would say, language is language actually, and knowing the structure of one can help you learn the structure of another. This is why multiple studies find strong correlations between ASL proficiency and English literacy (Andrew, Hoshooley, & Joanisse, 2014; Chamberlain & Mayberry, 2008; Hoffmeister, 2000; Scott & Hoffmeister, 2017; Strong & Prinz, 1997). When the arguments zoomed in on a possible sensory roadblock to learning to read words, research again stepped in to fill the void.

Remember the story of the deaf high school boys to whom Bob's dad taught typesetting skills? From today's vantage point, we can surmise that the deaf typesetters at major newspapers would have been better at the job than the hearing typesetters. We can infer this because research has found that deaf children are less prone to spelling errors arising from spelling-sound conflicts between how words are pronounced on how they are spelled. Deaf elementary school children educated strictly in oral-only methods who neither know nor use any sign language are not sensitive to the spelling-sound patterns of English (Seidenberg, 2017; Waters & Doehring, 1990). This means that knowing sign language is not the reason why deaf readers have mental forms in their heads that are only weakly related to sound. Adults born deaf read French words without recourse to spelling-sound mappings (Bélanger, Baum, & Mayberry, 2012). Across studies, the ability to associate sound with spelling has only small effects on deaf children's reading achievement (Mayberry, Del Guidicie, & Lieberman, 2011). ASL signing adults and children have wider visual-perceptual spans when reading English words than their hearing peers, meaning that they can see more letters ahead as they are reading a line of text, maybe because they are unencumbered by sound (Bélanger et al., 2012; Bélanger, Lee, & Schotter, 2017; Bélanger, Mayberry, & Rayner, 2013).

If ASL can't be banned from the classroom because a familiarity with sound is not necessary to learn to read, then what about the argument that ASL can impede reading development because it has a different morpho-syntactic structure than that of English? According to the radical idea that ASL is language, and that sublexical structure is sublexical structure, researchers have discovered that reading words activates their meanings and sublexical structures across the languages that are in their heads, that is, all the languages that they know. This happens for ASL signers reading English words, and DGS signers reading German words (Kubus, Villwock, Morford, & Rathmann, 2014; Morford, Occhino-Kehoe, Pinar, Wilkinson, & Kroll, 2017). Bob and his

xvi Foreword

team developed ASL curricula designed to foster meta-linguistic awareness of sign structure in elementary school children. But if ASL is going to be successfully used in all classrooms, then STEM (Science, Technology, Engineering, and Mathematics) signs in ASL need to have consistent lexical forms across the diverse classrooms using them. Understanding the principles of word formation in ASL allows signers to create new lexical items from old ones in a linguistic fashion faithful to STEM terminology and the sublexical structure of ASL, which is just what Bob and his research team did (Reis, Solovey, Henner, Johnson, & Hoffmeister, 2015).

The third part of Bob's vision came to fruition after countless years of brain-numbing work. According to Bob, not only must teachers of deaf children be able to use ASL to teach and be able to comprehend what the students' ASL expressions are telling them about how they are learning, but schools also need assessment tools to help them figure out the landscape of their students' ASL abilities in relation to their age and backgrounds (Schick, De Villiers, De Villiers, & Hoffmeister, 2007). Bob and his team of talented ASL signers edited and expanded an ASL assessment tool that Bob had been working on over the years for his research program and the undergraduate and graduate ASL and teacher training programs at BU. Again, fighting for the financial resources needed to launch the project, Bob and his team have created an online ASL assessment tool and have tested nearly 700 students in classrooms for deaf children across the United States. This remarkable achievement has netted the largest ASL proficiency data set available to date and is yielding unparalleled insights into the development of ASL by deaf students in classrooms across the nation (Henner, Caldwell-Harris, Novogrodsky, & Hoffmeister, 2016; Novogrodsky, Caldwell-Harris, Fish, & Hoffmeister, 2014; Novogrodsky, Fish, & Hoffmeister, 2013; Scott & Hoffmeister, 2017).

Professor Robert Hoffmeister's academic career has been driven by the radical idea that ASL is language. Not only was his insight prescient for such a young man wandering in a wilderness bereft of knowledge about ASL, but it guided him like the North Star going against the educational tide to create classrooms for deaf children that are rich with ASL learning nourishing their minds no matter their age. When asked what he envisions for the future of his radical idea, Bob stands firm, naturally, on his belief that we need to train teachers who are able to use ASL to foster deaf children's learning and who can translate research into educational practice. Progress in the educational domain, he also emphasizes, will be driven by progress in the research domain as well. I am certain that I am not alone in being especially grateful to Professor Hoffmeister for his insights into the nature of ASL and his courage and perseverance throughout his long and illustrious career to give life to his radical idea.

Notes

1 The American School for the Deaf in Hartford, Connecticut is one of the oldest in the United States, established in 1817 (Van Cleve & Crouch, 2002).
2 See also Tang, Yiu, and Lam (2015).

References

Andrew, K. N., Hoshooley, J., & Joanisse, M. F. (2014). Sign language ability in young deaf signers predicts comprehension of written sentences in English. *Plos One*, *9*(2), e89994. doi:10.1371/journal.pone.0089994

Babbidge, H. D., and others. (1965). *Education of the Deaf: A report to the Secretary of Health, Education, and WelfareED014188.pdf*. Washington DC: ERIC.

Bélanger, N. N., Baum, S. R., & Mayberry, R. I. (2012). Reading difficulties in adult deaf readers of French: Phonological codes, not guilty! *Scientific Studies of Reading*, *16*(3), 263-285. doi:10.1080/10888438.2011.568555

Bélanger, N. N., Lee, M., & Schotter, E. R. (2017). Young skilled deaf readers have an enhanced perceptual span in reading. *Q J Exp Psychol (Hove)*, 1-34. doi:10.1080/17470218.2017.1324498

Bélanger, N. N., Mayberry, R. I., & Rayner, K. (2013). Orthographic and phonological preview benefits: parafoveal processing in skilled and less-skilled deaf readers. *Q J Exp Psychol (Hove)*, *66*(11), 2237-2252. doi:10.1080/17470218.2013.780085

Chamberlain, C., & Mayberry, R. I. (2008). ASL syntactic and narrative comprehension in skilled and less skilled adult readers: Bilingual-bimodal evidence for the linguistic basis of reading. *Applied Psycholinguistics*, *28*(3), 537-549.

Chomsky, N. (1965). *Aspects of the Theory of Syntax*. Cambridge: M.I.T. Press.

Evolang13. (2019). *The Evolution of Language: Proceedings of the 13th International Conference (Evolang13)*, Brussels.

Furth, H. G. (1966). *Thinking Without Language: Psychological implications of deafness*. New York: The Free Press.

Henner, J., Caldwell-Harris, C. L., Novogrodsky, R., & Hoffmeister, R. (2016). American Sign Language syntax and analogical reasoning skills are influenced by early acquisition and age of entry to signing schools for the deaf. *Front Psychol*, 7. doi:10.3389/fpsyg.2016.01982

Hoffmeister, R. (1977). Analysis of possession in deaf children of deaf parents. *Research, Development, and Demonstration Center in Education of Handicapped Children Research Report #108*, University of Minnesota, Minneapolis.

Hoffmeister, R. (2000). A piece of the puzzle: ASL and reading comprehension in Deaf children. In C. Chamberlain, J. Morford, & R. Mayberry (Eds.), *Language acquisition by eye*. Mahwah, N.J.: Lawrence Erlbaum Associates.

Hoffmeister, R. (2004). Including deaf people as part of the learning process in families with deaf children. In L. Clara (Ed.), *Educating Deaf Children in Portugal*. Lisbon: Educational Press.

Hoffmeister, R., & Moores, D. (1975). Some procedural guidelines for the study of the acquisition of Sign Language. *Journal of Sign Language Studies*, *0*(7), 121-137.

Hoffmeister, R., & Wilbur, R. B. (1980). The acquisition of American Sign Language: A review. In H. Lane & F. Grosejan (Eds.), *Current Perspectives on Sign Language*. NJ: Lawrence Erlbaum.

xviii Foreword

Humphries, T. (2013). Schooling in American Sign Language: A paradigm shift from a deficit model to a bilingual model in deaf education. *Berkeley Review of Education, 4.* doi:10.5070/b84110031

Klima, E., & Bellugi, U. (1979). *The Signs of Language.* Cambridge: Harvard University Press.

Kourbetis, V., Hoffmeister, R., & Simpsa, T. (2004). *Curriculum of Greek Sign Language as a first language of deaf students.* Paper presented at the Proceedings of the 4th Pan-Hellenic Congress, "Greek Pedagogic and Educational Research", Alexandroupoli.

Kubus, O., Villwock, A., Morford, J. P., & Rathmann, C. (2014). Word recognition in deaf readers: Cross-language activation of German Sign Language and German. *Applied Psycholinguistics, 36*(4), 831-854. doi:10.1017/s0142716413000520

Lane, H., Bahan, B., & Hoffmeister, R. (1996). *A Journey into the Deaf World.* San Diego: Dawn Sign Press.

Liddell, S. K. (1984). Think and believe: Sequentiality in American Sign Language. *Language, 60*(2), 372-399. doi:Doi 10.2307/413645

Marmor, G. S., & Petitto, L. A. (1979). Simultaneous communication in the classroom: How well is English grammar represented. *Sign Language Studies, 23,* 99-136.

Mayberry, R. I., Del Guidicie, A. A., & Lieberman, A. M. (2011). Reading achievement in relation to phonological awareness in deaf readers: A meta-analysis. *Journal of Deaf Studies and Deaf Education, 16*(2), 164-188.

Mayberry, R. I., & Kluender, R. (2018). Rethinking the critical period for language: New insights into an old question from American Sign Language. *Bilingualism: Language and Cognition, 21*(5), 886-905. doi:10.1017/s1366728917000724

Mayberry, R. I., & Wille, B. (2021). Lexical representation and access in sign languages. In L. Gleitman, A. Papafragou, & J. Trueswell (Eds.), *The Oxford Handbook of the Mental Lexicon.* London: Oxford University Press.

Mindel, E. D. (1974). Deaf education: A child psychiatrist's view. *Peabody Journal of Education, 51*(3), 153-161. doi:10.1080/01619567409558519

Morford, J. P., Occhino-Kehoe, C., Pinar, P., Wilkinson, E., & Kroll, J. F. (2017). The time course of cross-language activation in deaf ASL-English bilinguals. *Biling (Camb Engl), 20*(2), 337-350. doi:10.1017/S136672891500067X

Myklebust, H. R. (1964). *The Psychology of Deafness: Sensory Deprivation, Learning, and Adjustment* (Second ed.). New York: Grune & Stratton.

Nover, S. M., & Andrews, J. F. (1999). *Critical pedagogy in deaf education: Bilingual methodology and staff development.* Washington D.C.

Novogrodsky, R., Caldwell-Harris, C. L., Fish, S., & Hoffmeister, R. (2014). The development of antonyms knowledge in American Sign Language (ASL) and its relationship to reading comprehension in English language learning. *Language Learning, 64*(4), 749-770.

Novogrodsky, R., Fish, S., & Hoffmeister, R. (2013). The acquisition of synonyms in American Sign Language (ASL): A further understanding of the components of ASL vocabulary knowledge. *Sign Language Studies, 14*(2).

Poizner, H., Klima, E., & Bellugi, U. (1987). *What the Hands Reveal about the Brain.* Cambridge: MIT Press.

Reis, J., Solovey, E. T., Henner, J., Johnson, K., & Hoffmeister, R. (2015). *ASL CLeaR: STEM education tools for deaf students.* Paper presented at the 17th International ACM SIGACCESS Conference on Computers & Accessibility.

Schick, B., De Villiers, P., De Villiers, J., & Hoffmeister, R. (2007). Language and theory of mind: A study of deaf children. *Child Development, 78*(2), 376-396. doi:10.1111/j.1467-8624.2007.01004.x

Scott, J. A., & Hoffmeister, R. J. (2017). American Sign Language and academic English: Factors influencing the reading of bilingual secondary school deaf and hard of hearing students. *Journal of Deaf Studies and Deaf Education, 22*(1), 59-71. doi:10.1093/deafed/enw065

Seidenberg, M. S. (2017). *Language at the Speed of Sight: How We Read, Why So Many Can't, and What Can be Done About It.* New York: Basic Books.

Stokoe, W. C., Casterline, D. C., & Croneberg, C. G. (1976/1965). *A Dictionary of American Sign Language on Linguistic Principles.* Silver Spring, MD: Linstok Press.

Strong, M., & Prinz, P. M. (1997). A study of the relationship between American Sign Language and English Literacy. *Journal of Deaf Studies and Deaf Education, 2*(1), 37-46.

Tang, G., Yiu, C. K.-M., & Lam, S. (2015). Awareness of Hong Kong Sign Language and Manually Coded Chinese by Deaf students learning in a sign bilingual and co-enrollment setting. In H. Knoors & M. Marschark (Eds.), *Educating Deaf Learners* (pp. 117-121). New York: Oxford.

Van Cleve, J. V., & Crouch, B. A. (2002). *A Place of Their Own: Creating the Deaf Community in America.* Washington D.C.: Gallaudet University Press.

Vernon, M., & Koh, S. D. (1971). Effects of oral preschool compared to early manual communication on education and communication in deaf children. *American Annals of the Deaf, 116*(6), 569-574.

Waters, G., & Doehring, D. (1990). The nature and role of phonological information in reading acquisition: Insights from congenitally deaf children who communicate orally. In T. Carr & B. Levy (Eds.), *Reading and Its Development: Component skills approaches*: psycnet.apa.org.

PREFACE

Charlotte Enns, Jonathan Henner, and Lynn McQuarrie

We have thoroughly enjoyed this project – compiling a Festschrift in honor of our mentor, guide, and critical friend, Dr. Robert Hoffmeister, or as most people know him, Bob. The process has given us the opportunity to connect with new and familiar colleagues and to learn more about Bob's work, and even more so, to understand the far-reaching impact of his work. The book was initiated as a tribute, but the result is a state-of-the-art resource for educators and researchers in the field of bilingual deaf education.

The collection is organized into three sections, which we named with sailing terms, to honor one of Bob's favorite activities. *Part 1: Seaworthy Construction* includes six chapters that outline the theoretical underpinnings of bilingualism in deaf children. In the first chapter **Brian H. Greenwald** provides a history of deaf education in the United States, with a particular emphasis on the origin and trajectory of American Sign Language (ASL) and how it has shaped, and been shaped, by Deaf communities. A key premise of bilingual deaf education is the requirement of a solid first language foundation for successful academic and social outcomes. The remaining chapters in this section address this premise in various ways. The acquisition of ASL is the focus of chapter two where **Jenny L. Singleton** and **Richard P. Meier** outline the importance of context and the variations that can occur in this process. The criticism of signed languages as lacking abstraction and consisting of iconic gestures is addressed by **Naomi Caselli**, **Amy Lieberman**, and **Jennie Pyers** in chapter three, as well as the role that iconicity plays in language acquisition. In chapter four, **Frances Conlin** discusses the acquisition of a unique aspect of signed languages, verbs of motion, and the insights this knowledge provides to improve the overall understanding of language, whether spoken, signed, or written. In addition to ASL acquisition, deaf bilingual education involves specific visual abilities and acquiring English via print for many deaf children. In the final two chapters of this section,

Preface **xxi**

Matthew Dye and **Brennan Terhune-Cotter** examine the development of visual functioning in deaf children, and **Catherine L. Caldwell-Harris** thoroughly outlines the theoretical underpinnings of language acquisition via print. They both conclude with the assertion, which is in keeping with the overall theme of this first section, that a strong first language foundation supports cognitive growth and subsequent academic outcomes.

If *Part 1* focuses on the underpinnings and construction of the vessel, then *Part 2: Launching the Voyage* takes that vessel out to sea. Here cutting-edge and effective bilingual teaching strategies and materials are shared and described. The section begins with **Marlon Kuntze** and **Debbie Golos** revisiting the components that contribute to literacy development in deaf children from a visually-based perspective. In chapter eight, **Vassilis Kourbetis** and **Spyridoula Karipi** extend the theoretical aspects of bilingual deaf education and outline specific online and interactive materials for teaching Greek Sign Language and Modern Greek via print. Curricular materials are also the focus of chapters nine and ten, with **Kristin A. Di Perri** outlining the Bedrock Literacy Curriculum and **Todd Czubek** presenting the key concepts of the Bilingual Grammar Curriculum. In chapter 11, **Jessica Scott** examines the evidence that supports the relationship between ASL fluency and English literacy, emphasizing the effectiveness of curricular approaches linking signed and written languages. In the final chapter in this section, **Claudia M. Pagliaro** and **Christopher Kurz** move beyond language arts and examine teaching mathematics in a bilingual deaf education classroom. Throughout this section, it is clear that effective teaching strategies and materials, which were once significantly lacking, do exist and are available for educators in the area of deaf bilingual education.

Part 3: Sailing into the Wind is focused on ASL assessment. This is the area where Bob made his most important contributions, but also where he, and many other researchers, have faced significant challenges. In chapter 13, **Patrick J. Costello** provides a retrospective of the beginnings of the *ASL Assessment Instrument (ASLAI)*, Bob's dream and the challenges that were involved in making it a reality. **Rama Novogrodsky** addresses the specific challenges of vocabulary assessment in ASL in chapter 14, which is a key feature of the *ASLAI*. ASL assessment measures, not part of the *ASLAI* but inspired by Bob and his team, are discussed by **Lynn McQuarrie** and **Charlotte Enns** in chapter 15. This section, and the book, concludes with a tribute by **Jonathan Henner, Patrick Rosenberg**, and **Rachel Benedict**, demonstrating and describing Bob's most important legacy – the pipeline he built for strengthening deaf leaders and scholars.

It is clear, from the scholarship presented in this volume, that Bob inspired critical thinkers, rigorous researchers, and conscientious educators. What might not be as clear is that through this process he also generated many friends. His quick wit, unwavering support, and generosity of time and heart have truly inspired and nurtured us all. We are so grateful for Bob's dedication to deaf people and hope that through this book his gift will continue to inspire researchers and educators to improve education for deaf children.

PART I

Seaworthy Construction

Theoretical Underpinnings of Bilingual Deaf Education

1

TWO CENTURIES OF DEAF EDUCATION AND DEAF AGENCY IN THE UNITED STATES

Brian H. Greenwald

Each Deaf person, myself included, is part of the continuum of Deaf history. We are influenced in ways by the generations of Deaf people who came before us. This chapter is an effort to summarize the history of Deaf life in the United States to provide something of a frame for the chapters that follow in this book. It is exceedingly difficult to distill such a complex story over two centuries. Below are threads that are merely a start to the topic, and it is my hope that this will be of value in considering how we got to this particular moment in history.[1]

The Grand Narrative

The grand narrative in American Deaf history typically recounts the fundraising prowess of Dr. Mason Fitch Cogswell and the subsequent transatlantic journey of Reverend Thomas Hopkins Gallaudet. Gallaudet first traveled from America to France, then returned to America with French master teacher Laurent Clerc to form the first permanent school for deaf students in Connecticut. Mason Fitch Cogswell was a prominent citizen in Hartford and well connected with successful Connecticut luminaries, including Daniel Wadsworth, Nathaniel Terry, Henry Hudson, John Caldwell, and Daniel Buck. Daniel Buck, for example, profited off the trade and sale of rum, molasses, and cotton produced by slave labor. Buck would go on to found an insurance company in Hartford, the predecessor of The Hartford (Sayres, 2017). Cogswell tapped into wealthy Hartford men and women, including Lydia Sigorney, who made their fortunes in banking, insurance, and the slave trade and raised money via subscriptions to fund the trip to Europe.

The grand narrative continues that Gallaudet, while in England, was rebuffed at the Braidwood Academy, as the school's founders sought to protect their pedagogy techniques which favored speaking and lipreading. They had wanted to

4 Brian H. Greenwald

keep their methods a proprietary secret, which would not have worked for Gallaudet since his chief aim was to bring a mechanism of teaching deaf children to the United States. That pushed Gallaudet from the United Kingdom toward Paris and a meeting with the Abbe Roch-Ambroise Sicard. Abbe Sicard worked under the Abbe de L'Epee at the Institut National de Jeunes Sourdes de Paris (at St. Jacques), where Gallaudet met star pupil and model teacher Laurent Clerc.

Clerc was ensconced at the Paris school, working in a familiar environment when Gallaudet asked him to uproot his work and community ties to relocate to an unfamiliar environment in the United States in the midst of the War of 1812. The agreement, bound by Gallaudet's promise, was that all expenses would be paid should Clerc decide to return to his native France. That never came to pass, however, as Clerc married a deaf woman and raised two children in the United States. On the Mary Augusta ship, the narrative continues with Clerc teaching Gallaudet French Sign Language and Gallaudet teaching Clerc written English. Clerc agreed to relocate to Hartford, Connecticut, essentially on a guarded leap of faith.

A gifted teacher, Clerc also established himself as a shrewd negotiator in his contract signed in Paris, France, on June 13, 1816, shortly after the end of the War of 1812. Clerc agreed to a three-year contract before a school was even founded in America. Gallaudet would cover all of Clerc's relocation expenses – transportation, lodging, meals, washing clothes – from France to the United States. Arriving at Hartford, Clerc was furnished with an apartment, and his laundry, lights, and wood for fire were supplied. He would eat with Thomas Gallaudet daily. In exchange for his work, Clerc was compensated 2,500 francs annually, paid in quarterly installments. Had Clerc decided to return to his native France, a separation package required Gallaudet to pay 1,500 francs in addition to all relocation expenses (*American Annals of the Deaf,* 1879).

Laurent Clerc was to teach six hours per weekday, three hours on Saturday, and was exempt from teaching on Sundays and all other holidays. The content areas were specified: grammar, language, arithmetic, the "globe', geography, and history. Clerc, a Roman Catholic, was not obligated to offer religious teachings that contradicted with Catholicism. Gallaudet would assume other teachings, "which may not be in accordance with this faith" (*American Annals of the Deaf,* 1879, p.117). Religious instruction remained prevalent in residential schools for more than a century.

Residential schools served as a cornerstone of the American Deaf community ever since the founding of the Connecticut Asylum for the Deaf-Mutes and Dumb (later American School for the Deaf (ASD)) in Hartford in 1817. Located on lands provided by state governments, residential schools created that critical mass of deaf students using sign language, and contributed to the rise and growth of the Deaf community in America. Starting with this first permanent school for deaf students in the United States, language passed from teacher to student, one generation to the next in hallways and classrooms. The majority of deaf students came from hearing families, so they acquired sign language at the residential schools and not at home. Thus, language, along with traditions and values, were transmitted from cohort to cohort over the years.

Thomas Hopkins Gallaudet and the Second Great Awakening

Working within the context of the Second Great Awakening, a Protestant religious revival that began in the north and swept throughout the south, Gallaudet developed educational and salvation plans for students enrolled at the ASD. Ministers in the Second Great Awakening led by Lyman Beecher, Henry Ward Beecher, and Charles Grandison Finney worked in Rochester and other locations in upstate New York before the movement spread to New England, and the South. The current reached Hartford and swept Reverend Thomas Hopkins Gallaudet into this movement, and he, like other ministers, pushed for closer, more direct access to God. Direct access to God, Gallaudet believed, lay in the salvation of deaf students through sign language. God, as the omnipresent being, could understand the natural language of signs. Gallaudet's ministry was tinged with paternalism, claiming older deaf students at ASD as childlike. The average age of ASD students at the time of admission was 18 years old, nearly adults. As a result, some students procured alcohol in Hartford, caused some property damage, and suspicious conversations occurred between male and female students at the school. Gallaudet struggled to impose discipline, and, therefore, he suggested raising the age of admission to over 20 years, along with some knowledge of writing, fingerspelling, and demonstration of the ability for self-discipline and sitting in a classroom (Sayres, 2017).

With Gallaudet as the Principal of ASD, hearing faculty maintained tight control on academic matters. An exception was made for a single deaf person, Laurent Clerc. Clerc not only commanded the highest salary but also retained voting privileges denied to other deaf faculty at ASD. It is not known to what extent Clerc argued for expanding voting rights to all deaf faculty. After Clerc's initial term expired, he took temporary leave to influence the inception of other schools in the United States emphasizing sign language in the curriculum. Students often learned from deaf teachers. Deaf teachers routinely earned less than their hearing counterparts and endured paternalism exhibited by school administrators who exercised tight administrative and fiscal control over school matters.

The ASD struggled to survive in the early years. To address some of the financial shortcomings and the need for a new building, the school sold the parcel of land in Alabama that was gifted to them from the Federal government. In addition, income from slave labor and the sale of slaves funded building construction at ASD, which in part, helped to bring the school on more sound financial footing (Sayres, 2017).

6 Brian H. Greenwald

The education of deaf children in the first half of the nineteenth century was largely modeled on the successes at the Hartford school. In residential schools, sign language was used to deliver the curriculum. There were speech training classes as early as the 1830s at the Virginia School for the Deaf, and the 1840s at the Kentucky School for the Deaf. It is important to note that education was focused primarily on white deaf children. Although a black student attended ASD as early as 1825, and reportedly the New York School for the Deaf had a black student in 1818, the numbers were small, with a total of only 11 black students enrolled at ASD between 1829 and 1870 (Edwards, 2012).

The Midpoint

At the midpoint of the nineteenth century, residential schools used sign language in the curriculum, and a professional journal, *American Annals of the Deaf*, became a mechanism for dissemination of information on the pedagogy of educating deaf students. As the nation found itself mired in the Civil War, several residential schools in the south contributed to the southern cause. Most schools experienced a decline in enrollment during the war, with Georgia School for the Deaf at Cave Spring suspending operations. Kentucky School for the Deaf was the only southern school that remained open throughout the Civil War.

Willie J. Palmer, a hearing principal at North Carolina School for the Deaf and Dumb and the Blind at Raleigh, "quickly turned the school into a major resource for Jefferson Davis…in no other Southern school for deaf children were the children more directly involved in aiding the Confederacy" (Lang, 2017, p. 124). Lang (2017) further credits Palmer for his acumen in running a school with a good academic and vocational program while working to "inspire the deaf children to the Southern cause" (p. 124). The North Carolina School for the Deaf and Dumb and the Blind in Raleigh printed Confederate dollars and made ammunition (Joyner, 2004).

Several hearing principals and some teachers, for example, from the Virginia School for the Deaf at Staunton, took leave from the school to participate in the war out of duty and to support the Confederate army (Lang, 2017; McPherson, 1997). Facilities at some schools were converted to hospital wards or barracks, as in the case of the Maryland School for the Deaf, to house Confederate soldiers. Some schools claimed these various services, providing necessities to the Confederate army, kept them open during the war.

Founding of the National Deaf-Mute College

In the midst of the Civil War that ripped the United States in half, the first college for Deaf people in the history of the world was established in Washington, DC. Known first as the Columbia Institution for the Instruction of the Deaf, Dumb, and Blind, the charter to establish the collegiate branch, the National Deaf-Mute

College, was signed by Abraham Lincoln. Laurent Clerc arrived in Washington, DC, to partake in the inauguration activities for the National Deaf-Mute College on June 28, 1864. Clerc would be dead three years later, but he had already been in the United States for 48 years, marrying a deaf woman, Eliza Boardman, and raising two children. The realization of an institution of higher learning was important to Clerc despite his belief that some fields such as medicine and law were closed to deaf people (Clerc, 1864).

The college, serving as the highest level in the education of deaf people, was founded in part to remove any doubts that deaf students could complete a rigorous program of study similar to other students. Following the spirit of Abraham Lincoln, who had signed the charter, the college allowed deaf students, according to the inaugural catalog, to "become better men, better citizens ... they may stand in fair competition with the more favored in the struggle of life" (National Deaf-Mute College Catalog, 1866, pp. 8–9). Lincoln's rhetoric of giving all a fair chance in the race of life resonated with deaf college students. That fair chance could be achieved with the removal of barriers faced elsewhere via access to sign language.

The National Deaf-Mute College in its inception trained deaf white males to become "educated men" (National Deaf-Mute College Catalog, 1866, p. 8). A white female student, Lydia Kennedy, matriculated in Fall 1866 as a first-year college student but did not return the following year. A few other women students attended the college in the 1860s, but none graduated. President Edward Miner Gallaudet closed the doors to women in 1871. After much resistance from the school's administration, women were accepted to be students on probationary status in 1887. However, two years later, in 1889, that status was removed (Parker, 2008).

Black students did not matriculate at the college (Jowers-Barber, 2008; Joyner, 2008). Hume Battiste graduated in 1913 but he had been listed as an Indian, hiding his racial heritage (Battiste, 2020). It was not until 1954 when Andrew Foster became the first openly known African-American male to graduate from Gallaudet (Peruzzi, 2019). Ida Wynette Hampton was the first African-American deaf woman to graduate from Gallaudet in 1957. Foster went on to establish at least 35 schools throughout Africa before his untimely death. The National Deaf-Mute College provided an opportunity for deaf students, although at first only white males, to attend an institution of higher learning, and to better their chances for upward social and economic mobility.

Towards the Twentieth Century

Amidst the rise of social and linguistic Darwinism being applied to deaf pedagogy, oralism, which had been spreading since shortly after the Civil War, gained traction. Oralism was in part a pedagogical approach emphasizing speech and lipreading in educating deaf children, and prohibiting the use of sign language in classrooms, dormitories, and in social settings.

Progressive educators sought to reshape public education. Low wages and unskilled jobs offered little in the way of upward economic mobility for immigrants and poor families. Child labor was a frequent problem and children endured hazardous working conditions at the turn of the twentieth century. Combined with the surging industry, reformers began to agitate for reforms in American education. Compulsory attendance laws, teacher training, vocational education, and establishing kindergartens would provide the impetus for improved social and economic opportunities to develop better citizenry.

Deaf schools reflected regional and national perspectives of their time, and were not immune to racism and discrimination. Southern schools lagged behind their northern school counterparts, allocating significantly less resources to programs for black students. Educational conditions were no better for Native Americans – the government forced Indian children apart from their tribal communities and herded them to Indian residential schools ostensibly to eradicate their language, clothes, and culture in the name of "Americanization." Schools like the Carlisle School and the Chilocco Indian school in Oklahoma were designed to force Indian children into mainstream America (Adams, 1995; Lomawaima, 1995). Reflecting the racism that tainted all US schools, deaf residential schools in the south remained segregated until the last school, Louisiana School for the Deaf, was finally integrated in 1978 (McCaskill, Lucas, Bayley, & Hill, 2011).

The ideology of Americanization predominated at the outset of the twentieth century. Progressivists sought to address a range of problems and institute reforms. Progressivists pushed for child labor laws and required public education for children, especially the growing immigrant population so they could learn English. Advocates strove to address a range of issues such as urban overcrowding, lack of public health, and workplace safety in the industrial age. Women's suffrage, they believed, would further the progressive platform. Child labor laws, compulsory education laws, and workers' compensation programs were passed.

In that context, oralism came to be viewed as forward progress, while sign language was seen as atavistic. Educators and other proponents of oralism unleashed a tidal wave that severely tested residential schools. In just one instance, for example, Frank Booth, the hearing child of deaf parents Edmund and Mary Walworth Booth, and superintendent of the Nebraska School for the Deaf in 1911, worked to institute state law that mandated oralism and not sign language to be used (Van Cleve, 1984). The oralists' insistence on learning to speak English when deaf people lacked residual hearing, with the expectation that these deaf people somehow would not only speak flawless English but also command mastery of the English language, was an illusion that seldom turned to reality.

Oralism gained further traction with its most famous advocate, Alexander Graham Bell. Bell testified at state legislatures in support for day schools, couching his argument in part on economics, that is, day schools were cheaper than state residential schools and students would have more interaction and could practice speech with their family (Van Cleve, 1993). Yet, in 1906, Bell conceded the value of residential schools in successfully training deaf students to lead independent and productive lives. The residential schools, Bell wrote, "are mainly responsible for the fact that the deaf from childhood no longer constitute a dependent class" (Bell, 1906, p. 149). Despite the contrarian position that Bell adopted in the 1900 Special Census report on "The Deaf," he continued promoting the hypothetical intrinsic and practical values of oralism. The value of residential schools was publicly contested by hearing educators who supported day schools and those who favored schools where speech and lipreading dominated, and sign language was prohibited. Oralism was viewed as a mechanism for upward mobility and homogeneity at a time when immigration in part dominated the nation's agenda.

Resistance

Residential schools did push back. Prominent examples include the consistent demonstration of citizenship and productivity of deaf people as members of American society. For example, in the early 1900s, the Deaf community challenged the Civil Service Exam as discriminatory as those exams excluded deaf people from government jobs based on the inability to hear. Through the National Association of the Deaf (NAD), deaf leaders such as Olof Hanson, convinced President Theodore Roosevelt to overturn this requirement in applying for federal jobs (Buchanan, 1999).

By 1910, there were some 45 newspapers printed at the residential schools. The chief and practical objective was to train students to become competent printers so they could obtain a salaried job after graduation. School newspapers included news articles, debates, shorter announcements such as weddings, funerals, job postings, and other articles that alumni or parents of students would find informative. These sections formed the cultural cornerstone; yet, in the same vein, these papers were especially important in demonstrating that the schools were responsible stewards of state funding by training pupils to become productive, working taxpayers (Haller, 1993).

By 1920, 78% of teachers at residential schools were white hearing women (Baynton, 1996). They supposedly possessed the maternal trait of patience with repetitive tasks, and they were paid less than hearing men, who generally did not desire the tedious work of teaching deaf students speech and lipreading (Baynton, 1996). Oralism was practiced in the white schools as it was thought to be a more superior approach to social integration with society at large. Sign language was considered by some educators more animalistic than human. Although residential schools did not completely abandon sign language in the early twentieth century, it was certainly unfavorable. At Texas School for the Deaf, which had separate buildings for black and white students, black students were left to use sign language while white students focused on speech and lipreading. The irony, of course, is that it was black students, and not white students, who benefited from more direct access to language (McCaskill *et al.* 2011; Tabak, 2006).

From "Hearing Loss" to Thriving Organizations

Discrimination on the basis of "hearing loss" continued to be a pressing matter. For example, insurance companies founded and run by hearing people discriminated against deaf people, and insurance was difficult for deaf people to purchase (Buchanan, 1999). Organizations, comprised of deaf people who graduated from state residential schools, responded forcefully.

The National Fraternal Society of the Deaf (NFSD) was an organization led by deaf people. It was critical in fending off legislation drafted by hearing people that sought to ban deaf drivers. Labeling deaf drivers as "dangerous," "defective," and a "menace," states pushed to deny licenses to deaf drivers who were deemed unfit and unsafe to drive. Ignatius Bjorlee, the hearing superintendent of Maryland School for the Deaf, who had two deaf brothers, challenged state efforts to ban driving rights (Burch, 2002). Maryland Department of Transportation Commissioner E. Austin Baughman, in 1924, fiercely opposed issuing licenses to deaf people. Drivers from the Maryland Deaf community, with support from NFSD, embarked on a public relations campaign emphasizing visual superiority over sound, and flipped eugenic rhetoric around arguing they were endowed with "superior sight and skills," while blasting hearing people with subpar driving records as "careless" and "dangerous."

American Patriotism: World War I and World War II

As the United States entered World War I in 1917, the Deaf community galvanized in support of the war effort. Schools such as the New York School for the Deaf (Fanwood) exemplified patriotism with their own military training drills, complete with uniforms and marching band. During World War II, students collected items and raised money for the American Red Cross in support of the war efforts. On the home front, deaf workers at Good Year, Firestone, and Boeing contributed to the war effort (Buchanan, 1999). While there was an upsurge in American patriotism and fear of those of Japanese descent following the bombing of Pearl Harbor in December 1941, President Franklin Delano Roosevelt issued Executive Order 9066 in 1942 that removed American citizens of Japanese ancestry to internment camps on the west coast, such Gila River in Arizona, Manzanar in California, and Topaz in Utah, among other places. The effect reached Deaf Japanese-American children at the California (Berkeley) School for the Deaf, who were forced to relocate with their families to internment camps. Deaf schools in the south remained segregated during both World War I and World War II (Knorr & Whatley, 2015).

The Great Depression

Between the two major World Wars, the nation weathered the Great Depression. By the time Franklin Delano Roosevelt, who himself suffered from polio, took office in January 1933, the nation's confidence in the uninsured banking system was in tatters. Some 25% of the nation was unemployed, complications of market saturation, and a very uneven distribution of wealth factored into the fallout that plunged the nation and most of the world into a decade-long depression. Roosevelt and the various New Deal programs made inroads into the Deaf community. Deaf people in the Works Progress Administration (WPA) program worked in the Indiana School for the Deaf, rebuilding portions of the school's main building. The Social Security Act, passed in 1935, did not provide financial support on the basis of deafness; therefore, members of the Deaf community, including its chief advocacy organization, the National Association of the Deaf, argued against receiving charitable funds from the government, declaring that deafness was not an impediment to one's ability to secure work.

Deaf organizations such as The National Fraternal Society of the Deaf proved astute during the nation's financial crisis. This fraternal society was formed in 1901 by a handful of alumni from the Michigan School for the Deaf. NFSD sold insurance policies to deaf people and the organization experienced rapid and impressive growth. On the eve of the Great Depression, the organization boasted some 7,000 members with US$900,000 in assets. By 1931, that had increased to US$1,500,000 in assets and throughout the Great Depression the society held US$2,000,000 in cumulative assets (*The Frat*, 1929). By 1932, nationwide unemployment soared to 25% and nearly 90% of the nation's banks had failed. Insurance companies folded by the dozens as subscribers ceased payment on premiums due to financial hardships. NFSD bucked this trend, and not only survived the debilitating financial effects of the depression but rather expanded its membership.

At the tail end of the Great Depression, Deaf education, particularly the residential school setting, was troubled. The precipitous decline of Deaf newspapers from the Little Paper Family (LPF) consortium removed a thread of local, regional, and national communication that was so vital to the community. The LPFs served several goals. First, they were a source of training for mostly deaf male students in the printing trade. Second, because these newspapers operated on funding provided by the state, the papers themselves served as tangible evidence of funds well utilized. Finally, they were also a mechanism to inform parents of students, friends of the school, and state legislators that the schools' vocational training programs were effectively using the latest skills and technology available at the time.

The decline of school newspapers also reflected the shift in pedagogical approaches in residential schools. The story of a deaf editor losing his position highlights this change. George Porter, from New Jersey, was terminated from his job after a showdown on the school's efforts to weed out sign language from the classroom by Superintendent Alvin Pope, a product of Gallaudet's Normal School (Buchanan, 1999). Alvin Pope first earned his undergraduate degree from the University of Nebraska, and taught using the oral method at the Nebraska School for the Deaf. Pope later came to Gallaudet and earned a master's degree

12 Brian H. Greenwald

before he became Superintendent at New Jersey School for the Deaf. Pope moved the New Jersey school from a sign-based curriculum to pedagogy that emphasized oralism. Deaf editors were not the only ones to lose their jobs with the rise of oral education. The notable decline in the number of deaf teachers throughout the residential schools further exacerbated the Deaf community's fragile hold on autonomy.

Uncovering Abuse

Sexual and physical abuse at a number of residential schools for the deaf occurred during the 1950s–1980s, typically by those who held positions of authority or exercised tight oversight of student life in the dormitories. Schools in New England, such as the American School for the Deaf, New York School for the Deaf at Fanwood, Governor Baxter School for the Deaf, and Clarke School for the Deaf, conducted investigations into physical and sexual abuse of deaf children and teenagers (Bravin & Burns, 2020; Vigdor, 2020). At the St. John's School for the Deaf in Wisconsin, a Catholic priest may have abused 200 boys over twenty years (Goodstein & Callender, 2010). These schools mirrored a larger pattern of physical and sexual abuse among elite private boarding schools, churches, and other institutions that were charged with safeguarding students away from home. Many of these stories have spilled out into major news outlets and have sparked a growing number of deaf adults coming forward with stories of corporal punishment, sexual abuse, and rape.

The 1960s: Academic Recognition of ASL, Education, and the Outgrowth of Deaf Culture

As the Civil Rights movement took root in the 1960s, an English professor from Cornell University who moved to Gallaudet in the previous decade began to observe ways that sign language had its own distinct syntax, orientation, semantics, grammatical structure, and other properties known in the study of linguistics. William Stokoe worked with two deaf colleagues, Dorothy Casterline and Carl Croneberg, and published the *Dictionary of American Sign Language* in 1965. Academic recognition of ASL came at a time when the value of residential schools was under extreme duress. Deaf people were initially uncomfortable with this paradigm shift; that American Sign Language (ASL) had its own linguistic properties was a completely unfamiliar notion. That same year, President Lyndon Baines Johnson signed into law the creation of the National Institute for the Deaf (NTID), a college within Rochester Institute of Technology (RIT). Deaf students now could choose between a college that focused on liberal arts studies versus technological training. In the 1970s and 1980s, hallmarks of culture became more prominent with published accounts of Deaf history, theatre, art, poetry, and most of all, self-determination.

The Rehabilitation Act of 1973 prohibited discrimination on the basis of disability in federal employment, or in programs that are funded by federal dollars. Contractors receiving federal funds were bound to follow guidelines for federal employment. Three years later P.L. 94–142 was adopted, mandating a free, appropriate public education for children with disabilities, including deaf children.

Deaf President Now

The first college for deaf people in the world had been run by hearing administrators ever since the founding of the National Deaf-Mute College (now Gallaudet University) in 1864. The protest known as the Deaf President Now (DPN) movement challenged this stronghold. Students, staff, faculty, alumni, parents, and community leaders participated in this nonviolent protest (support for DPN was not unanimous) in March 1988. A coalition of students, faculty, staff, and alumni issued four demands, including the removal of selected hearing President Zinser, the composition of the University's trustees had to be a Deaf majority, the Board's chair to step down, and no reprisals against the demonstrators who effectively shut down and controlled access to the 99-acre campus in northeast Washington, DC (see Christiansen & Barnhartt, 1995; Gannon, 1989; and Sign Language Studies, Fall 2014). The week-long protest culminated in the removal of a hearing president, Dr. Elisabeth A. Zinser, and replaced her with a deaf president, Dr. Irving King Jordan. For the first time in 124 years at the sole four-year collegiate institution for deaf students in the land, a deaf president was chosen.

It took over a century for Deaf people to claim agency in appointing the first deaf president in the university's history. Since the successful outcome of DPN over three decades ago, the field of Deaf education has changed dramatically. Some of the greatest benefits in technology have leveled the playing field in communication accessibility, the impact of mainstreaming, and increasing the number of deaf people in positions of leadership, including school superintendents.

Education policies reflected the social, economic, or political contexts of the times. While there were some successes in Deaf education, there were also failures. Most notable is the incredible shortchanging of students' access to a visual language and education. The one constant over the two centuries was that Deaf communities sought to build, structure, advise, and control the education of deaf students, who like themselves as deaf adults, understood what was necessary to succeed.

Moving Deeper into the Millennium

When there is a "discovery' through scientific methods that clearly demonstrates that deaf children acquire a visual language before spoken language, the world looks to this science, but glosses over the 200 years of lived experiences. Scientists are not detached from historical settings – they change their positions on race and ableism in response to criticism generated by historians and activists. The

14 Brian H. Greenwald

experiences that deaf people hold must be taken seriously for no one else possesses the breadth and depth of cumulative experiences over two centuries of Deaf education.

Two centuries of Deaf education have informed us of the value of a bilingual education. Our country, founded by hearing white males, had long exhibited hostilities to minorities in acquiring literacy in nineteenth-century America. The value of bilingualism or trilingualism is especially important in the twenty-first century. For America to succeed in the global marketplace, cultural literacy is essential. The goal of the Language Equality and Acquisition for Deaf Kids (LEAD-K) movement is to ensure language access at the earliest age possible. This movement, in part, was born out of the notion to halt language deprivation for deaf and hard of hearing children and placing a premium on equal access to ASL and written English.

Deaf people make positive contributions to humanity (Bauman & Murray, 2014). We have biological and cultural worth. Differences among ourselves and between deaf and hearing people bring new ideas and perspectives. In that context, we should consider the impact of genetic manipulation. Genetic tests in embryonic development hold the power and promise of information. Parents have additional tools to plan for education, seek resources, and options well before birth. Partnering with cochlear implant industries may be one avenue to push back against genetic manipulation that threatens to eradicate genetic deafness. The world has something to gain by having Deaf people as part of human diversity.

The approximate division of 85% of deaf students in America today are mainstreamed with the remainder in residential schools. Given that we may have passed the point of critical mass, it is worthwhile to consider expanding the borders of our Deaf community and who is defined as deaf. Deaf students who grew up speaking and lipreading can be allies if we welcome them to the signing world. Many do indeed gravitate to the Deaf world later in life, often as adults, and that assimilation can be a painful struggle for some.

Parent-infant programs, for hearing parents of deaf children, must be made available despite incredible budget constraints. These represent the next generation of deaf pupils at our schools. Should we follow what Clarke School has done, that is, cease the residential school program but become a day school in multiple major cities, including Boston, New York, Philadelphia, and Jacksonville? What promise does this model hold for residential schools? What would a decentralized school look like? How would it function?

Laurent Clerc undoubtedly would have been pleased to learn that there are over 350 known deaf lawyers in the United States, and a growing number of deaf people are entering the medical profession. Surely he would delight in seeing successful bilingual and bicultural models of Deaf education with a growing number of superintendents of schools who are themselves deaf.

Note

1 Portions of this paper were originally presented at Boston University in March 2018.

References

Adams, D. W. (1995). *Education for extinction: American Indians and the boarding school experience*. Lawrence, KS: University Press of Kansas.

American Annals of the Deaf (1879). Contract between Laurent Clerc and Thomas Hopkins Gallaudet, June 13, 1816. Reprinted in *American Annals of the Deaf*, Vol. 24 (April 1879), 115–117. Retrieved from https://www.disabilitymuseum.org/dhm/edu/detail.html?id=689&annotations=39&paragraphs=1-19.

Battiste, A. A., Sr. (2019). Hume LePrince Battiste: Passing through to success. *Deaf Life* (February), 20–26.

Bauman, H. D., & Murray, J. J. (2014). *Deaf gain: Raising the stakes for human diversity*. Minneapolis: University of Minnesota Press.

Baynton, D. C. (1996). *Forbidden signs: American culture and the campaign against sign language*. Chicago: University of Chicago Press.

Bell, A. G. (1906). 'The Deaf' in Department of Commerce and Labor, Bureau of the Census. *Special Reports: The Blind and the Deaf*, 1900, Washington, DC, 149.

Bravin, J. S., & Burns, C. S. (2020). Findings. *The New York Times*, February 21.

Buchanan, R. (1999). *Illusions of equality: Deaf Americans in school and factory, 1850–1950*. Washington, DC: Gallaudet University Press.

Burch, S. (2002). *Signs of resistance: American deaf cultural history, 1900–1942*. New York: New York University Press.

Christiansen, J. B., & Barnhartt, S. (1995). *Deaf president now!: The 1988 revolution at Gallaudet university*. Washington, DC: Gallaudet University Press.

Clerc, L. (1864). Address by Laurent Clerc, A.M. In *Inauguration of the College for the Deaf & Dumb at Washington, District of Columbia*, June 28.

Edwards, R. A. R. (2012). *Words made flesh: Nineteenth-century deaf education and the growth of deaf culture*. New York: New York University Press.

Gannon, J. (1989). *The week the world heard Gallaudet*. Washington, DC: Gallaudet University Press.

Goodstein, L., & Callender, D. (2010). For years, deaf boys tried to tell of priest's abuse. *The New York Times*, March 26.

Haller, B. (1993). The little papers: Newspapers at nineteenth-century schools for deaf persons. *Journalism History*, *19*(2), 43–50.

Jowers-Barber, S. (2008). The struggle to educate black deaf schoolchildren in Washington, DC. In B. H. Greenwald & J. V. Van Cleve (Eds.), *A Fair chance in the race of life: The Role of Gallaudet University in Deaf history* (pp. 113–131). Washington, DC: Gallaudet University Press

Joyner, M. (2008). Douglas Craig, 186?-1936. In B. H. Greenwald & J. V. Van Cleve (Eds.), *A Fair chance in the race of life: The Role of Gallaudet University in Deaf history* (pp. 65–84). Washington, DC: Gallaudet University Press.

Joyner, H. (2004). *From pity to pride: Growing up Deaf in the old south*. Washington, DC: Gallaudet University Press.

Knorr, R., & Whatley, C. (2015). *The Segregated Georgia School for the Deaf, 1882–1975*. Mechanicsburg, PA: Sunbury Press.

Lang, H. G. (2017). *Fighting in the shadows: Untold stories of Deaf people in the civil war*. Washington, DC: Gallaudet University Press.

Lomawaima, K. T. (1995). *They called it prairie light: The story of Chilocco Indian school*. Lincoln, NB: University of Nebraska Press.

McCaskill, C., Lucas, C., Bayley, R., & Hill, J. (2011). *The hidden treasure of black ASL: Its History and structure*. Washington, DC: Gallaudet University Press.

McPherson, J. M. (1997). *For cause & comrades: Why men fought in the civil war*. New York: Oxford University Press.

National Deaf-Mute College (1866). *Catalog, 1866*. Washington, DC: Joseph L. Pearson Printer.

Parker, L. M. (2008). The women of Kendall Green: Coeducation at Gallaudet, 1860-1910. In B. H. Greenwald & J. V. Van Cleve (Eds.), *A Fair chance in the race of life: The Role of Gallaudet University in Deaf history* (pp. 85–112). Washington, DC: Gallaudet University Press.

Peruzzi, M. (2019). Transforming the Narrative: Battiste, Foster, and the Status Quo. Poster session, Gallaudet University Research Expo, Spring 2019.

Sayres, E. E. (2017). *The Life and times of T.H. Gallaudet*. Hanover, NH: ForeEdge Press.

Sign Language Studies (Fall 2014). Special issue assessing the impact of DPN a quarter century later. *Sign Language Studies, 15*(1).

Tabak, J. (2006). *Significant gestures: A History of American Sign Language*. Westport, CT: Praeger.

The Frat, (October 1929). Issues of *The Frat* typically listed assets & liabilities of the national organization in issues published by NFSD.

Van Cleve, J. V. (1984). Nebraska's Oral Law of 1911 and the Deaf community. *Nebraska History, 65*, 195–220.

Van Cleve, J. V. (1993). The Academic integration of deaf children: A Historical perspective. In R. Fischer & H. Lane (Eds.), *Looking back: A reader on the history of deaf communities and their sign languages* (pp. 333–347). Hamburg, DE: Signum.

Vigdor, N. (2020). School for the deaf reports dozens of decades-old sexual abuse cases. *The New York Times*, February 24.

2

SIGN LANGUAGE ACQUISITION IN CONTEXT

Jenny L. Singleton and Richard P. Meier

Deaf signing communities vary in ways crucial to our understanding of first-language acquisition in the children of those communities and to our understanding of first-language acquisition in all children. We will touch on three variables in the demography of the deaf population, with a focus on the American deaf community: (1) Deaf children may have hearing or deaf parents; (2) If they have hearing parents, deaf children vary considerably in their age at first exposure to ASL; and (3) For deaf children of deaf parents, there is variation in the sign input that they receive at home, variation that depends in part on when their parents were exposed to ASL. Most deaf parents themselves have hearing parents; in some cases, these deaf parents may be late learners of ASL and may have incomplete knowledge of the language. We conclude this chapter by considering the role of teachers and peers as primary language models for deaf children – usually deaf children of hearing parents – who are not exposed to a signed language in the home.

Deaf Children of Deaf Parents

Most deaf children have hearing parents; only a small minority have deaf parents (Mitchell & Karchmer, 2004). In the United States and anglophone Canada, deaf children of deaf parents have early exposure to ASL. When we look at the acquisition of ASL by the children of deaf parents, we see that the timeline is broadly similar to the acquisition of spoken languages (Newport & Meier, 1985). We expect first signs at roughly 12 months of age, first two-sign sentences at 18 months or thereabouts. Like spoken languages, some aspects of signed languages take years to master, for example, handshape production (e.g., Karnopp, 2002, on Brazilian Sign Language; Takkinen, 2003, on Finnish Sign Language; reviewed in Meier, 2019) and wh-questions in ASL (Reilly, 2006). The broad similarity in the developmental milestones for signed and spoken languages affirms the fundamental plasticity of the child's language-learning capacity. The import of this conclusion can't be overstated. Although some hearing communities have auxiliary signed languages (e.g., Umiker-Sebeok & Sebeok, 1978) and some majority hearing communities are bilingual in sign and speech due to the presence of large numbers of deaf individuals in those communities (e.g., De Vos, 2012, Groce, 1985; Sandler et al., 2005), spoken languages are otherwise ubiquitous in hearing communities. We might, therefore, have expected children to be biased toward the acquisition of spoken languages, with consequent delay in the acquisition of a signed language. Not so.

But modality nonetheless matters. For example, there has been debate, pro and con, about whether first signs might appear before first words by perhaps a month or so (Anderson & Reilly, 2002; Meier & Newport, 1990; Petitto et al., 2001). On one influential account, all children – deaf and hearing – show an early gestural advantage. Volterra and Iverson (1995) found that the gestural lexicons of hearing, 12-month old Italian children were, on average, twice as large as their spoken vocabularies. Early in work on the acquisition of signed languages, the role of iconicity in the acquisition of first signs was discounted (Orlansky & Bonvillian, 1984), with the suggestion instead that the size of signs, or early motor control of the hands, or parents' ability to recognize infant signs might account for reports of a disadvantage for speech in the acquisition of first words (Newport & Meier, 1985). Recent years have seen new claims that iconicity facilitates the acquisition of early signs, as assessed by parental reports of when a child knows a sign (Thompson et al., 2012; Caselli & Pyers, 2017). Iconicity may have less of a role to play in how infants produce signs. Instead, infant production of signs is largely guided by motoric factors (Meier et al., 2008); some of those motoric factors may be common to the two language modalities (e.g., a tendency toward repeated movement), whereas others may be specific to one modality, such that proximalization of movement and a tendency for the nondominant hand to mirror the dominant hand constrain infant sign production. Particularly in atypically developing deaf children (Shield & Meier, 2012, 2018), children's acquisition of sign may be impacted by the fact that some parameters of sign formation – e.g., hand orientation – appear quite different from different angles of regard. Acquisition in the sign modality may also be vulnerable to particular nonlinguistic deficits that would have little or no impact on spoken language. For example, Quinto-Pozos et al. (2013) presented a case study of a native ASL-signing teenager with nonlinguistic perspective-taking difficulties – indeed, her role-shifting and other narrative coherence structures were impaired in her ASL signing. This case illustrates that the cognitive requisites for language may be different in the two modalities. For example, viewers of signed language must depend on mental rotation capacities to process language (Shield & Meier, 2018). Had this teenager been a hearing user of spoken language, she may not have experienced a negative impact on her language.

Simon: A Deaf Child of Deaf Late Learners

It is important to point out that not all deaf children of deaf parents experience "perfect" ASL input. A case study reported by Singleton and Newport (2004) described the unique case of Simon, a deaf child born to deaf parents, who was exposed to ASL from birth. However, both of his parents were late learners of ASL, and thus provided Simon with signing that had grammatical gaps and inconsistencies. Simon attended a "mainstreamed" school program for deaf students that used Manually Coded English (there were no other ASL using children in his school). The parents socialized primarily with other late learners, thereby limiting Simon's contact with fluent ASL signers.

Singleton and Newport gave Simon a comprehensive battery of ASL tests at age seven. He outperformed both of his parents on these tasks. That a child can improve upon the imperfections of his primary linguistic input speaks to the robust language-making capacity possessed by children. Singleton and Newport proposed that Simon performed a kind of statistical analysis of his input, searching for regularities and boosting weaker patterns into systematic rule-based structures in his own ASL. For example, Simon's parents did not use the VEHICLE (3-handshape) ASL classifier in their signing; instead they used a B-EDGE handshape (in which a flat B-hand is produced with the palm toward the midline) about half the time to represent vehicles. Simon also does not use the 3-handshape, evidence that he has not had contact with fluent ASL signers who would often use this classifier handshape. Instead, Simon chooses B-EDGE and produces that form with much higher regularity than his parents, thus regularizing a pattern seen somewhat frequently, but amid competing inconsistent forms. Newport (2016) went on to suggest that it is only children who respond to imperfect input in this way. Her artificial language-learning experiments (Hudson Kam & Newport, 2005, 2009) with adults and children show that adults more or less reproduce the inconsistencies modeled in the input (i.e., "probability matching"), whereas children will improve upon the input with a more rule-governed output that has "cleaned up" the inconsistency (i.e., "probability boosting").

Deaf Children of Hearing Parents

What is the effect of early experience – or lack thereof – on the acquisition of a first language, whether signed or spoken? With rare exceptions (Curtiss, 1977; Lane, 1976), hearing children do not vary in whether or not they have early exposure to language. Not so for deaf children of hearing parents. Particularly in the years before early hearing screening, hearing parents might not recognize their child's hearing loss for months or even years; prior to the advent of universal neonatal hearing screening, the average age in Colorado at which a child's hearing loss was detected was 23 months (Yoshinaga-Itano, 2003). Thus, there was substantial variation in when these deaf children gained their first exposure to ASL.

First exposure to ASL might come when those children entered a state residential school for the deaf, but even this context differs in the extent of contact with fluent ASL language models that a child experiences (i.e., not all teachers, dormitory counselors, or peers are fluent in ASL). For other children, first exposure to ASL might not come until adolescence after the child had spent years in an oral program or in an inclusive classroom at a school that serves mostly hearing children (Henner, 2016, found that 66% of deaf children of hearing parents in their study entered ASL-using schools around age ten). For many deaf children of hearing parents, delayed first exposure to ASL effectively meant delayed first exposure to language of any sort.

Even for highly homogeneous groups of subjects (e.g., deaf adults who had all attended the Pennsylvania School for the Deaf and who had 30 or more years of exposure to ASL), age of acquisition matters, as reported by Newport (1990). Early learners (first exposed to ASL at ages 4–6) showed small, but consistent, differences from native learners (deaf children of deaf parents) in their responses to a battery of tests examining the production and comprehension of ASL morphology. Late learners (first exposed to ASL after age 12) showed even more robust differences, both from native and early learners. In contrast, age at first exposure to ASL did not predict performance on a test of ASL word order; all subjects were near ceiling. Mayberry and Eichen (1991) report a similar study, in which they examined memory for ASL sentences in native learners, early learners (exposed on entry to a residential school at ages 5 to 8), and adolescent learners (exposed on entry to a residential school at ages 9 to 13). Performance decreased with later age of acquisition; adolescent learners showed errors that suggested shallow processing of the stimulus sentences (e.g., remembering the sign SLEEP as the formationally-similar, but semantically unrelated, sign AND). A recent case study that examined the initial sign learning period of three adolescent late-learners (Cheng & Mayberry, 2018) suggests that their sign order was somewhat variable in the early stages (just like ASL-learning toddlers, as reported by Hoffmeister, 1978; see Lillo-Martin and Chen-Pichler, 2006, for discussion of the acquisition of sign order). They eventually settle to canonical ASL word order, but their learning period was more protracted than a toddler acquiring ASL.

Henner (2016) compared 371 deaf children of hearing parents (DCHP) to 193 deaf children of deaf parents (DCDP) between ages 8 and 18 on various tasks requiring advanced language and cognitive skills (e.g., analogical reasoning, advanced vocabulary). In his study, the earlier a DCHP entered an ASL school context, the better their scores were on relational thinking tasks. The DCDP in his sample show appropriate developmental growth on these tasks each year, always outperforming the DCHP, but there was an interesting downward dip on these measures in the DCDP age cohort around age 10. Interestingly, 66% of the DCHP sample did not enter the deaf school until after age 10. Henner suggests that, with the influx of DCHP around this age period, teachers are accommodating the large percentage of

Sign Language Acquisition in Context **21**

their students with weak relational thinking skills and weak vocabularies and may be pitching their discourse at a lower level for those students to "catch up"; doing this may adversely affect the DCDP by dampening their upward trajectory for a period.

Deaf Children with No Formal Sign Language Input

Many deaf children of hearing parents do not receive any signed language input at home; some of these children will create a family-based communication system from gestures (Goldin-Meadow & Mylander, 1990; Goldin-Meadow et al., 2009). These "homesigning" systems show that the deaf child can innovate basic gesture order, some limited morphology, and other grammatical systematicities. While they do not create a full-blown, complex signed language on their own, the fact that these children create homesigns is a testament to the linguistic resiliency of children.

In certain contexts where multiple homesigners or non-signing deaf children are brought together in a critical mass (e.g., Nicaragua) and given the opportunity to interact daily, researchers documented advances in grammatical complexity from an ontogenetic perspective (within an individual signer) and from the historical perspective of changes in patterns of interaction among the generational cohorts of signers (Senghas, 2003). For example, when a "next generation" of signers (i.e., children) is exposed to a nascent ("first generation") signed language, that second cohort introduces advances in grammatical complexity such as increased frequency of spatial modulation, greater coherence in the use of spatial modulation, greater fluency, and use of pointing signs as nominals (Senghas & Coppola, 2001, 2011). For both the first and second cohorts, children with early exposure to the emergent signed language show superior performance to those exposed after age ten.

This body of work on children who confront a break in the generation-to-generation transmission of language also reveals how important it is for children (and adults) to have contact with a community of language users (see, for recent discussion, Neveu, 2019). In the case of NSL, deaf children very quickly formed a language community because they came together daily in the deaf schools that had been established for them. In contrast, isolated homesigners with no peer networks, who may establish standards of well-formedness for their gestures and some rudimentary grammatical structure in their utterances, nevertheless remain tethered to more iconic or simpler gestural communication (Singleton et al., 1993). One possible impetus for continuing iconicity or simplicity in homesign is to ensure that hearing family members can understand the homesigner. Carrigan and Coppola's (2017) study of parents and siblings of homesigners in Nicaragua shows that hearing family members have poor comprehension of the home-signer's productions. Sensitivity to a linguistically fragile interlocutor may inhibit a child's progress in developing language complexity; for example, Gagne (2017) showed that on an experimental production task hearing children of adult deaf

22 Jenny L. Singleton and Richard P. Meier

homesigners in Nicaragua produced "unrotated" spatial modulations, an accommodation that would presumably make comprehension easier for their parents because the child's sign would not require the parent to "do the mental rotation or perspective-taking necessary to interpret rotated productions" (p. 120).

The Role of Schools

The relationships between schools and language are complex. Public schools are frequently on the front lines of government language policies, whether to suppress minority languages (e.g., the suppression of Native American languages in government-run boarding schools, Hinton, 1994), to foster learning of the national language by immigrant children (McEachron & Bhatti, 2005; Valdés, 1998), or to teach standard dialects (witness debates about the place of mainstream English versus African-American Vernacular English in classrooms with large numbers of African-American children; see Baugh, 2000, and for a recent critique, Flores & Rosa, 2015). On rarer occasions, schools can be the venue for language revival. For example, Ravid (1995, p. 6) writes that, although the revival of Hebrew was carried out by literate adults, Hebrew "first came to life again in the schools where children and adolescents learned it from their teachers; and at home – since by the 1920s the language already had native speakers ...." But, as Ravid further notes, what "those youngsters made of the language ... was not always in accord with what the adult [language] planners had envisioned ...."

The impacts that deaf schools have had on the lives of deaf people have sometimes had little to do with the stated policies of these schools but have been the product of the roles those schools have played in the formation of deaf communities. Residential schools have been the locus around which national signed languages such as French Sign Language or ASL have formed, such that the American School for the Deaf in Hartford, CT has sometimes styled itself as "the birthplace of American Sign Language" (American School for the Deaf, 2019). Sex-segregated schools for the deaf- and differences in signing practices between boys' and girls' schools – led to substantial gender differences in the basic vocabulary of Irish SL (LeMaster & Dwyer, 1991). Importantly, residential schools have been the place where deaf children of non-signing hearing parents have acquired national signed languages such as ASL. As a result, residential schools have been the wellsprings of deaf communities (Baynton, 1996; Padden & Humphries, 1988; Van Cleve & Crouch, 1989).

Historically, the majority of deaf children have not experienced signed language in their homes; see Lucas and Schatz (2003) for results of a survey showing that most American deaf adults use some form of English with their family members, whereas they use ASL with their deaf peers. Classrooms, and other settings such as dormitories and playgrounds, may offer primary sites for language exposure to ASL. Daily access to signing teachers and interaction with other deaf children who sign

Sign Language Acquisition in Context **23**

can provide deaf children from non-signing homes with rich sign language experience (Erting & Kuntze, 2017). While classroom arrangements are strikingly different from the typical caregiver-child social interactions that foster language development, it seems that generations of deaf individuals validate the effectiveness of this school-based primary language acquisition model.

We know that historically in the United States, up through the 1970s, most deaf children were educated in residential schools (typically one major campus in every state). There they lived among hundreds of deaf children of differing ages who signed – a real linguistic community. From the early 1800s to the early 1900s, most of these state residential schools used ASL and fingerspelling in the classroom and even employed deaf teachers and dormitory counselors. But around the early 1900s, the educational tides within state residential schools shifted to "oralism" and sign language was no longer used in the classroom. By 1919, 80% of deaf children in the United States were communicating with their teachers without any "manual language" (Van Cleve & Crouch, 1989, p. 122). It is reported that many deaf teachers lost their jobs (Burch, 2004), but that a small core of deaf teachers remained in the vocational education department or taught students who were referred to as "oral failures" (Van Cleve & Crouch, 1989, p. 141). Linguists and historians have suggested that deaf children of deaf parents who had acquired ASL in the home then became responsible for the survival of ASL through the decades of oralism, by passing it along to deaf children of hearing parents in the dormitories around the country (Baynton, 1996, p. 150). The impact of these residential schools extended beyond access to ASL. "The schools helped deaf young people to learn that they were not strange or alone, but members of a larger community of similar individuals …. They shared not only their own language, but also social rules, group norms, values, and ASL poetry and storytelling traditions" (Krentz, 2000, p. xvii–xviii). An interesting piece of this survival history comes from the residential schools that were established for African-American deaf children during the segregation era. Unlike the schools for white children, the schools for African-American children were not forced to adopt an oralist philosophy and many continued to use manual approaches to education (McCaskill et al., 2011; Settles, 1940). Thus, these schools may have been a refuge for ASL.

Since the 1970s, and the passage of various parts of the Individuals with Disabilities Education Act (IDEA), the majority (reportedly 88.3%) of deaf children in the United States are "mainstreamed" in public schools (U.S. Department of Education, National Center for Education Statistics, 2019). There are a variety of educational arrangements available now, from self-contained classrooms on a public school campus with a signing teacher (who most likely uses an English-based signing system, not ASL), to full inclusion in general education classrooms where the deaf student learns from a hearing, non-signing teacher with the support of an educational sign language interpreter. The majority of deaf students no longer live in dormitories; instead, they go home at the end of each school day to their hearing families. The small minority of deaf students who attend residential schools (9.7%) experience classrooms full of deaf peers (many of whom are native or early-learning ASL signers); around half of the staff working at state residential schools are themselves deaf, with some schools as high as 78% (see the Suggs, 2018 survey of 26 state schools).

The prevalence of deaf teachers in today's residential schools contrasts with a 2008 report of a national survey of 313 programs serving deaf students that found only 22% of teachers were deaf (with an even lower percentage being deaf teachers of color) (Simms et al., 2008). Thus, in a residential school that uses signed communication in its approach, deaf children should have ample opportunity to learn ASL (Stinson & Foster, 2000) and "deaf ways of being" (Graham & Tobin, 2020; Singleton & Morgan, 2006). Even so, primary language acquisition in a school environment is likely to be quite different than in a family home. It is interesting to note that among several qualitative studies or ethnographies of the "lived experience" of deaf individuals in residential versus mainstreamed educational environments, few of these narratives give details about language acquisition. There are instead many vignettes about social isolation in mainstreamed settings, and full social participation, a sense of belonging, but lowered academic expectations, within residential school settings (Foster, 1989; Foster, 1998; Steinberg, 2000; Stinson & Foster, 2000).

With the 1986 reauthorization of the IDEA, and the approval of PART C in 2011, young deaf and hard of hearing children in the United States began receiving early intervention services in the home before they entered a school setting. States vary in their models of early intervention for deaf or hard of hearing infants and toddlers. The National Center for Hearing Assessment and Management (NCHAM, 2020) maintains a database about early intervention programs across the United States that involve deaf/hard of hearing adults as role models, guides, or mentors. Even with ASL exposure through such early intervention programming, it likely occurs only on a weekly or bi-weekly basis for a short visit.

Classroom Learning

In some ways, deaf children of hearing parents – especially those who attend state residential schools for the deaf – are newcomers to the Deaf world. For newly-arrived children, whether to the United States or to a state residential school, the classroom may be an important venue for language acquisition. Singleton and Morgan (2006) discuss primary language acquisition in the classroom for deaf children. The residential-school classroom may be the first time that the deaf child – and likely the majority of their deaf classmates – experiences a signing environment with consistent access to a fluent-signing adult language model. Yet even with signing teachers, how this primary language is experienced by deaf children in the classroom varies depending on whether the linguistic ecology

Sign Language Acquisition in Context **25**

created by the teacher invites the child into "natural language" discourse. For example, Harris's (2010) qualitative study includes a description of a deaf teacher in a preschool classroom and how she used extended discourse to facilitate her students' ASL acquisition. Importantly, teachers will have to recognize the effects of language delay in many of their deaf students and be mindful of how these effects may vary across students within their classroom.

Classroom observational studies of signing teachers in the UK (in "SimCom" classrooms where teachers sign and speak simultaneously) revealed that the teacher often adopted a "therapeutic" language approach with her deaf students, controlling conversational turn-taking with the expectation that the students would produce clear speech while signing (Wood & Wood, 1991, 1997; Wood et al., 1986; Wood et al., 1991). The teachers dominated the exchanges, asking many questions, and often made requests for children to repeat their responses. There was little extended discourse between teachers and students. Teachers rarely provided elaborations on children's utterances. Erting (1988) found similar results in her ethnographic observation of a hearing teacher of the deaf in the United States, adding that the teacher often began signing before she even had the deaf students' attention.

For deaf children who are mainstreamed in classrooms with a hearing, non-signing teacher and a sign language interpreter, different challenges are present in both the quality and nature of the linguistic input offered to the young deaf learner. Schick et al. (2006) evaluated the sign proficiency of approximately 2,100 educational interpreters in the United States who used ASL, MCE (Manually Coded English), or PSE (signing that includes features of both ASL and MCE). They found that nearly 60% of these interpreters had inadequate signing skills to provide children in K–12 settings with linguistic access to their hearing teacher's spoken English. Moreover, interpreters with the weakest skills were disproportionately placed in early grades. The interpreted message was not just "simplified" to younger deaf students; rather these researchers found many random errors, distortions, and deletions in the presented message. To our knowledge, how well a deaf child can acquire their signing skills directly from a sign language interpreter model has not been systematically studied.

Even though signing is theoretically being modeled to the deaf child by the interpreter, the dynamics of "interpreted-speech" are unlike everyday, conversational turn-taking. Classroom sign language interpreters often adapt the teacher's talk into more "instructional forms" based on their own assessment of the student's understanding of the material (Cawthon, 2001). Interpreted speech does not reflect the natural turn-taking synchrony and contingent response patterns characteristic of first-language acquisition settings that involve caregivers and their children. Fitzmaurice (2017) reports an ethnographic study of three uncredentialed educational sign language interpreters working in rural settings. He found that these interpreters had considerable autonomy in how they controlled the flow of communication experienced by the deaf child, for instance by not signing ambient peer talk when the deaf child was not looking, or by prioritizing chatting with the deaf student over-interpreting content instruction. Notably, these interpreters took on a wide range of roles in the classroom besides interpreting content instruction and functioning as a conversational partner with the deaf student; for example, they might tutor the deaf student or manage the classroom behavior of hearing students.

Studies of hearing children in preschool settings have suggested the importance of the teachers' linguistic responsivity for children's language development. Linguistic responsivity includes language facilitating behaviors (e.g., following the child's lead, contingent responding, encouraging participation in turn-taking) and language developing behaviors (e.g., recasts, expansions, and other strategies that model increasingly complex syntax and vocabulary) (Justice et al., 2018). These characteristics are typical of the language-promoting behaviors observed in child-directed speech produced by caregivers. Adult talk to children, from both parents and teachers, also provides the corpus (or "input data") for the child to analyze as they internalize the pattern of rules of their target language. For example, the number of different words used and percentage of syntactically complex sentences produced by mothers is associated with their children's developing vocabulary and grammar skills (Hoff, 2003; Huttenlocher et al., 2002). Justice et al.'s (2013, 2018) studies of preschool teachers suggest that when teacher talk "aligns with" known language-promoting styles of talk used by caregivers, positive impacts are observed in the language development of the children.

Because so many deaf children enter preschool classrooms with a language delay, teachers may lean into a "therapeutic style" of interaction (as described above by Wood & Wood) rather than a "parent-like" discourse style. Harris's (2010) study comparing deaf and hearing preschool teachers of the deaf found that deaf teachers used more language facilitating styles of talk. Singleton and Morgan (2004; Morgan, 2004) observed three deaf teachers in their preschool classrooms and documented numerous examples of the teachers engaging in an "everyday talk" style of communication, offering personal narratives, engaging in extended discourse, and following into topics raised by the child. Yet, Singleton and Morgan noted that the adult-child ratio of a classroom setting distinguishes it from a family setting. For example, with some four to eight students in a class, it would seem there would be diminished opportunity for one-on-one teacher-student interaction that would simulate a parent-child dyad. The authors suggested that other deaf adults could contribute to natural language interaction in the classroom, for example, early intervention professionals or paraprofessionals.

The crosscultural language socialization and language acquisition ideology literature shows us that caregivers also vary in how they present the primary language acquisition experience of their infants and children (Brown & Gaskins, 2014; Riley, 2011). For example, in some cultures, parents rarely speak directly to their children, nor do they modify their speech patterns (Schieffelin & Ochs, 1986). In such settings, children are often with their parents (e.g., being carried on their mother's back while she works or prepares meals) and are *overhearing* the multi-party communication going on in their midst. It is impressive that these children acquire their native language in a roughly similar fashion as those children raised in communities where parents behave almost like teachers (e.g., by asking their children to label objects or by exaggerating their speech to make phrases salient to their pre-linguistic infant). That the bandwidth for diversity in infant-directed speech styles is rather wide suggests that, even with four to eight deaf children in a classroom with one linguistic model, those children would still benefit from the ambient conversations between the teacher and other students, or from observing interactions among their peers.

Learning from Peers

Peers may be especially important for deaf children's primary signed language acquisition. We know from homesigners that when a child is isolated their self-created signed systems remain limited in terms of linguistic complexity. Having a critical mass of peers to negotiate meaning with, to use language for creative and pretend play, to teach less-fluent peers, and to learn from more-fluent peers are all factors that could arguably advance a deaf child's language and cognition. Adult language models are critically important, but peers may also influence the learning process in significant ways. How this happens is underexplored (Erting & Kuntze, 2017; Singleton & Morgan, 2006).

Let's begin by looking at the language socialization literature: Kyratzis (2004) explains how important peers are among hearing children, establishing pragmatic uses of language, and using language and rituals to solidify peer culture and resist adult social expectations. Blum-Kulka and Snow (2004) review evidence of the great importance of native-speaker peers in second language learning, but note that native-speaker preschoolers may be unhelpful to non-English-speaking children, until those children have learned at least a few English words (Tabors & Snow, 1994). Furthermore, Blum-Kulka and Snow observe that peer groups lacking native-speaker members (e.g., French immersion programs in Canadian schools) may settle on ungrammatical usages, even when they have access to native-speaker teachers.

It has been said that native-signing deaf peers deserve credit for the survival of ASL through the "oralism years" in the United States (Baynton, 1996, p. 163). It may also be that residential schools have attracted and continue to attract more deaf children of deaf parents than do other educational placements, given the historical importance of these schools to the Deaf community; deaf children of deaf parents may thus represent a larger fraction of the residential-school population than would be expected based on the demographics of deafness (i.e., greater than the 5–10% of the deaf population that we might have expected). [Note again that segregated schools serving African-American deaf students may

28 Jenny L. Singleton and Richard P. Meier

have used ASL both in and out of the classroom during the oralism years (McCaskill et al., 2011; Settles, 1940).]

How native-signing peers may serve as language models in residential schools is not fully understood, but there is an interesting study of the language acquisition process among deaf peers in one residential school in Thailand (Reilly & Reilly, 2005). There older deaf students were observed teaching younger deaf peers and sharing with them "news of the day" and other personal narratives. In the absence of deaf children of deaf parents at this Thai deaf school, the frequent experience of contact with older, more proficient signing peers may have been adequate for promoting effective language socialization. Another residential school where there apparently were no deaf models among the children is the school in Managua, Nicaragua that was established in 1977; in 1997, Polich (2005, p.107) identified just one 17-year-old deaf individual with a deaf parent in the country of Nicaragua, and that deaf mother was a home sign user, not a signer of Nicaraguan Sign Language.

Foster (1998) summarizes vignettes from over 150 interviews with deaf individuals, some of whom came from hearing non-signing families and who attended state residential schools for the deaf. These deaf adults often mentioned learning to sign from their peers and teachers (in fairly general terms) and commonly expressed the joy of being able to understand everyone around them. Steinberg (2000) interviewed one deaf adult who remembered back when she was four years old and entering a signing school for the first time. She recalls observing that everybody seemed to know what to do except her and that, without realizing that their moving hands was the key to this mystery, she surmised that she must have thought that those people have Extrasensory Perception (pp. 99–100).

Conclusions

A small, but crucial, fraction of the American deaf population acquires ASL at home; these are deaf children of deaf parents. The larger fraction of the deaf population may be exposed to ASL in schools and by peers, but not all deaf children are. The spread of ASL out of its core population within deaf-parented families is impacted – to an extent we don't fully understand – by many recent changes in education and in medicine. Because of the ubiquity of neonatal hearing screening, deaf children born to hearing parents don't go undetected for months or years. Hearing parents who have a deaf infant and who are interested in learning ASL may now find it easier to do so because of the availability of ASL language programs at local community colleges and residential schools, and early intervention services that include home visits by deaf adults, but we have no idea how often hearing parents avail themselves of these resources. There is a changing menu of audiological and educational interventions, including cochlear implants, that parents – and later the deaf children themselves – may choose from.

Compared to what was once true, a smaller fraction of deaf children go to residential schools; most children are mainstreamed. Yet, some families move to cities like Austin, Texas to be close to state schools for the deaf; in the process, large deaf communities emerge. Most deaf children who attend state schools now do so as day students; a smaller fraction live in the dorms where they once would have received intense exposure to ASL from fluent peers. We also know from Henner's study (2016) that many of these students do not enter these state schools until middle school, around age ten. Yet, in the classrooms of those residential schools, the large fraction of deaf teachers and the advent of bilingual/bicultural programs may mean that children receive effective exposure to ASL, even during instructional time.

We are unsure how all these changes are affecting the size of the ASL-signing community, nor are we sure of the impacts these changes will have on the long-term viability of ASL, although we worry. As we have written this essay, we have searched again and again for statistics that would help us to understand where ASL, the deaf signing community, and deaf education are headed. We hope that future research on the demography of the American Deaf community will fill the gaps that we have noticed. We also hope that studies will soon appear that will help us to better understand how hearing parents can promote their deaf child's language acquisition, how the acquisition of ASL can take place in children's classrooms, and how peers affect the mastery of ASL and its spread to new generations of users. One thing we know from decades of research on the language learning experiences of deaf children is that these children are powerfully resilient and will attempt to communicate within even the most meager linguistic ecology. Still, we must ask ourselves whether the educational and technological advances of the day truly enable deaf children to reach their linguistic and cognitive potential.

Acknowledgment

We thank Tony Woodbury and Ceil Lucas for help in tracking down references.

References

American School for the Deaf (2019, November). *Employment opportunities.* https://www. asd-1817.org/about/employment-opportunities.

Anderson, D., & Reilly, J. (2002). The MacArthur Communicative Development Inventory: Normative data for American Sign Language. *Journal of Deaf Studies and Deaf Education*, 7, 83–106.

Baugh, J. (2000). *Beyond Ebonics: Linguistic pride and racial prejudice.* Oxford University Press.

Baynton, D. (1996). *Forbidden signs: American culture and the campaign against sign language.* University of Chicago Press.

Blum-Kulka, S., & Snow, C. E. (2004). Introduction: The potential of peer talk. *Discourse Studies*, 6, 291–306.

30 Jenny L. Singleton and Richard P. Meier

Brown, P., & Gaskins, S. (2014). Language acquisition and language socialization. In N. J. Enfield, P. Kockel-man & J. Sidnell (Eds.), *Handbook of linguistic anthropology* (pp. 187–226). Cambridge University Press.

Burch, S. (2004). *Signs of resistance: American deaf cultural history, 1900 to World War II.* NYU Press.

Carrigan, E. M., & Coppola, M. (2017). Successful communication does not drive language development: Evidence from adult homesign. *Cognition, 158,* 10–27.

Caselli, N., & Pyers, J. (2017). The road to language learning is not entirely iconic: Iconicity, neighborhood density, and frequency facilitate acquisition of sign language. *Psychological Science, 28,* 979–987.

Cawthon, S. W. (2001). Teaching strategies in inclusive classrooms with deaf students. *Journal of Deaf Studies and Deaf Education, 6,* 212–225. https://doi.org/10.1093/deafed/6.3.212.

Center for Disease Control (2019, November). 2016 Summary of hearing screening among total occurrent births. https://www.cdc.gov/ncbddd/hearingloss/2016-data/02-screen.html.

Cheng, Q., & Mayberry, R. (2018). Acquiring a first language in adolescence: the case of basic word order in American Sign Language. *Journal of Child Language, 46,* 214–240.

Curtiss, S. (1977). *Genie: A psycholinguistic study of a modern-day "wild child."* Academic Press.

De Vos, C. (2012). The Kata Kolok perfective in child signing: Coordination of manual and nonmanual components. In U. Zeshan & C. de Vos (Eds.), *Sign languages in village communities: Anthropological and linguistic insights* (pp. 127–152). DeGruyter Mouton.

Erting, C. J. (1988). Acquiring linguistic and social identity: Interactions of deaf children with a hearing teacher and a deaf adult. In M. Strong (Ed.), *Language Learning and Deafness* (pp. 192–219). Cambridge University Press.

Erting, C., & Kuntze, M. (2017). Signed language socialization in Deaf communities. In P. Duff & S. May (Eds.), *Language Socialization, Encyclopedia of Language and Education* (pp. 383–396). Springer.

Fitzmaurice, S. (2017). Unregulated autonomy: Uncredentialed educational interpreters in rural schools. *American Annals of the Deaf, 162*(3), 253–264.

Flores, N., & Rosa, J. (2015). Undoing appropriateness: Raciolinguistic ideologies and language diversity in education. *Harvard Educational Review, 85*(2), 149–171.

Foster, S. B. (1989). Reflections of a group of deaf adults on their experiences in mainstream and residential school programs in the United States. *Disability, Handicap, & Society, 4*(1), 37–56.

Foster, S. B. (1998). Communication experiences of deaf people: An ethnographic account. In I. Parasnis (Ed.), *Cultural and language diversity and the Deaf experience* (pp. 117–135). Cambridge University Press.

Gagne, D. L. (2017). *With a little help from my friends: The contributions of a peer language network on the conventionalization of space in an emerging language.* University of Connecticut Dissertation. www.opencommons.uconn.edu.

Goldin-Meadow, S., & Mylander, C. (1990). Beyond the input given: The child's role in the acquisition of language. *Language, 66*(2), 323–355.

Goldin-Meadow, S., Özyürek, A., Sancar, B., & Mylander, C. (2009). Making language around the globe: A crosslinguistic study of homesign in the United States, China, and Turkey. In J. Guo, E. Lieven, N. Budwig, K. Nakamura & S. Ozcaliskan (Eds.), *Crosslinguistic approaches to the psychology of language: Research in the tradition of Dan Isaac Slobin* (pp. 27–39). Psychology Press.

Sign Language Acquisition in Context **31**

Graham, P., & Tobin, J. (2020). The body as a canvas: Developing a Deaf bodily habitus in deaf signing preschools. In I.W. Leigh & C.A. O'Brien (Eds.), *Deaf Identities: exploring new frontiers* (pp. 145–161). Oxford University Press.

Groce, N. E. (1985). *Everyone here spoke sign language: Hereditary deafness on Martha's Vineyard.* Harvard University Press.

Harris, R. L. (2010). *A case study of extended discourse in an ASL/English bilingual preschool classroom.* (*Unpublished dissertation*). Gallaudet University.

Henner, J. (2016). *The relationship between American Sign Language vocabulary and the development of language-based reasoning skills in deaf children* (Doctoral dissertation). Boston University.

Hinton, L. (1994). *Flutes of fire: Essays on California Indian languages.* Heyday Books.

Hoff, E. (2003). The specificity of environmental influence: Socioeconomic status affects early vocabulary development via maternal speech. *Child Development, 74*(5), 1368–1378.

Hoffmeister, R. J. (1978). *The development of demonstrative pronouns, locatives and personal pronouns in the acquisition of American Sign Language by deaf children of deaf parents.* (Unpublished doctoral dissertation). University of Minnesota.

Hudson Kam, C. L., & Newport, E. L. (2005). Regularizing unpredictable variation: The roles of adult and child learners in language formation and change. *Language Learning and Development, 1*(2), 151–195.

Hudson Kam, C. L., & Newport, E. L. (2009). Getting it right by getting it wrong: When learners change languages. *Cognitive Psychology, 59*(1), 30–66.

Huttenlocher, J., Vasilyeva, M., Cymerman, E., & Levine, S. (2002). Language input and child syntax. *Cognitive Psychology, 45*, 337–374.

Justice, L. M., McGinty, A. S., Zucker, T., Cabell, S. Q., & Piasta, S. B. (2013). Bi-directional dynamics underlie the complexity of talk in teacher–child play-based conversations in classrooms serving at-risk pupils. *Early Childhood Research Quarterly, 28*(3), 496–508.

Justice, L. M., Jiang, H., & Strasser, K. (2018). Linguistic environment of preschool classrooms: What dimensions support children's language growth? *Early Childhood Research Quarterly, 42*, 79–92.

Karnopp, L. B. (2002). Phonology acquisition in Brazilian Sign Language. In G. Morgan & B. Woll (Eds.), *Directions in sign language acquisition* (pp. 29–53). John Benjamins.

Krentz, C. (2000). *A mighty change: An anthology of deaf American writing, 1816-1864* (Vol. 2). Gallaudet University Press.

Kyratzis, A. (2004). Talk and interaction among children and the co-construction of peer groups and peer culture. *Annual Review of Anthropology, 33*, 625–649.

Lane, H. (1976). *The wild boy of Aveyron.* Harvard University Press.

LeMaster, B., & Dwyer, J. P. (1991). Knowing & using female & male signs in Dublin. *Sign Language Studies, 73*, 361–396.

Lillo-Martin, D., & Chen-Pichler, D. (2006). Acquisition of syntax in signed languages. In B. Schick, M. Marschark & P. E. Spencer (Eds.), *Advances in sign language development by deaf children* (pp. 231–261). Oxford University Press.

Lucas, C., & Schatz, S. (2003). Sociolinguistic dynamics in American Deaf communities: Peer groups versus families. In L. Monaghan, C. Schmaling, K. Nakamura & G. Turner (Eds.), *Many ways to be Deaf: International variation in Deaf communities* (pp. 141–152). Gallaudet University Press.

Mayberry, R. I., & Eichen, E. B. (1991). The long-lasting advantage of learning sign language in childhood: Another look at the critical period for language acquisition. *Journal of Memory and Language, 30*(4), 486–512.

McCaskill, C., Lucas, C., Bayley, R., & Hill, J. (2011). *The hidden treasure of Black ASL: Its history and structure*. Gallaudet University Press.

McEachron, G., & Bhatti, G. (2005). Language support for immigrant children: A study of state schools in the UK and US. *Language, Culture and Curriculum, 18*(2), 164–180.

Meier, R. P. (2019). Acquiring signed languages as first languages: The milestones of acquisition and the form of early signs. In N. Grove & K. Launonen (Eds.), *Manual sign acquisition in children with developmental disabilities* (pp. 59–86). Nova Science Publishers.

Meier, R. P., Mauk, C., Cheek, A., & Moreland, C. J. (2008). The form of children's early signs: Iconic or motoric determinants? *Language Learning and Development, 4*, 63–98.

Meier, R. P., & Newport, E. L. (1990). Out of the hands of babes: On a possible sign advantage in language acquisition. *Language, 66*, 1–23.

Mitchell, R. E., & Karchmer, M. (2004). Chasing the mythical ten percent: Parental hearing status of deaf and hard of hearing students in the United States. *Sign Language Studies, 4*, 138–163.

Morgan, D. D. (2004). *Deaf teachers' practices: Supporting and enabling preschool deaf children's development of a participative identity*, (Unpublished doctoral dissertation). University of Illinois Urbana-Champaign.

National Center for Hearing Assessment and Management (NCHAM) (2020, March). http://www.infanthearing.org/dhhadultinvolvement/states/index.html.

Neveu, G. K. (2019). *Lexical conventionalization and the emergence of grammatical devices in a second generation homesign system in Peru*. (Unpublished doctoral dissertation). University of Texas at Austin.

Newport, E. L. (1990). Maturational constraints on language learning. *Cognitive Science, 14*(1), 11–28.

Newport, E. L. (2016). Statistical language learning: Computational, maturational, and linguistic constraints. *Language and Cognition, 8*(3), 447–461.

Newport, E. L., & Meier, R. P. (1985). The acquisition of American Sign Language. In D. I. Slobin (Ed.), *The crosslinguistic study of language acquisition. Volume 1: The data* (pp. 881–938). Lawrence Erlbaum Associates.

Orlansky, M. D., & Bonvillian, J. D. (1984). The role of iconicity in early sign language acquisition. *Journal of Speech and Hearing Disorders, 49*(3), 287–292.

Padden, C., & Humphries, T. (1988). *Deaf in America*. Harvard University Press.

Petitto, L. A., Katerelos, M., Levy, B. G., Gauna, K., Tétreault, K., & Ferraro, V. (2001). Bilingual signed and spoken language acquisition from birth: Implications for the mechanisms underlying early bilingual language acquisition. *Journal of Child Language, 28*(2), 453–496.

Polich, L. (2005). *The emergence of the deaf community in Nicaragua*. Gallaudet University Press.

Quinto-Pozos, D., Singleton, J., Hauser, P. C., Levine, S. C., Garberoglio, C. L., & Hou, L. (2013). Atypical signed language development: A case study of challenges with visual-spatial processing. *Cognitive Neuropsychology, 30*, 332–359.

Ravid, D. D. (1995). *Language change in child and adult Hebrew: A psycholinguistic perspective*. Oxford University Press.

Reilly, J. (2006). How faces come to serve grammar: The development of nonmanual morphology in American Sign Language. In B. Schick, M. Marschark & P. E. Spencer (Eds.), *Advances in the sign language development of deaf children* (pp. 262–290). Oxford University Press.

Reilly, C. B., & Reilly, N. (2005). *The rising of lotus flowers: Self-education by deaf children in Thai boarding schools*. Gallaudet University Press.

Riley, K.C. (2011). Language socialization and language ideologies. In A. Duranti, E. Ochs & B. B. Schieffelin(Eds.), *The handbook of language socialization* (pp. 493–514). Wiley Blackwell.

Sandler, W., Meir, I., Padden, C., & Aronoff, M. (2005). The emergence of grammar: Systematic structure in a new language. *Proceedings of the National Academy of Sciences, 102*, 2661–2665.

Schieffelin, B. B., & Ochs, E. (1986). Language socialization. *Annual Review of Anthropology, 15*(1), 163–191.

Schick, B., Williams, K., & Kupermintz, H. (2006). Look who's being left behind: Educational interpreters and access to education for deaf and hard-of-hearing students. *Journal of Deaf Studies and Deaf Education, 11*(1), 3–20.

Senghas, A. (2003). Intergenerational influence and ontogenetic development in the emergence of spatial grammar in Nicaraguan Sign Language. *Cognitive Development, 18*(4), 511–531.

Senghas, A., & Coppola, M. (2001). Children creating language: How Nicaraguan Sign Language acquired a spatial grammar. *Psychological Science, 12*, 323–328.

Senghas, A., & Coppola, M. (2011). Getting to the point: How a simple gesture became a linguistic element in Nicaraguan signing. In G. Mathur & D. J. Napoli (Eds.), *Deaf around the world: The impact of language* (pp. 127–143). Oxford University Press.

Settles, C. J. (1940). *Normal training for colored teachers. American Annals of the Deaf, 85*(2), 209–217.

Shield, A., & Meier, R. P. (2012). Palm reversal errors in native-signing children with autism. *Journal of Communication Disorders, 45*, 439–454.

Shield, A., & Meier, R. P. (2018). Learning an embodied visual language: Four imitation strategies available to sign learners. *Frontiers in Psychology, 9*. doi:10.3389/fpsyg.2018.00811.

Simms, L., Rusher, M., Andrews, J. F., & Coryell, J. (2008). Apartheid in deaf education: Examining workforce diversity. *American Annals of the Deaf, 153*(4), 384–395.

Singleton, J. L., Morford, J. P., & Goldin-Meadow, S. (1993). Once is not enough: Standards of well-formedness in manual communication created over three different timespans. *Language, 69*(4), 683–715.

Singleton, J. L., & Morgan, D. D. (2004). *Becoming Deaf: Deaf teachers' engagement practices supporting deaf children's identity development.* Paper presented at the annual meeting of the American Educational Research Association, San Diego, CA.

Singleton, J. L., & Morgan, D. D. (2006). Natural signed language acquisition within the social context of the classroom. In B. Schick, M. Marschark & P. E. Spencer (Eds.), *Advances in sign language development by deaf children* (pp. 344–373). Oxford University Press.

Singleton, J. L., & Newport, E. L. (2004). When learners surpass their models: The acquisition of American Sign Language from inconsistent input. *Cognitive Psychology, 49*(4), 370–407.

Steinberg, A. (2000). Autobiographical narrative on growing up deaf. In P.E. Spencer, C.J. Erting & M. Marschark (Eds), *The deaf child in the family and at school: Essays in honor of Kathryn P. Meadow-Orlans* (pp. 93–108). Taylor & Francis.

Stinson, M. S., & Foster, S. (2000). Socialization of deaf children and youths in school. In P.E. Spencer, C.J. Erting & M. Marschark (Eds), *The deaf child in the family and at school: Essays in honor of Kathryn P. Meadow-Orlans* (pp. 191–209). Taylor & Francis.

Suggs, T. (2018, December). *Deaf Schools: True Business Deaf? 20 years later.* http://www.trudysuggs.com/deaf-schools-true-business-deaf-20-years-later/.

Tabors, P. O., & Snow, C. E. (1994). English as a second language in preschool programs. In F. Genesee Ed., *Educating second language children: The whole child, the whole curriculum, the whole community* (pp. 103–125). Cambridge University Press.

Takkinen, R. (2003). Variations of handshape features in the acquisition process. In A. Baker, B. van den Bogaerde, & O. Crasborn (Eds.), *Cross-linguistic perspectives in sign language research: Selected papers from TISLR 2000*, (pp. 81–91). Signum.

Thompson, R. L., Vinson, D. P., Woll, B., & Vigliocco, G. (2012). The road to language learning is iconic: Evidence from British Sign Language. *Psychological Science, 23*, 1143–1448.

Umiker-Sebeok, D. J., & Sebeok, T. (1978). *Aboriginal sign languages of the Americas and Australia. Volume 1: North America Classic Comparative Perspectives*. Plenum.

U.S. Department of Education, National Center for Education Statistics (2019, November). Fast facts: Inclusion of Students with Disabilities. https://nces.ed.gov/fastfacts/display.asp?id=59

Valdés, G. (1998). The world outside and inside schools: Language and immigrant children. *Educational Researcher, 27*, 4–18.

Van Cleve, J. V., & Crouch, B. A. (1989). *A place of their own: Creating the deaf community in America*. Gallaudet University Press.

Volterra, V., & Iverson, J. M. (1995). When do modality factors affect the course of language acquisition? In K. Emmorey & J. Reilly (Eds.), *Language, gesture, and space* (pp. 371–390). Erlbaum.

Wood, D., & Wood, H. (1991). Signed English in the classroom, I. Teaching style and child participation. *First Language, 11*, 189–217.

Wood, D., & Wood, H. (1997). Communicating with children who are deaf: Pitfalls and possibilities. *Language, speech, and hearing services in schools, 28*, 348–354.

Wood, D., Wood, H., Griffiths, A., & Howarth, I. (1986). *Teaching and talking with deaf children*. John Wiley & Sons.

Wood, D., Wood, H., & Kingsmill, M. (1991). Signed English in the classroom, II. Structural and pragmatic aspects of teachers' speech and sign. *First Language, 11*, 301–325.

Yoshinaga-Itano, C. (2003). Early intervention after universal neonatal hearing screening: Impact on outcomes. *Mental Retardation and Developmental Disabilities Research Reviews, 9*, 252–266.

3

ICONICITY

A Threat to ASL Recognition or a Window into Human Language Acquisition?

Naomi Caselli, Amy Lieberman, and Jennie Pyers

The now uncontroversial premise that sign languages are indeed real languages required a radical reimagining of some of the core design features of language, including "duality of patterning" and "arbitrariness" (Hockett, 1960). Duality of patterning is the idea that a finite set of meaningless units (e.g., phonemes) are combined and recombined to generate the meaningful units of language, including bound and unbound morphemes (e.g., words). Crucially, for phonological units to be re-used across different words, the idea was that they must be relatively context-independent and not tied to a single meaning. A second design feature, "arbitrariness," draws on this context-independent nature of phonemes and posits that the form of any word is unrelated to its meaning – the link between linguistic form and meaning is entirely arbitrary. Yet, even a superficial examination of sign languages around the world revealed linguistic systems replete with iconically motivated forms, such as the American Sign Language (ASL) sign TREE, where the arm in the sign corresponds to a tree trunk and the extended fingers correspond to the branches. The presence of iconic forms throughout sign languages seemed to violate these two design features of language, and initially led to a central conflict: either sign languages were lesser linguistic systems than spoken languages, or our understanding of what constitutes a language was inaccurate.

In the first half of this chapter, we explore the often politically fraught journey to resolve the apparent conflict between the "necessary" properties of human language and the linguistic characteristics of sign languages. We argue that this journey led to a reimagining of the nature of language, regardless of modality, and with this new understanding a line of inquiry into iconicity in language has blossomed. We conclude with a brief survey of a few of the questions about the role of iconicity in language acquisition.

36 Naomi Caselli et al.

A Brief History of Iconicity and the Linguistic Status of Sign Languages

Central figures in the study of language made strong claims about the role of iconicity in sign languages. For example, in 1978, Roger Brown, a Harvard University professor and leading researcher in the field of language acquisition, suggested that iconicity may be the answer to the question that he laid out in the title of a paper, *Why are signed languages easier to learn than spoken languages*:

> I think iconicity, which is pervasive and productive in signed languages but very limited in spoken languages, is an aid to learning in humans and in chimpanzees.
>
> *(Brown, 1978, p. 33)*

Our view is that such comparisons between any two languages or varieties, particularly when the languages differ in prestige and the language users differ in privilege, primarily serves to strengthen power imbalances. We include it here to illustrate that Brown's argument contained a series of assumptions about iconicity. We take the following assumptions as empirical questions: (1) Is iconicity very limited in spoken languages but pervasive and productive in sign languages? (2) Does iconicity facilitate sign language learning?

Brown acknowledged that his claims were provocative, and we argue that the historical context in which he wrote this paper made these ideas uniquely so. ASL was and still is a minoritized language, and its nascent status as a real language made it especially vulnerable at the time. It was only in 1965 that a small group of linguists began to argue that ASL should be thought of as a language rather than as unorganized gestures[1] (Stokoe, Casterline, & Croneberg, 1965). Some 35 years later the Linguistic Society of America found the need to pass a resolution recognizing sign languages as "full-fledged languages" (Linguistic Society of America, 2001). Notably, with the exception of ASL and African American Vernacular English, the organization is generally not in the business of passing resolutions validating languages. Still today, many universities in the United States do not allow ASL courses to satisfy foreign language requirements, and efforts to change such rules are often met with resistance because of a continued failure to recognize the linguistic properties of ASL (Armstrong, 1988; Wilcox, 1989; Reagan, 2011; "Tufts Daily," 2013). Moreover, around the world, many governments have yet to recognize sign languages despite ongoing movements for their legal recognition (De Meulder, 2015; Murray, 2015; Kusters, De Meulder, Friedner, & Emery, 2015). The idea that sign languages differ in a central way from spoken languages jeopardized the fight for linguistic equity of signed and spoken languages.

A second major threat to ASL at the time of Brown's paper was that the use of sign language was, and in some ways still is, widely discouraged for deaf children.

For example, in 1988 a superintendent of a school for deaf children said, "ASL is a beautiful, conceptual language ... but it has no place in the education process, if deaf citizens ever wish to compete with their hearing counterparts, with any kind of efficiency" (Bellefleur, 1988). The continued push to eliminate ASL from deaf educational settings in the late 1970s was bolstered by the advent of cochlear implants, which many saw as a means to "ensure that deaf children grow up to use a spoken language rather than ... signed languages" (Sparrow, 2005, p.136; Lane, Hoffmeister, & Bahan, 2001). Pushing back against the tide, deaf educators and linguists developed a Bilingual-Bicultural model of education with the goal that deaf children would at minimum become proficient in both written English and ASL (Hoffmeister, 1990; Johnson, Liddell, & Erting, 1989), with the Learning Center for the Deaf in Framingham, Massachusetts, becoming the first school to adopt this model in 1985. The proposal that sign languages were easier to learn than spoken languages blunted arguments that ASL was equal to English and worth pursuing as a means of supporting healthy language and cognitive development for deaf children.

Ironically, while many deaf children were prohibited from accessing ASL during this time period, the rest of the country was enamored by stories of chimpanzees and gorillas learning ASL (e.g., the 1981 National Geographic documentary "Gorilla"). In actuality, non-human primates never learned more than a small number of signs (Terrace, 2019). Nevertheless, Brown's suggestion that sign languages were so easy that chimpanzees can learn them was an affront to the validity of sign languages during a period in which their legitimacy was tenuous.

Moreover, the apparent prevalence of iconicity in sign languages compared to spoken languages seemed to violate a fundamental property of language, arbitrariness (de Saussure, 1919; Hockett, 1960). Hockett's design features of language were widely accepted as a means of separating animal communication and human language; thus, Brown's argument that sign languages were easy to learn because they were highly iconic lent support to the idea that sign languages might not be as sophisticated as spoken languages.

Early Research on Iconicity and Acquisition

These historical undercurrents focused the field of sign language research on identifying parallels between signed and spoken language acquisition, paying close attention to the possible role of iconicity driving children's language learning. The earliest approach was to observe and record children's early expressive sign vocabularies, and then analyze them either for the proportion of iconic signs present or for any systematic patterns of errors. A study of the sign productions of 13 native-signing children starting as young as four months of age found that less than one-third of children's expressive sign vocabulary was transparently iconic (Orlansky & Bonvillian, 1984). Children's first signs looked much like the first words of children learning a spoken language, and included signs like MOMMY, MILK, and COOKIE, which vary in both iconicity and transparency. Whereas iconicity broadly refers to the mapping between the physical form of the sign and its meaning, transparency specifically captures the degree to which meaning can be surmised solely on the basis of form. Moreover, like children learning a spoken language, sign-exposed children made articulatory errors. Crucially, their errors did not enhance the iconicity of the sign, but rather systematically reflected developmental motor constraints of initially articulating signs with proximal body joints like the shoulders and elbows and later with more distal joints like the wrist and fingers (Meier, Mauk, Cheek, & Moreland, 2008). Children's errors in their production of morphosyntax also suggested that iconicity was not driving acquisition. For example, children's early pronoun use in ASL revealed reversal errors that paralleled those observed in spoken language acquisition, demonstrating that a seemingly highly iconic gesture (i.e., pointing to the self to indicate "self") was part of a linguistic, not gestural, system (Petitto, 1987). Similarly, errors in verb agreement confirmed that the majority of young children's production errors decreased rather than increased the iconicity of target signs (Meier, 1987). The relatively low proportion of iconic signs in children's early vocabulary and the observation that children do not make signs more iconic in their productions suggested that iconicity was not the main mechanism of acquisition in sign languages.

A second approach to studying the role of iconicity in sign language learning focused on how accessible or transparent iconicity was to a novice adult sign language learner. The rationale for this line of inquiry was that the meaning of iconic signs, which have a close mapping between form and meaning, should be easily guessed by non-signers. Yet, non-signers seemed to only correctly come up with the meaning of an iconic sign about 10% of the time, and their performance increased only to 18% when they had to select among five possible meanings (Klima and Bellugi, 1979). Thus, although some signs have iconic form-meaning mappings, these mappings were largely inaccessible to learners.

In sum, a body of work suggested that children's early sign productions did not favor iconicity, and that iconicity was far less transparent than anticipated and thus was a suboptimal strategy for children to access meaning. The drive to disprove the role of iconicity in acquisition led Wilcox and Wilcox (1995) to lament that iconicity seemed to be "something of an embarrassment to ASL linguists" and that linguists seemed to be trying to "explain away iconicity in ASL" (p. 151). We imagine that rather than suppressing a role for iconicity in sign language, sign language researchers were simply focused on testing the extreme proposals that sign languages are largely iconic and that learners rely on iconicity over other factors during acquisition. They found that contrary to Brown's claim, children learning a sign language, like those learning a spoken language, may disregard iconicity in order to attend to the formal properties of all symbols, treating them as arbitrary despite any possible iconic origin (Newport & Meier, 1985). At a time when Hockett's (1960) design features of language were widely accepted as a means of distinguishing human communication from animal communication, the demonstrated irrelevance of iconicity in sign language raised the status of sign languages in the eyes of researchers and practitioners.

Revisiting the Role of Iconicity in Language and Language Learning

After the first wave of research describing and documenting the linguistic structure of sign languages identified striking similarities between signed and spoken languages (e.g., Stokoe et al., 1965; Klima and Bellugi, 1979), researchers began to write about the ways that the visuo-spatial modality of sign languages led to characteristics unique to sign languages. Cognitive linguists, members of a branch of linguistics that strives to align the study of language with what is known about human cognition, delved deep into analyzing the ways that signers use their hands and bodies to depict actions, dialogue, and psychological states (Liddell, 1995; Wilcox, 2004; Dudis, 2004; Ferrara & Hodge, 2018; Young, Morris, & Langdon, 2012). Their approach to linguistic analysis uncovered the multidimensionality of iconicity in sign languages and highlighted the range of possible iconic mappings between form and meaning that spanned from relatively simple direct mappings (e.g., pointing to a body part to refer to that body part) to more complex, multilayered metaphorical mappings (e.g., in Israeli Sign Language the sign ANGRY is performed on the chest as metaphor for the heart as the locus of emotion) (Taub, 2001, Meir, Padden, Aronoff, & Sandler, 2013). As these unique characteristics of the visuo-spatial modality took the spotlight, there was a renewed interest in how signers leverage iconic mappings. Differences between the visuo-spatial and auditory-oral modalities began to be seen as linguistic affordances of the modality instead of as threats to sign languages' linguistic status.

In tandem with recognizing the unique features of sign language, sign linguists, rather than disregarding the iconicity in sign language, pushed against the notion of arbitrariness as a hallmark of language and called for a deeper examination of iconicity in all languages.

> Iconicity has been devalued in linguistic theory and arbitrariness hailed as the thing that separates human language from lesser communication systems. Yet iconicity is not merely a matter of 'imitating' or 'miming' sounds or movements; instead it is a conventionalized part of languages' resources. It is in fact common in both signed and spoken languages, in grammar as well as lexicon.
>
> *(Taub, 2001, p. 32)*

40 Naomi Caselli et al.

This movement opened the door for the development of different accounts of the way that iconicity functions. We briefly summarize several theoretical perspectives on iconicity here: one way of thinking about iconicity is as an analogue-building model, in which the cognitive process of comparing a form to a meaning is critical to our determination of iconicity (Taub, 2001). According to this model, iconic forms are created through the selection of an image that represents a concept, the schematization of that image, and encoding of the schematized image in a linguistic form. A related theory of "cognitive iconicity" (Wilcox, 2004) suggests that iconicity occurs when pairings of semantic and phonological structure are near one another in the same conceptual space. Similarly, in the structure mapping theory of iconicity (Emmorey, 2014 which builds on Gentner's 1983 structure mapping theory of analogical reasoning), iconicity is seen as a mapping between structured phonological representations and structured semantic representations. Meir (2010) considered how iconicity might interact with metaphor, and posited that iconicity and metaphor are two different kinds of form-meaning mappings that can work in tandem (e.g., the Israeli Sign Language sign LEARN iconically depicts a metaphor of learning: grasping something and putting it in one's head). Perniss, Thompson, and Vigliocco (2010) described iconicity as a way of "reducing the gap between linguistic form and conceptual representation to allow the language system to "hook up" to motor, perceptual, and affective experience" (p. 1). Recent considerations of iconicity include the concept of patterned iconicity (Padden et al., 2013), which suggests that systematic iconic mappings can appear across a group of signs that share a semantic class. Indeed, researchers began suggesting that iconicity in language was not random but rather had a specific purpose in language creation and indeed in language acquisition.

With the growing interest in the linguistic status of iconicity, studies over the past decade that examined iconicity have provided some empirical answers to the assumptions embedded in Brown's (1978) question. In the following sections, we present the evidence that addresses these two assumptions in turn:

1. Is iconicity limited in spoken languages but pervasive in sign languages?
2. Does iconicity facilitate language learning?

Is Iconicity Limited in Spoken Languages but Pervasive in Sign Languages?

In spoken language, iconicity, which is often called "sound symbolism," has long been recognized by researchers as existing to some degree, but has not generally been considered a dominant or influential property in language acquisition and processing. Sound symbolism has been most associated with onomatopoeia (words like *meow, ding,* and *sizzle*, which refer to sounds), but iconicity in spoken languages can extend well beyond onomatopoeia. In fact, a wide range of phonological features systematically participates in iconic mappings, particularly in languages other than English. For example, in some languages syllable reduplication can indicate repetition in an action (e.g., in Japanese, *goro* means heavy rolling object and *gorogoro* means heavy rolling object moving multiple times), changing the length of a vowel can map on to relative differences in size of a referent, and changes in consonant voicing often indicate differences in mass or weight (Dingemanse, Blasi, Lupyan, Christiansen, & Monaghan, 2015). Also, the length of a word can correspond to its meaning; for example, longer adverbs convey more intensity than shorter ones (e.g., *very* vs *extremely*; Bennett & Goodman, 2018) and, more humorously, the length of Pokemon character names positively correlates with character size and weight (Kawahara, Noto, & Kumagai, 2018). Strikingly, some speech sounds are systematically associated with some meanings across different, unrelated languages. The sounds "l" and "n" are commonly used in words that label *tongue* and *nose*, respectively (Blasi, Wichmann, Hammarström, Stadler, & Christiansen, 2016). The growing evidence of the cross-linguistically similar ways that phonological form can iconically map to meaning in spoken languages has highlighted that iconicity not only exists in spoken languages, but also that it is far more prevalent than once assumed. Today, iconicity is taken seriously as an important aspect of the linguistic structure that can contribute to spoken language evolution (e.g., Hofer & Levy, 2019), processing (e.g., Schmidtke & Conrad, 2018), and even acquisition (e.g., Massaro & Perlman, 2017).

With a growing acknowledgment of the presence of iconicity in spoken languages, it remains unclear whether there is relatively more iconicity in signed versus spoken languages as many have previously claimed. One tantalizing piece of evidence in support of a greater prevalence of iconicity in signed languages is that iconicity ratings are more correlated between different sign languages than between different spoken languages (Perlman, Little, Thompson, & Thompson, 2018), indicating that iconic symbols appear more consistently across signed than spoken languages. The possible difference in prevalence may be because the signed and spoken modalities lend themselves to different types of iconic mappings: signed languages are better able to represent spatial relationships iconically, and spoken languages are better able to represent auditory relationships iconically (Dingemanse et al., 2015). Indeed, there seem to be modality-specific interactions between iconicity and lexical class, with verbs for example rated more highly iconic in signed languages and adjectives more highly iconic in spoken languages (Perlman et al., 2018). If iconicity does turn out to be more prevalent in sign than spoken languages, the transparency of this iconicity is nevertheless low. Echoing early findings from Klima and Bellugi (1979), recent evidence suggests that non-signers' accuracy in guessing the meanings of isolated signs is very low, and that using iconicity as a "guessing" strategy can yield incorrect guesses (Sehyr & Emmorey, 2019), even for signs produced in child-directed signing contexts (Fitch, Arunachalam, & Lieberman, 2018).

Does Iconicity Aid Language Learning?

With more robust ways of understanding the mappings involved in linking an iconic symbol to its referent (e.g., Emmorey, 2014; Meir, 2010; Taub 2001; Wilcox, 2004), researchers began to recognize that symbols were not merely either iconic or arbitrary. Rather iconicity could be seen as falling on a continuum from low iconicity to high iconicity, a metric that often reflects the transparency of iconicity to either a novice learner or a fluent speaker (Dingemanse, Perlman, & Perniss, 2019). In addition to a gradient measure of iconicity, iconicity can be categorized into different types (e.g., Lepic, Börstell, Belsitzman, & Sandler, 2016; Occhino, 2017; Ortega, Sümer, & Özyürek, 2017). More refined ways of defining and measuring iconicity have allowed researchers to better test whether and under what conditions language learners leverage iconicity.

Adult language learners seem to be exquisitely sensitive to iconicity during natural language learning and in language learning in the lab. In general, sign-naive adults learn highly iconic signs better than signs with little iconicity (Baus, Carreiras, & Emmorey, 2013; Lieberth & Gamble, 1991). In the same vein, speakers learn sound-symbolic words better than non-sound symbolic words (Lockwood, Dingemanse, & Hagoort, 2016). Although iconicity seems to help during adults' initial learning phase, it can also lead them astray; adult sign language learners make sign errors that maintain the iconic motivation often at the expense of phonological information (e.g., remembering that the sign COW depicts a cow's horns, but forgetting the correct handshape; Ortega & Morgan, 2015). That adult learners show sensitivity to iconicity during language learning may be relatively uncontroversial; they have the conceptual knowledge and cognitive abilities necessary to see the different ways a symbol can iconically map to a referent. Infants and toddlers, on the other hand, may not have such tools to leverage iconicity during early language development.

A growing body of literature, however, suggests that iconicity matters in children's first-language acquisition as well. Hearing children produce iconic spoken words more frequently than non-iconic spoken words (Imai, Kita, Nagumo, & Okada, 2008; Massaro & Perlman, 2017; Perry, Perlman, & Lupyan, 2015). Similarly, iconic signs are overrepresented in deaf children's early signed vocabularies (Caselli & Pyers, 2017; Caselli & Pyers, 2019; Thompson, Vinson, Woll, & Vigliocco, 2012). Crucially, the effects of iconicity do not wash out the effects of other properties of words. Frequency and phonological composition play important roles in children's growing vocabularies (Caselli & Pyers, 2017; Caselli & Pyers, 2019; Thompson et al., 2012). Nevertheless, some evidence suggests that the ability to leverage iconicity emerges with age. In laboratory studies, children's ability to learn novel iconic signs seems to get progressively better over the early preschool years (Magid & Pyers, 2017; Tolar, Lederberg, Gokhale, & Tomasello, 2007; Chen, Magid, & Pyers, 2016). Systematic analyses of large datasets of parental reports of children's vocabularies, either signed or spoken, have shown that iconicity seems to exert its greatest effect during the window of development most associated with rapid vocabulary growth. Among signing children, iconic signs were most prevalent in their vocabularies between the ages of 22–36 months (Thompson et al., 2012), and among children learning English, systematic sound-meaning relationships were stronger among words frequently acquired between the ages of two and six years (Monaghan, Shillcock, Christiansen, & Kirby, 2014). This developmental pattern indicates that for the youngest language learners, the cognitive demands of detecting the analogous relationship between phonological form and meaning may be too difficult (although see Massaro and Perlman (2017) for a discussion of the early productive use of animal sounds). Only once this cognitive ability is in place can children reliably use iconicity to acquire new words, though this ability seems to emerge relatively early in language learning.

A number of open questions about the role of iconicity in language acquisition remain. For example, we do not yet understand the nature of the mechanisms that underlie the effects of iconicity. Some evidence suggests that parents modify their signs to highlight iconicity by repeating and lengthening them during child-directed signing (Fuks, 2018; Perniss, Lu, Morgan, & Vigliocco, 2017). Thus, children's apparent early sensitivity to iconicity may arise because parents provide more helpful learning contexts for iconic than non-iconic signs. Additionally, while we have a good understanding of how age affects the ability to leverage iconicity in the native acquisition of a first language and in adult second-language acquisition, we know little about how the unfortunately common experience of delayed first-language acquisition of a sign language by deaf children with hearing parents affects their sensitivity to iconicity. Perhaps the more mature brain of late learning children allows these children to readily access iconicity during the earliest stages of their vocabulary development. These and many other questions make clear that there is still much work to be done to understand the function and effect of iconicity across modalities for both language acquisition and processing.

Conclusion

As we have illustrated throughout this chapter, the study of iconicity has been politically and philosophically fraught, and scientific inquiry has come into conflict with the interests of a marginalized group of people. Acknowledging the unique properties of sign languages once meant jeopardizing their linguistic status. The iconicity in sign languages initially made them seem somehow lesser or less linguistically structured than spoken languages, which were thought to be almost entirely arbitrary. As the linguistic status of sign language gained widespread acceptance, the unique properties of sign languages were reframed as affordances of the modality. Consequently, the study of iconicity in signed and

44 Naomi Caselli et al.

spoken languages has blossomed, and iconicity is seen as a fundamental feature of human language, regardless of modality. Iconicity presents a level of linguistic structure that has complex relationships with phonological, morphological, lexical, and syntactic structure.

We see the evolving scientific framework of iconicity as an example of how serious investigation of sign language not only benefits Deaf people and sign language users but can contribute to our understanding of the human capacity for language broadly construed. Insights from a feature widely recognized and examined in the signed modality have now enriched our understanding of an important feature of all human languages. By looking at the full range of human experiences, we can better understand human language and development more broadly.

Note

1 The notion that gestures are, by definition, non-linguistic has also undergone a perhaps parallel history, and is no longer an uncontroversial view.

References

Armstrong, D. F. (1988). Some notes on ASL as a "Foreign" Language. *Sign Language Studies*, *59*(1), 231–239.

Baus, C., Carreiras, M., & Emmorey, K. (2013). When does iconicity in sign language matter? *Language and Cognitive Processes*, *28*(3), 261–271.

Bellefleur, Philip A. (1988). Letter to the editor, *Deaf Life 2*, 23.

Bennett, E. D., & Goodman, N. D. (2018). Extremely costly intensifiers are stronger than quite costly ones. *Cognition*, *178*, 147–161.

Blasi, D. E., Wichmann, S., Hammarström, H., Stadler, P. F., & Christiansen, M. H. (2016). Sound–meaning association biases evidenced across thousands of languages. *Proceedings of the National Academy of Sciences*, *113*(39), 10818–10823.

Brown, R. (1978). *Why are signed languages easier to learn than spoken languages? Part two. Bulletin of the American Academy of Arts and Sciences*, *32*(3), 25–44.

Caselli, N. K., & Pyers, J. E. (2017). The road to language learning is not entirely iconic: Iconicity, neighborhood density, and frequency facilitate acquisition of sign language. *Psychological Science*, *28*(7), 979–987.

Caselli, N. K., & Pyers, J. E. (2019). *Degree and not type of iconicity affects sign language vocabulary acquisition. Journal of Experimental Psychology: Learning, Memory, and Cognition*, *46*(1), 127–139.

Chen, J., Magid, R., & Pyers, J. (2016, November). *The effect of iconicity type on preschoolers' gesture learning: A role for embodiment? Conference on Language Development*. Poster presented at the 41st Annual Boston University Conference on Language Development, Boston, MA.

Dingemanse, M., Blasi, D. E., Lupyan, G., Christiansen, M. H., & Monaghan, P. (2015). Arbitrariness, iconicity, and systematicity in language. *Trends in Cognitive Sciences*, *19*(10), 603–615.

Dingemanse, M., Perlman, M., & Perniss, P. (2019). *Experimental approaches to iconicity: Operationalizing form-meaning resemblances in language. Language and Cognition.*

Dudis, P. G. (2004). Body partitioning and real-space blends. *Cognitive Linguistics, 15*(2), 223–238.

Emmorey, K. (2014). Iconicity as structure mapping. *Philosophical Transactions of the Royal Society, B: Biological Sciences, 369*(1651), 20130301.

Ferrara, L., & Hodge, G. (2018). Language as description, indication, and depiction. *Frontiers in Psychology, 9,* 716.

Fitch, A., Arunachalam, S., & Lieberman, A. (2018, November): *Learning words from context in ASL: Evidence from a Human Simulation Paradigm.* Poster presented at the 43rd Boston University Conference on Language Development.

Fuks, O. (2018). *Two styles of infant-directed signing in Israeli Sign Language (ISL).* Paper presented at the Sign Language Acquisition and Assessment Conference, Haifa, Israel.

Hockett, C. (1960). The origin of speech. *Scientific American, 203,* 88–96.

Hofer, M., & Levy, R. P. (2019). Iconicity and Structure in the Emergence of Combinatoriality. *Psyarxiv.* Retrieved from https://psyarxiv.com/vsjkt/.

Hoffmeister, R. (1990). ASL and its implications for education. In H. Bornstein (Ed.), *Manual Communication in America.* Washington, DC: Gallaudet University Press.

Imai, M., Kita, S., Nagumo, M., & Okada, H. (2008). Sound symbolism facilitates early verb learning. *Cognition, 109*(1), 54–65.

Johnson, R. E., Liddell, S. K., & Erting, C. J. (1989). *Unlocking the curriculum: Principles for achieving access in Deaf education.* Working Paper. 89–83.

Kawahara, S., Noto, A., & Kumagai, G. (2018). Sound symbolic patterns in Pokémon names. *Phonetica, 75*(3), 219–244.

Klima, E. S., & Bellugi, U. (1979). *The signs of language.* Cambridge, MA: Harvard University Press.

Kusters, A., De Meulder, M., Friedner, M., & Emery, S. (2015). *On "diversity" and "inclusion": Exploring paradigms for achieving sign language people's rights.* Working paper.

Lane, H., Hoffmeister, R., & Bahan, B. (2001). The Hearing Agenda II. In L. Bragg (Ed.),*Deaf World: A Historical Reader and Primary Sourcebook* (p. 365). New York University Press.

Lepic, R., Börstell, C., Belsitzman, G., & Sandler, W. (2016). Taking meaning in hand. *Sign Language & Linguistics, 19*(1), 37–81.

Lieberth, A. K., & Gamble, M. E. B. (1991). The role of iconicity in sign language learning by hearing adults. *Journal of Communication Disorders, 24*(2), 89–99.

Liddell, S.K. (1995). Real, Surrogate, and Token Space: Grammatical Consequences in ASL. In K. Emmorey & J.S. Reilly (Eds.), *Language, Gesture, and Space.* Hillsdale, NJ: Lawrence Erlbaum Associates.

Linguistic Society of America. (2001, July 1). *Resolution: Sign Languages.* Retrieved from https://www.linguisticsociety.org/resource/resolution-sign-languages.

Lockwood, G., Dingemanse, M., & Hagoort, P. (2016). Sound-symbolism boosts novel word learning. *Journal of Experimental Psychology: Learning, Memory, and Cognition, 42*(8), 1274.

Magid, R. W., & Pyers, J. E. (2017). "I use it when I see it": The role of development and experience in Deaf and hearing children's understanding of iconic gesture. *Cognition, 162,* 73–86.

Massaro, D. W., & Perlman, M. (2017). Quantifying iconicity's contribution during language acquisition: Implications for vocabulary learning. *Frontiers in Communication*, 2, 4.

Meier, R. P. (1987). Elicited imitation of verb agreement in American Sign Language: Iconically or morphologically determined? *Journal of Memory and Language*, 26(3), 362–376.

Meier, R. P., Mauk, C. E., Cheek, A., & Moreland, C. J. (2008). The form of children's early signs: Iconic or motoric determinants? *Language Learning and Development*, 4(1), 63–98.

Meir, I. (2010). Iconicity and metaphor: Constraints on metaphorical extension of iconic forms. *Language*, 86(4), 865–896.

Meir, I., Padden, C., Aronoff, M., & Sandler, W. (2013). Competing iconicities in the structure of languages. *Cogn Linguist*, 24(2). doi:10.1515/cog-2013-0010.

De Meulder, M. (2015). The legal recognition of sign languages. *Sign Language Studies*, 15(4), 498–506.

Monaghan, P., Shillcock, R. C., Christiansen, M. H., & Kirby, S. (2014). How arbitrary is language? *Philosophical transactions of the Royal Society of London, series B, 369*(1651), 20130299.

Murray, J. J. (2015). Linguistic human rights discourse in deaf community activism. *Sign Language Studies*, 15(4), 379–410.

National Geographic (1981). *Gorilla*.

Newport, E. L., & Meier, R. P. (1985). *The acquisition of American Sign Language*. Hillsdale, NJ: Lawrence Erlbaum Associates, Inc.

Occhino, C. (2017). An introduction to embodied cognitive phonology: claw-5 hand-shape distribution in ASL and Libras. *Complutense Journal of English Studies*, 25, 69.

Orlansky, M. D., & Bonvillian, J. D. (1984). The role of iconicity in early sign language acquisition. *Journal of Speech and Hearing Disorders*, 49(3), 287–292.

Ortega, G., & Morgan, G. (2015). Phonological development in hearing learners of a sign language: The influence of phonological parameters, sign complexity, and iconicity. *Language Learning*, 65(3), 660–688.

Ortega, G., Sümer, B., & Özyürek, A. (2017). Type of iconicity matters in the vocabulary development of signing children. *Developmental Psychology*, 53(1), 89.

Padden, C. A., Meir, I., Hwang, S. O., Lepic, R., Seegers, S., & Sampson, T. (2013). Patterned iconicity in sign language lexicons. *Gesture*, 13(3), 287–308.

Perlman, M., Little, H., Thompson, B., & Thompson, R. L. (2018). Iconicity in Signed and Spoken Vocabulary: A Comparison Between American Sign Language, British Sign Language, English, and Spanish. *Frontiers in Psychology*, 9, 1433.

Perniss, P., Lu, J. C., Morgan, G., & Vigliocco, G. (2017). Mapping language to the world: The role of iconicity in the sign language input. *Developmental Science, 21*(2), 10.1111/desc.12551.

Perniss, P., Thompson, R., & Vigliocco, G. (2010). Iconicity as a general property of language: evidence from spoken and signed languages. *Frontiers in Psychology*, 1, 227.

Perry, L. K., Perlman, M., & Lupyan, G. (2015). Iconicity in English and Spanish and its relation to lexical category and age of acquisition. *PLoS One*, 10(9), e0137147.

Petitto, L. A. (1987). On the autonomy of language and gesture: Evidence from the acquisition of personal pronouns in American Sign Language. *Cognition*, 27(1), 1–52.

Reagan, T. (2011). Ideological barriers to American Sign Language: Unpacking linguistic resistance. *Sign Language Studies*, 11(4), 606–636.

de Saussure, F. (1919). *Corso di Linguistica Generale, introduction*. Italian translation and commentary by Tullio de Mauro. Bari, Italy: Laterza (1967).

Schmidtke, D., & Conrad, M. (2018). Effects of affective phonological iconicity in online language processing: Evidence from a letter search task. *Journal of Experimental Psychology: General, 147*(10), 1544.

Sehyr, Z. S., & Emmorey, K. (2019). The perceived mapping between form and meaning in American Sign Language depends on linguistic knowledge and task: evidence from iconicity and transparency judgments. *Language and Cognition, 11*(2), 208–234.

Sparrow, R. (2005). Defending deaf culture: The case of cochlear implants. *Journal of Political Philosophy, 13*(2), 135–152.

Stokoe, W., Casterline, D., & Croneberg, C. (1965). *A dictionary of ASL on linguistic principles*. Washington, DC: Gallaudet Press.

Taub, S. F. (2001). *Language from the body: Iconicity and metaphor in American Sign Language*. Washington, DC: Cambridge University Press.

Terrace, H. S. (2019). *Why Chimpanzees can't learn language and only humans can*. New York: Columbia University Press.

Thompson, R. L., Vinson, D. P., Woll, B., & Vigliocco, G. (2012). The road to language learning is iconic: Evidence from British Sign Language. *Psychological Science, 23*(12), 1443–1448.

Tolar, T. D., Lederberg, A. R., Gokhale, S., & Tomasello, M. (2007). The development of the ability to recognize the meaning of iconic signs. *Journal of Deaf Studies and Deaf Education, 13*(2), 225–240.

Tufts Daily (2013, May 19). *Faculty approves American Sign Language for Part I of foreign language requirement*.

Wilcox, S. (1989). *Foreign language requirement? Why not American Sign Language? ERIC Digests*.

Wilcox, S. (2004). Cognitive iconicity: Conceptual spaces, meaning, and gesture in signed language. *Cognitive Linguistics, 15*(2), 119–148.

Wilcox, S., & Wilcox, P. (1995). The gestural expression of modality in ASL. In J. Bybee & S. Fleischman (Eds.), *Modality in grammar and discourse* (pp. 135–162). Philadelphia: John Benjamins.

Young, L., Morris, C., & Langdon, C. (2012). "He said what?!" Constructed dialogue in various interface modes. *Sign Language Studies, 12*(3), 398–413.

4

THE ACQUISITION OF MOTION EVENTS IN VERBS OF MOTION

Frances Conlin

Children's understanding of spatial relations represents an important feature of their semantic proficiency and allows them to construct meaning from the world around them. Signed languages offer a unique glimpse into the means through which this acquisition process occurs in a visual language. Verbs of motion (VOM) in signed languages can be analyzed according to the features of motion events – including figure, ground, path, and manner. In this chapter, we examine these verbs of motion and how deaf children develop an understanding of these as they occur in motion events.

Motion Event Theory

Talmy (1985, 1991, 2000, 2003) described motion events as "containing movement or maintenance of a stationary location" (1985, p. 85). These events are further analyzed into the features of figure, motion, ground, path, manner, and cause. The entity (or entities) whose movement or location is specified is referred to as the *figure(s)*. A verb serves as the means by which the *motion* component is indicated. As the figure undergoes motion, its' relationship with other entities is observable through the *ground* component. The *path* is demonstrated through the course a figure takes as it moves or remains located with respect to the ground. Moreover, the way in which the figure moves indicates its' *manner* within a motion event. Finally, as its name suggests, the *cause* remains the reason for which the figure moves or is located in position. Talmy related the following examples to demonstrate how each of these components is united into a single motion event (Talmy, 1985, p. 61).

Motion Event signifying movement:
The pencil   rolled   off   the table
[FIGURE][MOTION + MANNER][PATH][GROUND]

Motion Event signifying location:
The pencil   lay   on   the table
[FIGURE][MOTION + CAUSE] [PATH][GROUND]

Motion Events in Signed Languages

In signed languages, motion events may be expressed through the employment of signs or through constructions involving verbs of motion and location (Conlin-Luippold, 2015). Figure 4.1 demonstrates how a signer incorporates signs of American Sign Language (ASL) into discourse in order to delineate each of the components within a motion event.

As the above example shows, signs effectively demonstrate spatial relations in signed discourse because each sign represents a semantic role. In addition to signs, verbs of motion and location also serve as a means for expressing motion events in signed languages. In the present, we now turn our attention specifically to verbs of motion and the way in which signed languages utilize these structures to communicate motion events[1].

Verbs of Motion

In signed languages, verbs of motion are depicted on small-scale space or large-scale space (Smith & Cormier, 2014). Both types of space utilize classifier handshapes to allow a signer to demonstrate the whole or part of an action in the space in front of the signer's body[2]. For small-scale space, the signer's hands represent entities being located or undergoing an action. In Figure 4.2 below,

  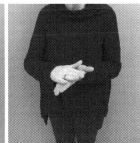

FIGURE 4.1   A Motion Event With Signs

50 Frances Conlin

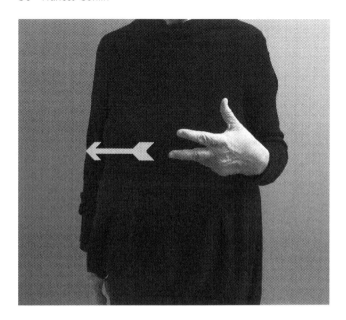

FIGURE 4.2 ASL Verb of Motion 1

the signer has employed a "3CL vehicle" classifier handshape to show the action of a car moving through a scale that is limited to the area in front of the signer's body.

In contrast, large-scale space refers to when the signer moves "as if they were interacting with people or objects on a real-world scale" (Smith & Cormier, 2014, p. 277). Figure 4.3 offers an example of this scale as a signer adopts an "S" classifier handshape on both hands to depict the action of "rolling out dough."

Along with classifier handshapes, signers also rely on specific types of movement to communicate the action within a motion event (Supalla, 1982; Engberg-Pedersen, 1993). For verbs of motion, signers typically utilize motion-active movement to show the active motion of an entity (as shown in Figure 4.2). A second movement type, referred to as manner-imitative movement, allows the signer to demonstrate how an action is taking place through the imitation of the action being described (as shown in Figure 4.3). Taken together, these movements, combined with classifier handshapes and the locations designated within the signing space provide the framework through which signers convey motion events.

As can be observed from the ensuing examples, verbs of motion provide a productive means of relaying a host of information. This differs from a signed lexical utterance where signs are set – and therefore limited – in the amount of information they can convey. In the next section, we can observe how each of the parts of a motion event blend together within a verb of motion (VOM)).

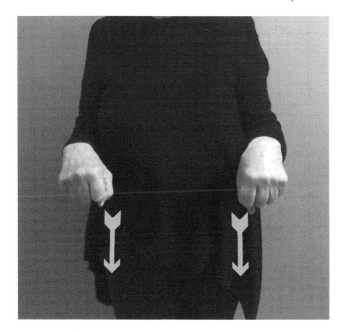

FIGURE 4.3 ASL Verb of Motion 2

Motion Events within Verbs of Motion

In Figure 4.4, we can observe how each of the components of a motion event combines through a verb of motion. After introducing a context involving a rabbit (with the sign for RABBIT), the signer adopts a "bent V" classifier handshape (typically employed to describe animals) to indicate the RABBIT as *figure*. Using the arm of their non-dominant hand for the *ground*[3], the signer employs an upward movement to depict both *path* and *motion*. At the same time, the movement occurs in a hopping fashion to demonstrate *manner*.

Acquisition of Motion Event Structure within Verbs of Motion

A small but promising pool of studies has investigated how motion event structure in verbs of motion is acquired by deaf children. These studies have explored the development of motion event understanding across a range of deaf children from homesigners (Morford, 2002) to young signers (Morgan, Herman, Barriere, & Woll, 2008) and adolescent teens (Slobin, et al., 2003; Tang, Sze, & Lam, 2007). Across different signed languages, commonalities have emerged. Most notably, findings have revealed that while deaf children slowly develop ease in their command of the figure component, the ground component remains a challenge. Tang et al. (2007) suggested this circumstance is likely due to the "conceptually more prominent role" (p. 308) of the figure handshape. Likewise,

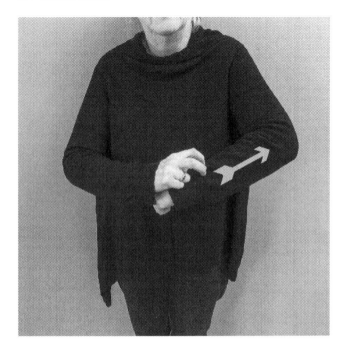

FIGURE 4.4 ASL Verb of Motion 3

with ground bearing its own unique handshape on the non-dominant hand, children wrestle with the challenge of attending to it within the verb of motion.

While an understanding of how the repertoire of figure and ground handshapes develops is advantageous, what is lacking in the literature is a more thorough examination of how deaf children acquire each of the components that structure a motion event. With this in mind, the current investigation explores how deaf children develop an understanding of each component of a motion event within a verb of motion. Along with figure and ground, this study addresses how the acquisition process proceeds for the components of motion, manner, and path and how each of these components develops amid the variables of age and parentage.

Methodology

Subjects

A total of 350 subjects were recruited for the present study. These subjects were deaf students enrolled in day and residential programs for the deaf in the Northeast of the United States. Of these students, 111 (32%) were Deaf Children of Deaf Parents (DCDP) while 239 (68%) were Deaf Children of Hearing Parents (DCHP)[4]. The ages of the students ranged from 4 to 18 years with a mean age of 11.44 years.

Subjects were assigned to one of five age groups in years: 4–6, 7–9, 10–12, 13–15 and 16–18. The reasoning for this was twofold. On the one hand, combining ages in this way allowed for the observation of any critical period effects arising in the data (Mayberry & Kluender, 2018). On the other hand, as in previous studies (Novogrodsky, Caldwell-Harris, Fish, & Hoffmeister, 2014), the advantage of this two-year grouping ensured that each age group included an ample number of DCDP.

Materials

For the purposes of this study, a task of the American Sign Language Assessment Instrument (Hoffmeister, Fish, Benedict, Henner, & Rosenburg, 2013) was administered to subjects. The ASLAI, developed by Robert Hoffmeister and colleagues at the Center for the Study of Communication and the Deaf (CSCD), consists of 15 different receptive and expressive tasks for evaluating ASL proficiency. In the present investigation, the Real Objects, Plurals and Arrangements task (ROPL) was selected as a measure of assessing competency in verb of motion constructions.

Procedure

For testing, students underwent a training phase prior to testing. In the practice items, students were shown a stimulus video and asked to select from one of four possible signed answers (A, B, C, or D). Students were instructed to select the item that clearly matched what was shown in the stimulus video. Practice items provided answers in "green" when the correct answer was selected and "red" when an incorrect answer was chosen. Following training, students were administered the actual test. During testing, no feedback was offered regarding the correctness of their selections.

Of the 45 total test items within the ROPL, 30 are designed to assess verbs of location (VOLs) while the remaining 15 items address verb of motion proficiency. Thus, for the current study, the 15 verb of motion test items were selected for analysis.

Results

Results were first analyzed according to overall receptive comprehension of each motion event component as they appeared in verbs of motion. As shown in Table 4.1, the means and standard deviations for the components of motion ($M = .848$, $SD = .142$) and manner ($M = .838$, $SD = .148$) were acquired with greater ease compared to the components of path ($M = .806$, $SD = .161$), figure ($M = .782$, $SD = .158$) and ground ($M = .724$, $SD = .169$). Scores were then further analyzed according to how different age groups performed in relation to each motion event component. As can be observed in Table 4.1, results

TABLE 4.1 VOM Means (St. Devs.) Total Correct & Age Groups

Age Group	N	Correct	Figure	Ground	Manner	Motion	Path
Total	350	0.587(0.206)	0.782(0.158)	0.724(0.169)	0.838(0.148)	0.848(0.142)	0.806(0.161)
4 to 6	46	0.401(0.21)	0.693(0.216)	0.601(0.212)	0.742(0.226)	0.749(0.229)	0.681(0.23)
7 to 9	73	0.504(0.192)	0.762(0.153)	0.666(0.155)	0.806(0.157)	0.838(0.129)	0.762(0.163)
10 to 12	73	0.627(0.18)	0.799(0.137)	0.758(0.138)	0.873(0.106)	0.871(0.108)	0.838(0.124)
13 to 15	96	0.657(0.161)	0.818(0.119)	0.77(0.136)	0.861(0.098)	0.873(0.094)	0.846(0.107)
16 to 18	62	0.667(0.197)	0.799(0.164)	0.773(0.165)	0.871(0.137)	0.869(0.141)	0.854(0.146)

The Acquisition of Motion Events **55**

demonstrated advancing competency for each semantic component with increasing age.

As a further means of analyzing scores, an ANOVA test was performed to investigate whether any of the differences for age between each of the motion event components within a VOM were significant. Table 4.2 offers the results of this analysis as well as tests for significance between the individual age groups. The results indicated that the most significant differences were seen between the youngest and oldest subjects. Likewise, there appeared to be a ceiling effect for performance once subjects reached the 10- to 12-year-old age group, as there were no differences between this group and any of the older groups of students (all p's > .999).

Along with age, results were analyzed to examine if there was any difference according to parental hearing status. Initial observations suggested no significant differences between the scores of DCDP and DCHP (Table 4.3). Though initially surprising, this finding became understandable when it was revealed that the mean age differed between the two groups (DCHP: $M = 12.14$, $SD = 3.83$; DCDP: $M = 10.01$, $SD = 3.80$). Furthermore, this difference in age based on parentage was significant, $t(348) = 4.86$, $p = .001$. Therefore, given that the DCHP group were older, this provided them with the opportunity to perform more similarly to DCDP on the VOM task items.

TABLE 4.2 Test of Significance Between Age Groups (all two-tailed p-values)

Comparison	Correct	Figure	Ground	Manner	Motion	Path
ANOVA	<0.001	<0.001	<0.001	<0.001	<0.001	<0.001
4-6 v. 7-9	0.034	0.176	0.306	0.164	0.006	0.047
4-6 v. 10-12	<0.001	0.003	<0.001	<0.001	<0.001	<0.001
4-6 v. 13-15	<0.001	<0.001	<0.001	<0.001	<0.001	<0.001
4-6 v. 16-18	<0.001	0.004	<0.001	<0.001	<0.001	<0.001
7-9 v. 10-12	0.001	>0.999	0.005	0.047	>0.999	0.022
7-9 v. 13-15	<0.001	0.185	<0.001	0.134	>0.999	0.004
7-9 v. 16-18	<0.001	>0.999	0.001	0.087	>0.999	0.004
10-12 v. 13-15	>0.999	>0.999	>0.999	>0.999	>0.999	>0.999
10-12 v. 16-18	>0.999	>0.999	>0.999	>0.999	>0.999	>0.999
13-15 v. 16-18	>0.999	>0.999	>0.999	>0.999	>0.999	>0.999

TABLE 4.3 VOM Parentage Tests for Means and Significance

	DCHP (n = 239)	DCDP (n = 111)	t-stat	p-value
Correct	0.589(0.201)	0.583(0.218)	0.238	0.812
Figure	0.78(0.156)	0.789(0.161)	-0.494	0.622
Ground	0.726(0.165)	0.721(0.177)	0.262	0.793
Manner	0.841(0.142)	0.832(0.161)	0.556	0.579
Motion	0.848(0.14)	0.849(0.146)	-0.024	0.981
Path	0.809(0.158)	0.801(0.168)	0.465	0.642

56 Frances Conlin

As a final means of investigation, a Multiple Linear Regression analysis was performed examining how both age and parentage affected VOM scores (Table 4.4). Significant, positive coefficients were found for both age (p = .001) and parentage (p = .047) among performance on VOM test items.

Discussion

The foregoing study investigated deaf children's comprehension of motion events in verbs of motion (VOM). The data indicated that for all deaf children, the motion event components of motion and manner are acquired with greater ease over those of path, figure, and ground. Previous research has demonstrated that knowledge of handshapes alone represents a formidable challenge in understanding verbs of motion (Slobin, et al., 2003; Morgan et al., 2008). This study has taken an additional step to compare how the handshapes within motion events (figure and ground) compare with motion, manner and path and demonstrates the need to provide for directed instruction of these components from the earliest ages.

In addition to insight into how each of the components of a motion event are acquired, this study also examined how the variables of age and parentage influence this acquisition process. In regards to age, children in the youngest group of subjects (aged 4–6) experienced the most errors across the semantic components. With increasing age, scores improved for each of the components until subjects reached the 10- to 12-year-old age group. At that point, subject performance on motion event components was no longer distinguishable from older subject groups.

Since a wealth of research proposes that deaf children born to Deaf parents (DCDP) enjoy an advantage in the acquisition process (Newport & Meier, 1985; Lane, Hoffmeister, & Bahan, 1996; Mayberry, 2007), the results for parentage were *initially* perplexing. It was expected that these children would automatically perform better as a group compared to deaf children born to hearing parents (DCHP). However, when it was discovered that the sample of DCHP tended to be older than their DCDP counterparts, this made sense. For one thing, the older children had the advantage of longer exposure over time to ASL than their younger peers. Likewise, research has found that when DCHP are placed in exemplar signing programs from a young age, their competency in a signed language mirrors that of native signing children (Henner, Caldwell-Harris, Novogrodsky, & Hoffmeister, 2016). This is the fortunate consequence of being immersed in a signed language environment.

TABLE 4.4 OLS Regression of VOM Correct by Age and Parentage

	Coefficient	Std. Error	t-stat	p-value
Intercept	0.304	0.034	8.950	<0.001
Age	0.023	0.003	8.940	<0.001
Parentage	0.044	0.022	1.996	0.047

The Acquisition of Motion Events **57**

Through exposure to fluent models of a signed language in and out of the classroom, DCHP are provided with plenty of opportunities to master the language. Moreover, many of these programs also offer support to hearing parents learning a signed language. These efforts produce DCHP signers whose fluency is closely on par with their native DCDP counterparts.

Additionally, the results compel insight into a further possibility pointing to the role of iconicity in certain types of verbs of motion. Given that some VOM test items involved a manner-imitative movement (in which a signer imitates how a movement is occurring), it is plausible to consider the possibility that the DCHP group may have been attending to the iconicity available in these items. In a study by Baus, Carreiras, and Emmorey (2013), a sign's iconicity allowed new adult signers greater recall over non-iconic signs. Similarly, with respect to DCHP, Caselli and Pyers (2017) noted that "it may be the case that children acquiring their first language later in childhood may rely to a greater degree on iconicity than on the phonological properties of the sign to learn their first signs" (p. 16). In their study of deaf children's sign acquisition, Caselli and Pyers found that iconicity played an important role in vocabulary development (along with the features of neighborhood density and frequency). On account of these findings, it is plausible to concede that the present results offer further testament to the impact iconicity has on the acquisition process.

The preceding study highlights the necessity of providing direct instruction of verbs of motion in signed languages. These structures provide an interface through which children can observe how language and meaning interconnect through motion events. Thus, in fostering an understanding of these structures, educators can ensure they are laying a strong foundation in both a *visual* and *accessible* language for deaf children.

Notes

1 For further reading on verbs of location, the reader is referred to Supalla (1982 & 1986), Hoffmeister (1992) and Conlin-Luippold (2015).
2 See Engberg-Pedersen (1993) and Benedicto & Brentari (2004) for reviews of major classifier handshape categories.
3 In cases where the non-dominant hand is not required to express a verb of motion, the ground is indicated by the relationship between the dominant figure handshape and its movement along the spatial plane from one point to another. See Tang (2003) for further analysis of this in Hong Kong Sign Language (HKSL).
4 Given that only 5% of deaf children are born to deaf parents (Mitchell & Karchmer, 2004), this sample size was fortuitous for the goals of the current study.

References

Baus, C., Carreiras, M., & Emmorey, K. (2013). When does iconicity in sign language matter? *Language and Cognition Processes*, *28*(3), 261–271.
Benedicto, E., & Brentari, D. (2004). Where did all the arguments go? Argument changing properties of classifiers in ASL. *Natural Language and Linguistic Theory*, *22*, 743–810.

Caselli, N., & Pyers, J. (2017). The road to language learning is not entirely iconic: Iconicity, neighborhood density and frequency facilitate acquisition of sign language. *Psychological Science*, *28*(7), 979–987.

Conlin-Luippold, F. M. (2015). *Deaf children's understanding of the language of motion and location in ASL (Doctoral dissertation)*. Available from ProQuest Dissertations & Theses Global database. (Accession Order No. AAT 3734035)

Engberg-Pedersen, E. (1993). *Space in Danish Sign Language: The semantics and morphosyntax of the use of space in a visual language*. Hamburg: Signum Press.

Henner, J., Caldwell-Harris, C., Novogrodsky, R., & Hoffmeister, R. (2016). American Sign Language syntax and analogical reasoning skills are influenced by early acquisition and age of entry to signing schools for the deaf. *Frontiers in Psychology*, *7*, 1–14.

Hoffmeister, R. (1992). *Why MCE won't work: ASL forms inside signed English*(Working Paper #16). Boston: Boston University, Center for the Study of Communication and Deafness.

Hoffmeister, R. (1999). *American Sign Language Assessment Instrument (ASLAI)*. Manuscript, Center for the Study of Communication and the Deaf, Boston University.

Hoffmeister, R., Fish, S., Benedict, R., Henner, J., & Rosenburg, P. (2013). *American Sign Language Assessment Instrument (ASLAI): Revision 4*. Boston University Center for the Study of Communication and the Deaf, Boston University.

Mitchell, R., & Karchmer, M. (2004). Chasing the mythical ten percent: Parental hearing status of deaf and hard of hearing students in the United States. *Sign Language Studies*, *4*(2), 138–163.

Lane, H., Hoffmeister, R., & Bahan, B. (1996). *A journey into the Deaf World*. San Diego, CA: Dawn Sign Press.

Mayberry, R. (2007). When timing is everything: Age of first language acquisition effects on second language learning. *Applied Psycholinguistics*, *28*(3), 537–549.

Mayberry, R., & Kluender, R. (2018). Rethinking the critical period for language: New insights into an old question from American Sign Language. *Bilingualism: Language and Cognition*, *21*(5), 938–944.

Morgan, G., Herman, R., Barriere, I., & Woll, B. (2008). The onset and mastery of spatial language in children acquiring British Sign Language. *Cognitive Development*, *23*, 1–19.

Morford, J. (2002). The expression of motion events in homesign. *Sign Language and Linguistics*, *5*(1), 55–71.

Newport, E., & Meier, R. (1985). The acquisition of American Sign Language. In D. Slobin (Ed.), *The crosslinguistic study of language acquisition. Vol. 1: The data* (pp. 881–938). Hillsdale, NJ: Lawrence Erlbaum Associates.

Novogrodsky, R., Caldwell-Harris, C., Fish, S., & Hoffmeister, R. (2014). The development of antonym knowledge in American Sign Language (ASL) and its relationship to reading comprehension in English. *Language learning*, *64*(4), 749–770.

Schembri, A. (2003). Rethinking 'classifiers' in signed languages. In K. Emmorey (Ed.), *Perspectives on classifier constructions in sign languages* (pp. 3–34). Mahwah, NJ: Lawrence Erlbaum Associates, Inc.

Slobin, D., Hoiting, N., Kuntze, M., Lindert, R., Weinberg, A., & Pyers, J. (2003). A cognitive/functional perspective on the acquisition of "classifiers.". In K. Emmorey (ed.), *Perspectives on classifier constructions in sign language* (pp. 271–296). Mahwah, NJ: Lawrence Erlbaum.

Smith, S., & Cormier, K. (2014). In or out? Spatial scale and enactment in narratives of native and non-native signing deaf children acquiring British Sign Language. *Sign Language Studies*, *14*(3), 275–301.

The Acquisition of Motion Events **59**

Supalla, T. (1982). *Structure and acquisition of verbs of motion and location in American Sign Language*. Unpublished doctoral dissertation, University of California, San Diego.

Talmy, L. (1985). Lexicalization patterns: semantic structure in lexical forms. In T. Shopen (Ed.), *Grammatical categories and the lexicon. Language typology and syntactic description* (Vol. III, pp. 57–149). New York: Cambridge University Press.

Talmy, L. (1991). Path to realization: A typology of event conflation, *Proceedings of the seventeenth annual meeting of the Berkeley Linguistics Society* (pp. 480–519). Berkeley, CA. Berkeley Linguistics Society.

Talmy, L. (2000). *Toward a cognitive semantics*. Cambridge, MA: Massachusetts Institute of Technology.

Talmy, L. (2003). Spatial structure in spoken and signed Language. In K. Emmorey (Ed.), *Perspectives on classifier constructions in signed languages* (pp. 169–195). Mahwah, NJ: Lawrence Erlbaum Associates.

Tang, G. (2003). Verbs of Motion and Location in Hong Kong Sign Language: Conflation and Lexicalization. In K. Emmorey (Ed.), *Perspectives on classifier constructions in sign languages* (pp. 143–165). Mahwah, NJ: Lawrence Erlbaum Associates Inc.

Tang, G., Sze, F., & Lam, S. (2007). Acquisition of simultaneous constructions by deaf children of Hong Kong Sign Language. In M. Vermeerbergen, L. Leeson & O. Crasborn (Eds.), *Simultaneity in signed languages: Form and function* (pp. 283–316). Amsterdam, The Netherlands: John Benjamins Publishing Company.

5

SUSTAINED VISUAL ATTENTION IN DEAF CHILDREN

A Deafcentric Perspective

Matthew Dye and Brennan Terhune-Cotter

> I call it *the law of the instrument,* and it may be formulated as follows: Give a small boy a hammer, and he will find that everything he encounters needs pounding.
>
> (Kaplan, 1964)

There is an ongoing debate in the field of early intervention and deaf education about the differences in executive functions between deaf and nondeaf children and what might give rise to them (Hall, 2020; Kronenberger & Pisoni, 2020; Morgan & Dye, 2020). Executive functions encompass cognitive abilities that allow a child to successfully perform tasks by planning and organizing their actions, and by maintaining focus on their goals and avoiding distraction (for a review, see Diamond, 2013). Executive functions include a range of abilities, often studied in isolation, such as working memory (Baddeley, 2012), inhibition (Bari & Robbins, 2013), and sustained attention (Fisher, 2019). Studies of deaf children from nondeaf families who have received a cochlear implant (CI) have reported deficits and large variability in outcomes for a number of these executive functions (Castellanos, Pisoni, Kronenberger, & Beer, 2016; Kronenberger, Beer, Castellanos, Pisoni, and Miyamoto (2014); Lyxell *et al.* 2008; Quittner *et al.* 2007). Several different proposals have been put forward to explain the large degree of variability in this population of children. Those proposals differ in what they see as the optimal approach to early intervention and/or remediation of executive function. Some argue that rehabilitation of hearing loss is the best approach (Kral, Kronenberger, Pisoni, & O'Donoghue, 2016), others that establishing healthy communication between caregiver and child is critical (Morgan & Dye, 2020), and yet others that early exposure to and acquisition of a natural sign language is the best approach (Hall, 2020). In this chapter we will focus on just one of the executive functions – *sustained attention* – and use that (1) to explore the evidence for and against different approaches and (2) to consider how some of those approaches interpret data based upon what we claim is an audiocentric perspective that fails to acknowledge or appreciate the experience and authority of deaf people.

Sustained Attention

The study of *attention* is the study of how information is selected and/or filtered by the human brain (Carrasco, 2011). One aspect of attention is called spatial attention. This is concerned with how information from different physical locations in the external world is selected and filtered. Visual spatial attention is the process by which we select/filter information from different parts of our visual field (Carrasco, 2018; Yeshurun, 2019). For example, as we drive down the road, we take in information from across our visual field. But while light from the deer grazing at the side of the road may fall upon our retina, we do not necessarily "see" the deer unless we are paying attention to that part of the visual field, a phenomenon called inattentional blindness (Simons & Chabris, 1999). While visual spatial attention has been well researched in deaf children and adults (Dye, Baril, & Bavelier, 2007; Daza & Phillips-Silver, 2013; Prasad, Patil, & Mishra, 2015; Bavelier *et al.* 2000; Dye, Hauser, & Bavelier, 2009; Loke & Song, 1991; Proksch & Bavelier, 2002; Stevens & Neville, 2006; Codina, Buckley, Port, & Pascalis, 2011), far less work has considered *temporal* aspects of visual attention in these populations. Temporal visual attention is concerned with how we attend to events or objects over time. For example, consider a child attending to a video on a tablet PC. That child must direct their eye gaze toward and attend to the spatial location of the video in order to understand what is happening. They must also sustain that spatial attention over time, not allowing their mind to wander or eye gaze to be averted. Sustained attention is one form of temporal attention (Fortenbaugh, DeGutis, & Esterman, 2017). A closely related process is vigilance (Oken, Salinsky, & Elsas, 2006; sometimes referred to as alerting: Posner, 2008), which refers to staying ready and alert for something to happen or appear within the visual field.

Why would we expect these temporal aspects of visual processing to be different for deaf compared to nondeaf individuals? In the spatial domain, it is anticipated that an information processing system that does not use hearing to attend to the world will instead devote more resources to doing so visually – this is referred to as a *compensation* hypothesis (Bavelier, Dye, & Hauser, 2006; Dye & Bavelier, 2010). Auditory systems are able to attend spatially to a larger field than visual systems, allowing nondeaf people to shift their visual attention to spatial locations that are prompted by peripheral sounds (Arnott & Alain, 2011). In deaf individuals, it seems that the visual system compensates by allocating more resources to the far visual periphery, making deaf people more "sensitive" to visual events occurring there (Bavelier *et al.* 2006; Pavani & Bottari, 2012). It is also

62 Matthew Dye and Brennan Terhune-Cotter

possible that such compensation can occur in the temporal domain, given the greater importance of vision for deaf children and adults. Contrary to this expectation, studies of temporal visual attention in deaf individuals have typically demonstrated performance in deaf children that is "worse" than that of nondeaf children, and have been used to support *deficit* hypotheses. These studies are summarized below.

Sustained Visual Attention and Deaf Children

One metaphor commonly used to discuss visual attention is that of the flashlight or spotlight of attention (Posner, Snyder, & Davidson, 1980). The idea is that by shining the "attentional beam" on a stimulus, it can be processed more accurately and efficiently. Attention, however, is effortful, and must be actively sustained in order to be effective (deBettencourt, Norman, & Turk-Browne, 2018). In the spotlight metaphor, one can think of the beam weakening in strength as resources are exhausted, with the amount of light on the target decreasing, and performance suffering. Sustained visual attention can be considered the ability to maintain that attentional beam over time. The ability to sustain visual attention over time has been assessed in deaf children using observational studies (Quittner et al., 2007) and surveys (Mitchell & Quittner, 1996; van Eldik, Treffers, Veerman, & Verhulst, 2004; Karchmer & Allen, 1999). Here, however, we focus on computerized assessments.

Computerized assessments of sustained attention have used variants of the continuous performance test (CPT). The purpose of a CPT is to determine how well an individual can maintain their attention for a relatively long time (typically ~9 minutes) in a task that is repetitive and requires infrequent responses. In one version of this task – the Gordon Diagnostic CPT (Gordon & Mettelman, 1988) – individuals must pay attention to a sequence of 540 digits appearing on an LED display at a rate of 1 digit/second and respond to a specific sequence of digits (a 1 followed by a 9) that occurs only 45 times. If attention cannot be sustained, and the attentional beam weakens, then the sequence will be missed. Conversely, responses to non-target sequences will produce false alarms. By examining the pattern of misses and false alarms, an index of *vigilance* can be derived that serves as a measure of the construct of interest – sustained attention.

The first study to use such a CPT with deaf children was reported by Quittner, Smith, Osberger, Mitchell, and Katz (1994) who compared three groups of children: nondeaf children, deaf children with hearing aids (HAs), and deaf children with CIs. The deaf children were in educational settings that implemented oral or Total Communication (a combination of speech, supporting signs, gestures, and drawing) approaches, so it is important to note that none of the children were proficient in, nor had they received early exposure to, American Sign Language (ASL). The children were further sub-divided into younger (6–8 years) and older (9–13 years) age groups: no *a priori* justification for this grouping was provided, although the two groups can be thought of as representing primary school and elementary school-aged children in a US context. Results suggested that (1) deaf children had worse sustained attention than nondeaf children in both age groups and (2) older deaf children looked more like their nondeaf peers if they had received a CI, but not if they used HAs. A subsequent study by the same research group recruited a larger sample and did not categorize based upon age (Smith, Quittner, Osberger, & Miyamoto, 1998). They reported that while all children started to show gains in sustained attention around the age of 8–9 years, those gains were greater for deaf children with CIs than those with HAs and neither group caught up with their nondeaf peers. Of course, caution must be taken in inferring a causal effect of being deaf on visual attention sustained from cross-sectional data that also lacks random assignment to groups: pre-existing differences between the deaf and nondeaf children unrelated to their hearing levels may have led to differences in performance on the CPT, a critique that can be leveled at all studies employing causal-comparative (ex post facto) designs.

Subsequently, Horn, Davis, Pisoni, and Miyamoto (2005) reported a retrospective longitudinal design that analyzed CPT performance prior to implantation (mean implantation age was 6.2 years), and at several time points 1–3 years post-implantation, in 88 deaf children. Again, these children used either oral communication or Total Communication (not ASL), and included a number of children who became deaf over time as a result of contracting meningitis in infancy. Due to a large amount of missing data, the researchers used a mixed effects model so that all of their data could be included. They reported the number of children for whom data was available at each age range, revealing that very few children provided data at three time points, and no children provided data at all four time points: this is a relatively sparse data set, and it is not clear that the missing data were missing-at-random (a key assumption of the statistical approach used). The authors reported that CPT performance improved each year following implantation, although the large amount of variability at pre-implant testing meant that there was no statistically significant improvement compared to that baseline score. While it is tempting to conclude that implantation led to improvements in sustained attention, there was no comparison group of deaf children who did not get CIs, and comparisons to nondeaf children were based on published norms that were likely collected under very different testing and recruitment conditions.

A study by Tharpe, Ashmead, and Rothpletz (2002) was the first to find no differences between 8- and 14-year-old nondeaf children and deaf children with HAs or CIs. Their study was careful to control for nonverbal IQ differences between the deaf and nondeaf samples, and suggested that nonverbal IQ differences may have driven the effects observed in prior studies. This study, and prior work, recruited and tested deaf children who were learning English as a primary language, with no studies reporting the inclusion of deaf children fluent in a natural sign language or deaf children from deaf families. It is possible, therefore, that these deaf children were experiencing the effects of language deprivation (Cheng, Roth, Halgren, & Mayberry, 2019; Mayberry, Davenport, Roth, & Halgren, 2018; Murray, Hall, & Snoddon, 2019). The full effect of delayed and impoverished access to natural language is still being determined by scholars, although it would not be surprising that decrements in nonverbal IQ were one corollary of such deprivation.

In yet another CPT study, Yucel and Derim (2008) compared deaf children who had received CIs at different ages with nondeaf children. All of the deaf children were enrolled in Auditory Verbal Therapy programs, and none used a sign language. The deaf children were split into two groups: those who received their implant before age four years, and those who were four years or older when they underwent the surgery – no *a priori* justification for dividing the children in this way was provided. While the performance of the two groups of deaf children with CIs did not significantly differ – suggesting age at implantation has little-or-no effect on sustained attention abilities – both groups were out-performed by a sample of nondeaf children. While the authors claimed that the deaf children who got implants later were "less mature" and "more careless" than their nondeaf peers, these claims appear to be both unsubstantiated by the data and reveal a logical fallacy in extending the results of a single CPT task to a population-level generalization about maturity and carelessness.

A study by Dye and Hauser (2014) recruited deaf children who used ASL as a first language, and compared their CPT performance with that of nondeaf children, in an attempt to determine whether being deaf was a necessary pre-condition for reported performance deficits on the CPT. In audiological terms, these signing deaf children were profoundly deaf, they did not use CIs, and all had acquired ASL as a first language from deaf parents. No differences were observed either for a younger (6–8 year) or older (9–13 year) age group – following the age grouping reported by Quittner et al. (1994). While it can be claimed that these children are not "typical" deaf children because they belong to the small proportion of deaf children with deaf parents (Mitchell & Karchmer, 2004), at a theoretical level they argue against the notion that a lack of audition alone is sufficient to bring about deficits in sustained visual attention.

Most recently, Hoffman, Tiddens, Quittner, and the CDaCI Investigative Team (2018) reported data from a large-scale longitudinal project (Childhood Development after Cochlear Implantation) that included CPT data from 106 deaf children who had received a CI five years previously. All of the deaf children were being educated using an oral-aural approach alongside nondeaf children. These children were compared with nondeaf children of the same age. The nondeaf children had mothers with higher levels of education and came from families with larger incomes – maternal education was controlled for, but family income was not. Their results suggested that the nondeaf children outperformed the deaf children, and that age of implantation was a predictor of sustained attention performance.

So, do deaf children have "deficits" in sustained visual attention? It would seem that some deaf children clearly do show performance decrements on computerized CPT assessments, yet some deaf children do not. In a recent article, Kronenberger and Pisoni (2020) highlight the importance of looking at both group differences and explaining individual variability within groups. All of the studies reported above have focused on group comparisons. Most of the studies compare nondeaf children with a specific group of deaf children: those from nondeaf families, who use HAs or CIs, and who do not know a natural sign language such as ASL. It is often argued that these deaf children are the "typical" case, with very few deaf children born to deaf parents (or born to hearing parents and provided access to a sign language from an early age). However, that does not mean that studies of deaf children from deaf families are uninformative: they provide important insights into the development of visual attention *without* auditory input. The Dye and Hauser (2014) study started from the viewpoint that enhancements in sustained visual attention were more likely than deficits, especially for deaf children who did not undergo language deprivation. Despite sample sizes much larger than previous studies, they did not find any deficits (although there were no compensatory enhancements either). At face value, this suggests that while there are undoubtedly sustained visual attention deficits in deaf children, it may not be being deaf itself that caused those deficits. This is important, as we shall see, when it comes to determining what an effective early intervention for cognitive development might look like.

Audiocentrism and Deficit Theorizing

In the extant literature, there are four different (albeit related) proposals for why being deaf in and of itself might result in weaker sustained visual attention, with some of those proposals extending to executive functions more broadly. The first, proposed by Smith et al. (1998), is the *division-of-labor* hypothesis, which claims that because deaf children cannot use hearing to attend to the world around them, they must spread their visual attention and use that to monitor their environment. This, the hypothesis proposes, results in a more diffused spread of limited attentional resources. Restoring auditory inputs via CIs, therefore, results in better visual attention skills as the children adapt to using the auditory channel to monitor their environment – an ironic claim that deaf children are better visual learners if they are given the ability to hear. This hypothesis is problematic in several ways. First, it cannot account for the lack of sustained visual attention deficits in deaf signing children – it predicts that these children would perform worse than non-signing deaf peers rather than equivalently to nondeaf children. Second, it also rests upon the notion of limited attentional resources that are spread thin, failing to consider possible compensatory mechanisms or the adoption of strategic behaviors by deaf children. Finally, its origins are in the notion of *deficit* and the idea that deaf children must "rely" upon vision in the absence of audition – the audist/linguicist equivalent of suggesting that deaf children are forced to "rely" upon a sign language for communication – betraying an audiocentrism that sees "hearing" and "speech" as aspirational and superior for deaf children (Bauman, 2004; Eckert & Rowley, 2013; Humphries, 1975).

Conway, Pisoni, and Kronenberger (2009) proposed the *auditory scaffolding hypothesis*. Simply stated, the auditory scaffolding hypothesis explains poor spoken language outcomes in deaf children with CIs as resulting from both a lack of access to the sound structure of speech *and* from cognitive deficits that also stem from a lack of access to sound. The auditory scaffolding hypothesis considers sound to be crucial for the development and support of sequencing abilities, although it can arguably be extended to other cognitive functions. Inherent in this view is that vision is superior for spatial processing whereas audition is superior for sequential statistical learning. There is not the space here to discuss studies of statistical learning in deaf individuals in depth (see Hall, 2020). Suffice to say that whereas studies of non-signing deaf children with CIs reveal sequence learning deficits (Conway, Pisoni, Anaya, Karpicke, & Henning, 2011; Lévesque, Théoret, & Champoux, 2014), studies with deaf signing children fail to replicate those findings (Hall, Eigsti, Bortfeld, & Lillo-Martin, 2017; von Koss Torkildsen, Arciuli, Haukedal, & Wie, 2018; Giustolisi & Emmorey, 2018). Like the division-of-labor hypothesis, the auditory scaffolding hypothesis seeks to attribute observed deficits to a lack of access to sound on the basis that being deaf must result in some kind of problem or performance decrement. It is important to state that audition is not a prerequisite for language – deaf individuals who are native users of signed languages are an existence proof that language does not depend upon any specific sensory modality. However, these deficit approaches commonly start from the audiocentric premise that acquiring *spoken* language is to be prioritized – given that deaf children commonly struggle to successfully acquire proficiency in spoken language, there is already a deficit (poor language) that may be explainable by other deficits (poor cognition). As we will suggest below, if one starts from the assumption that deaf children do not struggle to acquire *language*, then one does not seek to theorize deficits but instead to consider the optimal linguistic and social environment to promote language acquisition. A philosophical difference, but one which also has significant impacts upon how we as scientists theorize about deaf children.

Kral *et al.* (2016) proposed the idea of being deaf as suffering from a "*connectome disease.*" They argued that being deaf results in a disconnection of auditory processing regions of the brain from other brain areas that support memory, reasoning, language, and so on. The way that each deaf child's brain responds to this perturbation means that the disease may reveal itself differently in different children. However, all of those deaf children will essentially have an abnormal connectome, with a broad range of consequences for cognitive and linguistic functioning. Cochlear implantation, in this view, does more than restore sound, it rewires the brain and restores the normal equilibrium and balance between multiple, interconnected brain regions. Inherent in this approach is the view that the brain is supposed to be wired a certain way, and that deviations from that are abnormal and result in sensory, cognitive, linguistic, and emotional deficits because the deaf child no longer has a brain that allows them to function successfully. Deaf children, then, are not neuro-diverse, they are neuro-compromised with widespread trauma to brain connectivity because their primary auditory cortex has been decoupled. The evidence presented by Kral et al. in support of the "deaf connectome" – a heavily neuroscientific model – is based almost entirely on clinical and cognitive outcomes of deaf non-signing children with CIs, and fails to consider any of the research on the neuroscience of language processing. In fact, the idea that higher-order neural processes are contingent on any particular input modality runs contrary to the vast array of neuroimaging evidence that the frontotemporal classical language network is supramodal (Arana, Marquand, Hultén, Hagoort, & Schoffelen, 2020; Fedorenko, Behr, & Kanwisher, 2011), and that the brain is highly plastic and adaptable to input in early life. Language activation has been observed in both the occipital cortex of congenitally blind people (Bedny, Richardson, & Saxe, 2015) as well as frontotemporal neural areas commonly associated with audition and language processing in deaf people (Corina, Lawyer, & Cates, 2013). Such extensive neuroplastic changes in response to altered input do not track with the idea that such changes would cause a *deficit* in higher-level cognition. Rather, they suggest the converse: that the human brain is remarkably adaptable to input and there is no one "correct" configuration of neural connectivity which confers cognitive superiority. In summary, we find the idea that to be deaf is to have a brain disease to be highly misguided, once again reflecting audiocentric and audist views of deaf people. Nor does the approach explain the lack of cognitive deficits in the large number of deaf children who have typical linguistic abilities as a result of natural sign language acquisition in infancy.

Kral et al.'s deaf connectome proposal is a limited form of *biopsychosocial systems theory* (Engel, 1977). Recently, Kronenberger and Pisoni (2020) and Kronenberger (2019) have articulated an auditory-neurocognitive model that emphasizes the interconnectedness of the human brain (the "bio") but also takes into account the psychological and sociocultural factors that are known to influence cognitive development. Kronenberger and Pisoni (2020) argue that a myriad of such biological (auditory experience), psychological (intelligence, reduced early language exposure, social maturity), and sociocultural (family communication challenges, educational environment) factors combine in order to produce the precise pattern of executive function deficits observed in each individual deaf child. However, they return to "hearing loss" as the primary driver of deficit, as hearing loss is seen as the culprit behind disrupted biological, psychological, and sociocultural processes that bring about executive function deficits in deaf children.

Deafcentric Approaches to Cognitive Development

Interestingly, Kronenberger and Pisoni (2020) contrast biopsychosocial systems theory with arguments by others that early access to language is the primary driver of executive function deficits in deaf children. Ironically, in arguing against the importance of language for cognitive development, they describe studies in which *spoken* language accounts for little variability in executive function in Deaf children, ignoring the point that such "language based approaches" espouse the cognitive benefits of learning a *signed* language, as opposed to a spoken language. Furthermore, they argue, what they call "language based approaches" are just that – approaches and not theories. This is a mischaracterization of the arguments put forward by proponents of early language intervention for deaf children (Hall et al., 2017; Hall, 2020; Morgan & Dye, 2020). Indeed, Hall (2020) explicitly states that a "single factor view" that either auditory access or language access is the sole determinant of executive function development is a claim that no one has made. Similarly, Morgan and Dye (2020) propose a model of executive function development in deaf children that focuses on communication (rather than language) and which incorporates cascading interactions between multiple representational and processing systems.

Audiocentric approaches – such as the auditory scaffolding hypothesis and the auditory-neurocognitive model – see speech and hearing as the norm and the desired goal for deaf children. It is the fact that the children cannot hear is the researcher's focus. If one can fix the hearing, then the child will develop as a "normal hearing" child. In contrast, deafcentric approaches do not see being deaf as a problem intrinsic to the child that requires fixing or repair. Under the right conditions, the healthy cognitive, linguistic, and social development of the child is not seen as being at risk. Those conditions would include early access to a natural sign language such as ASL (not sign-and-speech, SimCom or Signed English), caregivers who can establish early communicative interactions with their deaf child, an educational system that understands the needs of a deaf child and provides an appropriate education, and a society that accepts the deaf child as a deaf child. Here, then, we start to see that Kronenberg and Pisoni's auditory-neurocognitive model is exactly what is being argued for by proponents of language-based approaches. Perhaps the only difference is that language-based proponents do not see the link between auditory access and language access in the same way. Indeed, from a deafcentric perspective, there is *no connection* between hearing and language. Language exists in the absence of audition – auditory access provides privileged access to but one form of human language: spoken language. Time and again, studies of deaf children who meet the optimal conditions from a deafcentric perspective reveal no deficits in executive function, sequence learning, or language development. The claim that auditory access is crucial for cognitive development is made despite these data, and by researchers whose field is speech and hearing science, or communication sciences and disorders. There is a failure to consider things from a deaf perspective, or to consider the inherent value of being deaf. This is perhaps most commonly revealed in the exhortation by clinicians that even if deafcentric sign language proponents are correct, nondeaf parents will never bother to learn sign language and, even if they did, could not do so well enough to support their deaf child's development. This reflects not just a lack of respect for the deaf child but also a lack of respect for nondeaf parents of deaf children, many of whom do choose to use a sign language to successfully communicate with their child and provide rich linguistic interactions as a result.

Acknowledgments

Matthew Dye's contribution is supported by the National Science Foundation under Grant No. 1550988. Any opinions, findings, and conclusions or recommendations expressed in this material are those of the authors and do not necessarily reflect the views of the National Science Foundation.

References

Arana, S., Marquand, A., Hultén, A., Hagoort, P. & Schoffelen, J. M. (2020). Sensory modality-independent activation of the brain network for language. *The Journal of Neuroscience, 40*(14), 2914–2924.

Arnott, S. R. & Alain, C. (2011). The auditory dorsal pathway: Orienting vision. *Neuroscience & Biobehavioral Reviews, 35*(10), 2162–2173.

Baddeley, A. (2012). Working memory: Theories, models, and controversies. *Annual Review of Psychology, 63*, 1–29.

Bari, A. & Robbins, T. W. (2013). Inhibition and impulsivity: Behavioral and neural basis of response control. *Progress in Neurobiology, 108*, 44–79.

Bauman, H. D. L. (2004). Audism: Exploring the metaphysics of oppression. *Journal of Deaf Studies and Deaf Education, 9*(2), 239–246.

Bavelier, D., Dye, M. W. & Hauser, P. C. (2006). Do deaf individuals see better? *Trends in Cognitive Sciences, 10*(11), 512–518.

Bavelier, D., Tomann, A., Hutton, C., Mitchell, T. V., Corina, D. P., Liu, G. & Neville, H. J. (2000). Visual attention to the periphery is enhanced in congenitally deaf individuals. *The Journal of Neuroscience, 20*, 1–6.

Bedny, M., Richardson, H. & Saxe, R. (2015). "Visual" cortex responds to spoken language in blind children. *The Journal of Neuroscience, 35*(33), 11674–11681.

Carrasco, M. (2018). How visual spatial attention alters perception. *Cognitive Processing, 19*(Suppl 1), 77–88.

Carrasco, M. (2011). Visual attention: The past 25 years. *Vision Research, 51*(13), 1484–1525.

Castellanos, I., Pisoni, D. B., Kronenberger, W. G. & Beer, J. (2016). Early expressive language skills predict long-term neurocognitive outcomes in cochlear implant users: Evidence from the MacArthur–Bates Communicative Development Inventories. *American Journal of Speech-Language Pathology, 25*(3), 381–392.

Cheng, Q., Roth, A., Halgren, E. & Mayberry, R. I. (2019). Effects of early language deprivation on brain connectivity: Language pathways in deaf native and late first-language learners of American Sign Language. *Frontiers in Human Neuroscience, 13*, 320.

Codina, C., Buckley, D., Port, M. & Pascalis, O. (2011). Deaf and hearing children: A comparison of peripheral vision development. *Developmental Science*, *14*(4), 725–737.

Conway, C. M., Pisoni, D. B., Anaya, E. M., Karpicke, J. & Henning, S. C. (2011). Implicit sequence learning in deaf children with cochlear implants. *Developmental Science*, *14*(1), 69–82.

Conway, C. M., Pisoni, D. B. & Kronenberger, W. G. (2009). The importance of sound for cognitive sequencing abilities: The auditory scaffolding hypothesis. *Current Directions in Psychological Science*, *18*(5), 275–279.

Corina, D. P., Lawyer, L. A. & Cates, D. (2013). Cross-linguistic differences in the neural representation of human language: Evidence from users of signed languages. *Frontiers in Psychology*, *3*, 587.

Daza, M. T. & Phillips-Silver, J. (2013). Development of attention networks in deaf children: Support for the integrative hypothesis. *Research in Developmental Disabilities*, *34*(9), 2661–2668.

deBettencourt, M. T., Norman, K. A. & Turk-Browne, N. B. (2018). Forgetting from lapses of sustained attention. *Psychonomic Bulletin & Review*, *25*(2), 605–611.

Diamond, A. (2013). Executive functions. *Annual Review of Psychology*, *64*, 135–168.

Dye, M. W. G., Baril, D. E. & Bavelier, D. (2007). Which aspects of visual attention are changed by deafness? The case of the Attentional Network Test. *Neuropsychologia*, *45*(8), 1801–1811.

Dye, M. W. & Bavelier, D. (2010). Attentional enhancements and deficits in deaf populations: An integrative review. *Restorative Neurology & Neuroscience*, *28*(2), 181–192.

Dye, M. W. G., Hauser, P. C. & Bavelier, D. (2009). Is visual selective attention in deaf individuals enhanced or deficient? The case of the useful field of view. *PLoS One*, *4*(5), e5640.

Dye, M. W. & Hauser, P. C. (2014). Sustained attention, selective attention and cognitive control in deaf and hearing children. *Hearing Research*, *309*, 94–102.

Eckert, R. C. & Rowley, A. J. (2013). Audism: A theory and practice of audiocentric privilege. *Humanity & Society*, *37*(2), 101–130.

Engel, G. (1977). A Need for a new medical model: A Challenge for biomedicine. *Science*, *196*, 129–136. doi: 10.1126/science.847460.

Fedorenko, E., Behr, M. K. & Kanwisher, N. (2011). Functional specificity for high-level linguistic processing in the human brain. *Proceedings of the National Academy of Sciences USA*, *108*(39), 16428–16433.

Fink, N. E., Wang, N. Y., Visaya, J., Niparko, J. K., Quittner, A., Eisenberg, L. S. & Tobey, E. A. and the CDaCI Investigative Team. (2007). Childhood Development after Cochlear Implantation (CDaCI) study: Design and baseline characteristics. *Cochlear implants international*, *8*(2), 92. 116.

Fisher, A. V. (2019). Selective sustained attention: A developmental foundation for cognition. *Current Opinion in Psychology*, *29*, 248–253.

Fortenbaugh, F. C., DeGutis, J. & Esterman, M. (2017). Recent theoretical, neural, and clinical advances in sustained attention research. *Annals of the New York Academy of Sciences*, *1396*(1), 70–91.

Giustolisi, B. & Emmorey, K. (2018). Visual statistical learning with stimuli presented sequentially across space and time in deaf and hearing adults. *Cognitive science*, *42*(8), 3177–3190.

Gordon, M. & Mettelman, B. B. (1988). The assessment of attention: I. Standardization and reliability of a behavior-based measure. *Journal of Clinical Psychology*, *44*(5), 682–690.

Hall, M. L. (2020). Dissociating the impact of auditory access and language access in deaf children's cognitive development. In M. Marschark & H. Knoors (Eds.), *The Oxford handbook of deaf studies in learning and cognition*. New York, NY: Oxford University Press.

Hall, M. L., Eigsti, I. M., Bortfeld, H. & Lillo-Martin, D. (2017). Auditory access, language access, and implicit sequence learning in deaf children. *Developmental Science, 21*(3), e12575.

Hoffman, M., Tiddens, E. & Quittner, A. L., and the CDaCI Investigative Team (2018). Comparisons of visual attention in school-age children with cochlear implants versus hearing peers and normative data. *Hearing Research, 359*, 91–100.

Horn, D. L., Davis, R. A., Pisoni, D. B. & Miyamoto, R. T. (2005). Development of visual attention skills in prelingually deaf children who use cochlear implants. *Ear & Hearing, 26*(4), 389–408.

Humphries, T. (1975). *Audism: The making of a word*. Unpublished essay.

Kaplan, A. (1964). *The conduct of inquiry: Methodology for behavioral science*. San Francisco, CA: Chandler Publishing Co.

Karchmer, M. A. & Allen, T. E. (1999). The functional assessment of deaf and hard of hearing students. *American Annals of the Deaf, 144*(2), 67–77.

Kral, A., Kronenberger, W. G., Pisoni, D. B. & O'Donoghue, G. M. (2016). Neurocognitive factors in sensory restoration of early deafness: A connectome model. *The Lancet Neurology, 15*(6), 610–621.

Kronenberger, W. G. (2019). Executive functioning and language development in children with cochlear implants. *Cochlear implants international, 20*(Suppl 1), 2–5.

Kronenberger, W. G. & Pisoni, D. B. (2020). Why are children with cochlear implants at risk for executive function delays?: Language only or something more? In M. Marschark & H. Knoors (Eds.), *The Oxford handbook of deaf studies in learning and cognition*. New York, NY: Oxford University Press.

Kronenberger, W. G., Beer, J., Castellanos, I., Pisoni, D. B. & Miyamoto, R. T. (2014). Neurocognitive risk in children with cochlear implants. *JAMA Otolaryngology—Head & Neck Surgery, 140*(7), 608–615.

Lévesque, J., Théoret, H. & Champoux, F. (2014). Reduced procedural motor learning in deaf individuals. *Frontiers in Human Neuroscience, 8*, 343.

Loke, W. H. & Song, S. (1991). Central and peripheral visual processing in hearing and nonhearing individuals. *Bulletin of the Psychonomic Society, 29*, 437–440.

Lyxell, B., Sahlén, B., Wass, M., Ibertsson, T., Larsby, B., Hällgren, M. & Mäki-Torkko, E. (2008). Cognitive development in children with cochlear implants: Relations to reading and communication. *International Journal of Audiology, 47*(Suppl. 2), S47–S52.

Mayberry, R. I., Davenport, T., Roth, A. & Halgren, E. (2018). Neurolinguistic processing when the brain matures without language. *Cortex, 99*, 390–403.

Mitchell, R. E. & Karchmer, M. A. (2004). Chasing the mythical ten percent: Parental hearing status of deaf and hard of hearing students in the United States. *Sign Language Studies, 4*(2), 138–163.

Mitchell, T. V. & Quittner, A. L. (1996). Multimethod study of attention and behavior problems in hearing-impaired children. *Journal of Clinical Child Psychology, 25*(1), 83–96.

Morgan, G. & Dye, M. W. G. (2020). Executive functions and access to language: The importance of intersubjectivity. In M. Marschark & H. Knoors (Eds.), *The Oxford handbook of deaf studies in learning and cognition*. New York, NY: Oxford University Press.

Murray, J. J., Hall, W. C. & Snoddon, K. (2019). Education and health of children with hearing loss: The necessity of signed languages. *Bulletin of the World Health Organization*, *97*(10), 711–716.

Oken, B. S., Salinsky, M. C. & Elsas, S. M. (2006). Vigilance, alertness, or sustained attention: Physiological basis and measurement. *Clinical Neurophysiology*, *117*(9), 1885–1901.

Pavani, F. & Bottari, D. (2012). Visual abilities in individuals with profound deafness A critical review. In M. M. Murray & M. T. Wallace (Eds.), *The neural bases of multisensory processes*. Boca Raton, FL: CRC Press/Taylor & Francis.

Posner, M. I. (2008). Measuring alertness. *Annals of the New York Academy of Sciences*, *1129*, 193–199.

Posner, M. I., Snyder, C. R. & Davidson, B. J. (1980). Attention and the detection of signals. *Journal of Experimental Psychology: General*, *109*(2), 160–174.

Prasad, S. G., Patil, G. S. & Mishra, R. K. (2015). Effect of exogenous cues on covert spatial orienting in deaf and normal hearing individuals. *PLoS One*, *10*(10), e0141324.

Proksch, J. & Bavelier, D. (2002). Changes in the spatial distribution of visual attention after early deafness. *Journal of Cognitive Neuroscience*, *14*, 687–701.

Quittner, A. L., Barker, D. H., Snell, C., Cruz, I., McDonald, L. G., Grimley, M. E., Botteri, M. & Marciel, K., CDaCI Investigative Team (2007). Improvements in visual attention in deaf infants and toddlers after cochlear implantation. *Audiological Medicine*, *5*(4), 242–249.

Quittner, A. L., Smith, L. B., Osberger, M. J., Mitchell, T. V. & Katz, D. B. (1994). The impact of audition on the development of visual-attention. *Psychological Science*, *5*(6), 347–353.

Simons, D. J. & Chabris, C. F. (1999). Gorillas in our midst: Sustained inattentional blindness for dynamic events. *Perception*, *28*, 1059–1074.

Smith, L. B., Quittner, A. L., Osberger, M. J. & Miyamoto, R. (1998). Audition and visual attention: The developmental trajectory in deaf and hearing populations. *Developmental Psychology*, *34*(5), 840–850.

Stevens, C. & Neville, H. (2006). Neuroplasticity as a double-edged sword: Deaf enhancements and dyslexic deficits in motion processing. *Journal of Cognitive Neuroscience*, *18*(5), 701–714.

Tharpe, A. M., Ashmead, D. H. & Rothpletz, A. M. (2002). Visual attention in children with normal hearing, children with hearing aids, and children with cochlear implants. *Journal of Speech, Language, and Hearing Research*, *45*(2), 403–413.

van Eldik, T., Treffers, P. D. A., Veerman, J. W. & Verhulst, F. C. (2004). Mental health problems of deaf Dutch children as indicated by parents' responses to the Child Behavior Checklist. *American Annals of the Deaf*, *148*(5), 390–395.

von Koss Torkildsen, J., Arciuli, J., Haukedal, C. L. & Wie, O. B. (2018). Does a lack of auditory experience affect sequential learning? *Cognition*, *170*, 123–129.

Yeshurun, Y. (2019). The spatial distribution of attention. *Current Opinion in Psychology*, *29*, 76–81.

Yucel, E. & Derim, D. (2008). The effect of implantation age on visual attention skills. *International Journal of Pediatric Otorhinolaryngology*, *72*(6), 869–877.

6

THEORETICAL UNDERPINNINGS OF ACQUIRING ENGLISH VIA PRINT

Catherine L. Caldwell-Harris

Why are deaf students' reading levels low, and so persistently low, despite innovations and changes in educational practices over the last 30 years? In our 2014 paper, Robert Hoffmeister and I argued that what deaf children must learn when faced with print is not just "reading," that is, learning to match graphic symbols to sounds and words. They must learn an unknown language at the same time as learning to read (Hoffmeister & Caldwell-Harris, 2014).

Many authors have noted this in the past decades. Barnum (1984) argued that a natural sign language be used as the primary language of instruction in the first four to six grades. This would allow students to develop cognitive/academic skills in a first language that could then facilitate learning English as a second, written language, using the first language to teach the second (Hoffmeister, 2008; Supalla, Wix, & McKee, 2001). Johnson, Liddell, and Erting (1989) argued that deaf children would not have academic success unless the curriculum could be "unlocked," with ASL used as the primary language of instruction. English would be learned as a written language only after ASL acquisition. Variations on this idea have been discussed by Bockmiller (1981), Strong (1988), Drasgow (1993, 1998), Wilbur (2000),Hoffmeister (2000), and numerous others. Koulidobrova, Kuntze, and Dostal (2018) wrote: "…the process of learning to read and write is more a task of learning a new language that is based on orthography, rather than a task of mapping print onto spoken language" (p. 112). Recent advocates of English as a second language for deaf children include Howerton-Fox and Falk (2019) and Hrastinski and Wilbur (2016).

In this chapter, I adopt a psycholinguistic perspective on why learning a language via print is hard, and why it is sometimes impossible. For convenience, I will refer to the written language as English, but the same principles apply to deaf children learning the written form of any spoken language. I review the

74 Catherine L. Caldwell-Harris

descriptive model of Hoffmeister and Caldwell-Harris (2014), which includes three stages that many deaf children pass through while learning English. The model describes why learning English (and thus progressing through reading grade levels) frequently stalls. I then review three empirical studies on deaf children's reading successes and failures, which illustrate the usefulness of the descriptive model.

The Neglect of an Interesting Problem

Psychologists and educators have no systematic evidence about how to learn a language from reading, nor is it a topic that is discussed in language acquisition textbooks or journals. There is literature on how to improve one's ability in a foreign language via reading (e.g., Krashen, 2004), but success is only documented for teenagers and adults. Some foreign language courses emphasize learning the written language, but these are also oriented toward teenagers and adults, and success depends on someone who is highly motivated. For these courses, a fluent first language is used as the basis for instruction; and the spoken language can be explained or taught should the learner desire that. So these cases are very different from a deaf child encountering print.

Learning a language via reading should be a topic of high interest to psycholinguists. Its neglect is because it hasn't been recognized as something humans need to do. Psycholinguists spent the 1960s and 1970s arguing that language developed via social learning, rather than via an innate language acquisition device (Menyuk, 1971). The proposal that any child could acquire a language, even a second language, via reading was not on anyone's radar. Some discomfort is apparent at the conclusion of Charrow and Fletcher's (1974) paper, published in *Developmental Psychology*. They hypothesized (and found) that because deaf students born to deaf parents had grown up with ASL as their first language, they would demonstrate a pattern of performance on The Test of English as a Foreign Language (TOEFL) that was similar to those of hearing EFL learners. The authors had the courage to title their paper "English as the Second Language of Deaf Children," but backed off in their final paragraph from any strong implications with the comment, "Whether or not deaf children learn English as a second language may be too broad an issue to investigate" (p. 469). Even academic researchers were cautious about pushing back against the hegemony of audism (Lane, 1992).

The Advantage of Learning via Social Interaction

Three theoretical ideas about the importance of social interaction are summarized below. The absence of these three aspects of social interaction contributes to the profound difficulty of learning a language via print.

Tracking Communicative Intent

The commonsensical, folk psychology view is that children learn the meaning of words when a word is uttered (or the sign is gestured) in spatial and temporal contiguity with a visible object, as in *Look at the ball!* Philosophers claimed this could not be sufficient because induction is too weak to allow learning from mere co-occurrences of an object and an utterance. This is the Gavagai problem, in which a speaker exclaims *Gavagai!* to someone who does not know his language, while pointing to a rabbit running across a field (Quine, 1960). The listener does not know whether *Gavagai* is the word for rabbit, run, animal, animal-parts, or fast. Language acquisition theorists initially solved this problem by proposing that infants and children are born with constraints to make learning possible despite the weakness of induction. An example is the whole object constraint: learners will initially assume a word refers to a whole object rather than a property of an object (Markman, 1990).

Theorists now believe something far more flexible and important facilitates word learning: intended meaning is constrained in real-world situations because learners track the communicative intention of the speakers (or signers) in the discourse context (Baldwin, 1993; Tomasello, & Barton, 1994). Consider the experimental scenarios used by Tomasello, Strosberg, and Akhtar (1996), where an adult brought out a large box of novel objects, announcing to a toddler, *Let's find the gazzer.* Without using language, the adult sequentially picked up objects, rejecting each with a frown or head shake and continued searching. At a random spot in the search, the adult held up the target with an expression of glee. Children were able to fast-map (i.e., one trial learning) the label "gazzer" to the object, as shown by subsequent tests. This was evidence that spatial-temporal contiguity was not necessary for word learning, but that what mattered was children's ability to track across multiple objects the adult's goal of finding a specific toy. On some trials, individual children even spontaneously cried out *Gazzer!* when the adult's facial expression indicated the sought object has been found.

Other research showed that children will resist learning a word label, even with spatial-temporal co-occurrence of object and word label, if communicative intention is absent. The experimental example of this used a free play situation with no adults in the room. Baldwin (1993) found that toddlers did not learn a word label when they reached for and touched an object, when the word label was pronounced from a loudspeaker. In contrast, learning was successful when all conditions were identical except an adult in the room uttered the label. We inherently intuit that children are tracking speakers' intentions: no one expects a child to fast map the frying pan to the word *damn* even though a parent touched the scorching hot frying pan and immediately yelled *damn!*

Krashen (1985) called utterances that are understandable from context "comprehensible input." One reason children easily learn a second language from social interaction, while adults have more difficulty, is that the language children hear is structurally simple and the meaning is comprehensible from the discourse context. The absence of feelings of achievement that accompany learning via social interaction decreases motivation to learn (Caldwell-Harris and MacWhinney, under review).

Embodied Learning

Learning a second language via social interaction has an additional advantage over explicit instruction: Figuring out the meaning of a word via inference leads to deeper and longer-lasting learning than can occur when one is provided a translation. This is because the act of generating an inference allows deep encoding of meaning (Jacoby, 1978). In contrast, learning from popular language teaching tools like duo-lingo or Rosetta Stone are decontextualized from actual experience.

Immediate Rewards

The satisfaction of social interaction, the feeling of achievement from successful communication, provides immediate rewards, which are absent from the rote memorization and grammar drills of a classroom (Caldwell-Harris, Goodwin, Chu, & Dahlen, 2013). Motivation from achieving communicative goals, together with the three advantages listed above, are the reasons why classroom foreign language learning is inferior to learning in an immersion context, and why children learn languages poorly from classroom instruction (Caldwell-Harris & MacWhinney, under review).

The necessity of learning with social interaction is why theorists have assumed language learning from reading is not possible, at least for children. But deaf children have been learning English (or whatever the spoken language may be) via print for the last hundreds of years since deaf communities have formed and have used their native sign language to teach themselves the written forms of spoken languages, as documented by Lane (1992) and described in auto-biographical reports (Coleman, 2012; Collins-Ahlgren, 1974; Dalby & Letourneau, 1991; Williams, 1976). Two recent studies have echoed the importance of ASL as the tool for learning written English. One is an ethnography of deaf reading practices (Mounty, Pucci & Harmon, 2014), the other used grounded interviews (Silvestri & Wang, 2019; described in detail below). Yet, psychologists and language acquisition researchers have not studied this process.

How is it possible to learn a language via print? Not easily, due to the absence of the advantages of learning from social interaction. The model described in the next section reflects the consistent themes that Hoffmeister extracted from his work as a researcher and educator of the deaf, and which resonated with what I knew about cognition and language learning as a cognitive scientist, psycholinguist, and researcher of ASL acquisition.

Learning English via Print, in an Uninstructed Context

Not all deaf or hard-of-hearing children will need to learn a language via print. Acquiring the spoken language may occur due to residual hearing, access to sound via hearing aids or cochlear implants, or because oral training/cued speech methods were successful. However, these methods often fail (Hoffmeister, 2000). Many deaf children are, thus, faced with the task of learning the written form of the language via print.

Hoffmeister and Caldwell-Harris (2014) outlined three broad stages that deaf children go through when trying to obtain meaning from print. We referred to this as a descriptive model of learning in uninstructed contexts. *Uninstructed context* means that deaf children interact with print in an ad-hoc manner; classrooms lessons are adapted from those designed for hearing children, and are not designed to teach English as a second language.

"English as a second language via print" (ESL-VP) has three stages, from initial exposure to forms, to the final stage of being able to obtain meaning from print in a bilingual learning mode.

Stage 1: Mapping Lexical Signs (simple translation equivalents)

High frequency, short print words are mapped to their American Sign Language (ASL) signs. This may occur when parents sign CAT or GIRL while pointing to printed words *cat* and *girl* in a picture book. Deaf parents have been observed performing direct mapping when signing picture books to their children; deaf parents frequently teach the manual alphabet with fingerspelling (Padden, 2006). Parents may point to the print words on food items while signing the meaning; this promotes early acquisition of the print forms for words such as *cereal, popcorn, candy, cookie,* and *potato chip.* Factors that influence ease of learning during this initial mapping process are the similarity in meaning between English and ASL forms, and their frequency. Also important are children and parents' conversational priorities; whether the goal is school readiness or helping with household chores, such as shopping.

The process of mapping single words to single signs continues for a variable period, but at some point, children attempt more complex mappings. Many common English print words must map to ASL phrases, as in the case of English *read* and the ASL phrase READ A BOOK. Slightly more difficult are nouns like *soup*, which map to the ASL verb+noun sequence EAT SOUP.

Stage 2: From Words to Sentences: Simple Translation Breakdown

For children with a rich first language (L1) and patient parents/teachers who provide mappings, the initial stage of learning can be heady, with rapid acquisition of many translation equivalents. But the success of this strategy can sow seeds of failure. Problems occur because single words in any language are only rarely directly mapped to words/signs in any another language or to single nonverbal concepts. The most frequent words in English, as is the case with many languages, are also those with the most idiosyncratic polysemy structure. English phrases like *take the bus* are confusing for deaf children, who think this must mean gain possession of the bus (see Hoffmeister & Caldwell-Harris, 2014).

At this stage, learners need to realize that English has unique methods for conveying meaning that need to be learned on their own, not as translations from ASL. This is the stage where children can stall in their reading progress because of the inherent difficulty of figuring out function words, polysemic variations, and English syntax. Academic failure and dislike of reading are likely outcomes.

Individuals with innate linguistic aptitude, or those with parents and teachers who explain the purpose of English grammar, can grapple with complex mappings. Interpreting larger word combinations puts learners in a position to process print in a bilingual learning mode.

Stage 3: Bilingual Learning Mode

Once learners understand that English print constitutes a separate language from ASL, and have a lexicon of basic mappings, they can proceed in a bilingual learning mode, such as Cummins' (1981) theory of the comparative learning process. A bilingual learning model enables learners to understand the lack of translation-equivalency, and how to compensate for this by inferring the meaning of new words from context (Drasgow, 1998). They can make analogies to ASL morphosyntactic and metalinguistic knowledge, and narrative skills gained from storytelling in ASL (Czubek, 2006). Perhaps most importantly, learners' fluent first language can be used as the medium of instruction for teaching English polysemy and morphosyntax (Wilbur, 2000).

Summary

The model describes when initial success is rapid (stage 1, mapping translation equivalents), and where learners typically get stuck (stage 2, when simple mappings are insufficient), and also the method of success (using ASL to teach English in a bilingual learning mode).

ESL-VP is too simple to represent the ideal method for using sign language as the medium of instruction for teaching English. Instead, it describes how it is logically possible for some children to accomplish a rather amazing feat, of learning a language without extensive social interaction, in the non-optimal conditions of lacking a curriculum designed for this purpose.

Theoretical and Practical Implications

As a descriptive model of a route to successful reading, ESL-VP offers implications for theory and practice. These have been noted before by diverse authors but are nonetheless a sharp contrast with mainstream practices.

Implication 1: Learning Spoken-Word Phonology Is not Necessary When Learning a Language via Print

The traditional view is that representing written words' auditory form is an essential component of reading (Ehri, 2005; Dehaene, 2009). Because of this, some researchers have reasoned that activation of auditory phonological codes must also be essential for reading for deaf readers (Paul, 1998; Perfetti, & Sandak, 2000). But this perspective is not rooted in the science of reading and the science of information processing (Hall & Bavelier, 2010).

There are several reasons to view auditory activation as unnecessary for reading. Humans can process many graphic representations that lack auditory components. Examples include road signs which don't easily activate words, such as a circle with a line through it or icons indicating lane reductions. Ancient writing systems are believed to have begun as pictographic systems (Dehaene, 2009). This is probably because humans' initial goals for writing were to record business transactions. Phonetic components were incorporated into writing systems as societal complexity increased, necessitating general systems for recording any phrase in the language. If the language of general use had been a gestural language, then the phonetic elements would have coded for gestural phonemes.

Modern writing systems have two routes for going from the written word to its meaning (*dual route theory*, see Dehaene, 2009). The semantic pathway causes meaning to be activated directly by graphemes, while the phonological pathway activates representations for sounds, resulting in the auditory image of hearing the sound in one's mind. But meaning can be activated alone, without phonological decoding. In English, semantic activation is often much faster than phonological activation. With increasing reading skill, readers activate less phonology, and may skip the step of phonologically decoding difficult words, because it is more efficient to access meaning directly via the semantic pathway (Dehaene, 2009; Bowers & Bowers, 2018). Low or no activation of phonology frequently occurs when reading Chinese, since cues to pronunciation are absent or unreliable in two-thirds of characters (Cheng & Caldwell-Harris, 2011).

An important piece of empirical evidence is that even good readers may not activate phonological codes during word recognition or recall (Bélanger, Baum, & Mayberry, 2011). This is evidence against the thesis that deficits in phonological codes are responsible for deaf children's reading difficulties (Mayberry, Del Giudice & Lieberman, 2011). But some skilled deaf readers show knowledge of the sounds of words – why? These readers may be employing their residual

80 Catherine L. Caldwell-Harris

hearing or may have gained this knowledge as a result of becoming fluent in English (Mayberry et al., 2011).

The irregularity of many spelling systems means that typical hearing readers have the burden of learning many exceptions (Bowers & Bowers, 2018). Ignoring spelling-to-sound patterns is the ideal option for deaf readers, as it allows more time for mapping between orthography and meaning (Grushkin, 1998). Without mapping subcomponents of letter strings to their sounds, in the early stages of learning, deaf individuals must memorize arbitrary strings of letters, sometimes helped by learning their fingerspelled analogues (Padden, 2006). Pertinent to this is Lane's (1992) discussion of Laura Bridgman, a deaf and blind woman of the nineteenth century. Bridgman recalled being corrected as a child for misspelling *cat*. She had responded why it mattered whether one spelled it "cta" or "act" or "tac". In the last decades, deaf children have been found to be highly sensitive to the orthographic morphological regularities in words (Grushkin, 1998).

The above research regarding auditory phonological coding suggests that drills in spoken word phonology may indeed be the "waste of childhood" lamented by critics of audism (Lane, 1992). But what about the reasonable goal of learning to interact with hearing persons via speaking and lipreading? It is time to investigate the following: learning to orally produce sounds via speech training can proceed with less effort and greater success after English has been learned as a written language.

This thesis was briefly mentioned by Johnson et al. (1989, p.17): "Understanding and producing speech are skills to be developed not as a means of acquisition, but as a result of acquisition, after competence in the language has been established through literacy." The authors did not elaborate on the statement, probably to avoid detracting from their main objective, which was arguing for the right of deaf children to learn a natural sign language and to use that in the classroom for academic learning.

Below I outline the general arguments for the "speech training is easier after learning English" thesis.

Before English is learned as a language:

- Speech training for deaf children is effortful, frequently requires hours a day with a professional speech therapist, and therefore detracts from other learning.
- Many children may not understand the purpose of hours spent with fingers on the speech pathologist's throat, trying to articulate sounds.

After English is learned as a language:

- Deaf learners can read and write for pleasure, information, and human connection.

- The purpose of the hours of speech training is more easily understood because the learner may have an emotional connection with the written language and thus can anticipate the benefits of additional opportunities to connect with speakers of that language.
- Learning to produce a sequence of sounds for a word is more meaningful because the sequence of sounds can be attached to a known meaning.

The following example elaborates the last point. In typical reading acquired by hearing children, the child has an "aha" moment of phonologically decoding "mother" and noting: "Wow, that spells a word I know well – *mother*." If speech training begins after language learning, a deaf child benefits from the same mapping but in reverse: "I am learning the auditory form of that word I've long seen written – *mother*."

There is currently no data regarding the speed, effort, and outcome of speech training before or after learning the written form of a spoken language. This should be prioritized as an area for future research.

Implication 2: The Model Addresses the Question of How ASL Is a Bridge to Reading

It has long been appreciated that acquiring ASL (or other native sign language) is associated with good reading and academic success (e.g., Drasgow, 1998; Hoffmeister, 2000; Wilbur 2000). At the same time, some theorists have been puzzled by how a fluent sign language, being in a different modality and lacking a written form, could be a "bridge to literacy" (Marschark, 2001; Mayer & Wells, 1996; Mayer, 2017). But "bridge to literacy" is not the correct way to understand why ASL helps reading, and is a phrase that biases people to focus on the modality difference and ASL being a language without a written form. The primary advantage of ASL for deaf children is foundational and humanitarian: early ASL (or other natural signed language) creates the necessary foundation for future learning, thereby allowing normal cognitive, social, and emotional development (Barnum, 1984; Bockmiller, 1981; Corina & Singleton, 2009; Drasgow, 1993, 1998; Humphries, Kushalnagar, Mathur, et al., 2016). ASL at birth thus indirectly helps reading English later in school, since children with normal cognitive and social skills are in the best position to master the difficult task of learning a language via print (or benefiting from any type of school instruction, even non-optimal methods).

There are two additional ways that ASL facilitates acquisition of written English that are part of the ESL-VP descriptive model:

- ASL provides the semantic and conceptual structures to which learners map inert print forms (stage 1).
- ASL is the medium of instruction for teaching children English as a second language via print (stage 3).

82 Catherine L. Caldwell-Harris

Recently, scholars have argued for the benefits of an additional type of bridge – written forms of ASL. These could be existing signwriting systems, or a to-be-designed alphabet (Grushkin, 2017). Also welcome is ASL glossing, a system of using English words with additional notation to write ASL (Supalla, Cripps, & Byrne, 2017). After the basics of the ASL writing system are learned, written ASL can be used to teach standard elementary school content, thus providing another means of unlocking the curriculum.

Implication 3: Exposing Deaf Children to ASL Is not Enough – Use ASL to Teach English

Over the last century, many deaf children suffered language deprivation from policies that replaced the deaf-centered education of the nineteenth century with the oral practices of the twentieth century (Humphries et al. 2014; Lane, 1992). The humanitarian need to provide deaf children access to sign language was (and is) so great that many ASL advocates promoted ASL as a way to help deaf children learn to read (e.g., Hoffmeister, 2000). ASL exposure ameliorates language deprivation (Drasgow, 1993; Humphries et al., 2014), but access to ASL does not automatically lead to English literacy (Goldin-Meadow & Mayberry, 2001; Padden, 2006). An example is Knoors and Marschark (2012), who observed that sign language aids deaf children initially by building reading vocabularies, but long-term reading achievement remains elusive. Those authors wrote, "… stagnation occurs, and the reading skills tend to lag or asymptote among deaf children both with and without cochlear implants" (p. 297). In their review of these and related findings, Howerton-Fox and Falk (2019, p. 12) noted: "If we are going to maximize the literacy outcomes for bi/multilingual deaf children, it will be important to understand both the mechanisms through which sign language supports literacy development and the reasons why so many signing deaf children do not become proficient readers and writers."

The answer to these disagreements is the purpose of this chapter: deaf children are asked to do a difficult task (learn a language via print), and the methods used for this are inadequate (Grushkin, 1998). To preview my argument, as proposed by the early advocates for bilingual education for the deaf (e.g., Barnum, 1984; Bockmiller, 1981; Drasgow, 1993, Johnson et al., 1989; Strong, 1988; Hoffmeister, 2000, 2008; Wilbur 2000), ASL must be taught first, to fluency, preferably in a naturalistic environment. Barnum (1984) suggested not introducing English until between grades four and six, to provide time for sufficient mastery of ASL. ASL should be used as the medium of instruction for all academic discourse, including how to teach English as a second language.

Drasgow wrote, "Implementing a bilingual program for deaf students in which ASL is acquired as their first language and English is taught as a second language is no simple matter. There is much to consider" (Drasgow, 1993,

p. 247). He reviewed three approaches to bilingual education. In an English-centered approach, English is the primary language, but ASL is used to clarify, to explain difficult material or to answer student questions if necessary.

In the second method, English and ASL are equal in the bilingual classroom even from the earliest grade levels, with both being used and taught at the same time. The drawback of this is lack of a fluent language for instruction and socialization. Lacking a fluent language for classroom discourse, what teachers can do is limited. Techniques like *sandwiching* and *chaining* can be helpful and are used frequently by teachers (Humphries & MacDougall, 1999). In sandwiching, a concept is signed in ASL, then the English word is written and pointed to and then the ASL sign is again presented. Alternatively, the English word "sandwiches" the ASL sign. The goal is for children to infer meaning identity from the rapid juxtaposition of these symbols. Chaining is similar but additional representations of the words can be inserted in the chain, such as a fingerspelled version or a picture or a spoken word version, if speech is used in the classroom. Note that if children were fluent in ASL, teachers could simply state the meaning equivalency using learners' fluent language, as is the norm in a second-language learning situation.

The third method is what was recommended by the early advocates of bilingual education (Johnson et al., 1989 and others cited above): A natural sign language is taught first, learned to fluency, and then used as the medium of instruction for teaching the written language. This method has been employed successfully for decades in Denmark and Sweden (Davies, 1991; Svartholm, 2014). Only the third method is adequate. Children need fluency in ASL first before that language can be used as a medium of instruction for teaching English. The logical result is that English and ASL cannot be equal in the bilingual classroom.

Implication 4: Learning English via Print without ASL

Learning the written form of a second language is especially difficult for learners who do not have a fluent first language. Indeed, when Hoffmeister and I developed the descriptive model, we purposely limited it to cases of ASL-using learners, following Hoffmeister's extensive experience with this population at The Learning Center in Framingham and various residential schools around the country. Learning English without fluent ASL skills is highly variable, as shown by larger variances in reading scores for deaf children with hearing parents compared to deaf children with deaf parents (as in Figure 3, Novogrodsky, Caldwell-Harris, Fish, & Hoffmeister, 2014).

When there is no fluent L1, there is no large storehouse of vocabulary items to be mapped to printed words, there is no model of linguistic structure to be used as a source domain for analogical explanations, no fluent language to be used to discuss motivation, career aspirations and the future long-term benefits of literacy (see Albertini, Kelly, & Matchett, 2011, for a discussion of motivation in deaf college students). From the cognitive, social, language development, and humanitarian perspectives, there can be only one recommendation for children who do not have a fluent first language: remediate language deprivation. The helpfulness of English literacy (which cannot be obtained without a fluent L1) pales compared to the intelligence and socialization to be gained by acquiring a fluent first language in a naturalistic learning context. Set aside a number of years to acquire a natural signed language in a naturalistic context, teaching the standard curriculum with ASL (plus ASL writing system), whenever possible (Barnum, 1984; Grushkin, 1998, 2017).

The perspectives about language acquisition reviewed in the introduction suggest that the written version of a spoken language cannot be fully acquired via print without a fluent L1. In the next sections, I review recent studies relevant to this claim.

The Heuristic Value of ESL-VP: A Review of Three Recent Studies

The first article reviewed describes accomplished readers, who grew up with ASL and who succeeded in learning English via print using a bilingual learning mode (Silvestri & Wang, 2018). The second article involves a group of profoundly deaf individuals who were orally trained yet as adults were identified as skilled readers (Domínguez, Carrillo, del Mar Pérez, & Alegría, 2014). The third study reports on sign-word mapping practices for children in a bilingual school (Van Staden, 2013).

Review 1: The Reading Strategies and Experiences of High Achieving Deaf Readers

Many authors have noted that the field of deaf education lacks "insight into effective reading processes used by deaf people" (Silvestri & Wang, 2018, p. 423). To fill this gap, Silvestri and Wang (2018) interviewed 30 deaf individuals on how they learned to read and assessed their reading strategies with a think-aloud protocol. This research address topics Hoffmeister and I have pursued in the past years in unpublished work (Caldwell-Harris& Hoffmeister, 2020). A prediction is that these individuals had access to ASL growing up and used it to learn English as their second language. This indeed was one of the main findings of the interviews.

The adult interviewees were selected so that 15 were categorized as high achieving readers (those with graduate degrees who reported reading extensively for professional-level jobs) and 15 as low achieving readers, self-identified as struggling readers with language barriers. The authors also included 15 high achieving hearing readers, with similar educational and professional attainments as

Acquiring English via Print **85**

the deaf group, and 15 low achieving hearing readers. The interviews focused on language experience, instructional methods, and reading activities while growing up. Using the think-aloud method, participants read a passage from Macbeth with rhyming verses. This allowed them to report on their awareness of rhyme and other poetic elements.

The first question I asked in scrutinizing Silvestri and Wang's (2018) data was what reading experiences and strategies differed most strongly between the high achieving and low achieving deaf readers. I subtracted the number of low achieving deaf who mentioned a strategy/experience from the number of high achieving deaf who mentioned that same strategy/experience, and then sorted these difference scores from highest to lowest. In Table 6.1 the top 20% of items on this list have been sorted into two broad categories, *Importance of ASL* and *Comprehension Strategies*.

"Signing at home" was the item that most strongly distinguished the high and low achieving readers. Also mentioned often by the good readers were the use of ASL in elementary school, reading with parents, and parents signing stories. The high achieving deaf participants resembled the high achieving hearing participants on their report of using comprehension strategies for attaining optimal comprehension.

The deaf high achievers used ASL to comprehend the Macbeth passage. High achievers reported translating character dialogue by using role-shift in ASL (e.g., "He said that they would...."). One assumes this is the feeling or bodily image of a shoulder shift, the ASL marker for dialogue change. However, it would be ideal to have more information about this, such as how frequently ASL users have a bodily experience of a shoulder shift when they are reading in a written language about reported language or other aspects of dialogue.

The interviews provide strong support for ESL-VP by showing that high achieving readers used ASL to support their learning. Indeed, the good readers mentioned using sign language in literacy instruction, and they used ASL for interpreting texts. The findings suggest that these readers learned by being in a bilingual learning mode, which Hoffmeister and I characterized as necessary for learning English and thereby attaining reading fluency.

Review 2: Gaining Information from Print via Keywords

Domínguez et al. (2014) open their detailed study of the reading abilities and strategies of orally trained deaf adults by remarking: "A vast body of literature has shown that deaf persons are generally handicapped at the syntactic level .... [multiple citations] ... Nevertheless, reading requires syntax, that is, the ability to integrate morphemes into larger linguistic units such as phrases...." (p. 1441). This quote motivated their research question: does a lack of syntactic knowledge limit the average reading abilities for deaf adults to the fourth- or fifth-grade level?

86 Catherine L. Caldwell-Harris

TABLE 6.1 Experiences and strategies of high and low achieving deaf readers (from Silvestri & Wang, 2018)

Importance of ASL	Difference Score*	Total out of 15 interviewees			
		Hi Ach Deaf	Low Ach Deaf	Hi Ach Hearing	Low Ach Hearing
Signing at home	12	14	2	0	0
Use of role-shift in ASL for character dialogue	11	12	1	0	0
ASL in elementary school	10	10	0	0	0
Connections between signs, pictures, and words	5	5	0	0	0
Identification of other phonetic devices	9	11	2	10	4
Reading with parents	8	9	1	10	6
Parents signing stories	7	7	0	0	0
Repeat handshapes to demonstrate rhyme	6	10	4	0	0
Use of sign language in literacy instruction	6	9	3	0	0
Comprehension Strategies					
Carefully analyzing information presented in text	9	12	3	13	4
Thinking of an analogy/ association to clarify	8	8	0	1	1
Seeking answers to self-generated questions	8	9	1	6	1
Generating elaborations – events/thoughts/ feelings	7	10	3	4	4
Relation of theme to broader social ideas	6	10	4	11	2
Modifying the main idea	6	7	1	5	1
Mental imagery	6	12	6	9	10
Identifying shape of text and/or patterns in text	6	8	2	5	0
Constructing alternative meanings for words	6	6	0	2	1

Items mentioned by deaf low achievers at greater rates than by deaf high achievers

Substituting familiar for unfamiliar words	−4	6	10	6	8

(Continued)

Acquiring English via Print **87**

TABLE 6.1 (*Continued*)

Importance of ASL	Difference Score*	Total out of 15 interviewees			
		Hi Ach Deaf	Low Ach Deaf	Hi Ach Hearing	Low Ach Hearing
Eliminating information to simplify text	−4	6	10	6	8
Reading word for word, line by line	−6	4	10	9	12

Table Notes: *__High Achieving Deaf__ minus __Low Achieving Deaf__.
Difference scores are followed by the counts provided by Silvestri and Wang, 2018

The deaf individuals studied by Domínguez et al. (2014) were exposed to Spanish via oral methods, although by adulthood these adults used sign language in their daily interactions. The authors selected deaf individuals, age range 18–55, who were good readers and read daily for information and enjoyment. Participants had a university degree or had pursued non-compulsory technical training.

In their prior work, the authors had observed orally trained deaf adults using semantic strategies when reading Spanish. In the "keyword" strategy, a reader uses the most frequent content words to infer sentence meaning, ignoring function words. The authors noted:

> [T]his strategy is not compatible with a thorough understanding of written material, so it can explain at least partially why deaf persons hardly ever achieve high levels of reading. The main problem, however, is to understand why the key word strategy is so widely used among deaf readers. It must necessarily be related to their linguistic competence at all levels, syntactic, lexical, and phonological.
>
> (*Domínguez et al., 2014, p. 1441*)

Reading level was measured using a forced-choice sentence completion test, the READ test. All choices were orthographically similar; two of the distractors were pseudowords. Targets included difficult vocabulary items, such as *submersible*, allowing the test to measure a wide range of reading levels. Additional tests assessed Spanish vocabulary, syntactic and morphological ability.

The primary finding was the reliance on the keyword strategy. Even individuals selected to be accomplished readers with university degrees and post-compulsory education used the keyword strategy, as revealed by their low scores on the sentence completion task. Their reading ability, when matched to hearing children, was either low (below fourth-grade level), intermediate (between sixth and seventh grade), or superior level, reading slightly beyond hearing readers of

88 Catherine L. Caldwell-Harris

tenth-grade level. Even those in the superior group overused semantic strategies and underutilized sentence-level syntax when reading.

The authors wondered if the key word strategy would disappear as syntactic ability increased. It did not. The authors concluded, "using the key word strategy during long periods of time increases knowledge of content words but not syntax, probably because function words are neglected by this strategy" (Domínguez et al., 2014, p. 1451).

This rich study provides a wealth of insights pertinent to deaf persons learning a language via print. Reading competence following oral training was highly uneven, with strong semantic and inferential capabilities, and weak morphosyntax. The findings fit the descriptive model of Hoffmeister and Caldwell-Harris as follows. The orally trained deaf Spaniards learned to map many words to concepts, as in our Stage 1. They became stuck at Stage 2. Without a fluent L1 for conversation, scaffolding, explicit instruction, these individuals had uneven success when grappling with meaning at the sentence level.

This study also raises questions and ideas for future research. The Domínguez et al. (2014) study indicates that, following oral training, semantic strategies curtail acquiring the syntax of the written language. What components of full linguistic competence can be learned when a language is learned via print without a fluent L1 to scaffold explicit instruction? When no sign language is available in the classroom due to oral training, sign language is typically learned either outside of the classroom or acquired later, often when deaf individuals socialize as teenagers (Lane, Hoffmeister and Bahan, 1996). How much and how often can this later-learned ASL correct for semantic reading strategies acquired during oral training? Can explicit instruction in the syntax of the written language in adulthood compensate for lack of explicit instruction during childhood?

Review 3: Elaborating the Print-to-Sign Mapping Task

Consistent with viewing deaf children's task as learning a language via print, Van Staden (2013) wrote, "The major impediment to deaf children's reading development is not simply an inability to speak English but rather insufficient language development.... A further complication is a discrepancy between deaf children's incomplete spoken language system and the demands of reading a speech-based system" (p. 306).

Van Staden (2013) reports on an English vocabulary intervention to boost deaf children's ability to grasp and retain the meaning of English print words, working with students at a residential school for the deaf in South Africa. The school had a bilingual sign policy, with South African Sign Language (SASL) taught alongside written English. The bilingual school appears to be the second option described in the prior section, where English and sign language had equal status as languages that needed to be taught. English print vocabulary was explicitly mapped to SASL signs, using the techniques of sandwiching and chaining (Humphries &

MacDougall, 1999). Additional multimodal methods were part of teaching, including tracing words on sandpaper, creating clay models of the words and their meanings, sorting vocabulary cards into different semantic categories, signing stories from a print book, and picture/word/sign matching exercises.

This vocabulary intervention represents stage 1 of ESL-VP, *Mapping translation equivalents*. Because SASL was being learned at the same time as English, a fluent sign language was not available to explain the challenges of stage 2, such as confronting complex word combinations, dealing with English polysemy or morphosyntax. However some practices are suggestive of the bilingual learning mode of stage 3: "... students using their sign language skills to establish an interactive reading environment, and guiding them, through scaffolding, to apply the comprehension strategies" (Van Staden, 2013, p. 308). According to ESL-VP, learners cannot develop full comprehension of English without a fluent L1 for explicit instruction in English grammar and difficult areas like polysemy. What is unknown is whether the students described by Van Staden (2013) are on a path to resemble the orally trained students described in the previous study – with vocabulary items mapped to meanings and signs, but not integrated into a language system – despite being educated at a bilingual school.

Developing the Conversation around Teaching a Language via Print

Below I outline some broad suggestions for enlarging the conversation about deaf children's reading, in addition to the four implications reviewed earlier (spoken word phonology not necessary; ASL is a bridge to reading via explicit instruction; exposure to ASL is not enough to facilitate English literacy; English cannot be learned via print without a fluent first language).

Acknowledge that for Many Deaf Children the Task is Language Learning, Not "Reading."

Changing our view from "learning to read" to "learning a language via reading" gives us a new perspective on many problematic aspects of the deaf education literature and mindsets of some researchers.

Signposts of inaccurate views will be familiar to readers of this volume and include:

- Teaching interventions that focus on increasing deaf children's reading vocabularies, without reference to the need to learn the target language (e.g., Van Staden, 2013). This practice can then deepen nascent semantic or "keyword' approaches to reading.
- Comparing deaf children's written language skills to those of hearing, monolingual children's written language skills. Deaf children can only be expected to

approximate the written language skills of hearing children when they are given the same advantage as hearing children, of an accessible language from birth. Even with that advantage, the comparison should be to bilingual hearing children.

- Drawing conclusions about deaf children's cognitive or other abilities while not recognizing they are being assessed in a non-proficient language (see discussion in Lane, 1992).
- Viewing deaf children's reading failures as occurring because of their deafness, their lack of access to phonology, and/or their poor language skills, rather than the difficulty of being asked to read an unknown language.

Teaching English Morphology Is Useful for Hearing and Deaf Learners

What sense should deaf learners make of the letter sequences composing words, if they are not learning letter-sound mappings? Words are composed of parts; and there is a structure to those parts that will facilitate learning English. Letter clusters like *un, re* and *ment* can be mapped to meanings. Parents and teachers can explicitly teach the morphology of English words, something that has recently been advocated by Humphries et al. (2014). It is thus provocative that reading experts have also recently argued that standard reading curricula should be revised to explicitly teach children English morphology (Bowers and Bowers, 2018). The reason is that English sacrifices spelling-to-sound consistency to make the meaning-bearing parts of words salient; consider the usefulness of spelling similarity across words like *southern* and *south; health* and *heal*. The morphemes *south* and *heal* can activate their meanings rapidly, independently of phonological activation.

Morphological awareness enables readers to partition and understand words based on meaning rather than surface features alone (Trussell and Easterbrooks, 2017). Skilled deaf readers tend to have good command of English morphology (Clark, Gilbert, & Anderson, 2011). Interventions to teach deaf children morphology has led to improvement in reading comprehension and writing skills (Nunes, Burman, Evans, & Bell, 2010).

Draw on Foreign Language Learning Curricula which Use Written Materials or Emphasize Reading as Part of Language Learning

Foreign language learning materials for children typically emphasize face-to-face social interaction, such as routines for greeting and friendly information exchange. These could be adapted to text-based media such as texting and computer chats for educating deaf students. I briefly describe two examples that teach L2 via print.

A technique called enhanced subtitling helps connect written vocabulary words to their real-world referents and conceptual knowledge (Hassan & Neves, 2019).

Written vocabulary words were taught to deaf children in Qatar by superimposing the written label on the object that is part of the ongoing video story. Students acquired these vocabulary words better than did those assigned a control lesson.

The company One-third Stories developed a technique to teach foreign languages to young children via picture books, captured by their slogan, *Stories that start in English and end in a different language* (onethirdstories.com). An inherently interesting story begins in the first language, with a rich context established with full-color illustrations. Phrases in the second language are inserted in places where the context will make them interpretable, as in, "The little boy looked into the sky at the bright, round, yellow *soleil*." By the end of each book, one-third of the text is in the second language. This program is unusual in teaching a second language via print to young children, using the fluent L1. This method could be easily adapted for deaf learners, for those who know a writing system like ASL Gloss (Supalla et al., 2017), or other writing system to be developed (Grushkin, 2017).

Conclusions: Looking Forward

Arguments that the deaf are a linguistic and cultural minority and thus have a right to use their native language in the classroom have been repeatedly made and ignored (Drasgow, 1998; Hoffmeister, 2008; Lane 1992). There is now new momentum to make changes in deaf education. Koulidobrova et al. (2018) argue that deaf children should be identified as English language learners, thus eligible for federal resources to facilitate using their native language in the classroom. Howerton-Fox and Falk (2019) renew and elaborate the call for bilingual education. Withholding a visual language from deaf children is now understood to be a human rights violation; this may also spur a paradigm shift in deaf education (Grosjean, 2001; Humphries et al., 2016).

When the task facing deaf children is conceptualized as reading, deaf children are on their own to figure out the English language. When they are successful, this represents a human achievement akin to the famous mathematician Srinivasa Ramanujan discovering advanced mathematical principles while growing up in nineteenth-century India. A different mathematical example highlights the extraordinary in all of us: Probabilistic thinking gradually became part of the intellectual toolkit of people in the developed world in the centuries after the pioneering writing of Blase Pascal and Pierre de Fermat in the seventeenth century (Gigerenzer, Swijtink, Porter, & Daston, 1990). The result of that shift is that contemporary children easily learn to use probabilistic thinking, because of its omnipresence in everyday life and scaffolding in school. Yet the concepts of percentages and probabilities eluded the mathematicians of Renaissance Europe for centuries, despite their necessity to the everyday dice or cards gambler. My point is that seemingly difficult problems, when scaffolded by the larger culture and the school system, become tractable. This suggests that the problem of teaching a language via print, when it becomes normative to educators, can similarly be submitted to the engines of human ingenuity: studied by scientists, curricula developed by informed educators, debated and discussed by teachers, tested, revised, developed again. Humankind will crack the problem of how to teach a language via print, and children will learn. We just need to recognize that learning a language via print is something humans need to do.

References

Albertini, J., Kelly, R., & Matchett, M. (2011). Personal factors that influence deaf college students' academic success. *Journal of Deaf Studies and Deaf Education, 17*(1), 85–102. 10.1093/deafed/enr016.

Baldwin, D. A. (1993). Early referential understanding: Infants' ability to recognize referential acts for what they are. *Developmental Psychology, 29*(5), 832.

Barnum, M. (1984). In support of bilingual/bicultural education for deaf children. *American Annals of the Deaf, 129*(5), 404–408.

Bélanger, N. N., Baum, S. R., & Mayberry, R. I. (2011). Reading difficulties in adult deaf readers of French: Phonological codes, not guilty! *Scientific Studies of Reading, 16*, 263–285.

Bockmiller, P. R. (1981). *Hearing-impaired children: Learning to read a second language.* American Annals of the Deaf, 810–813.

Bowers, J. S., & Bowers, P. N. (2018). Progress in reading instruction requires a better understanding of the English spelling system. *Current Directions in Psychological Science, 27*(6), 407–412.

Caldwell-Harris, C.L., & Hoffmeister, R.J. (2020). *Reading thru your eyes: How deaf college students learn to read.* Survey approved by Boston University Institutional Review Board; available at https://bostonu.qualtrics.com/jfe/form/SV_41tceIC13jE5HW4?Q_JFE=qdg.

Caldwell-Harris, C.L., & MacWhinney, B. (under review). *Age effects in second language acquisition: Expanding the emergentist account. Behavioral and Brain Sciences.*

Caldwell-Harris, C.L., Goodwin, K.S., Chu, E., & Dahlen, K. (2013). Examining the advantage of a live instructor vs. video in a laboratory study. *Innovation in Language Learning and Teaching, 7*, 1–14.

Charrow, V. R., & Fletcher, J. D. (1974). English as the second language of deaf children. *Developmental Psychology, 10*(4), 463.

Cheng, H., & Caldwell-Harris, C. (2011). *When semantics overrides phonology: Semantic substitution errors in reading Chinese aloud.* Paper presented at the 85th Annual Meeting of the Linguistic Society of America. Pittsburgh, USA.

Clark, M. D., Gilbert, G., & Anderson, M. L. (2011). Morphological knowledge and decoding skills of deaf readers. *Psychology, 2*(02), 109.

Coleman, R. (2012). *My two cents: Cochlear implants. The Endeavor: A Publication for Families and Professionals Committed to Children who are Deaf and Hard of Hearing, Fall 2012.* Published by the American Society for Deaf Children.

Collins-Ahlgren, M. (1974). Teaching English as a second language to young deaf children: A case study. *Journal of Speech and Hearing Disorders, 39*(4), 486–499.

Corina, D., & Singleton, J. (2009). Developmental social cognitive neuroscience: Insights from deafness. *Child Development, 80*, 952–967.

Cummins, J. (1981). The role of primary language development in promoting educational success for language minority students. In California State Department of Education (Ed.), *Schooling and language minority students: A theoretical framework* (pp. 3–49). Los Angeles: Evaluation, Dissemination and Assessment Center, California State University.

Czubek, T. A. (2006). Blue Listerine, parochialism, and ASL literacy. *Journal of Deaf Studies and Deaf Education, 11*, 373–381.

Dalby, K., & Letourneau, C. (1991). *Survey of Communication history of deaf adults.* Paper presented at the biennial meeting of the Association of Canadian Educators of the Hearing Impaired, Calgary, Alberta.

Davies, S. (1991). The transition toward bilingual education of deaf children in Sweden and Denmark: Perspectives on language. *Sign Language Studies, 71*, 169–195.

Dehaene, S. (2009). *Reading in the brain: The new science of how we read.* New York: Penguin.

Domínguez, A. B., Carrillo, M. S., del Mar Pérez, M., & Alegría, J. (2014). Analysis of reading strategies in deaf adults as a function of their language and meta-phonological skills. *Research in Developmental Disabilities, 35*(7), 1439–1456.

Drasgow, E. (1993). Bilingual/bicultural deaf education: An overview. *Sign Language Studies, 80*(1), 243–266.

Drasgow, E. (1998). American Sign Language as a pathway to linguistic competence. *Exceptional Children, 64*(3), 329–342.

Ehri, L. C. (2005). Learning to read words: Theory, findings, and issues. *Scientific Studies of Reading, 9*(2), 167–188.

Gigerenzer, G., Swijtink, Z., Porter, T., & Daston, L. (1990). *The empire of chance: How probability changed science and everyday life* (Vol. 12). Cambridge University Press.

Goldin-Meadow, S., & Mayberry, R. I. (2001). How do profoundly deaf children learn to read? *Learning Disabilities Research and Practice, 16*, 222–229. 10.1111/0938-8982.00022

Grosjean, F. (2001). The right of the deaf child to grow up bilingual. *Sign Language Studies, 1*, 110–114.

Grushkin, D. A. (1998). Why shouldn't Sam read? Toward a new paradigm for literacy and the deaf. *The Journal of Deaf Studies and Deaf Education, 3*(3), 179–201.

Grushkin, D. A. (2017). Writing signed languages: What for? What form? *American Annals of the Deaf, 161*(5), 509–527.

Hall, M., & Bavelier, D. (2010). Working memory, deafness and sign language. In M. Marschark & P. E. Spencer (Eds.), *The handbook of deaf studies, language and education* (pp. 458–472). Oxford, UK: Oxford University Press. 645.

Hassan, R. H., & Neves, J. (2019). Teaching vocabulary to deaf students through enriched subtitling: A case study in Qatar. *International Journal of Language, Translation and Intercultural Communication, 8*, 10–27.

Hoffmeister, R. (2008). Language and the deaf world: Difference not disability. In C. Chamberlain, J. Morford, & R. Mayberry (Eds.), *Language, Culture, and Community in Teacher Education* (pp. 71–98). Mahwah, NJ: Lawrence Erlbaum Associates.

Hoffmeister, R. J. (2000). *A piece of the puzzle: ASL and reading comprehension in deaf children. Language Acquisition by Eye,* 143–163.

Hoffmeister, R.J., & Caldwell-Harris, C.L. (2014). Acquiring English as a second language via print: The task for deaf children. *Cognition, 132*, 229–242.

Howerton-Fox, A., & Falk, J. L. (2019). Deaf children as 'English learners': The psycholinguistic turn in deaf education. *Education Sciences, 9*(2), 133.

Hrastinski, I., & Wilbur, R.B. (2016). Academic achievement of deaf and hard-of-hearing students in an ASL/English bilingual program. *Journal of Deaf Studies and Deaf Education, 21*, 156–170.

Humphries, T., & MacDougall, F. (1999). "Chaining" and other links: Making connections between American Sign Language and English in two types of school settings. *Visual Anthropology Review, 15*(2), 84–94.

Humphries, T., Kushalnagar, P., Mathur, G., Napoli, D. J., Padden, C., Rathmann, C., & Smith, S. (2016). Avoiding linguistic neglect of deaf children. *Social Service Review, 90*(4), 589–619.

Humphries, T., Kushalnagar, P., Mathur, G., Napoli, D.J., Padden, C., & Rathmann, C. (2014). Ensuring language acquisition for deaf children: What linguists can do. *Language 2014, 90*, e31–e52.

Humphries, T. (2014). Schooling in American Sign Language: A paradigm shift from a deficit model to a bilingual model in deaf education. *Berkeley Review of Education, 4*, 7–33.

Jacoby, L. L. (1978). On interpreting the effects of repetition: Solving a problem versus remembering a solution. *Journal of Verbal Learning & Verbal Behavior, 17*, 649–667.

Johnson, R. E., Liddell, S. K., & Erting, C. J. (1989). *Unlocking the curriculum: Principles for achieving access in deaf education (Gallaudet Research Institute Working/Occasional Paper Series,* No. 89-3). Washington, DC: Gallaudet Research Institute.

Knoors, H., & Marschark, M. (2012). Language planning for the 21st century: Revisiting bilingual language policy for deaf children. *Journal of Deaf Studies and Deaf Education, 17*, 291–305.

Koulidobrova, E., Kuntze, M., & Dostal, H.M. (2018). If you use ASL, should you study ESL? Limitations of a modality-b(i)ased policy. *Language, 94*, 99–126.

Krashen, S. (1985). *The input hypothesis: Issues and implications.* New York: Longman.

Krashen, S. (2004). *The power of reading: A review of research.* Portsmouth, NH: Heinemann.

Lane, H. L. (1992). *The mask of benevolence: Disabling the deaf community* (p. 104). New York: Knopf.

Lane, H. L., Hoffmeister, R., & Bahan, B. J. (1996). *A journey into the DEAF-WORLD.* Dawn Sign Press.

Markman, E.M. (1990). Constraints children place on word meanings. *Cognitive Science, 14*, 57–77.

Marschark, M. (2001). *Language development in children who are deaf: A research synthesis.* National Association of State Directors of Special Education, Alexandria, VA. Downloaded February 28, 2020, from https://eric.ed.gov/?id=ED455620.

Mayberry, R.I., Del Giudice, A.A., & Lieberman, A.M. (2011). Reading achievement in relation to phonological coding and awareness in deaf readers: A meta-analysis. *Journal of Deaf Studies and Deaf Education, 16*, 164–188.

Mayer, C. (2017). Written forms of signed languages: a route to literacy for deaf learners? *American Annals of the Deaf, 161*(5), 552–559.

Mayer, C., & Wells, G. (1996). Can the linguistic interdependence theory support a bilingual–bicultural model of literacy education for deaf students? *Journal of Deaf Studies and Deaf Education, 1*, 93–107.

Menyuk, P. (1971). *The acquisition and development of language (p. xv).* Englewood Cliffs, NJ: Prentice-Hall.

Mounty, J. L., Pucci, C. T., & Harmon, K. C. (2014). How deaf American Sign Language/English bilingual children become proficient readers: An emic perspective. *Journal of Deaf Studies and Deaf Education, 19*(3), 333–346.

Novogrodsky, Caldwell-Harris, Fish, & Hoffmeister (2014). The development of antonym knowledge in American Sign Language (ASL) and its relationship to reading comprehension in English. *Language Learning, 64*(4), 749–770.

Nunes, T., Burman, D., Evans, D., & Bell, D. (2010). *Writing a language that you can't hear.* In *Reading and dyslexia in different orthographies* (pp. 127–146).

Padden, C. (2006). Learning to fingerspell twice: Young signing children's acquisition of fingerspelling. In M. Marschark, P. E. Spencer, B. Schick (Eds.), *Advances in the Sign Language Development of Deaf Children* (pp. 189–201). New York, NY: Oxford University Press..

Paul, P.V. (1998). *Literacy and deafness: The development of reading, writing, and literate thought.* Boston: Allyn and Bacon.

Perfetti, C.A., & Sandak, R. (2000). Reading optimally builds on spoken language: Implications for deaf literacy. *Journal of Deaf Studies and Deaf Education, 5*, 31–50.

Quine, W. V. O. (1960). *Word and object.* Cambridge. MA: MITPress.

Strong, M. (1988). A bilingual approach to the education of young deaf children: ASL and English. In M Strong (Ed.), *Language learning & deafness.* NY: Cambridge University Press. 113–129.

Supalla, S., Wix, T. R., & McKee, C. (2001). Print as a primary source of English for deaf learners. In J. Nichol & T. Langendoen (Eds.), *One mind, two languages: Studies in bilingual language processing.* Oxford: Blackwell.

Supalla, S. J., Cripps, J. H., & Byrne, A. P. (2017). Why American sign language gloss must matter. *American Annals of the Deaf, 161*(5), 540–551.

Svartholm, K. (2014). 35 years of bilingual deaf education-and then? *Education Review, 2*, 33–50.

Silvestri, J. A., & Wang, Y. (2018). A grounded theory of effective reading by profoundly deaf adults. *American Annals of the Deaf, 162*(5), 419–444.

Tomasello, M., & Barton, M. E. (1994). Learning words in nonostensive contexts. *Developmental Psychology, 30*(5), 639.

Tomasello, M., Strosberg, R., & Akhtar, N. (1996). Eighteen-month-old children learn words in non-ostensive contexts. *Journal of Child Language, 23*(1), 157–176.

Trussell, J. W., & Easterbrooks, S. R. (2017). Morphological knowledge and students who are deaf or hard-of-hearing: A review of the literature. *Communication Disorders Quarterly, 38*(2), 67–77.

Van Staden, A. (2013). An evaluation of an intervention using sign language and multi-sensory coding to support word learning and reading comprehension of deaf signing children. *Child Language Teaching and Therapy, 29*(3), 305–318. 10.1177/0265659013479961.

Wilbur, R. B. (2000). The use of ASL to support the development of English and literacy. *Journal of Deaf Studies and Deaf Education, 5*(1), 81–104.

Williams, J. S. (1976). Bilingual experiences of a deaf child. *Sign Language Studies, 10*(1), 37–41.

PART II
Launching the Voyage
Bilingual Teaching Strategies for Deaf Students

7

REVISITING RETHINKING LITERACY

Marlon Kuntze and Debbie Golos

The growing literature on the severe impact that language deprivation has on deaf children (e.g., Glickman & Hall, 2018; Hall, 2017; Hall, Levin, & Anderson, 2017; Humphries et al., 2012) puts a sharper focus on the critical relationships between access to comprehensible language and literacy development. In this chapter, we revisit the model, *the visual basis for literacy* (Kuntze et al. 2014), for the purpose of elucidating how different factors that support a visually based approach to literacy development have roots in unabridged access to communication during the early years. The 2014 model (see Figure 7.1) delineates five areas that we argue as being crucial for supporting the development of visually based literacy: acquisition of ASL and development of visual engagement, emergent literacy, social mediation and English print, literacy and Deaf culture, and media. In this chapter, we draw on arguments made in the 2014 paper to help illustrate a framework (see Figure 7.2) for showing the relationship between accessible communication and early literacy development. We posit that communication supports not only language development but also supports emergent literacy and written language development, especially when used with media and literature. We see identity development as having an important relationship to literacy and attempt to pinpoint factors that support identity development. In short, the chapter attempts to foreground the centrality of interactive communication in fully accessible language for building a necessary foundation for supporting a child becoming literate.

The immense repercussions that language deprivation has on the development of deaf children are very relevant to our discussion about the key components of robust literacy development. We propose that the principles of the whole child approach (Slade and Griffith, 2013) are useful for framing the question of literacy

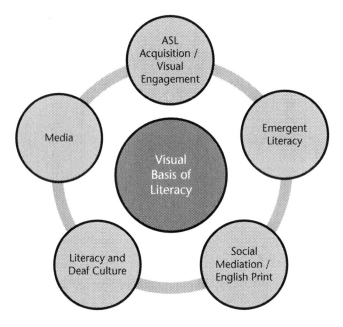

FIGURE 7.1 *Visual basis for literacy*

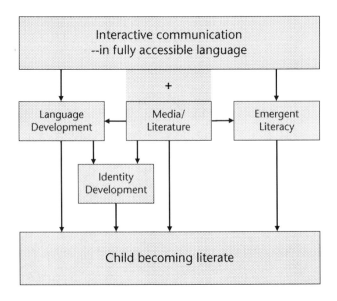

FIGURE 7.2 *Framework for early literacy*

development. Deaf children's progress in literacy development will not be equitable until we start to put individual students' needs first. It is critical to contemplate foundational skills that students need so they can actively engage in learning at school. Children need to feel connected to what is happening in school and to what is being taught. The goal of whole child education is premised on access to these key ingredients to ensure academic success.

The 2014 model is based on the perception that development should capitalize on strengths inherent in deaf children. Deaf children's orientation to the world is by nature already visually based from the very start; their eyes provide the best access to the world. This calls for making their environment visually based, and this is what helps make their development more optimal. Communication that is visually based is fully accessible; otherwise language will not be readily comprehensible. Deaf children are entitled to communication that is socially satisfying and intellectually nourishing, and this is what will help children be all they can be and become literate.

An important premise from the 2014 paper is that for deaf children the task of learning to read also involves the task of learning a *new* language. (Also see Erting & Kuntze, 2007; Hoffmeister & Caldwell-Harris, 2014; Kuntze, 1998; Singleton & Morgan, 2006 for further discussion.) We need to appraise literacy development in the context of an expansive framework as proposed by the proponents of multiliteracies (New London Group, 1996). The key point of that group is that literacy teaching will only be effective if it expands beyond a linear, text-based literacy approach ("mere literacy," i.e., the Simple View of Reading, SVR, originally proposed for reading comprehension by Gough & Tunmer, 1986). The SVR proponents claim that learning to read is simply a task of learning to decode words on paper and applying language comprehension skills that one already has as a part of spoken language competence. One reason this formula is problematic for deaf children is because it is based on the assumption that learning to read predicates on linking the print to spoken language. Learning to read in that way puts deaf children at a huge disadvantage. It does not take into account additional factors that are important, at least from the whole child perspective, in the task of learning to read without knowing spoken language. We need to be mindful of what it takes for deaf children to become successful as readers.

The SVR also does not take into account the cognitive aspects that support a child becoming literate, such as thinking critically and making inference. Those are important literacy skills needed for comprehension that do not develop exclusively through reading but can be developed through ASL (see Kuntze, 2004). The framework for early literacy as outlined in Figure 7.2 demonstrates how interactive communication is linked to language development, emergent literacy/written language development, and identity development and how each of these components supported by media and literature lay the foundation for helping the child become literate. The scope of development in the aforementioned areas rests on the extent to which a child has an opportunity for sustained and meaningful communication with multiple individuals.

As discussed in the 2014 paper, literacy development has its roots in emergent literacy development for which accessible communication is a key factor.

102 Marlon Kuntze and Debbie Golos

Emergent literacy development stems from the child having interactions with print from birth in multiple and frequent contexts (Sulzby & Teale, 1991). The breadth of topics covered in the child-adult communication, along with interaction with print in the environment, is instrumental in the development of language and literacy (NAEYC/IRA, 1998). This includes an appreciation not only of how the development of ASL and written English skills may take place within the process of socialization (Erting & Kuntze, 2007) but also the impact that ASL and Deaf cultural role models have on a child's identity development (Cawthon, Johnson, Garberoglio, & Schoffstall, 2016). Finally, we look at resources (books/media) that can be used as supplemental tools for a strong foundation for literacy.

Language Development

A newborn, deaf or hearing child, is primed for language acquisition. Language deprivation in the case of deaf children is simply a product of the lack of exposure to *psycholinguistically accessible* language (Gulati, 2019). Language accessibility refers to the extent to which the language modality (hearing or vision) renders the language input complete and unfiltered to a given child. For deaf children, the visual modality of ASL is what makes it accessible in ways that spoken language can never be. It is not enough for deaf children to get pieces of spoken language through lipreading even if it is supplemented by residual hearing. A child needs to experience a wide range of language uses, especially those that provide concomitant benefits for cognitive, social, and emotional developments (Fivush, Haden, & Reese, 2006).

In addition to the merits of ASL as the psycholinguistically accessible language, it is important to also argue for making ASL *sociolinguistically* accessible. Deaf children need to be constantly surrounded by ASL for language acquisition to take place naturally. Unfortunately, many parents are not informed about sign language and focus only on spoken language. They are mostly responding to the fact that their deaf child is not picking up speech, and as a result, they are driven by a desire to do something to remediate it. Further, some parents who consider sign language as a possibility, may opt for a "wait and see approach," choosing to see first how the child may progress with spoken language development before making a decision. Often this decision is put off if the child is making progress, albeit progress that is slow and delayed. Without appropriate advice and information, families often make choices that may not be in the best interest of the deaf child and make decisions without understanding the risks of linguistic deprivation (see Humphries et al., 2012 for a discussion on parents' vulnerability and misinformation given by the medical professionals).

The first five years of a child's life are the most crucial period of language acquisition. Any child with limited access to language before age five is in danger of never acquiring native-like fluency in any language (Kam & Newport, 2009). With limited access to language, a child is in a situation of being "linguistically deprived."

The term language deprivation encompasses the consequence resulting from lack of fully accessible language input during the formative years up to age five (Gulati, 2019; Shonkoff & Phillips, 2000). Linguistic deprivation also diminishes one's educational and career possibilities, since the cognitive consequence that comes with a strong foundation in language is an important factor that correlates highly with literacy (Chamberlain & Mayberry, 2008; Fischer, 1998; McGuinness, 2006; Wilbur, 2001).

There is a strong association between the amount of talk directed to children and vocabulary growth (Hart and Risley, 1995; Huttenlocher, Haight, Bryk, Seltzer, & Lyons, 1991). De Temple and Snow (1992) show a similar association on the basis of measures of emergent literacy and print-related skills. Shonkoff and Phillips (2000, p. 145) note that "wide individual differences at school entry in vocabulary and other early literacy skills do not diminish as children move through school, rather they typically become exacerbated." The limited communication exposure deaf children have with adults may indeed have long term repercussions.

The majority of deaf children experience language deprivation, and evidence is accumulating on the detrimental and long-lasting effects of language deprivation on deaf children's language, literacy, and social-emotional development; yet there is very little activity in research or policy in response to the effects that limited language input during the early years has on later school success. In fact, a recent survey of early childhood educators in the United States revealed that the majority of these teachers are not including quality language and literacy activities on a sufficiently regular basis (Golos, Moses, Roemen, & Cregan, 2018). Findings indicate that few teachers regularly incorporate Deaf role models, ASL stories, poems, rhythm, and rhyme, which are key factors in providing a strong foundation for early language and literacy development.

Emergent Literacy

Proponents of an emergent literacy perspective posit that language and literacy skills develop simultaneously (Sulzby & Teale, 1991; Teale & Sulzby, 1989) and that the needed attributes for literacy should start in infancy. Researchers who subscribe to this perspective have found that early experiences with language, books, print, and especially, extended discourse, is crucial for later literacy success (e.g., Dickinson & Tabors, 2001; Mayberry, del Giudice, & Lieberman, 2011; Ricasa, 2010; Whitehurst & Lonigan, 2001); they emphasize that adults play an important role in facilitating this development by engaging children in rich discourse and various literacy events as early as infancy.

Our premise is that communicative access to others is a valuable means for learning about written language prior to learning how to read or write. For deaf children, spoken language is not a viable pathway for making connection with words in print. ASL, on the other hand, serves as a viable pathway to make that connection.

For children who do not have an opportunity to learn ASL or who do not have access to others who know ASL, the opportunity to learn about written language and the words in print is very limited. The conventional view of deaf children and literacy is largely shaped by the literature on communication disorders. Deaf children are often perceived as having problems with language acquisition, and this perception drives language remediation efforts. Often overlooked is the lack of communication access the child has to others in the home and in the school. Without a viable communication milieu, the opportunity to learn about print that may have come about through communicating and learning about the world in early childhood settings just does not take place. Without the ability to carry out communicative interaction with the child, it is challenging for parents to participate in literacy activities such as bookreading with their deaf child.

In preschool classrooms where an emergent literacy environment is emphasized, children are exposed to print before they are able to read. They learn about concepts of print (e.g., that print, images, and text on a page or on the walls all have meaning). They also start developing word recognition skills which can easily take place through dialogue in ASL about what different printed words in their environment mean. Quality emergent-literacy classrooms should provide a good deal of interactions with print (NAEYC/IRA, 1998). However, as previously outlined, educators interacting with deaf children in early childhood settings often do not provide the much-needed high quality and frequent interactions with ASL and print (e.g., Golos et al., 2018).

In interacting with children during literacy activities, there are many ways teachers can mediate children's understanding of what they are reading: asking children open-ended questions, answering their questions, and encouraging them to interact with print and to talk about it with them throughout the day in various contexts (e.g., shared reading, outside time, drama time, and snack time). These activities that involve children interacting with English print are examples of how children are given the scaffolding to achieve a comprehensible exposure to English.

One of the most important activities to support emerging literacy skills (which includes the foundational knowledge needed for the development of written language) is reading aloud (Schleper, 1997; Trelease, 2006; Wauters & Dirks, 2017). Reading "aloud" in ASL provides the teacher with an excellent forum for telling stories in a visual way, thus making them fully accessible. By utilizing both languages (signing in ASL and pointing to printed English), the teacher not only makes the story comprehensible but also helps children begin to make connections with meaning through written English. Using ASL allows the teacher to check the children's comprehension of a story by inviting them to comment on or ask questions about it. The teacher is also in a position to call children's attention to important elements of the story or to the ways that some of the events in the story parallel or contrast with what the children may already know or have experienced.

In 1997, Erting and Pfau recommended the following to facilitate literacy development and these still apply today: (1) building metalinguistic awareness (i.e., helping children become aware of both ASL and written English); (2) effective strategies for shared reading, in which the teacher and the students make meaningful connections with print through ASL; and (3) writing that is facilitated by using ASL to discuss ideas and topics to write about. In essence, they and others (e.g., Golos & Moses, 2013) advocate the use of mediating interaction to promote both language, literacy, and identity development in the preschool classroom.

Identity Development

For the purpose of our discussion, identity development in relation to literacy development covers at least two areas. One is related to literacy identity which Seban and Tavşanlı (2017) defined (p. 1) "... as readers' proficiency and willingness to engage the meaning systems embedded within texts and to consider adopting them as part of their own personal meaning system – that system within which they define themselves and their relation to the world." The other is related to cultural identity – an identity formed through communication in a shared language. Kadar-Fulop (1988) points to the development of "language loyalty" and the encouragement of positive attitudes toward language as an important function for literacy education. While these two areas of identity development represent a timeline that extends beyond that for early literacy development, it is important that identity development starts as early as possible. In our framework we have shown how ASL acquisition (i.e., language development) and interactive exposure to media and literature serve to support identity development.

Identity development is rarely included in the discussion about deaf children's literacy development. When teachers or families model a cultural perspective of Deaf people by providing cultural and linguistic role models, valuing their students as visual beings and using bilingual strategies to connect ASL to written language, it not only fosters a positive sense of self but can also positively impact students' literacy development (Hermans, Ormel, Knoors, & Verhoeven, 2008).

The words adults use with children and the people and materials children interact with can impact children's feelings about themselves, which, in turn, can impact their motivation to engage in classroom activities including interacting with print (Derman-Sparks and Edwards, 2010). Hearing families or early childhood educators who have been influenced by a medical perspective of Deaf people, may unwittingly in their words or actions focus on what their child doesn't have (i.e., hearing ability) and on how they can help mitigate the consequence of the inability to hear (i.e., learn to speak). Because children may start developing an understanding about themselves and others as young as age three (Bishop, 1990; NAEYC/IRA, 1998), they may internalize these messages and grow to believe that they are less than others, feeling they are not accepted or valued for who they are. Further, educators who subscribe to a medical or audist approach to Deaf education, typically place greater value on spoken language development as a result of the belief that the action of making the connection between sound and print is the sole path to literacy. This creates an environment that may not only negatively impact the child's identity development as a result of not valuing their language(s) or cultures but that could also cause further delays in literacy development due to limited communication interaction. Further, children who experience delays in language may lack the ability to engage in conversations that concern negative or audist views others may have of them.

Resources are needed at home and school to provide deaf children with exposure to ASL and Deaf cultural role models to help foster positive self-identity (Cawthon et al., 2016; Stinson & Foster 2000). In regard to home, Solomon (2012) describes two different means of cultural transmission: vertical and horizontal. While hearing families can hand down "vertically" (from parent to child) the traits and values that families feel are important, deaf children also need to access values and knowledge horizontally from those who share a distinguishing characteristic with them which is not present in the homes of deaf children with hearing parents (i.e., Deaf people). Traditionally, this "horizontal" facilitation of identity development has happened at residential schools that employ Deaf people as teachers, aides, or caretakers in the dorms (e.g., Lane, Hoffmeister, & Bahan, 1996; Parasnis, 1996). However, nowadays the majority of deaf children go to public schools, where ASL and Deaf cultural models, particularly those from diverse backgrounds, are often absent; particularly in early childhood programs (Golos et al., 2018). Many of these children may not even socialize with deaf peers.

Teachers can also help foster identity development in educational settings by providing positive and diverse cultural and linguistic role models and utilizing bilingual strategies. These connections with role models help make deaf children feel whole (Lyle & Oliva, 2016) and help instill a positive sense of self. This, in turn, gives children added confidence and language to communicate their thoughts, ask questions, and express concerns all of which will ultimately increase their ability to actively engage in literacy activities (Cawthon et al., 2016; Holcomb, 1997). It is also important that teachers take into consideration the multilingual, multicultural homes that an increasing number of Deaf children come from. Students need support developing multiple and intersecting identities (García-Fernández, 2014). To foster this intersectional identity development, children need to be able to see both themselves and others, in multiple contexts on a regular basis and from a young age (Derman-Sparks & Edwards, 2010). This includes interactions with role models invited into the classroom, through print literature in which Deaf characters are portrayed, or through video literatures in which ASL is used by Deaf people (Moses, Golos, & Holcomb, 2018; Bishop, 1990; Golos & Moses, 2011). They also need to see other deaf children and Deaf adults from diverse backgrounds (i.e., gender, race, and culture) interacting with one another to support healthy development of identity and self-esteem (Derman-Sparks & Edwards, 2010; Corenblum & Annis, 1993; Parasnis, 1996). These interactions may also have a positive impact on the social aspect of literacy development and increase motivation to engage with print (Singer & Smith, 2003).

Teachers are an important part of this process. While exposure to Deaf adults is of critical importance, hearing teachers can also foster their students' identity development. In addition to providing interactions with Deaf people, they can facilitate important discussions with their students to foster their own self-awareness through shared-reading activities. Also, when the teachers attempt to have a better understanding of their own multiple and ever-changing intersecting identities, the better they will be able to select appropriate literature and media to facilitate these conversations. The greater understanding they have of themselves, the better they will also be able to connect to the families of their students, which is important for understanding the diversity of the family backgrounds that their students come from.

Media/Literature

Literature and media are a valuable resource for literacy development. Their value will be boosted when adults use them in interaction with children and their value will continue later on when children are able to use them independently. During the early years, children need adult engagement to help them make a connection with books and videos. When used with ASL, books can introduce children to the world of reading and are a valuable resource for emergent literacy activities. At that early stage, children can learn key English words that are important to the concepts and storyline related to each individual book. This is how they can be introduced to reading, and it is also how their knowledge of the world is augmented. Through reading the book "aloud" in ASL children can learn how a story is structured and how they may make meanings out of it. Children can enhance their ASL skills not only through adults who read the book aloud but also through media such as educational videos. Media may range from stories told in ASL to educational programming done in ASL. For deaf children, media is as valuable as books. They need to be exposed to ASL "in text" (i.e., ASL on video) as much as they need to be exposed to English in text.

Media incorporating ASL and Deaf characters also fosters identity development as it offers an opportunity for deaf children to make a greater connection with the content. It is important that deaf children see themselves as well as diverse others in various books/media. However, before selecting resources, adults should review messages with any materials students engage with (Moses et al. 2018). These representations can either foster children to form and appreciate knowledge about self and others or they can have an opposite effect depending on whether messages portrayed are negative or positive and how adults engage in discussion about these messages.

It is important to remember that educational media is to be used as a supplement, and not intended to replace live adults and peers who sign. The impact educational media can have is compounded when adults view it with children and engage in discussions about what they are watching and what they are seeing in it. However, children may still benefit when they watch it on their own. ASL in text (i.e., media) is a powerful way to expose children to the world of ASL, ASL signers, and Deaf characters. For example, programs such as *Peter's Picture* (Golos, 2010) or the *Hands Land* (http://www.handsland.com) rhythm and rhyme videos (developed by a completely Deaf team) showcase Deaf adults and deaf children learning language and literacy by interacting through ASL and modeling written English. They also integrate an interactive component that encourages viewer participation (Golos & Moses, 2013). It is important for hearing families and their deaf children to see quality models of interactions in ASL and how ASL helps make communication so effective as well as how it is used to support connections with print. Recent apps in ASL have also been created, such as *Peter's Picture,* VL2 apps (e.g., *Baobob)* or Isigntv *Signed Stories* which allow children to physically interact with the sign and text through interactive games. More recently the new genre of video presenting songs in ASL promotes the development of ASL rhythm and rhyme (e.g., *Hands Land*). The rationale is that those activities help nurture awareness of the structure and shape of ASL signs (i.e., ASL phonological awareness), and it is based on the premise that those activities help bolster competence at the level of the "building blocks" of ASL (Holcomb, 2019). These types of resources could serve as models of how resources may be developed for deaf children, their hearing families, and deaf educators.

Many deaf children often do not meet a Deaf adult or even a deaf peer until they are older (Marschark, Lang, & Albertini, 2002; Weisel & Reichstein, 1990). Children can benefit from seeing and realizing that there are many successful Deaf people in the world. They need to be exposed to a wide range of Deaf people: different ages, cultures, races, gender, abilities and to see them in a broad range of careers. When exposed to role models, children are provided with someone they can look up to (e.g., Cawthon et al., 2016) and see what fluently-signed communication looks like. Exposure to linguistic and cultural role models can aspire them to push the limit of their communicative world and achieve academic and social success. However, as mentioned, recent evidence suggests that early childhood educators are not incorporating linguistic or cultural Deaf role models into their classrooms on a consistent and regular basis (Golos et al., 2018). Technology and literature again can help fill the void as a supplemental tool when teachers are not fluent in ASL or if they do not have easy access to the Deaf community.

All deaf children need early access to fluent signers and exposure to both signed language and written language from birth (both of which can be augmented by media and literature). All children can benefit from role models they can look up to and learn from. Students should always have access to multiple types of literature and resources (e.g., fiction, stories, informational text, and media in ASL) and multiple opportunities to engage with them in meaningful ways, throughout the day both at home and in school.

Conclusion

The literature on language deprivation is critical not only for framing the discussion on early literacy development but also for highlighting the importance of accessible communication for facilitating deaf children's literacy development. Literacy is not about deaf children developing spoken language skills. It is also not about making the connection between spoken language and print. It is about language development and emergent literacy development, both of which are dependent on the extent of accessible communication deaf children have with peers, teachers, and family. Communication also allows children access to media and literature, which, in turn, further propel language development as well as initiating emergent literacy development. These are also key to identity development, fostering the child's multiple and intersecting identities so they grow to understand others and feel positive about themselves.

The framework presented in this chapter emphasizes that the first step must start with communication that is fully accessible and rich. It is crucial for engaging the child as a whole child. Interaction in a language the child can understand nurtures development in three main areas: primary language (ASL), emergent literacy (i.e., written English as a secondary language), and identity. Development in these three areas will be enhanced through media and literature when used with ASL. Each component complements one another and is essential to support a deaf child in becoming literate.

References

Bishop, R. S. (1990). Mirrors, windows, and sliding glass doors. *Perspectives: Choosing and Using Books for the Classroom*, 6(3), ix–xi.

Cawthon, S. W., Johnson, P. M., Garberoglio, C. L. & Schoffstall, S. J. (2016). Role models as facilitators of social capital for Deaf individuals: A research synthesis. *American Annals of the Deaf*, 161(2), 115–127. 10.1353/aad.2016.0021.

Chamberlain, C. & Mayberry, R. (2008). American Sign Language syntactic and narrative comprehension in skilled and less skilled readers: Bilingual and bimodal evidence for the linguistic basis of reading. *Applied Psycholinguistics*, 29(3), 367–388.

Corenblum, B. & Annis, R. C. (1993). Development of racial identity in minority and majority children: An affect discrepancy model. *Canadian Journal of Behavioural Science*, 25(4), 499–521.

Derman-Sparks, L. & Edwards, J. O. (2010). *Anti-bias education for young children and ourselves*. Washington, DC: National Association for the Education of Young Children.

De Temple, J. & Snow, C. (1992, April). *Styles of parent-child book reading as related to mothers' views of literacy and children's literacy outcomes* Paper presented at biennial Conference on Human Development, Atlanta, GA.

Dickinson, D. & Tabors, P. (2001). *Beginning literacy with language.* Baltimore: Paul H. Brooks Publishing Co., Inc.

Erting, C. & Kuntze, M. (2007). Language socialization in deaf communities. In P. A. Duff & N. H. Hornberger (Eds), *Encyclopedia of Language and Education* (Volume 8, 2nd edition). Language Socialization New York NY: Springer.

Erting, L. & Pfau, J. (1997). Becoming bilingual: Facilitating English literacy development using ASL in preschool, *Sharing Ideas.* Washington, DC: Gallaudet University Pre-College National Mission Programs.

Fischer, S. (1998). Critical periods for language acquisition: Consequences for deaf education. In A. Weisel (Ed.), *Issues Unresolved: New Perspectives on Language and Deaf Education.* Washington: Gallaudet University Press.

Fivush, R., Haden, C. A. & Reese, E. (2006). Elaborating on elaborations: Role of maternal reminiscing style in cognitive and socioemotional development. *Child Development,* 77(6), 1568–1588.

García-Fernández, C. (2014). *Deaf-Latina/Latino Critical Theory in Education: The Lived Experiences and Multiple Intersecting Identities of Deaf-Latina/o High School Students.* PhD dissertation, The University of Texas at Austin.

Glickman, N. S. & Hall, W. C. (Eds.). (2018). *Language deprivation and deaf mental health.* New York, NY: Routledge.

Golos, D. (2010). *Peter's picture: Our trip to Paulie's Pizza.* Retrieved from www.peterspicture.com.

Golos, D. B. & Moses, A. M. (2011). The representation of deaf characters in children's picture books. *American Annals of the Deaf,* 156(3), 270–282.

Golos, D. & Moses, A. (2013). Developing preschool deaf children's language and literacy learning from an educational media series. *American Annals of the Deaf,* 158(4), 411–425. 10.1353/aad.2013.0039.

Golos, D., Moses, A., Roemen, B. & Cregan, G. (2018). Cultural and linguistic role models: A survey of early childhood educators of the deaf. *Sign Language Studies,* 19(1), 40–74. 10.1353/sls.2018.0025.

Gough, P. B. & Tunmer, W. E. (1986). Decoding, reading, and reading disability. *Remedial and special education,* 7(1), 6–10.

Gulati, S. (2019). Language deprivation syndrome. In N.S. Glickman & W.C. Hall (Eds.), *Language deprivation and deaf mental health* (pp. 24–53). New York, NY: Routledge.

Hall, W. (2017). What you don't know can hurt you: The risk of language deprivation by impairing sign language development in deaf children. *Maternal and Child Health Journal,* 21(5), 961-965. doi:10.1007/s10995-017-2287-y.

Hall, W. C., Levin, L. L. & Anderson, M. L. (2017). Language deprivation syndrome: A possible neurodevelopmental disorder with sociocultural origins. *Social Psychiatry and Psychiatric Epidemiology,* 52(6), 761–776.

Hart, B. & Risley, T. (1995). *Meaningful differences in the everyday experiences of young American children.* Baltimore: Brookes Publishing Company.

Hermans, D. H., Ormel, E., Knoors, H. & Verhoeven, L. (2008). The relationship between the reading and signing skills of deaf children in bilingual education programs. *Journal of Deaf Studies and Deaf Education,* 13(4), 518–530.

Hoffmeister, R. J. & Caldwell-Harris, C. L. (2014). Acquiring English as a second language via print: The task for deaf children. *Cognition*, *132*(2), 229–242. 10.1016/j.cognition.2014.03.014.

Holcomb, L. K. (2019). Rhyme and rhythm on deaf children's engagement behavior and accuracy in recitation (PhD diss.). University of Tennessee. Retrieved from https://trace.tennessee.edu/utk_graddiss/5350.

Holcomb, T. (1997). Development of deaf bicultural identity. *American Annals of the Deaf*, *142*(2), 89–93. 10.1353/aad.2012.0728.

Humphries, T., Kushalnagar, P., Mathur, G., Napoli, D. J., Padden, C., Rathmann, C. & Smith, R. (2012). Language acquisition for deaf children: Reducing the harms of zero tolerance to the use of alternative approaches. *Harm Reduction Journal*, *9*(1), 16.

Huttenlocher, J., Haight, W., Bryk, A., Seltzer, M. & Lyons, T. (1991). Early vocabulary growth: Relation to language input and gender. *Developmental Psychology*, *27*, 236–248.

Kadar-Fulop, J. (1988). Culture, writing, and curriculum. In A.C. Purves (Ed), *Writing across languages and cultures: Issues in contrastive rhetoric* (pp. 25–50). London: Sage Publications.

Kam, C. L. H. & Newport, E. L. (2009). Getting it right by getting it wrong: When learners change languages. *Cognitive Psychology*, *59*(1), 30–66.

Kuntze, M. (1998). Literacy and deaf children: The language question. *Topics in Language Disorders*, *4*, 1–15. 10.1097/00011363-199818040-00003.

Kuntze, M. (2004). *Literacy acquisition and deaf children: A study of the interaction between ASL and English. Unpublished doctoral dissertation. Retrieved from ProQuest. (UMI3128664)*.

Kuntze, M., Golos, D. & Enns, C. (2014). Rethinking literacy: Broadening opportunities for visual learners. *Sign Language Studies*, *14*(2), 203–224.

Lane, H., Hoffmeister, R. & Bahan, B. (1996). *A journey into the deaf world*. San Diego, CA: Dawn Sign Press.

Lyle, L. & Oliva, G. (2016, April). *Raising the whole Child: Addressing social-emotional development in deaf children*. (Research Brief No. 11, Visual Language and Visual Learning Science of Learning Center). Washington, DC.

Marschark, M., Lang, H. G. & Albertini, J. A. (2002). *Educating deaf children: From research to practice*. New York, NY: Oxford University Press.

Mayberry, R. I., del Giudice, A. A. & Lieberman, A. M. (2011). Reading achievement in relation to phonological coding and awareness in deaf readers: A meta-analysis. *Journal of Deaf Studies and Deaf Education*, *16*(2), 164–188.

McGuinness, D. (2006). *Language development and learning to read: The scientific study of how language development affects reading skill*. Cambridge: MIT Press.

Moses, A., Golos, D. & Holcomb, L. (2018). Creating and using educational media with a cultural perspective of Deaf people. *Language Arts Journal*, *96*(1), 66–71.

NAEYC/IRA (1998). Learning to read and write: Developmentally appropriate practices for young children: A joint position statement of the International Reading Association and the National Association for the Education of Young Children, *Young Children*, *53*(4), 30–46.

New London Group (1996). A pedagogy of multiliteracies: Designing social futures. *Harvard Educational Review*, *66*(1), 60–92.

Parasnis, I. (1996). On interpreting the Deaf experience within the context of cultural and linguistic diversity. In I. Parasnis (Ed.), *Cultural and language diversity and the deaf experience* (pp. 3–19). NY: Cambridge University Press.

Ricasa, R. M. (2010). *Extended discourse in ASL between a deaf child and her teachers in ASL/ English preschool classrooms: Implications for literacy development. Unpublished doctoral dissertation. Retrieved from ProQuest. (UMI3532186).*

Schleper, D. R. (1997). *Reading to deaf children: Learning from deaf adults.* Washington, DC: Gallaudet University Press.

Seban, D. & Tavşanlı, Ö. F. (2017). Children's sense of being a writer: Identity construction in second grade writers' workshop. *International Electronic Journal of Elementary Education, 7*(2), 215–232.

Shonkoff, J. P. & Phillips, D. A. (2000). *From neurons to neighborhoods: The science of early childhood development.* Washington, DC: National Academy Press.

Singer, J. Y. & Smith, S. A. (2003). The potential of multicultural literature: Changing understanding of self and others. *Multicultural Perspectives, 5*(2), 17–23.

Singleton, J. L. & Morgan, D. (2006). Natural signed language acquisition within the social context of the classroom. In B. Schick, M. Marschark & P. E. Spencer (Eds.), *Advances in the Sign Language Development of Deaf Children..* Oxford: Oxford University Press.

Slade, S. & Griffith, D. (2013). A whole child approach to student success. *KEDI Journal of Educational Policy, 10*(3), 21–35.

Stinson, M. & Foster, S. (2000). Socialization of deaf children and youths in school. In P. Spencer, C. Erting & M. Marschark (Eds.), *The deaf child in the family and at school* (pp. 151–174). Mahwah, NJ: Lawrence Erlbaum Associates.

Solomon, A. (2012). *Far from the tree: Parents, children, and the search for identity.* New York, NY: Scribner.

Sulzby, E. & Teale, W. (1991). Emergent literacy. In R. Barr, M. L. Kamil, P. Mosenthal & P. D. Pearson (Eds.), *Handbook of reading research* (*Vol. II*, pp. 727–758). New York: Longman.

Teale, W. H. & Sulzby, E. (1989). Emergent literacy: New perspectives on young children's reading and writing development. In D. Strickland & L. Morrow (Eds.), *Emerging literacy: Young children learn to read and write* (pp. 1–15). Newark, DE: International Reading Association.

Trelease. (2006). *The read aloud handbook.* (*6th Edition*) NY: Penguin.

Wauters, L. & Dirks, E. (2017). Interactive reading with young deaf and hard-of-hearing children in eBooks versus print books. *The Journal of Deaf Studies and Deaf Education, 22*(2), 243–252.

Weisel, A. & Reichstein, J. (1990). Acceptance of hearing loss and adjustment of deaf and hard of hearing young adults. *Journal of the American Deafness and Rehabilitation Association, 24*(1), 1–6.

Whitehurst, G. J. & Lonigan, C. J. (2001). Emergent literacy: Development from pre-readers to readers. In S. B. Neuman & D. K. Dickinson (Eds.), *Handbook of Early Literacy Research* (pp. 11–29). New York: Guilford Press.

Wilbur, R. (2001). Sign language and successful bilingual development of deaf children. *Journal for General Social Issues, 10*(6), 1039–1079.

8

HOW CAN YOU TALK ABOUT BILINGUAL EDUCATION OF THE DEAF IF YOU DO NOT TEACH SIGN LANGUAGE AS A FIRST LANGUAGE?

Vassilis Kourbetis and Spyridoula Karipi

Over 90% of Deaf children are born to hearing parents who do not know or use Greek Sign Language (GSL); thus, the majority of Deaf children have little receptive experience with any fully accessible language (Kourbetis & Hatzopoulou 2010). Deaf children's lack of exposure to an accessible natural Sign Language (SL) delays their language acquisition and development, which, in turn, impairs their linguistic fluency (Hoffmeister & Caldwell-Harris, 2014; Morford & Hänel-Faulhaber, 2011; Woll & Ladd, 2011). Deaf children are frequently brought up in impoverished linguistic environments (Lane, Hoffmeister, & Bahan, 1996; Mitchell & Karchmer, 2004; Singleton & Newport, 2004). We accept the notion that "the world is facing a serious crisis in educating deaf students" (Humphries, 2013, p. 8) in Greece as well.

International studies demonstrate that academic progress and social and emotional growth of Deaf children is directly related to the acquisition of sign language as a first language (e.g., Hatzopoulou, 2008; Hoffmeister, 2000; Hoffmeister & Caldwell-Harris, 2014; Hrastinski & Wilbur, 2016; Kourbetis & Hatzopoulou 2010; Mayberry, 2007; Niederberger, 2008; Ormel, Hermans, Knoors, & Verhoeven, 2012; Woll, 1998). Also, empirical findings on the acquisition of sign languages by Deaf children of Deaf parents who learn a sign language in a natural way have been shown to achieve similar maturational milestones as hearing children in the acquisition of spoken languages (Emmorey, 2002; Hoffmeister & Wilbur, 1980). In our opinion, teaching Sign Language as a first language (L1) and as an academic subject in schools is a matter of paramount importance to learning. Similarly, knowing a visual, accessible language – such as GSL – is directly related to knowing and understanding a written language by Deaf children, and thus consequently impacts their literacy development (Albertini & Schley, 2003; Hatzopoulou, 2008; Hoffmeister & Caldwell-Harris, 2014; Hrastinski & Wilbur, 2016; Scott & Hoffmeister, 2017).

Research on the implementation of bilingual (SL and print) programs in the education for the Deaf in Sweden (Svartholm, 2010), Denmark (Bergmann, 1994), and the United States (Hoffmeister & Caldwell-Harris, 2014) demonstrates positive results in the academic development of Deaf students and stresses the advantages of acquiring the national Sign Language from preschool age (Baker & Wright, 2017; Hrastinski & Wilbur, 2016; Kourbetis & Hatzopoulou, 2010; Scott & Hoffmeister, 2017). A recent report (Kourbetis, 2018) on a survey conducted on the state-of-the-art of teaching signed languages as a first language contains information about the status of the 30 (n = 30) European and 31 (n = 31) other national signed languages in the world for their role in (special) education and the status of sign language curricula and teaching materials. Among other things, the study found that teaching SL as a first language to Deaf students was not listed as an objective for schools for the majority of Deaf schools. Unsurprisingly, the same was found for the mainstream schools where Deaf students study next to hearing students. The countries that teach SL as a first language are Norway, Nigeria, Germany, France, Finland, and, most recently (and by law), Greece (Kourbetis, 2018). For the full Report of the Survey, see http://www.sign1st.eu/en/intellectual-output/.

There are two other issues of importance, especially for Greece, to mention before our main presentation. The first refers to schooling of Deaf children, and the second refers to the use of national laws and the international treaties as legal instruments for teaching sign language. In terms of schooling, residential schools for Deaf children – the oldest type of schooling – have been the petri dish for sign language acquisition, development, and interaction for most Deaf children worldwide. There has been a decline in the enrollment and operation of residential schools for Deaf children in Greece and worldwide in recent years. This has resulted in droves of Deaf children enrolling in mainstream schools, which often do not emphasize sign language use and development (Humphries et al., 2012; Kourbetis & Gargalis, 2006; Kourbetis & Hatzopoulou, 2010). At the same time, however, the United Nations Convention on the Rights of Persons with Disabilities (CRPD, 2007) promotes sign language environments for Deaf children. As the first international treaty unambiguously referring to sign language (Article 24) as a human right, this instrument is of great importance to Deaf people all over the world.

Greece's experience with bilingual education and the Convention both propose that teaching and utilizing sign language as a first language in bilingual education should be the first priority for the linguistic, academic, social, and emotional development of Deaf children. It is a human right that we all must support. To meet these challenges, we are working to develop curricula and other instructional tools to promote the accessible bilingual education of Deaf children in Greece. We now present some of these tools.

The Curriculum and Other Greek Sign Language Teaching Tools in Greece

The first Curriculum for teaching Greek Sign Language as a first language was published by the Greek Pedagogical Institute in 2004. It was designed to cover grades K-9 (Kindergarten to Junior High School, a total of ten grades). The GSL curriculum development began as an adaptation of a curriculum for the teaching of ASL as a first language to Deaf children with the help of Todd Czubek, Bob Hoffmeister, and Janey Greenwald. As technology improved, curricula ideas were adjusted to incorporate the availability of new technical platforms and Universal Design (CAST, 2018). The Curriculum for teaching Greek Sign Language as a first language is available in Greek at http://prosvasimo.iep.edu.gr/el/. It was modified and updated up to the second-grade level in 2008, and it is available in English as well at http://www.sign1st.eu/en/intellectual-output/.

One of the major obstacles Greek teachers of the Deaf are faced with is the design and creation of sign language educational material for classroom use (Kourbetis, 2018). In the next section, we will introduce some of the teaching tools developed to support implementation of the curriculum. We will present innovative educational material that has been developed and is currently under development, the demanding process underlying the tools' creation, and, finally, the results of the production of sign language material for bilingual education of Deaf children.

Production of Teaching Materials

We have been designing, testing, and implementing innovative materials to promote academic and language learning in Greek Deaf children since 2004. One of our goals is to develop materials for young Deaf children and their hearing parents to help learn GSL. Specifically, based on the National Curriculum for teaching GSL as a first language (Pedagogical Institute, 2004), we created, designed, and implemented a grammar teaching program for Deaf students from preschool through fourth grade (Karipi, 2015). This program consists of a multimedia presentation focusing on the teaching of GSL phonology, morphology, syntax, and discourse features. We now turn to the innovative practices of the GSL as a first language teaching program.

1. The Online Interactive Digital Sign Language Library application
2. The Online Greek Sign Language Dictionary, which is linked to the digital library so that the dictionary entries can be seen in various contexts
3. Signing Books for GSL learning
4. The interactive, digital e-Books for bilingual teaching of Greek Sign Language and Modern Greek via print

The Online Interactive Digital Sign Language Library

The Online Interactive Digital Sign Language Library (DSLL), a web-based application, was designed and created to host accessible materials using GSL. The DSLL draws from the principles of Universal Design for Learning (UDL) (CAST, 2018). The DSSL application offers the potential to archive, search, and explore academic and social content delivered in GSL. We have developed two separate Digital Libraries, which are both free and accessible to all. One is designated for GSL teaching, the other for bilingual teaching needs (GSL and Greek print). Both applications have the same structure but different content. Both libraries prohibit users from uploading their own videos. The administrator of the project can upload such videos (if needed) and can modify other videos. Video downloading is available to anyone.

The DSLL application for teaching and learning signed language as a first language is presented on an independent platform (http://digital-library.sign1st. eu/). It contains video-recorded stories in the following Signed Languages: Greek, Cyprian, Swiss German, and Dutch. It includes signing stories ranging in duration from 29 seconds to 8 minutes and 13 seconds. The Digital Library for bilingual education (SL and Print) (Figure 8.1) is the second independent platform used in promoting Deaf education. It includes signed videos with both voice translation and subtitles for all textbook content from first through fourth grade (http://multimedia-library.prosvasimo.gr/DZ/player/E). The DSLL for bilingual education includes signed stories ranging from 38 seconds to 35 minutes in length. A GSL corpus of more than forty thousand signed videos has been constructed and is open to all, making it the largest GSL trove available for field research. The signed stories can be viewed in several different ways to meet the pedagogical needs of the users. For example, the stories can be viewed as video clips to display story structure in sequential videos, or viewed as a grid that displays the video as a cover page showing screenshots from the first scene in the video – like a book cover (Figure 8.1) – accompanied by a timeline illustrating the duration of the video (Figure 8.2 D).

The interactive subtitles are an important and useful tool, allowing the user to browse the video by selecting subtitles presented in a box on the right (see Figure 8.2, section A). The user is able to search for words and phrases included in the subtitles. When a phrase is selected, a simultaneous signed playback of the segment identified will occur in the large window on the left (Figure 8.2, section B). The total number of search results are tabulated and can be displayed (Figure 8.2, section B). Users can then navigate the search results. It is also possible for users to search subtitle content within and across all videos (Figure 8.2, section C) of the platform. This allows the user to view and compare all the available video clips matching the searched word or phrase. The timeline (Figure 8.2, section D) shows, in a visual manner, at what timestamp the specified word appears in the video. Clicking the highlighted area of the timeline moves the video to the corresponding

Teaching Sign Language as a First Language 117

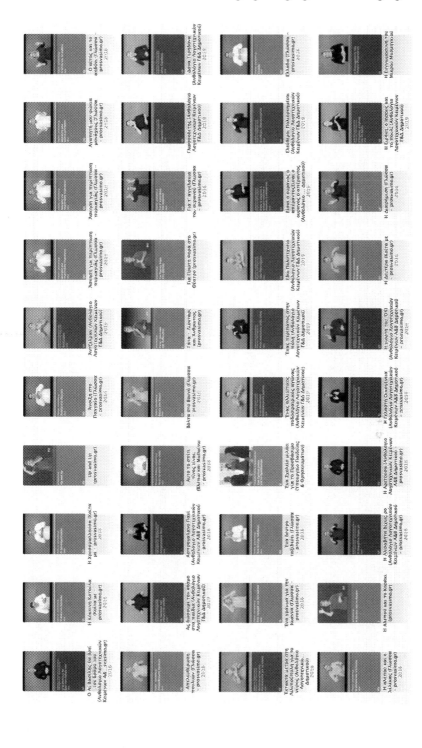

FIGURE 8.1   Digital Library for Bilingual Education

118 Vassilis Kourbetis and Spyridoula Karipi

FIGURE 8.2 Playback of educational material with interactive video subtitles

Note. Sections: A. Browse video using interactive subtitles, B. Search for subtitles in the video being played, C. Search for subtitles in all the videos of the platform, D. Visual search in the timeline of the video.

scene. Users can download the presented videos in a WebM format, which is not space demanding, using direct download.

Other innovative features include the ability to identify and save the URL address of the video for later use in homework assignments, in self-evaluation, in assessment, or in research. As well, the videos are stored and played on a local server, and thus do not depend on video services like YouTube. The entire application (with its material) can be installed onto a personal computer or connected to a local area network. These novel features enable students, parents, and teachers alike to access a large, digital GSL database effectively, something that until recently was impossible in the realm of Greek Deaf education (Kourbetis, Boukouras, & Gelastopoulou, 2016).

All of the material needed for teaching GSL as an L1 (for five grade levels) is also available as a stand-alone, interactive e-Book. This format meets the technological needs of many schools and families of Deaf children that do not have adequate internet access. This multisensory (Visual: SL and print; Audio: spoken translation) approach may be used in a bilingual educational environment to motivate students. We anticipate that an increase in motivation will result in a corresponding increase in classroom participation. As information becomes more accessible, students will better comprehend the content (Darrin, 2018; Hoffmeister & Caldwell-Harris, 2014; Moe & Wright, 2013; Tuomi, 2013). With the same multisensory approach, we have developed the Online Greek Sign Language Dictionary, which we present now.

The Online Greek Sign Language Dictionary

Our aim has been clear: Develop a Greek Sign Language Dictionary as a much-needed resource for the education of Deaf children. The Online Greek Sign Language Dictionary (http://prosvasimo.iep.edu.gr/dblexiko/) is the largest fully accessible interactive online dictionary for Greek Sign Language. It contains more than 3,500 signed lexical entries (lemmas), organized in 38 categories (e.g., animals, food, weather, technology, and math). It also includes 1,815 phrases and sentences sorted into five categories (i.e., Questions, Statements, Negation, Simple, and Conjoined). It will be enriched with content from bilingual educational materials that are currently being developed by our team, and it is expected to cover the educational needs of Deaf children in elementary education and beyond.

The database includes concepts signed by several native signers from various geographical areas of Greece, which demonstrates regional variations in sign production. The user is able to search for Greek words or phrases in the GSL Lexicon database using several filters and selections from display menus, by alphabetic search, or by a scroll-down list (see Figure 8.3). The search can be completed within 38 categories, some of which have already been mentioned. We are presently working to develop the capability to search the database using Signed Language properties (handshape or location).

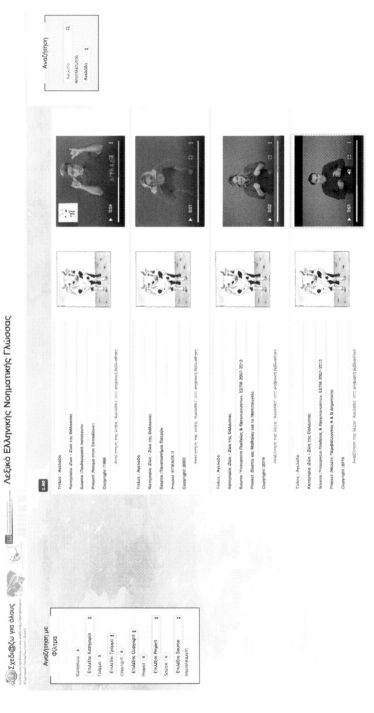

FIGURE 8.3 A search for the word/sign "COW" in the dictionary

Because students cannot learn a language from a dictionary, which presents words out of context, our main goal has been to connect the dictionary to the Online Interactive Digital Sign Language Library presented in the previous section. Relating the dictionary to the DSLL permits students to have access to and see signs in meaningful contexts. All GSL content in the DSLL and the GSL Lexicon is signed by native signers, providing access to more meaningful and useful content. This visual presentation of information is especially helpful for Deaf children in Greece that previously had limited access to native signed language input. Consider this example: A search in the dictionary for the word/sign "COW" (presented in Figure 8.3) depicts four variations of the sign for "COW." The word is signed by three different native signers who are more than 20 years apart in age, allowing Deaf students to view variations of signs used by the Deaf community of Greece. Additionally, you can search for any sign in the DSLL, and you will receive further information regarding that sign. The DSLL locates signed stories and connects to video clips that contain the sign for the searched word. The dictionary and DSLL were tested in three schools for the Deaf in Greece. Professionals who participated in the beta testing reported that the DSLL search and production feature was a valuable teaching tool and the materials were easily accessible for teachers, students, and caretakers. To complement the Dictionary and the Library, we have started to develop signing books, which we turn to now.

Signing Books

The Kindergarten for the Deaf in Argyroupolis, Greece, recently participated in the project *Sign First.*[1] Throughout the project, signed materials were created for young Deaf children and their hearing parents to learn Sign Language. The most common material that was created was books. These books covered a variety of topics, including signs, sign handshapes, the manual alphabet, and storytelling. The Deaf children – under the guidance of their teacher – were able to create signing books for future use. It is impressive that the Deaf children at such a young age (with such limited sign language exposure before coming to school!) were able to create a GSL signing book after participating in our project. We consider it worthwhile to offer a short description of two of the produced materials: "A book with … signs" and "My manual alphabet."

"A Book with … Signs"

The picture book "A book with … signs" (in Greek: "Ena viblio me … noima") contains 19 sentences that 21 Deaf children (11 kindergarten and 10 first-grade students) produced working alongside their five teachers and the second author of this paper (Spyridoula Karipi[2]) in a three-month period. Manoliou Ioanna, a Deaf artist, drew the illustrations, and a Deaf native signer and GSL teacher, Nikos

Isaris, signed the final video recording. They both worked closely with the children and the teachers. All sentences are made with three basic handshapes: The "1" handshape (7 sentences), the "B" handshape (5 sentences), and the "5" handshape (7 sentences). Of the 19 total sentences, 12 were produced with 3 signs; 6 were produced with 3 or 4 signs; and 1 sentence featured 6 signs. The story is comprised of 79 total signs (78 unique signs and one sign, EAT, twice). The book was created after the children had been taught a number of GSL grammatical structures. Each sign within a particular sentence of the book is made with the same handshape. For example, the GSL sentence SNAKE EAT CAKE (The snake eats a cake) (Figure 8.4) is signed with entirely handshape "1" (Index figure extended). Samples from the signing book created by the Deaf children are presented in Figure 8.4. The book is produced in both a signing version (video) and a printed version.

"My manual alphabet"

To achieve the goal of learning the Manual Alphabet of GSL, we developed a humorous story using the manual alphabet to produce signs. A screenshot of the video book is presented in Figure 8.5. To make it more understandable for children, we presented illustrations created by a Deaf artist (who wishes to remain anonymous) that depict the story. We then linked these illustrations to video recording of a Deaf native signer, Theodore Rikkou, so that the Deaf students have two visual ways to use to understand the story. The story is uploaded at http://digital-library.sign1st.eu/JD/player/A. A poster titled "My manual alphabet" was also developed for the children and displayed at school.

All of the presented applications and teaching materials are designed to teach GSL as an L1. The purpose of these materials was to expose Deaf children in the school to as much GSL as possible. This visual exposure produced results beyond even our expectations. The Deaf children were engaged, excited, and communicative about their work. We will next present the digital, accessible e-Books that are designed for bilingual teaching of academic content.

Digital Accessible e-Books

Digital, accessible e-Books are multimedia applications that enable the user to follow written content in the form of either audio or video-recorded signed language. Similar recent technology has been used by the Masaryk University in a web application known as "Hybrid Book" (Hladík & Gůra, 2012) for the creation of study materials aimed at users with different disabilities. The format that we adopted followed the guidance of the national curriculum books, which are aimed at specific age groups. The multimedia electronic form of the e-Books (either in the form of a single copy or a web application) combines the printed book and GSL translation of that book. There are also subtitles below the GSL

Teaching Sign Language as a First Language 123

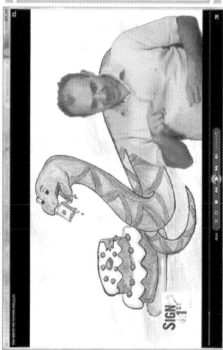

FIGURE 8.4 The video (left) and printed (right) versions of "A book with…signs" (SNAKE CAKE EAT)

FIGURE 8.5 The signing book "My manual alphabet."

Teaching Sign Language as a First Language **125**

video in addition to an oral reading of the text. The components of this app are presented in Figure 8.6. The multimedia data is shown as a.pdf, while the video and audio files are available as independent files.

Figure 8.6 depicts three main sections: the video window (upper right), individual video clip frames (lower right), and the story in print (left). This application's hallmark is its flexibility. The GSL translation can be viewed either continuously or in parts, depending on the user's preference. The user is also able to modify (1) the speed at which the text is signed, (2) the size of the video player, and (3) the presence of subtitles. Finally, and most importantly from a pedagogical standpoint, the user is able to take snapshots (still frames) of the signed videos whenever she wishes. The user can then use the snapshots alone or proceed to add text to the still frame. These snapshots can then be deleted, printed, or used to develop instructional materials.

We paid close attention to the relationship between written and signed languages, especially at the word and phrase level. Understanding this relationship is crucial for effective bilingual education. A text's accessibility depends on the quality of the text in GSL. The translation of a printed text into GSL can either closely parallel the original content or slightly diverge from the text itself to reflect an adaptation. Using the national curriculum textbooks, the native signers focus on either content comprehension or vocabulary learning. If the objective is to understand the meaning of the text, then the Deaf native signers follow an approach that tolerates distance from the text for the sake of improving clarity. If the objective is grammatical, syntactic, or phonological awareness, then interpretation mostly follows the original source. Research demonstrates that signing Greek texts is an extremely demanding and difficult task (Kourbetis, 2013). The signing of the texts is done, on the one hand, in cooperation with experienced, native signers, Deaf tutors, or consultants (all fluent in Greek). On the other hand, an additional translation component of the text is done with professional interpreters of GSL. These two categories of professionals work collaboratively to form a team of bilingual translators. The team's content and linguistic knowledge, combined with the knowledge of the target group, are important factors that have been taken into account to make all textbooks fully accessible to Deaf students. When converting written textbooks into accessible educational materials for Deaf students, the signed text was treated with the utmost importance. We treated the signed texts with such care because the core of the project is promoting GSL communication skills. We anticipate that this app will eventually contain all of the textbooks needed for elementary school.

Results and Impact

Twenty-three teachers of the Deaf evaluated the effectiveness of the applications we developed. The teachers work in five day-schools of the Deaf (K-12) on the mainland of Greece. These teachers completed the evaluation of the material after

126 Vassilis Kourbetis and Spyridoula Karipi

FIGURE 8.6 Screenshot from an e-Book (Modern Greek 3rd grade) whose accessible interface presents the text with the use of Greek Sign Language

Teaching Sign Language as a First Language **127**

implementation and an in-school training. Most teachers were female (n = 21) and hearing (n = 18). Fifteen teachers were below 40 years old, while 8 were above 40. All teachers had a certificate of GSL adequacy (functional communication), which is mandatory in Greece.

Respondents reported that using accessible educational materials in class and having separate materials dedicated teaching GSL as an L1 helped teachers who are not proficient in SL in three critical ways: (1) by providing teachers with all the visual materials, especially pre-recorded video narratives by native signers; (1) by providing curriculum-based assessment material (not presented in this chapter due to length limitations) in both GSL and printed Greek; and (3) by providing teachers with access to video narratives by native signers to improve their learning of GSL in a supportive way. Observational data following implementation of the teaching tools suggests that the use of the educational material is a cohesive and successful pedagogical practice for the bilingual-bicultural education of Deaf children.

Conclusions

Sign language teaching should involve the understanding and assimilation of the linguistic and grammatical elements of the target language through authentic, natural language learning situations. Learning in a bilingual (GSL-Greek) environment provides skills that are useful in encountering situations outside the classroom and within the Deaf community. One purpose of learning Sign Language is to comfortably interact with the Deaf community. Another is that learning Sign Language facilitates one's overall learning process by presenting information in two languages, Sign Language and written language, simultaneously.

The benefits of the presented applications are multiple, and they affect students, teachers, parents, and everyone else involved in the educational process of Deaf children. These applications (1) minimize barriers to learning among Deaf students and (2) foster an environment conducive to the implementation of bilingual educational programs (Booth & Ainscow, 2011). The innovative use and development of interactive subtitles make it an appropriate tool to serve the needs of Deaf students. These applications may also be used as a repository for the collection and processing of new material. Moreover, by using the instruments described in this chapter, Deaf students can acquire knowledge and information at a much earlier age. As a corollary, their ability to understand and handle incoming information will improve (Fajardo, Parra, & Cañas, 2010; Gentry, Chinn, & Moulton, 2004; Hockings, Brett, & Terentjevs, 2012; Mich, Pianta, & Mana, 2013; Smith & Throne, 2007; Tomlinson, 2001). Moreover, teachers can use these applications in the design and implementation of other educational programs. Parents can use these applications, not only to support their children but also to support their learning of GSL comfortably in their home. Finally, any other professionals interested in expanding their skills and understanding the issues in Deaf education may also take advantage of these applications.

We hope that the GSL translation of storybooks and the other interactive, curriculum-based applications will benefit all Deaf children in nursery schools and primary schools – as well as their hearing parents. We hope that these Sign Language materials will positively support change in the current situation in Greece. For those parents who want to use Greek Sign Language with their children, using the aforementioned resources will make it much easier to do so. The open-access online material for using, teaching, and learning Greek Sign Language was the chief priority for our project, and we are happy to offer such access to all.

Acknowledgments

This work is co-financed:

- By Greece and the European Union (European Social Fund – ESF) through the Operational Program "Human Resources Development, Education and Lifelong Learning 2014–2020" in the context of the project "Universal Design and Development of Accessible Digital Educational Material" bearing the Acronym title "Prosvasimo" and code number MIS 5001313, and
- By the European Programme Erasmus +, KA2 – Cooperation for Innovation and the Exchange of Good Practices, Strategic Partnerships for school education, in the context of the project "Teaching European Sign Languages as a First Language" bearing the Acronym title "Sign First" and code number 2016-1-EL01-KA201–023513. The State Scholarship Foundations (IKY) is the National Agency of the Erasmus+ Programme.

We wish to acknowledge all the people that support our work by name, but that would mean a list of hundreds of people, so we chose not to even attempt making a short list.

Special thanks goes to our Partners in the Projects "Sign First" and "Prosvasimo" for their helpful input and for their valuable contributions on earlier outputs. We are particularly indebted to our colleagues in the schools for the Deaf in Greece for their comments and suggestions. We are grateful to the families and their Deaf children for putting their trust in us.

We are particularly indebted to our Deaf native signer colleagues and our signed language interpreters who gave their best energy, knowledge, cooperation, and enthusiasm with the hopes of making our projects a success.

A special tribute goes to Dr. Robert J. Hoffmeister. Bob has been a mentor, friend, and supporter of our projects even before they began. Thank you for this long journey that started in 1980 and is still going strong. We will always be indebted to your vision and support, Bob!

Notes

1 Sign First is a project funded by the European Programme Erasmus + . Signed materials, including assessment tools, were developed that are available to be implemented in programs serving Deaf children in four countries in Europe (Cyprus, Greece, The Netherlands, and Switzerland) http://www.sign1st.eu/en/.
2 Spyridoula Karipi is the principal of The Kindergarten for the Deaf of Argyroupolis, Greece.

References

Albertini, J. A., & Schley, S. (2003). Writing: Characteristics, Instruction, and Assessment. In M. Marschark & P. E. Spencer(Eds.), *Oxford handbook of deaf studies, language, and education* (pp. 123–135). New York: Oxford University Press.

Baker, C., & Wright, W. (2017). *Foundations of bilingual education and bilingualism* (6th ed.). Clevedon, UK: Multilingual Matters.

Bergmann, R., Ahlgren, I., & Hyltenstam, K. (1994). Teaching sign language as the mother tongue in the education of deaf children in Denmark In I. Ahlgren & K. Hyltenstam (Eds.), *Bilingualism in education: Proceedings of the international conference on bilingualism in deaf education* , Stockholm, Sweden (pp. 83–90). Hamburg, Germany: Signum.

Booth, T., & Ainscow, M. (2011). *Index for inclusion: Developing learning and participation in schools* (3rd ed.). London: Centre for Studies on Inclusive Education (CSIE).

CAST (2018). *Universal design for learning guidelines(version 2.2)*. Wakefield, MA: Author.

CRPD (2007). *Convention on the Rights of Persons with Disabilities*. NY: UN General Assembly. Retrieved from http://www.refworld.org/docid/45f973632.html.

Darrin, G. (2018). American Sign Language and English bilingualism: Educators' perspectives on a bicultural education. *International Journal of Bilingual Education and Bilingualism*. Advance online publication doi:10.1080/13670050.2018.1512552.

Emmorey, K. (2002). *Language, cognition and the brain: Insights from sign language research*. Hillsdale, NJ: Lawrence Erlbaum Associates.

Fajardo, I., Parra, E., & Cañas, J. J. (2010). Do sign language videos improve web navigation for deaf signer users? *Journal of Deaf Studies and Deaf Education, 15*(3), 242–262. 10.1093/deafed/enq005.

Gentry, M. M., Chinn, K. M., & Moulton, R. D. (2004). Effectiveness of multimedia reading materials when used with children who are deaf. *American Annals of the Deaf, 149*(5), 394–403. 10.1353/aad.2005.0012.

Hatzopoulou, M. (2008). *Acquisition of reference to self and others in Greek Sign Language. From pointing gesture to pronominal pointing signs*. (Doctoral dissertation). Stockholm,SE: Stockholm University.

Hladík, P., & Gůra, T. (2012). The hybrid book – One document for all in the latest development. In K. Miesenberger, A. Karshmer, P. Penaz & W. Zagler (Eds.), *Computers helping people with special needs. ICCHP 2012. Lecture notes in computer science* (Vol. 7382, pp. 18–24). Berlin, Heidelberg: Springer.

Hockings, C., Brett, P., & Terentjevs, M. (2012). Making a difference-inclusive learning and teaching in higher education through open educational resources. *Distance Education, 33*(2), 237–252. 10.1080/01587919.2012.692066.

Hoffmeister, R. (2000). A piece of the puzzle: ASL and reading comprehension in deaf children. In C. Chamberlain, J. P. Morford & R. I. Mayberry (Eds.), *Language acquisition by eye* (pp. 143–163). Mahwah, N.J: Lawrence Erlbaum Associates.

Hoffmeister, R., & Caldwell-Harris, C. (2014). Acquiring English as a second language via print: The task for deaf children. *Cognition*, *132*(2), 229–242. 10.1016/j.cognition.2014.03.01S.

Hoffmeister, R., & Wilbur, R. (1980). The acquisition of American Sign Language: A review. In H. Lane & F. Grosjean (Eds.), *Reent perspectives on sign language,* (pp. 61–78). Hillsdale, N.J: Lawrence Erlbaum Associates.

Hrastinski, I., & Wilbur, R. (2016). Academic achievement of deaf and hard-of-hearing students in an ASL/English Bilingual Program. *Journal of deaf studies and deaf education*, *21*(2), 156–170. 10.1093/deafed/env072.

Humphries, T. (2013). Schooling in American Sign Language: A paradigm shift from a deficit model to a bilingual model in deaf education. *Berkeley Review of Education*, *4*(1), 7–33. 10.5070/B84110031.

Humphries, T., Kushalnagar, P., Mathur, G., Napoli, D. J., Padden, C., Rathmann, C., & Smith, S. (2012). Language acquisition for deaf children: Reducing the harms of zero tolerance to the use of alternative approaches. *Harm Reduction Journal*, *9*(16), 1-9. doi:10.1186/1477-7517-9-16.

Karipi, S. (2015). *Koíta me! Káti sou léo…[Look at me! I am telling you something… In Greek] Greek Sign Language for a-b grade.* Athens, GR: Institute of Educational Policy.

Kourbetis, V. (2013). Design and development of accessible educational and teaching material for deaf students in Greece. In C. Stephanidis & M. Antona (Eds.), *Universal access in human-computer interaction. Applications and services for quality of life. UAHCI 2013. Lecture notes in computer science* (Vol. 8011, pp. 172–178). Berlin, Heidelberg: Springer.

Kourbetis, V. (2018) *Survey for the State-of-the-art of teaching signed languages as a first language.* Retrieved from http://www.sign1st.eu/en/presentations-of-international-conference-28–29-september-2018/.

Kourbetis, V., Boukouras, K., & Gelastopoulou, M. (2016). Multimodal accessibility for deaf students using interactive video, digital repository and hybrid books. In M. Antona & C. Stephanidis (Eds.), *Universal access in human-computer interaction. Users and context diversity. UAHCI 2016. Lecture notes in computer science*(Vol. 9739, pp. 93–102). Berlin, Heidelberg: Springer.

Kourbetis, V., & Gargalis, K. (2006). Deaf Empowerment in Greece. In H. Goodstein, (Ed.), *The deaf way II reader* (pp. 42–48). Washington, DC: Gallaudet University Press.

Kourbetis, V., & Hatzopoulou, M. (2010). *Mporó kai me ta mátia mou, [I can do it with my eyes as well, In Greek].* Athens, GR: Kastaniotis Editions.

Lane, H., Hoffmeister, R., & Bahan, B. (1996). *A journey into the Deaf world.* San Diego, CA: Dawn Sign Press.

Mayberry, R. (2007). When timing is everything: Age of first-language acquisition effects on second-language learning. *Applied Psycholinguistics*, *28*(3), 537–549. 10.1017/S0142716407070294.

Mich, O., Pianta, E., & Mana, N. (2013). Interactive stories and exercises with dynamic feedback for improving reading comprehension skills in deaf children. *Computers & Education*, *65*, 34–44. 10.1016/j.compedu.2013.01.016.

Mitchell, R., & Karchmer, M. (2004). Chasing the mythical ten percent: Parental hearing status of deaf and hard of hearing students in the United States. *Sign Language Studies*, *4*(2), 138–163.

Moe, S., & Wright, M. (2013). Can accessible digital formats improve reading skills, habits and educational level for dyslectic youngsters? C. Stephanidis & M. Antona (Eds.),

Universal access in human-computer interaction. Applications and services for quality of life. UAHCI 2013. Lecture notes in computer science (Vol. 8011, pp. 203–1212). Berlin, Heidelberg: Springer.

Morford, J., & Hänel-Faulhaber, B. (2011). Homesigners as late learners: Connecting the dots from delayed acquisition in childhood to sign language processing in adulthood. *Language and Linguistics Compass*, 5(8), 525–537. 10.1111/j.1749-818X.2011.00296.x.

Niederberger, N. (2008). Does the knowledge of a natural sign language facilitate deaf children's learning to read and write? Insights from French Sign Language and written French data. In C. Plaza-Pust & E. Morales-Lopeze (Eds.), *Sign bilingualism* (pp. 29–50). Philadelphia, PA: John Benjamins Publishing Company.

Ormel, E., Hermans, D., Knoors, H., & Verhoeven, L. (2012). Cross-language effects in visual word recognition: The case of bilingual deaf children. *Bilingualism: Language and Cognition*, 15(2), 288–303. 10.1017/S1366728911000319.

Pedagogical Institute (2004). *A.P.S. gia mathites me provlimata akois noimatiki [Greek Sign Language Curriculum, in Greek]*. Retrieved from http://www.prosvasimo.gr/docs/pdf/Analytika-Programmata-Eidikhs-Agwghs-kai-Ekpaideushs/A.P.S.-Ellhnikhs-Nohmatikhs-Glwssas.pdf.

Scott, J. A., & Hoffmeister, R. (2017). American Sign Language and academic English: Factors influencing the reading of bilingual secondary school deaf and hard of hearing students. *Journal of deaf studies and deaf education*, 22(1), 59–71. 10.1093/deafed/enw065.

Singleton, J., & Newport, E. (2004). When learners surpass their models: The acquisition of American Sign Language from inconsistent input. *Cognitive Psychology*, 49(4), 370–407. 10.1016/j.cogpsych.2004.05.001.

Smith, G., & Throne, S. (2007). *Differentiating instruction with technology in K-5 classrooms*. Belmont, CA: International Society for Technology in Education.

Svartholm, K. (2010). Bilingual education for deaf children in Sweden. *International Journal of Bilingual Education and Bilingualism*, 13(2), 159–174. doi: 10.1080/13670050903474077.

Tomlinson, C. (2001). *How to differentiate instruction in mixed-ability classrooms* (2nd ed.). Alexandria, VA: Association for Supervision and Curriculum Development (ASCD).

Tuomi, I. (2013). Open educational resources and the transformation of education. *European Journal of Education*, 48(1), 58–78. 10.1111/ejed.12019.

Woll, B. (1998). The development of signed and spoken language. In S. Gregory, P. Knight, W. McCracken, S. Powers & L. Watson (Eds.), *Issues in deaf education* (pp. 58–69). Abingdon, GB: David Fulton Publishers.

Woll, B., & Ladd, P. (2011). Deaf communities. In M. Marschark & P. E. Spencer, (Eds.), *Oxford handbook of deaf studies, language, and education* (Vol. 1, 2nd ed., pp. 159–172). New York: Oxford University Press.

9

THE BEDROCK LITERACY CURRICULUM

Kristin A. Di Perri

Statement of the Problem

Too many Deaf and Hard of Hearing (DHH) students continue to graduate high school having minimally developed English literacy skills (Traxler, 2000; Goldin-Meadow & Mayberry, 2001, Qi & Mitchell, 2012). These students can be characterized as readers who lack strong reading comprehension abilities and writers who are ill-equipped to handle the daily literacy requirements of life in an information age. Though cognitively capable, DHH students are expected to become literate in English without full access to the language or the spoken language components used for phonological coding in literacy. To exacerbate matters further, teacher training programs often lack the depth and breadth of instruction that professionals require in order to effectively meet the range of their student's needs. Finally, instructional materials and methodologies are heavily grounded in spoken language phonics-based approaches, which are often incompatible with the DHH students' developing language abilities and needs. Consequently, a major disconnect results between the DHH teacher's literacy instruction and the actual linguistic abilities of their students in either language – ASL or English.

Teachers of the Deaf have continually been expected to deliver effective instruction without the proper training, applicable instructional approaches, or materials. The result of these combined factors often results in teacher burnout and frustration within a relatively short span of time (Kennon & Patterson, 2016). DHH teachers are often expected to attend professional development on literacy strategies in which the proffered suggestions are designed for hearing children and their linguistic needs. When the incongruencies are pointed out, DHH teachers are often told to "adapt" the strategies. This suggestion further prompts feelings of frustration as instructional support is not being adequately provided.

The Bedrock Literacy Curriculum   **133**

College and university training programs for pre-service DHH teachers are often brief when contrasted with the amount of information teachers are expected to comprehend (Jones & Ewing, 2002). The typical graduate school training program is 1.5–2 years in length. When we consider the extensive list of coursework topics that pre-service D/HH teachers need (e.g., ASL language fluency, instructional methodology in all content areas, addressing deaf students with special needs, fair and accurate assessment tools), it becomes evident that there is insufficient time to adequately prepare them (Scales, Wolsey, Lenski, Smetana, & Yoder, 2018). Without extensive coursework, especially in literacy instruction, teachers will logically resort to their default instruction or the way they learned to read and write. This can become a problematic issue when we realize that the majority of teachers are hearing and acquired English from birth. By virtue of their biology, they have never experienced the task of reading or writing a spoken language without using spoken language phonological information. Without clear direction, some hearing teachers will understandably use ASL as the language of instruction and assume that this practice alone will provide a parallel path to literacy for their students. However, literacy instruction devoid of clear strategies and organized procedures will continue to result in student achievement that falls far short of expectations.

The resources and tools that teachers are often required to use for literacy instruction are incompatible with many of their Deaf students' linguistic abilities and needs (Cummins, 1996, Smetana, Odelson, Burns, & Grisham, 2009). Mass marketed English curricula are naturally predicated on specific assumptions about the student population using them. The designers of curricula expect that hearing students using the materials arrive at school with age-appropriate language skills. These designers take advantage of the inherent language connection: the known (previously established spoken language skills) to the new (phonics instruction). Focused instruction in the curricula will then provide students with instructional opportunities for practice and reinforcement of skills. However, mass-marketed English literacy materials are inappropriate for some groups of DHH students. Bilingual Deaf students who have ASL as a first language require an approach that takes advantage of their developing knowledge in two languages (i.e., ASL and English). Deaf students who arrive at school with no language base are also at risk (Humphries et al., 2016; Hall, 2017; Hall, Hall, & Caselli, 2019). Widely available English literacy resources will not address the conceptually appropriate or developmentally designed sequence these students need in order to become strong English users. Despite these challenges, teachers of the deaf are often directed to "tweak" these resources to fit their student's needs. This directive manifests the clear lack of understanding of how literacy materials are designed for hearing students (Lane, Hoffmeister, & Bahan, 1996).

Despite these extraordinary challenges, we know that English literacy success among a specific group – Deaf children with Deaf parents – is well documented (Johnson, Liddell, & Erting, 1989; Lane et al., 1996; Hoffmeister, 2000,

134 Kristin A. Di Perri

Goldin-Meadow & Mayberry, 2001; Supalla, Wix, & McKee, 2001). Rather than extrapolating the nature of their success, the field of Deaf education has remained stalled in trying to leverage their literacy achievements by creating comparable instructional approaches. Moreover, the vast majority of research in reading instruction with DHH students has focused on using the English phonological system as a means for literacy attainment (Mayer & Wells, 1996; Mayer & Akamatsu, 1999; Wang, Trezek, Luckner, & Paul, 2008). However, consider what is being expected of DHH students who have minimal access to the sound stream of English. They are presented with an ominous task – to learn all of the components of English despite having limited or no natural access to the language. This does not happen to children in any other world language environment. Further, they have been expected to do this without a viable instructional intervention that allows them to connect their thoughts to print. Finally, they have been required to do this while simultaneously learning English (see Czubek, 2006; Hoffmeister & Caldwell-Harris, 2014; Kuntze, et al., 2014). In recent years, there have been renewed efforts in the field to develop viable alternatives that take account of DHH students' linguistic starting points. The Bedrock Literacy Curriculum is one example and is described below.

Rationale for the Bedrock Literacy Curriculum

The Bedrock Literacy Curriculum was designed to support DHH teachers as they create a literacy program tailored to the specific language needs of students who do not follow the typical monolingual, auditory-based trajectory for becoming literate in English. The program is intended for beginning literacy students (e.g., ages 5–8). However, older students who do not have solid foundational literacy abilities can also benefit from the suggested strategies, explanations, and tools. The Bedrock approach is not a curriculum in the traditional sense. Rather, it is a way to provide teachers with information about literacy development – particularly for bilingual Deaf students who do not use sound-based phonemic information for the purpose of encoding and decoding English. The instructional components are not based on grade-level English expectations. Instead, it is a developmentally ordered sequence for building skills in a logical and coherent manner for these DHH students.

The Bedrock curriculum recognizes the challenges that teachers face in finding instructional approaches that appropriately address the literacy needs of bilingual and/or language deprived students and reasserts the primary tenet that "adapting" literacy approaches designed for hearing children (and predicated on their vast acquired stores of linguistic information) is of little help for the teacher of the DHH who is struggling to find a starting place with their students. Instead, the Bedrock approach describes ways to develop student's literacy by using visually based strategies in a developmental framework that is appropriate for them. While the principles discussed are applicable to all literacy learners, a special focus is on bilingual learners.

The components of the Bedrock Literacy Curriculum are 15 instructional units. The first two units focus on how to teach beginning reading and writing. These units describe daily, non-negotiable activities that are critical to a comprehensive literacy program. Units 3 and 4 suggest ways for teachers to strengthen cognitive categorizing skills (i.e., Schema Development and Beginning Word Categorization). Units 5, 6, and 7 focus on vocabulary instruction, spelling, and how to employ specific strategies for deducing unknown words while reading. Units 8–11 focus on specific grammar skills. The three foundational units (i.e., Reading, Writing, and Vocabulary instruction) will be discussed in-depth in the next section.

Daily Non-Negotiable Literacy Activities

The most critical aspect of Bedrock Literacy is the focus on three crucial components for beginning literacy instruction: Vocabulary Development, Reading Comprehension, and Independent Writing. The principles and strategies discussed in each component provide a durable foundation for all subsequent literacy building. Time invested in developing each of these components cannot be overstated. An immense amount of time in school is spent in developing hearing children's spoken language phonemic capabilities. Likewise, Deaf ASL users need sufficient time to participate in literacy strategies that will provide a fully accessible system for actively engaging with print. For example, a visually based intervention (i.e., using signed language phonology) is presented as a means for connecting thought to print. To aid spelling recall during vocabulary instruction, a technique that focuses on fingerspelling words according to specific movement "chunks" of the hand (as opposed to sound-based syllabication) is discussed. For reading, translation skills (i.e., ASL to English and vice versa) are outlined in a specific way to ensure students learn to comprehend what they read. The discussion of instructional principles and suggested activities for these components provides the teacher with a solid means for developing literacy that is concept-based and focused on the students emerging linguistic abilities. The following sections will review the fundamental components and principles/strategies for developing skills.

Vocabulary Instruction and Spelling Practice

As a beginning teacher of predominantly profoundly deaf, middle school students, it became quickly apparent that the methods I was employing to teach vocabulary were not productive. My students had significantly below grade-level reading abilities. Without specific guidelines or materials, I was left to create my own vocabulary lists. I followed the traditional Teacher of the Deaf (TOD) approach of creating a list of words using a theme (e.g., Native Americans, and holidays) or choosing words from a book my students would be reading that week.

There was no structure, sequence, or connectedness to this compilation of vocabulary items. Two major problems emerged: the students were neither retaining the vocabulary nor recognizing them *if* the lexical item showed up during reading instruction at a later date.

It was evident that many of the students, though they were chronologically middle-school-aged, did not recognize and comprehend high frequency words in print (e.g., *each, about, and enough*). Though they certainly knew the related ASL sign(s) and concepts, their reading comprehension was hindered by their lack of immediacy in recognizing these words in print. Further, some students lacked word recognition skills of what would be considered simple lexical items (e.g., *small, now, and mouth*). It was clear that a different approach to creating vocabulary lists for direct instruction was vital. For a lexical item to be readily used during reading, it must be accessed immediately from long term memory (LTM) stores. The process for storage depends on the individual experiencing a particular item *in context* a specific number of times (McKeown, Beck, Omanson, & Pople, 1985, Beck & McKeown, 2007). The main problem with my instructional approach was that after working with a word list for a week, the words were not reviewed, revisited, and rarely encountered in print again. As can be seen, this disconnected approach to vocabulary instruction disregarded two very important principles: a rationale for how to select vocabulary words for instruction and instructional strategies to support how brain architecture stores lexical items in LTM.

The Bedrock approach to vocabulary development underscores two main tenants: (1) creation of lists that integrate the need for a developmentally appropriate hierarchy of words (concrete to abstract) and (2) a means for ensuring that lexical items are stored in LTM. Falk, Di Perri, Howerton-Fox, and Jezik (2020) reports on the Bedrock intervention showing the efficacy of this approach.

1. Word Lists: If a DHH student does not use English phonemic information for learning printed words then in essence these words will initially be learned via whole word memorization and established as sight words. However, unlike the "sight word" lists employed by teachers of hearing children (e.g., Dolch), the Year One Bedrock vocabulary list is focused on concrete, meaningful words that can be immediately visualized (e.g., *cat, eye, red, and girl*). There are no function words included (e.g., *is, of, and the*) as they cannot be visualized and, therefore, lack meaning. Function words will be addressed in the Bilingual Grammar Curriculum (Czubek & Di Perri, 2019 and Chapter 10 in this volume). Bedrock's Years Two through Five vocabulary lists are taken from the Fry high frequency word list (the first 1,000-word list) because of the natural expectation of their regularity in print.

2. Establishing words in LTM: Ensuring LTM storage is a critical aspect of vocabulary instruction. Bedrock's assessment procedure includes a rarely

utilized but critical step – the Cumulative Vocabulary Recognition Test (CVRT) (Falk et al., 2020). The CVRT is simply a list of all of the vocabulary words the teacher has presented since the beginning of the year. Words are individually printed on index cards or presentations slides. The teacher has a score sheet listing all the words being tested. The teacher presents the index card or slide for a total of three seconds. The student has to provide the related sign(s) within that time. If the student is unsure of the sign, the teacher can ask them to provide a definition or use the word in a contextualized sentence. The teacher tallies up the score. Words that were missed are listed for continued practice in sentences.

The CVRT assessment provides an expedient way to gauge which words have been efficiently stored in LTM and to highlight those that need more contextual exposures. Lists are individualized according to each student's progress. Each student has a list of those words that were incorrect (e.g., no response and error of response). This individualized student information, also provides the teacher with the means for differentiating instruction especially when students represent a wide range of linguistic backgrounds, experiences, and abilities. The CVRT assessment of rapid sight word recognition is only assessing the student's ability to instantly recall at least the most general entry-level meaning for a word.

While immediately recognizing vocabulary items is essential, the ability to spell them independently is also important. Without the aid of spoken language phonological information for decoding, recalling the specific sequence of letters in a word can be quite challenging. A word over 3–4 letters becomes very difficult to remember using a single letter sequence approach. Hearing children learn to use syllabication to aid their recall of "chunks" of sound information that relates to letter sequences. Using the same principle, the Bedrock approach to memorizing letter sequences for spelling takes advantage of a motoric rather than sound-based strategy (see Table 9.1).

Each week, the teacher takes the list of vocabulary items and divides each word into smaller "chunks" of letters. These chunks or letter groupings are not

TABLE 9.1 *Letter "chunking" categorization to aid recall when fingerspelling vocabulary words*

Examples:	Double letters	Combination "snap" of wrist	Natural hand rest	Palm orientation-facing front	Total letters to recall	Total "chunks" to recall
eight		gh	t	ei	5	3
cheese	ee	ch		se	6	3
liquid		qu		li / id	6	3
balloon	ll / oo		n	ba	7	4
kangaroo	oo	ng		ka / ar	8	4

based on sound. Instead they are derived from four basic categories of hand movement while fingerspelling. These categories (i.e., double letters, combination snaps, palm orientation, and hand rest) are used to group letters as the signer produces individual manual alphabet letters in the sequence of a word. The goal is twofold: (1) reduce the total number of individual letters in a word into smaller units for easier memory storage and (2) equate a spelling chunk with muscle memory on a specific movement while forming manual alphabet letters. For example, in Table 9.1, the word "balloon" has seven letters that can be categorized into four "chunks" for greater ease of recall.

This fingerspelling for spelling technique is not the same as regular fingerspelling employed by ASL users. Instead, it is a tool to connect distinct hand movements with specific types of manual letter combinations. This is a parallel process to the hearing child who employs English phonemic information and syllabication to recall spelling sequences of words. As an illustration, hearing children generally learn how to spell "February" by exaggerating the medial syllable (i.e., Feb-RU-ary) as a means for ensuring that the initial "r", though silent, is included. Of course, this technique is only employed to aid spelling. No hearing person would say, "Valentine's Day is on FebRUary 14th." The same principle is intended with the visually based fingerspelling technique for Deaf students. It is simply a means for remembering letter sequence when spelling.

Reading Instruction and Comprehension

Planning effective reading instruction for bilingual deaf students requires an understanding of the basic elements of the reading process and the role language translation plays in comprehension (see Hoffmeister & Caldwell-Harris, 2014). To address the needs of signing Deaf students, it is essential that we design an approach that takes into account the necessity of three essential strategies specific to these students: develop an understanding the reading should make sense, use non-sound-based repair strategies when comprehension is compromised, and learn to comprehend what is read by translating English into ASL.

While the cognitive processes that support reading are both varied and complex, information from various models of reading can provide assistance to teachers to augment their understanding of effective reading instruction. The Bedrock reading instructional approach was derived from a synthesis of some of the main reading models. To illustrate the design, consider the specific requirements in the reading process for bilingual deaf students. Students initially look at the print as linearly presented in English. Though phonics-based strategies are not the focus, the Bottom-Up reading model (Gough, 1972) outlines the importance of attending to the words and punctuation to derive initial word meaning in a sentence. However, to translate the entire sentence to ASL, words cannot be perceived as isolated meanings. Instead, meaning develops from the *context* of the sentence or the relationship between the words in a sentence.

The Bedrock Literacy Curriculum **139**

Therefore, attending only to the words at a "surface level" while reading will not necessarily result in comprehension. The Top-Down reading model (Smith, 2004) suggests that meaning is constructed as the student interacts with the print. This "deep level" interaction provides an opportunity to think about the words, not as separate entities, but as meaningful units dependent on the context Importantly, for reading comprehension to occur, both levels of language processing require consideration.

Understanding the relationship between the surface and deep levels of language processing while reading is especially important when teaching bilingual deaf students (Chamberlain & Mayberry, 2008). Effective reading instruction takes into account the principal difference between the act of transliteration (or individual word for individual sign mapping) and translation when moving from L_1 to L_2 and vice versa. In transliteration, there is a mapping of one language system to the other with no regard for inherent meaning. When translating, the meaning of a sentence in L_1 can only be conveyed once the entire sentence has been completely provided in L_2 and vice versa.

To understand the significance of the relationship between signed and written (or spoken) languages in translation, teachers of Deaf bilingual students need to also appreciate the difference between words and sentences and their relative functions. You can exchange a word in isolation in L_1 and get the equivalent word in L_2. For example, if you ask a Norwegian what is the word for "*light*" they would probably reply "*lys.*" However, if you attempt to use that word in the sentence "*I ate a light lunch*" you would be in error as "lys" refers to an object that emits light. Thus, attempting to exchange words in a sentence in L_1 using this 1:1 mapping approach will not guarantee the meaning will be similar in L_2. Depending on the dictates of each language, issues of syntax, morphology, and semantics have various roles. For example, as shown in Table 9.2, consider the following sentences transliterated.

At the surface level, each word in Spanish was exchanged by mapping an equivalent word in English. This process takes no account of the actual meaning of the original sentence but instead simply replaces each lexical item as singular entities in isolation. Using this approach, an individual attempting to read text in this way will have a difficult time understanding the original intent of the sentence. When rendered as single lexical items and strung together using identical syntax the English version becomes non-sensical. Using transliteration, there is no way the reader can discern the actual translation or true meaning of the Spanish sentence (i.e., *It is raining very heavily.* or *It's a downpour!*)..

TABLE 9.2 *Transliterating or mapping word exchanges in sentence examples of Spanish to English*

Spanish	Es	un	aguacero!
English	Is	a	water zero!

Many DHH students are taught to read using this type of transliteration or word for sign mapping approach. They are directly instructed to process text by attempting to exchange one English word for an ASL sign and then attempt to piece them together to determine the meaning. However, as we saw in the above example this approach does not allow for the construction of meaning between two disparate languages. Let's examine an English to ASL example as shown in Figure 9.1.

When Deaf students transliterate the sentence "Take your time." they are erroneously led to conclude that the meaning must have something to do with physically (*take*) removing a personal (*your*) clock or watch (*time*). Unlike the first transliteration example (i.e., Spanish-English), this at least appears plausible. However, the actual meaning of the sentence has nothing to do with physically removing anything. This is an English idiom which means: *Slow down, don't hurry* (see Figure 9.2).

Teachers of bilingual Deaf students are often confused with how to facilitate this translation process since hearing children are regularly taught to read aloud. However, during the read-aloud process, the hearing child who is a good reader is simultaneously integrating information in an interactive manner (Goodman, 1998). As hearing children encode reading at the surface level, the auditory feedback system allows them to connect word production (phonological level) to stored meanings (semantic level) in the brain while understanding the structure (syntax) of the sentence. In marked contrast, the Deaf student who is directed to read by transliterating or exchanging single words in a sentence for single signs is not considering the relationship between the words in a sentence. Additionally, they are not deriving information from phonological or syntactic sources in English if the sentence is unfamiliar. Thus, the hearing and deaf child are not following parallel processes. Unwittingly, teachers are training their DHH students to read by employing a contradictory word for sign transliteration process that will render the majority of sentences as incomprehensible. In order for a

FIGURE 9.1 Transliterating example of an English sentence to ASL: "Take your time."

Note: Thanks to Carey Ballard, ASL model.

FIGURE 9.2 Translation example of an English sentence to ASL: "Take your time."

beginning bilingual reader to truly comprehend reading in the L_2, they must learn to translate from L_2 (English) to L_1 (ASL). The Bedrock program describes a daily activity that will support students' conceptual understanding of the reading process and aid their development of becoming readers who are active constructionist meaning makers.

Daily Reading Comprehension Activity. The goal of this daily activity is to provide students with an interactive means for navigating the linguistic systems of ASL and English by actively constructing meaning during reading via a translation process. The basic objective is for each student to look at a target English sentence, independently create a mental representation, and then provide the translation (i.e., meaning equivalent) in ASL. The various target sentences used each day are teacher-constructed from instantly recognizable words. For the student to focus cognitive energy on constructing meaning making, it is critical that words are instantly identifiable. At the beginning level, students will have a generalized meaning for most of the Year One Bedrock words. Since this is a foundational effort, including figurative language such as multiple meaning and idioms are not included yet. As time goes on and the students become more fluent in their ability to quickly process English to ASL, the teacher can begin including figurative language. As students' skills improve, the English targets can be developed to include 2–3 sentences or short paragraphs that can be summarized.

Instructional Routine for the Daily Reading Comprehension Activity. The teacher creates two laminated mats on which the students will stand during the activity. One mat has the word ENGLISH on it and the other, ASL. Prior to the activity the teacher has created the list of sentences for that day's activity using known words. The sentence target is placed on the board (e.g., *The cat ran up the* *tree*.). The student stands on the English mat and is directed to read the full sentence with their eyes-no signing or speaking the word. When the student feels they understand the meaning of the sentence, they walk to the ASL mat and sign the relevant meaning in ASL. If the student makes an error (e.g., omitted/misunderstood word, and incorrect translation), they are directed to go back to the English mat. At this point, the teacher can mediate the miscue and/or model the correct translation.

The activity is intended as a daily skill-building reading exercise that will develop the student's ability to effectively process text in a comprehensible manner. It is critical that the activity is done daily in order to help students ingrain the concept that reading requires attentive thought and active meaning making. This attention to practicing a bilingual "process" for reading can lead to reading experiences that result in comprehension rather than confusion. The goal of this daily 20-minute activity is for students to learn how to negotiate meaning between two languages (English/ASL) and at two levels (surface/deep structure).

Independent Writing Instruction

Teachers of DHH students who are beginning literacy users often struggle to answer questions related to beginning writing instruction. How do you teach DHH students to write independently and enjoy it? How are these Deaf students expected to develop a phonological to alphabetic mapping process, such as assumed to be required in reading and writing, when the necessary physiological link to sound does not exist (Grushkin, 2017)? To respond to these important concerns, my dissertation focused on an alternative path to independent writing (Di Perri, 2004). The investigation focused on a visually based mediating system that connected Deaf students' independent thoughts to print. Rather than using sound-based phonology, this system was derived from the phonological parameters of ASL and provided a parallel process for writing development (see DiPerri, 2004). Similarly, Supalla and his colleagues devised the Grapheme System, using the ASL parameters of handshape, location, and movement to represent ASL signs for the purpose of encoding thought to print (Supalla et al, 2001).

Teachers of hearing children readily acknowledge the developmental sequence in learning to write. For example, young beginning hearing students are not expected to master the code known as the Alphabetic Principle (i.e., equating the 44 sounds to the 26 letters) until they have had sufficient, in-depth practice with it (National Reading Panel, 2000; Ziegler & Goswami, 2005). Thus, teachers expect to see a developmentally appropriate range of writing attempts as the individual hearing child learns the systematic relationship between sounds and letters as they recode words. A typical example of a phase in this development is manifested in examples of "invented spelling" (e.g., "My cat is pretty." might be rendered "mi kt iz prite"). Sanctioning these natural stages of writing development ensures that hearing students will be motivated and enjoy writing as an independent task from a very early age.

For Deaf bilingual students, using two language modalities that are very different, creates a challenging issue when learning how to write. Deaf students need writing instruction that is conceptually based, developmentally sequenced, and provides an intermediary tool for encoding thought that is not predicated on aural/oral abilities (Grushkin, 2017). Understandably, omitting English phonics instruction, if non-accessible, leaves a significant hole in the "typical" developmental process for learning to become a writer. Without a viable alternative, Deaf students are relegated to using teacher-dependent, ineffective strategies as developing writers. Common strategies include raising their hand for assistance whenever an English word is needed, using pre-made word banks, or simply copying teacher written sentences. The most unfortunate byproduct of this approach is frequently manifested when students become resistant to writing and internalize the idea that their written output does not equate with their actual linguistic or cognitive abilities.

In the Bedrock approach, bilingual Deaf students are presented with a range of developmentally appropriate strategies that will help them encode their thoughts into print. Initially, DHH students learn to formulate ideas that can be articulated in ASL. They are then taught how to represent those ASL ideas using a logo-graphic handshape holder technique. Students are simultaneously building English vocabulary during this writing instruction period (see the section on Vocabulary in this chapter). As students continue to strengthen independent abilities, their writing will manifest a combination between logographic re-presentations of words (in ASL) and English words. Eventually, the students will write in English as they generate greater control using English vocabulary.

The Handshape Holder Technique. Conveying internal ASL thoughts into a logographic form requires a technique that must be explicitly taught. Since the auditory channel is not accessible, a phonological parameter of the DHH students signed language is isolated to serve as a connection to semantic intent – the parameter of handshape. During a daily independent writing activity, students are taught to use a "Handshape Holder" to substitute for an unknown English word. This technique allows the student to maintain fluency of thought without seeking external assistance (Di Perri, 2004). The Handshape Holder technique takes approximately 30 minutes to master. After the initial training, most students are able to write by applying the encoding principle in an unlimited manner. The basic premise is that anything a student can sign can be written using an alphanumeric symbol. For example, "My cat is pretty" might be rendered: *B F 50* (i.e., *B* -my *F*-cat *5 0* -pretty). The limitation of this technique is that it is very difficult to recode a day after the initial writing is done. Thus, a highly focused daily writing task was designed.

Daily Independent Writing Activity – "Quick Writes." Students are given individual blank writing notebooks. Each day they view a specific target picture (e.g., a dog chasing a cat). The teacher takes two to three minutes asking students to explain, in ASL, what is happening or to provide their own rendition of a "story." When all students have articulated at least two sentences, they are directed to write their stated ideas into sentences in their writing books. Students know that writing means "English" but if they do not know the English word for a concept, they are to continue writing by using an alphanumeric symbol related to the handshape as a placeholder (e.g., "1 5" for leaf, "5 0" for pretty). When finished, the student meets briefly with the teacher. If a handshape was used, the teacher writes it on the opposite side of the notebook with the English equivalent word (see Figure 9.3). Teachers do not write on the student's actual work. The goal is to help students internalize the idea that a developmentally appropriate bilingual process is at work as opposed to the impression that an error or miscue has been made. After that day, if the same word is desired again, the student is directed to retrieve the English word rather than using a handshape holder.

This daily activity is strictly limited to 15 minutes per day. The main rationale for this is to reinforce with teachers the precept that writing is a skill that must be practiced with continuity in order to see internalized improvements. Additionally, there will be many other writing tasks students must learn how to do (e.g., writing poetry, summarizing, and writing fact vs opinion essays). However, other writing activities are a moot point unless the student knows how to express themselves confidently. Consistent integration of this task into the student's daily language arts block will result in students who become writers who enjoy expressing themselves independently. They will internalize the notion that writing is a bilingual process between ASL and English. This process will include rough drafts and editing but simultaneously maintains the integrity of their own thoughts and feelings.

FIGURE 9.3 Example of Daily Quick Write Activity

The Bedrock Literacy Curriculum   145

The Handshape Holder technique modeled in the daily quick write activity has been demonstrated in numerous workshops and trainings throughout the United States, and abroad. Observations and anecdotal outcomes collected in baseline and later students' independent writing samples indicate that:

- Students gain confidence and motivation to write
- Believe they can write anything they want
- Strengthen risk-taking skills
- Understand that writing is a *process*
- Write longer sentences
- Be accountable for exchanging Handshape Holders codes for English words
- Teachers obtain ongoing real data on individual abilities

Both students, whose work is featured below in Figure 9.4 and Figure 9.5, learned how to use the Handshape Holder technique during a pilot Bedrock program at a school for the deaf. The examples below show writing samples taken at baseline and again four years later. All writing samples were produced independently with no external aid from instructional staff.

The teacher of student #2 (see Figure 9.5) was concerned that given the student's additional challenges (i.e., language processing difficulties, and memory issues), the Handshape Holder technique might not work. However, the teacher

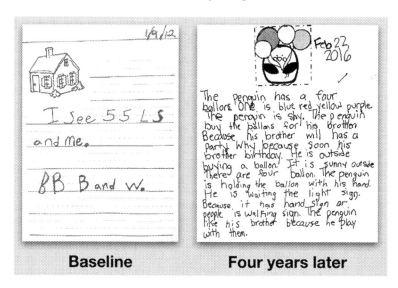

Baseline   **Four years later**

FIGURE 9.4 Student #1 Independent writing using the Handshape Holder techniques

Note: This student is a typical bilingual deaf student placed in a regular DHH classroom. Translation of the baseline sample: I see 5 (mom) 5 (dad) L (older sister's name) S (younger sister's name) and me. B B (house) B (brown) and W (white).

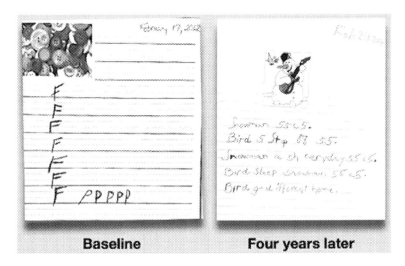

FIGURE 9.5 Student #2 - Independent writing using the Handshape Holder techniques
Notes: Translation of the baseline sample FFFFFFF PPPPP: The buttons (F) on my shirt are purple (P). Translation of the 4 years later sample: Snowman 55 (music) C 5 (guitar). Bird 5 (please) stop 8 8 (loud) 55 (music). Snowman a (sorry) sh (too bad) everyday 55 (music) C 5 (guitar). Bird sleep snowman 55 (music) C 5 (guitar). Bird go different home.

was encouraged to try it and then make a determination after sufficient time had been invested (i.e., 6 months).

Student #2 had definite language processing issues that affected her writing process. However, if we look closer at the student's intent, an incredibly intact and humorous story emerges. Additionally, her story contains many of the essential elements outlined in state standards for written language (e.g., plot, sequencing, problem/resolution, character motivation, and development).

The following is a translation of her story:

> *The snowman played music on his guitar.*
> *The bird said, "Please stop playing that loud music."*
> *The snowman said, "Sorry, too bad, I'm playing my guitar music every day."*
> *The bird sleeps and the snowman keeps on playing music with his guitar.*
> *The bird went to a different home.*

Summary

It is said that doing the same thing repeatedly and expecting different results (whatever the iteration) is the very definition of insanity. The time has come and is, in fact, long overdue for the field of deaf education to consider how to incorporate strategies that maximize abilities utilized by visual language users.

The Bedrock Literacy Curriculum **147**

Further, students who remain in language deprived environments deserve an approach that takes their intensely different linguistic needs into consideration for this task that is markedly different from the predominant status quo of literacy instruction. The Bedrock Literacy Curriculum, though fairly narrow in scope, is one such effort that hopes to support a new direction in radically revised literacy instruction approaches.

References

Beck, I., & McKeown, M. (2007). Increasing young low income children's oral vocabulary repertoires through rich and focused instruction. *The Elementary School Journal*, *107*(3), 251–271.

Chamberlain, C., & R. Mayberry, R. (2000). Theorizing about the relationship between American Sign Language and reading. In C. Chamberlain, J. Morford & R. Mayberry (Eds.), *Language acquisition by eye* (pp. 221–248). Mahwah, NJ: Lawrence Erlbaum Associates.

Chamberlain, C., & Mayberry, R. I. (2008). American Sign Language syntactic and narrative comprehension in skilled and less skilled readers: Bilingual and bimodal evidence for the linguistic basis of reading. *Applied Psycholinguistics*, *29*(3), 367–388.

Cummins, J. (1996). *Negotiating identities: Education for empowerment in a diverse society*. Los Angeles: California Association for Bilingual Education.

Czubek, T. A. (2006). Blue listerine, parochialism, and ASL literacy. *Journal of Deaf Studies and Deaf Education*, *11*, 373–381.

DiPerri, K. (2004). *ASL phonemic awareness in deaf children*. Unpublished doctoral dissertation Boston University.

Falk, J. L., Di Perri, K. A., Howerton-Fox, A., & Jezik, C. (2020). Implications of a sight word intervention for Deaf students. *American Annals of the Deaf*, *164*(5), 592–607.

Goldin-Meadow, S., & Mayberry, R. I. (2001). How do profoundly deaf children learn to read? *Learning Disabilities Research & Practice*, *16*, 222–229.

Goodman, Kenneth S. (1998). *Defense of good teaching: What teachers need to know about thereading wars*. York, Me: Stenhouse.

Gough, Philip B. (1972). One second of reading. In James F. Kavanagh & Ignatius G. Mattingly, (Eds.), *Language by ear and by eye* (pp. 331–358). Cambridge, MA: MIT Press.

Grushkin, D. A. (2017). Writing signed languages: What for? What form? *American Annals of the Deaf*, *161*(5), 509–527.

Hall, W. C. (2017). What you don't know can hurt you: The risk of language deprivation by impairing sign language development in deaf children. *Maternal and Child Health Journal*, *21*, 961–965. 10.1007/s10995-017-2287-y.

Hall, M. L., Hall, W. C., & Caselli, N. (2019). *Deaf children need language, not (just) speech*. *First Language*, 1–29. doi.org/10.1177/0142723719834102.

Hoffmeister, R. J. (2000). A piece of the puzzle: ASL and reading comprehension in Deaf children. In C. Chamberlain, J. Morford & R. Mayberry (Eds.), *Language acquisition by eye* (pp. 142–161). Mahwah, NJ: Lawrence Erlbaum Associates.

Hoffmeister, R, & Caldwell-Harris, C. (2014). Acquiring English as a second language via print: The task for deaf children. *Cognition*, *132*, 229–242.

Humphries, T., Kushalnagar, P., Mathur, G., Napoli, D. J., Padden, C., Rathmann, C., & Smith, S. (2016). Avoiding linguistic neglect of deaf children. *Social Service Review, 90*, 589–619. 10.1086/689543

Jones, T., & Ewing, K. (2002). An analysis of teacher preparation in deaf education: Programs approved by the Council on Education of the Deaf. *American Annals of the Deaf, 147*, 71–78.

Johnson, R. E., Liddell, S. K., & Erting, C. J. (1989). *Unlocking the curriculum: Principles for achieving access in deaf education*. Washington, DC: Gallaudet Research Institute.

Kennon, J., & Patterson, M. (2016). What I didn't know about teaching: Stressors and burnout among deaf education teachers. *Journal of Human Services: Training, Research, and Practice, 1*, 1–39.

Kuntze, Golos, & Enns (2014). Rethinking literacy: Broadening opportunities for visual learners. *Sign Language Studies, 14*, 203–224.

LaBerge, D., & Samuels, S. J. (1974). Toward a theory of automatic information processing in reading. *Cognitive Psychology, 6*(2), 293–323.

Lane, H. L., Hoffmeister, R., & Bahan, B. J. (1996). *A journey into the deaf-world*. San Diego: DawnSignPress.

Mayer, C., & Akamatsu, C. (1999). Bilingual–bicultural models of literacy education for deaf students: Considering the claims. *Journal of deaf studies and deaf education, 4*, 1–8.

Mayer, C., & Wells, G. (1996). Can the linguistic interdependence theory support a bilingual– bicultural model of literacy education for deaf students? *Journal of deaf studies and deaf education, 1*, 93–107.

McKeown, M., Beck, I., Omanson, R., & Pople, M. (1985). Some effects of the nature and frequency of vocabulary instruction on the knowledge and use of words. *Reading Research Quarterly, 20*(5), 522–535.

National Reading Panel. (2000). *Report of the National Reading Panel: Teaching children to read—An evidence-based assessment of the scientific research literature on reading and its implications for reading instruction*. Jessup, MD: National Institute for Literacy at EDPubsMD: Bethesda.

Qi, S., & Mitchell, R. E. (2012). Large-scale academic achievement testing of deaf and hard-of- hearing students: Past, present, and future. *Journal of deaf studies and deaf education, 17*, 1–18.

Scales, R., Wolsey, T., Lenski, S., Smetana, L., & Yoder, K. (2018). Are we preparing or training teachers? Developing professional judgment in and beyond teacher preparation programs. *Journal of Teacher Education, 69*, 7–21.

Smetana, L, Odelson, D., Burns, H., & Grisham, D. (2009). Using graphic novels in the high school classroom: Engaging deaf students with a new genre. *Journal of Adolescent & Adult Literacy*, Hoboken *53*(3), 228–240.

Smith, F. (2004). *Understanding reading* (6th ed). Mahwah, NJ: Lawrence Erlbaum Associates.

Supalla, S., Wix, T. R., & McKee, C. (2001). Print as a primary source of English for deaf learners. In J. Nichol & T. Langendoen (Eds.), *One mind, two languages: Studies in bilingual language processing*. Oxford: Blackwell.

Traxler, C. B. (2000). The Stanford Achievement Test 9th-Edition: National norming and performance standards for deaf and hard of hearing students. *Journal of Deaf Studies & Deaf Education, 5*, 337–348. 10.1093/deafed/5.4.337

Wang, Y., Trezek, B., Luckner, J., & Paul, P. (2008). The role of phonology and phonologically related skills in reading instruction for students who are deaf or hard of hearing. *American Annals of the Deaf, 153*(4), 396–407.

Weaver, C. (1988). *Reading process and practice: From socio-psycholinguistics to whole language*. Portsmouth: Heinemann Educational.

Ziegler, J. C., & Goswami, U. (2005). Reading acquisition, developmental dyslexia, and skilled reading across languages: A psycholinguistic grain size theory. *Psychological Bulletin, 131*(1), 3–29.

10

CROSSING THE DIVIDE

The Bilingual Grammar Curriculum

Todd Czubek

People have been motivated to cross chasms large and small for as long as history has been recorded. Whether we think about the early Polynesians traveling 2,000 miles in canoes to discover Hawaii's Big Island, NASA sending humans to the moon and back, or Evel Knievel jumping over 50 cars in the Los Angeles Coliseum, this desire echoes throughout the history of humankind in various and sundry ways.

The field of Deaf Education has been similarly inspired, as it has long sought to conquer the challenges posed by the modality divide between signed languages and spoken/written languages. The implications of these efforts have also been far-reaching, and in many ways, they have determined the course of Deaf Education. That is to say, it is easy to see that the moorings of most methodologies, philosophies, and trends all tie to the common anchor of bridging divides. What is sometimes not so obvious is how our field's approaches to language instruction have been unwittingly carried by the currents of common assumptions about the architecture of language itself.

Because the vast majority of languages are spoken/written, they wield what some have termed "Microsoft Power" (Purdy, 2007). In other words, theirs are the default structures and templates for how we understand and see the features of language. This idea should be familiar to many of us. For example, if we use templates that are not "Microsoft," we often run the great risk of rendering our content incompatible with, or inaccessible to, the broadest audience. Far from being an indictment of Microsoft, this merely serves as an illustration of how the network effect enjoyed by conventional templates can sometimes obscure the potential of other unique options for organizing our world. This is certainly true as it applies to how many of the stakeholders in Deaf Education have understood and applied language instruction. It is in this spirit, with an intention to proceed

Crossing the Divide **151**

against the conventional current, that the Bilingual Grammar Curriculum (hereafter, BGC) was developed.[1]

Incompatible Systems

We can all point to examples of schools and programs serving Deaf and hard of hearing children who have looked for ways to find meaningful roles for natural signed languages (e.g., ASL) in their language arts programming. Interestingly, in many of these cases, schools arrive at their answers by "working backward" as they base their plans for teaching about signed language on the progressions and structures outlined in ready-made spoken/written curricula, or on those that appear in national standards. Thus, those language features and applications that appear "first, second, and third" in a standard template's sequence are adapted to signed language so that the equivalent features and applications are also introduced "first, second, and third." This methodology, despite its flaws, often describes what happens in the best-case scenarios where there is a notable desire to develop skills in both the natural signed language and in the written language.

In most other circumstances, schools and programs don't set up any meaningful plan for studying signed language at all. For example, an informal survey of language arts faculty and administrators from 15 schools who consider themselves bilingual (i.e., they state that they are bilingual schools on their websites) found that 14 of the 15 describe their ASL and English programming/instructors as having little to no comprehensive coordination. In these (more common) cases, schools adopt examples of local or national language arts curricula from "exceptional schools" (i.e., English curricula that serve consistently successful hearing children) and attempt to implement them with Deaf and hard of hearing children. Similarly, schools in this category do their best to teach "language" by adapting national or state language arts standards for Deaf and hard of hearing students. These forms of programming seek to mirror the process and strategies that happen in hearing schools.

In both approaches outlined above, including many program permutations that fall somewhere in between, what consistently emerges is the realization that an overwhelming percentage of students are ill-equipped to meaningfully engage with the content of language arts instruction (Lederberg, Schick, & Spencer,2012; Spencer & Marschark, 2010; Easterbrooks, Lederberg, Miller, Bergeron, & Connor, 2008; Traxler, 2000). This is especially true as it applies to grammar study. The reasons why this occurs are complex. The implications of impoverished language input and experiences that many Deaf and hard of hearing children encounter as they grow up loom large. Unsurprisingly, these experiences have been shown to have pernicious effects on meta-linguistic skills (Boudreault & Mayberry, 2006; Mayberry, 2002). In addition to these fundamental challenges, the designs that guide our instruction almost never take into account accessible "starting points" for Deaf and hard of hearing children. It is even less

152 Todd Czubek

likely that those plans recognize the unique visuo-spatial architecture of signed language. Again unsurprisingly, what commonly results from this mix are frustrated teachers and even more frustrated students. Despite the broad consensus that the "typical templates" for learning the structure of language are inaccessible to many Deaf and hard of hearing children, Deaf Education continues to look to curricula designed for native users of spoken/written languages.

One reason this is true is related to the earlier discussion of Microsoft Power. In that discussion, we stated that our explanatory systems matter. This is because they necessarily privilege certain orientations and marginalize others. Rather than falling into the easy trap of suspecting malice, we must understand that this quality is part of the nature of perspectives. Any vantage point that an individual assumes inevitably serves to make some things more obvious and others less so. This is why including a variety of perspectives is valuable; with a diverse range of vantage points, we miss less. Our explanatory systems for teaching about language are no exception; they matter. As such, including multiple vantage points can help to broaden what we might mistakenly assume are comprehensive orientations.

Consider the following assumption: Languages are organized in a "linear" fashion. It is true that spoken/written languages are produced sequentially; the structural constraints of articulation (as well as those of most written systems) make this necessarily so. We simply cannot articulate pronouns, verbs, adverbs, and prepositions concurrently using spoken languages (but we can in signed languages!). Because this quality doesn't appear in the languages for which the overwhelming majority of curricula are developed, their "templates" never consider the need to acknowledge concurrently occurring elements of language. An unwitting result of this orientation is that – having become reliant on this template – we are conditioned to believe that all languages should fit nicely into linear models. This is obviously problematic for signed languages that leverage *both* linear and spatial affordances. As an example, consider the strong and unfortunate tendency for even the most enlightened programs to encourage children in the United States and Canada to "ASL-ize" state of being verbs (i.e., to find ways to more appropriately represent "is," and "are") in their signed renditions of various sentences.

In part, this practice is tied to the belief that ASL is enhanced by finding ways to have it conform to more standard, linear architectural principles. This influence is so profound that it justifies the use of artificial forms masquerading as legitimate signs (see Figure 10.1). But rather than sailing into the shoals of language purity debates, suffice it to say that Microsoft Power is alive and well as it applies to ASL.

Without changing course too much, we can also see how Microsoft Power can portray differences in linguistic structure as linguistic deficiencies. Consider how the visuo-spatial nature of ASL (when juxtaposed against the linear architecture of English) has contributed to the following common claims: ASL

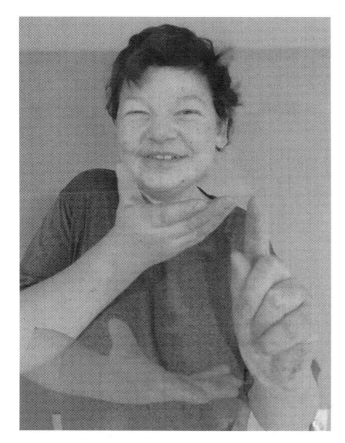

FIGURE 10.1 Depicting an "acceptable" form of signing the English word "is"
Note: There is no difference between this practice and using the more stigmatized, initialized, signed English form of "is".

is abbreviated, simple, and missing words such as "the" and "is," as well as other formal functional elements. The well-documented history of negative attitudes toward signed languages, which have enjoyed only recent acknowledgment as full-fledged languages, also serves to illuminate the impact of limited perspectives.

In order to advance against these prevailing winds, the BGC adopts an unconventional tack to overcome the natural forces that discourage progressing in alternative directions. This "unconventional tack" is a model we employ throughout the curriculum that encourages children to see languages in both linear and spatial terms. This model, the Santa Fe/New York City Template (SF/NYC) (Czubek, 2009), allows for insights that are often overlooked in standard, explanatory systems for language study. The application of this model will be detailed below.

154 Todd Czubek

The result of a fortunate metaphor, the SF/NYC template is valuable in the way that all metaphors are valuable; it provides an accessible way to think about an idea that can be complex. Metaphors frame one idea in terms of another, and we leverage those new conceptual pathways to illuminate relationships and potentials that we may have otherwise never considered.

As one of those frustrated teachers I previously mentioned, it was an auspicious circumstance to find myself living in Santa Fe, New Mexico. Like many teachers, I struggled in my efforts to understand how to effectively take advantage of my students' dominant language skills (ASL) in order to support their English learning. It became clear that I wasn't getting far by relying on natural exposure to ASL and English. But one fortuitous, informal tour of Santa Fe inspired the metaphor that helped to open the channel I was having such difficulty crossing. On that tour, I learned that in an effort to maintain the architectural integrity of historical Santa Fe, certain areas prohibited building two-floor structures. Joking, my guide informed me that despite those constraints, it alleviated any concern over the purchase of "air rights" (Marcus, 1983).

After long and thoughtful discussions about zoning in Santa Fe and air rights in places like New York City, it suddenly became clear that this idea had great potential for showcasing the architecture of ASL and English. As we discussed previously, English is linear; it operates under Santa Fe rules with one-floor constraints. But ASL operates under New York City rules. It is a language that builds outward *and* upward. Importantly, to ignore the parts of New York City that are built upward is to miss much of what makes it New York City.

In this metaphor, most languages operate under the Santa Fe rules, exclusively concerned with one-floor structures. Because the Santa Fe rules represent the dominant model (think Microsoft Power), stakeholders in Deaf education – both Deaf and hearing – often unconsciously fail to realize that appreciating the architecture of ASL requires that we *look up*. This unconventional model helps us to see and appreciate the concurrent structures that characterize ASL, and it represents one of the many novel contributions of the BGC. As a result of this new vantage point, children and teachers gain a more comprehensive perspective on the architecture of visual language. As a consequence, they are afforded more opportunities to make appropriately informed comparisons between ASL and English. Figure 10.2 provides an example of how an NYC template can illuminate the range of co-occurring elements of grammar in an ASL predicate.

Incompatible Expectations

An additional assumption built into all language curricula is an expectation that children arrive at school already having mastered much of the language facility they will ever use. Jim Gee (2002) argues that schools are consistently terrible at teaching, but they are highly effective at *practicing*. What he means by this is that if students arrive at school well-equipped to learn – if their inventory of skills and

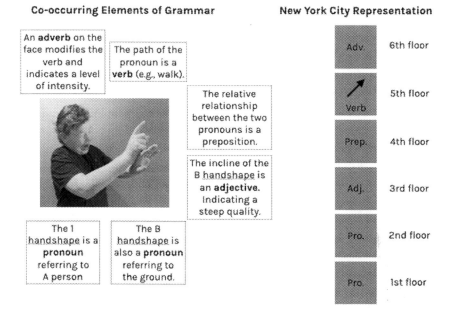

FIGURE 10.2 Illustrating the co-occurring features of an ASL predicate

Note: In this example, the predicate includes six "floors" of grammatical features.

routines are aligned with those that schools expect – then we have nothing to worry about because schools, and the curricula they use, are designed to support practicing and honing skills that students *already have*. However, if students lack strong academic fundamentals – if they are unfamiliar with school-based skills and especially if their language foundations are weak – then practicing what you don't know doesn't help much, if at all. Without teaching, these students are set up to be unsuccessful at school.

The reality is that we cannot expect curricula or standards designed for the vast majority of hearing children to include the unique, and low-incidence considerations of Deaf and hard of hearing children. Additionally, "adapting" curricula proves ineffective for two main reasons. First, it is difficult to do, and teachers cannot reasonably be expected to adapt every instructional resource. Second, the standard resources fail to consider (1) the experiences and abilities of Deaf and hard of hearing students, (2) a progression for instruction that lets students see the visual-spatial architecture of signed languages, and (3) the role of signed language grammar as a complementary approach for learning the grammar of written language. Instead, we need alternative options that address all of these considerations. This was the motivation for developing the Bilingual Grammar Curriculum, the first-ever comprehensive plan for bilingual grammar instruction based on the architecture of a signed language.

156 Todd Czubek

Starting Points

Language is a miracle. In simple terms, if we stop to consider what is made possible with language, we will see that through language we can raise ideas in our minds *and* make those same (or similar) ideas emerge in the minds of an audience. And as our ideas become more complex, we simply use proportionately more complex language structures to effectively share them. Understanding the nexus between conceptual frameworks and language was profound because it allowed us to get to the foundations of language and language instruction: complete ideas. This became our starting point. The consequences of this decision cannot be overstated because at the *idea level*, the chasm between modalities shrinks substantially. Finding this access point, where building bridges between otherwise dissimilar languages became manageable, is another important contribution of the BGC.

For example, any complete idea that we can possibly imagine has two basic components: a subject and a predicate. This fundamental quality is language-neutral. In other words, without context, any language requires those two elements to effectively transmit or elicit an idea. More explicitly, subjects are manifest in two basic forms: (1) *who* or (2) *what* the idea is about. Predicates assume one of three forms detailing: (1) *what happened* with the subject, (2) what the subject *has*, or (3) *describing* the subject. Some combination of these subject and predicate types generates a complete idea. In grammatical terms, we refer to this consolidation as a *sentence*. This unit of language is the North Star of the Bilingual Grammar Curriculum. All other grammatical features are understood in relation to their roles in sentences. Without this reference point, most elements of grammar are difficult to determine or understand.

As has been described, almost all language/grammar curricula will assume that children arrive at school already well-versed in forming complete ideas. And for most of us who are raised in environments with accessible language models, this ability is part of our primary discourse identity (Gee, 2007). We gain this proficiency automatically. Those skills we get "for free" are implicit results of our primary language acquisition and socialization experiences. Forming complete ideas is such a fundamental skill that at the point when children are typically expected to engage in the earliest stages of grammar study, models of instruction take it for granted. We presume that children are able to communicate using complete ideas and that they are capable of evaluating whether sentences are complete/grammatical. According to standard models, children have already developed the sense that sentences *sound right* as they begin grammar study. Curricula are designed to leverage these implicit foundations in order to practice recognizing *and* using elements of children's largely complete language abilities.

The BGC's design makes no such assumptions. As it begins, the BGC focuses on providing direct instruction about, and apprenticeships to, the central architecture of ideas (or sentences). Grounding the approach in language instruction at this fundamental level helps to build a foundation that contextualizes all subsequent elements of grammar. In and of itself, developing the underpinnings of meta-linguistic awareness as one learns about grammar is hard enough. Asking children (and teachers) to accomplish this task in a language with which learners have limited facility makes little to no sense. We sought to avoid the additional barriers that result from limited facility in English by ensuring that grammar study occurs first in ASL.

The Architecture of the BGC

A natural dividend of this progression is that it encourages schools and programs to establish bilingual language arts teams. The form a bilingual language arts team assumes is always subject to the resources that schools enjoy, but regardless of how it emerges, the BGC helps to establish clear expectations for the co-ordination of ASL *and* English instruction. Figure 10.3 outlines the sequence of Anchor Standards for three levels of the BGC.

Bilingual Grammar Curriculum
Anchor Standards Overview

Anchor Standard	Level 1	Level 2	Level 3
Standard #1 Sentence Components	X	X	X
Standard #2 Nouns	X	X	X
Standard #3 Pronouns		X	X
Standard #4 Adjectives	X	X	X
Standard #5 Adverbs	X	X	X
Standard #6 Prepositions			X
Standard #7 Verbs	X	X	X
Standard #8 Tense		X	X

FIGURE 10.3 An Overview of the Bilingual Grammar Curriculum

Note: The sequence of Anchor Standards taught in each level proceeds vertically from top to bottom in each column.

158 Todd Czubek

The BGC requires that students complete entire Anchor Standards in ASL before proceeding to the equivalent Anchor Standard in English. For example, if students are learning about Sentence Components in ASL, grammar instruction in English does not occur until students successfully complete this Anchor Standard. When students finish, they are assessed using an end-of-Anchor Standard evaluation. Earning a score of at least 80% meets the threshold for demonstrating mastery. At this point (having earned 80% or better), students move on to the next Anchor Standard in ASL (nouns) while they concurrently begin studying Sentence Components in English. Thus, students will always be one Anchor Standard "behind" in English. This coordination guarantees that students arrive at English grammar study already well-equipped to access the concepts and applications they will encounter.

The revolutionary idea behind this organization is that the entirety of the curriculum is based on a progression that makes sense for a visual language. We resisted the urge to "work backward" and rejected models designed for spoken and written languages. The sequence was intentionally and meticulously arranged so that Deaf and hard of hearing children would have ready access to each grammar element, as well as to the visual-spatial architecture that characterizes this modality. As they proceed, both ASL and English grammar study focus on developing conceptual frameworks. The BGC features an innovative, task-analyzed progression ensuring that instruction is comprehensible, internalized, and realized in student output. In order to do accomplish this, Anchor standards are divided into three Benchmarks: (1) *concept-building*, (2) *articulating* or *defining* a grammar feature's role, and (3) *applications and evaluations*. Framing instruction within this natural, developmental sequence is another substantial contribution that this model makes.

This structure has especially significant implications for the responsibilities of ASL instruction. As step one for every element of grammar study, ASL class is where foundations are built. In this model, much of the *heavy lifting* is done in ASL class, and students' success in both languages depends on how effectively instruction happens here. This is doubly critical for the work done in Benchmark 1, as this section is dedicated to building concepts that set the stage for Benchmarks 2 and 3 (where more applied interactions with grammar take place). In fact, Benchmark 1 is important for both ASL and English, and it is here that users will see the greatest concentration of creative frameworks designed to illuminate the grammar concepts that children will study. Students gain access to ideas through ingenious and language-free visual, tactile, or experiential activities that will prepare them for their interactions with grammar. This design becomes vital as students encounter more and more divergent grammatical forms in ASL and English.

Using a task-analysis approach, each Benchmark is then broken down into objectives that explicitly address complementary skills that progress sequentially toward our end of *conceptual*, *descriptive*, and *applied* mastery. Collectively, they contribute to a comprehensive engagement with different levels of grammar study.

Access to the BGC

After being beta tested at sites around the United States, the BGC website is now available for distribution (see Figure 10.4). This is an important step in the evolution of the BGC as it will serve to lessen the workload on teachers implementing bilingual grammar instruction. This resource provides over 300 objectives, each accompanied by an extensive lesson plan that includes materials lists, supporting resources, explicit procedures, native-users signing example and stimuli videos in ASL, example and stimuli sentences in English, printable activities, and assessments.

Included below are examples of objectives and their accompanying lesson plans taken from the online version (one for ASL and English, respectively).

FIGURE 10.4 An image of the Bilingual Grammar website

160 Todd Czubek

Objectives are labeled using our four-digit conventions. Each number refers to specific stage in the curriculum hierarchy:

> The first number indicates the Level
> The second number indicates the Anchor Standard
> The third number indicates the Benchmark
> The fourth number indicates the specific objective

For example, Objective 3.1.1.12. indicates that this is:

> Level 3
> Anchor Standard #1: Sentence Components
> Benchmark #1: Concept Building
> Objective # 12 in the sequence of objectives

The first example (see *Lesson Plan Example #1)* is taken from Level 3 and deals with transitive verbs. (At this point students have already studied transitivity and object nouns in HAS predicates.)

Objective 3.1.2.12.

Given sentences with WHAT HAPPENED predicates (both complete and incomplete) where the verb is transitive (i.e., it must have an object noun), distinguish between grammatical and ungrammatical examples.

Lesson Plan Example #1

Lesson Materials:

- LCD projector
- Laptop or tablet
- Images showcasing transitive verbs and object nouns
- Sentence stimuli with predicates including complete and incomplete transitive verbs
- Transitive verb stimuli
- OBJ label

Note for Teachers:

This objective extends our understanding of transitive verbs and how they impact WHAT HAPPENED predicates. We will take advantage of the foundation we have built as we move to this next predicate type.

HAS predicates set us up to see how transitive properties work. The nature of HAS predicates includes the idea that we must "have something" (i.e., something is being "had"). Now, we will turn to applying this idea to action verbs.

We will begin by introducing the idea of transitive action verbs "acting on" object nouns. In other words, transitive verbs are those that can "verb something." When you chase, you chase something; when you buy, you buy something; when you hug, you hug something. If we visualize the idea of chasing, buying, or hugging, we know that the idea should include an object noun. Something is being acted upon. Therefore, CHASE, BUY, and HUG are transitive verbs.

Other action verbs (which are also used in WHAT HAPPENED predicates) are intransitive. These verbs do not take an object noun. Consider the following examples:

BOY **SNEEZE**, GIRL **SIT**, and MOM **FALL.**

When we visualize these ideas in our minds we don't wonder, "what is being sneezed?," "what is being sat?," or "what is being fallen?" These verbs stand on their own. Therefore, **SNEEZE**, **SIT**, and **FALL** are all examples of intransitive verbs.

Our job will be to distinguish between these two forms.

Lesson Procedure:
1. Show the following image. Ask your students to think of **the verb** the sequence represents. They should arrive at the conclusion that the verb is **LIFT**.

2. Then, ask your students if the image looks complete (it doesn't). This is because we don't know what is being "lifted." The image (or idea) needs something more to be complete.
3. Show the next image. Ask your students to think of **the verb** the sequence represents. They should arrive at the conclusion that the verb is **PUSH**.

4. Then, ask your students again if the image looks complete (it doesn't). This is because we don't know what is being "pushed." State that the image (or idea) needs something more in order to be complete.
5. Show the next image. Ask your students to think of **the verb** the sequence represents. They should arrive at the conclusion that the verb is **CHASE**.

6. Then, ask your students, once again, if the image looks complete (it still doesn't). This is because we don't know what is being "chased." State that the image (or idea), once again, needs something more to be complete.
7. At this point, assess whether your students understand the dilemma (we need to know what the object noun is!). If everyone is clear that these ideas need something more, we are ready for the next step. If you want to review more examples you can create similar, additional stimuli using the following transitive verbs: HIT, BUY, KISS, and KICK.
8. Once your students are ready, return to our first example-image.

Ask them to generate a sentence using only the information we have in the image. Record their answer. Students should sign something like:

MAN LIFT

As you review it, discuss whether that sentence makes sense. You should arrive at the conclusion that it does not. Just as in HAS predicates that have to *have* something, we have to lift *something*. State that this sentence is incomplete because it needs an OBJECT NOUN. Ask students to generate some ideas and record them. Be ready to compare them soon.

9. Now reveal the following image:

10. Ask students to re-evaluate the image. Is it now complete? Do we know what is being lifted? (Yes!) Ask students to identify the object noun and tape/paste our OBJ label to the CAR in the image.
11. Once they do, have them sign a sentence using all of the new information we have. They should sign:

MAN LIFT CAR.

12. Show the following two sentences in ASL and ask students to compare them.

MAN LIFT.

MAN LIFT CAR.

13. Review each example as many times as is needed. Ask students to choose which of the sentences is grammatical (MAN LIFT CAR is). Ask them to explain why. They should be able to state that without knowing what is being lifted, the sentence isn't complete. It simply doesn't make sense. For predicates using the verb LIFT, we need an Object Noun.

14. Tell students that some verbs (like HAS) are special and need OBJECT NOUNS. In order to be fully understood.
15. Have students generate new LIFT sentences using the OBJECT NOUNS that they proposed earlier.

The procedure outline above is repeated using "WOMAN PUSH" and "DOG CHASE" as additional examples of how this feature of grammar is realized in context.

164 Todd Czubek

After reviewing these examples, we engage in the following applied activities to further support meta-linguistic awareness skills.

16. Tell students that we will now be discussing these special verbs as we look at ASL sentences with WHAT HAPPENED predicates. Our task will be to look at the predicate to see if it is complete (grammatical).
17. Show students the following sentences and ask them to (1) evaluate each example, describing what (if anything) is missing, (2) identify the OBJECT NOUN in the sentence (if it is there), and (3) repair the sentence if it is incomplete. Appropriate sentences with OBJECT NOUNS are bolded.

    1. ARTISTS PAINT BEAUTIFUL PICTURE.
    2. TALL MAN HIT.
    3. EVERY WEEK GRANDMOTHER BUY.
    4. MY DADDY OPEN PEANUT BUTTER JAR.
    5. YESTERDAY MY UNCLE COOKED CHICKEN.
    6. LITTLE GIRL HELP.
    7. MY TEAM WON SOCCER GAME.
    8. HANDSOME MECHANIC FIX.
    9. CHILDREN WANT.
    10. CURIOUS BOY TOUCH.

18. Show the following transitive verbs on video. Ask students to explain why they need OBJECT NOUNS. Then ask students to generate two sentences for each example. Ensure that each sentence uses a novel OBJECT NOUN.

    - HUG
    - STUDY
    - COPY
    - READ
    - DRINK

19. Label these special verbs as TRANSITIVE (spelled). TRANSITIVE verbs take object nouns in order to communicate ideas clearly and completely. Without OBJECT NOUNS, predicates including TRANSITIVE verbs are missing important information.

Note to teachers*
There are occasions when verbs appear in both transitive and intransitive forms. For example, the verb WIN is normally assumed to be a transitive verb (i.e., you have to win *something*, a GAME, or a PRIZE). However, we can also say, "WE WON!" without using an OBJECT NOUN. In these cases, the OBJECT NOUNS are often understood. For our purposes, all verbs that **can** (or normally) take an OBJECT NOUNS are considered TRANSITIVE. Those that do not take OBJECT NOUNS are intransitive.

Crossing the Divide 165

The next example (see *Lesson Plan Example #2*) is taken from English, Level 1 and involves awareness of sentence boundaries and their commensurate punctuation conventions. This lesson-plan combines two objectives.

Objective 1.1.3.10.

Capitalize the beginning of an English sentence and state that the capital letter indicates the beginning of a new sentence.

Objective 1.1.3.11.

Add a period at the end of a written English sentence and state that the period indicates the end of that sentence.

Lesson Plan Example #2
Lesson Materials:
- Masking tape, 6–8 feet long
- Ball
- Lid to a plastic container
- English target sentences
- Whiteboard
- Markers

Note to Teachers:
Before class begins, ask one or two adults to enthusiastically volunteer for demonstrating the actions you will describe. They will be confederates, intentionally demonstrating the sequence *incorrectly* so that students can explicitly critique their errors.

Lesson Procedure:
1. Explain to the class that you are going to play a memory game. Describe that your goal is to see who can remember a precise sequence of actions that you will demonstrate. State that they must follow the sequence exactly.
2. Apply your tape to the floor in a straight line. Ask a student to help you. After you have taped it down, ask students where you started and where you ended.

3. Give the container lid to a student volunteer and direct her to place it at the *right end* of the line. It must be placed at the right end of the line, and *it must remain there*. This is a rule.

4. Review your progression with the students by asking:
   - Where did I start applying the tape? (Students should indicate the left end.)
   - Where does the tape stop? (Students should indicate the right end.)
   - Can we move the lid from the end of the tape to the middle of the line? (No.)
   - How about to the beginning? (No.)

5. Now, add an additional feature to this memory game. Stand at the starting point of your line (opposite the lid) while holding a ball (preferably one that can bounce). Jump up and throw the ball into the air. Catch it as it comes down, landing in exactly the same spot as you jumped from.

6. Next, bounce the ball along the line until you reach the other end (with the lid). Once there, place the ball on the lid in order to keep the ball stationary.

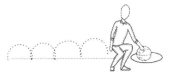

7. Ask for a volunteer who can recall all of our "rules" and perform them in exactly the same way. Choose your confederate teacher-volunteer, not a student.
8. Before she begins, ask a student volunteer to restate the four rules in order:
   I. Stand at the left end of the taped-line.
   II. Throw the ball into the air while jumping up, and catch it while landing in the same spot.

Crossing the Divide **167**

    III. Dribble the ball down the line.
    IV. Place the ball on the lid at the end of the tape line.

9. Ask your confederate to demonstrate the sequence (recall that the confederate will intentionally make mistakes for students to correct). She will begin from the wrong end (i.e., she will start at the right side of the line). Ask students to evaluate the demonstration. They should recognize that the confederate did not obey the first rule.
10. This time, ask *a student* volunteer to come up to correctly demonstrate the sequence. Ask the student to repeat the rules to the confederate to reinforce the procedure.
11. Choose a second confederate volunteer. Have her start at the appropriate beginning point, but, this time, arrange for her to dribble the ball without first jumping up, throwing, and catching the ball. Once at the end, have her put the ball on the lid.
12. Once again, ask students to evaluate the demonstration. They should all note that it was, again, wrong! Reiterate to the confederate that in order to be right, she must follow the rules exactly.
13. Ask another student to demonstrate the correct sequence. Ask them to, again, restate the rules to the confederate. By now, everyone should be clear on the rules that we have created.
14. Ask a student to help you remove the tape from the floor and to help you apply it to the board (horizontally). Point to the masking tape and ask students where we should start. After they point to the left-most edge, ask them where we start when we write in English. They should once again point to the left-most edge.

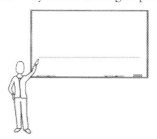

15. Explain that when we write using English, we must follow inviolable rules, and our memory game is illustrative of these rules.
    Write the following sentence on the line:

    mom works

16. After you write the sentence, ask your students if anyone sees anything missing from this example. If a student recognizes that the first word should be capitalized, or that there should be a period after "works," let her fix the sentence on the line. If not, explain the grammatical rules that "mom works" violates.

17. Draw a parallel between the required capital letter at the beginning of any sentence and our jumping, throwing, and catching the ball. Additionally, draw a parallel between our lid at the end of the line and periods.
18. State that when we write in English there are two critical rules:

    1. *The first letter of any sentence must be BIG (capitalized).*
    2. *The end of a sentence must have a period.*

19. Write the following sentence on the board:

    The cat is white

    Ask students to check your sentence to see if you have incorporated our two rules for writing. Have a volunteer correct the sentence by adding a period. Ask the student to restate the two rules.
20. Write another sentence on the board:

    pizza is hot.

    Once again, ask students to check your sentence to see if it obeys our two rules. Have a volunteer correct the sentence by capitalizing the first letter of the sentence. Ask the student to reiterate the two rules.
21. Write the following English target sentences on the board one at a time (or have them pre-written on sentence strips). Have students take turns repairing the sentence (or leaving it intact, if it is correct). As they repair, ask them to restate our rules.

    English target sentences:

    1. the ball is red.
    2. My car is blue
    3. fish swim
    4. Superman is strong.
    5. Dad runs.
    6. pizza is hot

7. The baby has milk
8. Snow is cold.
9. mom has a ball
10. the sun is yellow.

Important: Holding students accountable for what they are learning is essential. It will take time for grammar skills to become internalized to the point that students use them independently. In order to support this process, whenever students engage in writing rough drafts, it is helpful to provide them with simple editing checklists that include the elements that they are learning. Once they become automatic (when the grammar skill is now stored in long-term memory), the grammar feature can be removed, and the checklist can be updated with new grammar skills.

Conclusion

The comprehensive approach to bilingual grammar study outlined in the BGC can be an effective resource that navigates a course across the chasm that we have had such great difficulty crossing. We seek to do this by equipping the stakeholders in our field with a variety of tools. First among them is a progression of instruction that respects the role and architecture of ASL. Another is a plan for learning English that meets students where they truly are rather than where traditional templates assume they are. This plan uses conceptually accessible, developmentally appropriate examples in both languages, and makes use of lessons that illuminate the role that grammar features play. These lessons will show students how increasingly complex grammar elements help to communicate more and more sophisticated ideas. By providing a structure that lowers affective filters, we promote success in both ASL and English. In the end, we expect that grammar study, if done well, will support students' successful engagement in independent composition and comprehension of both ASL and English.

There is no debate that the journey we're describing is long. Language learning is no "day sail." But as with any worthwhile endeavor, we must keep at it. Venturing 2,000 miles into the open ocean with canoes required impressive fortitude; we chose to go to the moon because it was hard; and Evel Knievel broke the world record for jumping over 14 Greyhound buses *after* the Snake River and Wembley Stadium disasters. It is our hope that with the BGC, *keeping at it* is made significantly easier in the field of Deaf Education.

Note

1 The Bilingual Grammar Curriculum was co-authored by Todd Czubek and Kristin DiPerri with help and consultation from many Deaf individuals throughout its decade-long development.

References

Boudreault, P., & Mayberry, R. I. (2006). Grammatical processing in American Sign Language: Age of first-language acquisition effects in relation to syntactic structure. *Language and cognitive processes, 21*(5), 608–635.

Czubek, T. A. (2009). *ASL Instructional Guide.* [Unpublished manuscript]

Easterbrooks, S. R., Lederberg, A. R., Miller, E. M., Bergeron, J. P., & Connor, C. M. (2008). Emergent literacy skills during early childhood in children with hearing loss: Strengths and weaknesses. *The Volta Review, 108,* 91–114.

Gee, J. P. (2002). *Literacies, identities, and discourses. Developing Advanced Literacy in First and Second Languages: Meaning with Power,* 159–175.

Gee, J. P. (2007). *Social linguistics and literacies: Ideology in discourses.* New York, NY: Routledge.

Lederberg, A., Schick, B., & Spencer, P. (2012). *Language and Literacy Development of Deaf and Hard-of-Hearing Children.* Successes and Challenges.

Marcus, N. (1983). Air rights in New York City: TDR, zoning lot merger and the well-considered plan. *Brooklyn Law Review, 50,* 867–911.

Mayberry, R. I. (2002). Cognitive development in deaf children: The interface of language and perception in neuropsychology. *Handbook of Neuropsychology, 8*(Part II), 1–107.

Purdy, J. (2007). *Being America: Liberty, commerce, and violence in an American world.* Vintage.

Spencer, P. E., & Marschark, M. (2010). *Evidence-based practice in education deaf and hard-of-hearing students.* New York, NY: Oxford University Press.

Traxler, C. B. (2000). The Stanford Achievement Test, 9th Edition: National norming and performance standards for deaf and hard-of-hearingstudents. *Journal of deaf studies and deaf education, 5,* 337–348. 10.1093/deafed/5.4.337.

11

THE RELATIONSHIP BETWEEN ASL FLUENCY AND ENGLISH LITERACY

Jessica Scott

Introduction

An enduring interest of researchers in deaf education has been the examination of how literacy skills develop. For decades, scholars and teachers in the field have sought best practices and instructional approaches that would improve literacy outcomes for deaf children. A small number of studies have found promise in one or another instructional practice (e.g., explicit instruction in a variety of areas of English literacy, Miller, Lederberg, & Easterbrooks, 2013; Wolbers, Dostal, & Bowers, 2011; shared reading practices, Maxwell, 1984; morphological awareness instruction, Gaustad & Kelly, 2004; Trussell & Easterbrooks, 2015; Trussell, Nordhaus, Brusehaber, & Amari, 2018). In addition, there is a growing body of evidence exploring how reading develops among bilingual deaf learners who use American Sign Language (ASL) or another natural-signed language. Such evidence includes research on the relationship between ASL language proficiency and English literacy. There is also a related debate regarding whether the path to reading is qualitatively similar to or different from how hearing learners develop reading skills (see Andrews & Wang, 2015; Paul & Lee, 2010 for an introduction to the Qualitatively Similar Hypothesis and surrounding debate).

A number of researchers have found a relationship between ASL proficiency and the English literacy of deaf learners (Allen, 2015; Allen, Letteri, Choi, & Dang, 2014; Clark et al., 2016; DeLana, Gentry, & Andrews, 2007; Golos, 2010; Golos & Moses, 2011; Golos & Moses, 2015; Hoffmeister, 2000; Hoffmeister & Caldwell-Harris, 2014; Hratinski & Wilbur, 2016; McCann, 2018; McQuarrie & Abbott, 2013; Novogrodsky, Caldwell-Harris, Fish, & Hoffmeister, 2014; Scott & Hoffmeister, 2017; Scott & Hoffmeister, 2018; Strong & Prinz, 1997; Wolbers et al., 2015; Wolbers et al. 2014). These researchers measured ASL proficiency in

172 Jessica Scott

a variety of ways. Measurements included (1) using proxy measures (e.g., years of enrollment in an ASL-using school, parent signing proficiency, or presence of a deaf family member; DeLana et al. 2007; Golos, 2010; Golos & Moses, 2011, 2015; Hoffmeister, 2000; McCann, 2018); (2) self- or teacher-report (Clark et al., 2016; Hratinski & Wilbur, 2016; Wolbers et al., 2014); (3) a global or holistic measure of ASL proficiency, which often meant classification of individuals as more or less proficient (Allen, 2015; Allen et al. 2014; Strong & Prinz, 1997); and (4) a measure of ASL that included scores in one or several language subskills as well as a global score (McQuarrie & Abbott, 2013; Novogrodsky et al. 2014; Scott & Hoffmeister, 2017; Scott & Hoffmeister, 2018). In this chapter, I summarize what research has uncovered about the relationship between ASL proficiency and English literacy, a relationship that Dr. Hoffmeister extensively explored, and close with suggestions for new metaphorical research shores for which we might set sail.

The Theoretical Underpinnings for a Connection between ASL and English Literacy

There are a number of theoretical frameworks that could be employed to explain the potential for a relationship between ASL proficiency and English literacy. In this chapter, we will explore only two, though it should be noted that these are certainly not the only avenues for considering such a relationship. The first is Cummins' (1979) interdependence hypothesis, and the second is Krashen's (1985) input hypothesis. As these hypotheses were developed and published concurrently with the first research exploring ASL as a potential source of linguistic resource for deaf children, they were highly influential on the foundational research in this area.

Cummins' (1979) linguistic interdependence hypothesis has been an enduring theoretical model of how language can develop bilingually. In his groundbreaking paper, Cummins (1979) combined two existing theoretical models. First, the developmental interdependence hypothesis stated that learning a second language was at least partially related to the existence of a foundational first language. Second, the threshold hypothesis asserted that a certain level (threshold) of linguistic ability is needed for students to experience the benefits of bilingualism. Taken together, Cummins' (1979) hypothesis asserts that home language experiences, first language proficiency, and second language proficiency can all impact the academic achievement of bilingual children. The consequence of this hypothesis for deaf children was that first-language proficiency in ASL was finally considered a contributor toward achievement, including achievement in English literacy. Research has explored the linguistic interdependence hypothesis across a variety of spoken languages and found evidence to support the theory (Abu-Rabia, 2001; Bournot-Trites & Reeder, 2001; Verhoeven, 1994). Cummins (2006) himself, in a paper about deaf children, argued that the

ASL Fluency and English Literacy **173**

linguistic interdependence hypothesis was applicable to bilingual deaf children who learned ASL as their first language and were acquiring English as their second language. Although some deaf education researchers argued that this hypothesis was too narrow to describe the bilingual development of deaf children (Hermans, Ormel, & Knoors, 2010), others have noted its usefulness for exploring this population (Easterbrooks, 2008).

Krashen (1985) developed the Input Hypothesis, which argued that language development only occurs with the availability of "comprehensible input." Comprehensible input is defined as language plus "extra-linguistic information" that makes linguistically unfamiliar concepts accessible (e.g., the addition of visual aids such as pictures or objects, or connecting new information with known information) (Krashen, 1985). Krashen argued that language is not *taught* but develops naturally through interactions with others that are accessible to and understood by the language learner. Researchers have tested and found support for this hypothesis with second language learners and non-native English speakers (Loschky, 2008; Pica, Doughty, & Young, 1986), although there has been criticism against Krashen for theoretical assumptions made without sufficient supporting evidence (Gregg, 1984). Deaf education re-searchers, including Hoffmeister, have used Krashen's (1985) work as a theo-retical foundation to argue for the need for bilingual deaf students to have "comprehensible input" in ASL, which can then support the acquisition of English literacy (Hoffmeister & Caldwell-Harris, 2014). Others have even ar-gued that text that is generated from student explanations in ASL and then translated to English can then serve as comprehensible written English input for deaf learners (Wolbers et al. 2014).

Evidence for a Relationship between ASL and Literacy

As the theoretical frames explored above emerged, this alongside the signed language linguistic work of Stokoe (1970), and his deaf colleagues Casterline and Croneberg, allowed for deaf education researchers to pioneer studies examining the relationship and potential impact of ASL proficiency on English literacy skills for deaf students. The majority of this type of research fell into three areas: emergent literacy skills, reading comprehension, and writing. The evidence base for each of these areas is explored in further detail below.

Emergent Literacy. Emergent literacy skills among deaf students who use ASL is somewhat understudied, as a great deal of emergent literacy research is focused on spoken language phonemic awareness and phonics skills (for example, see Miller et al. 2013; Wang, Spychala, Harris, & Oetting, 2013; Webb, Lederberg, Branum-Martin, & Connor, 2015) and less research is available on other types of early skills. This is unfortunate, as there is strong evidence that a variety of emergent literacy skills (for example, recognizing symbols, playwriting, beginning understandings of conventions of print; Morrow, Tracey, & Del Nero, 2011)

174 Jessica Scott

are often predictive of later academic outcomes – and phonological level skills are only half of the emergent literacy framework as it is widely understood (Whitehurst, et al., 1999; Whitehurst & Lonigan, 1998). The research that exists on ASL's effects on emergent literacy skills has two foci: describing literacy abilities among young deaf children, and examining the effects of an ASL-oriented intervention on early literacy skills.

The Early Education Longitudinal Study (EELS) conducted by the National Science Foundation funded Visual Language/Visual Learning (VL2) initiative collected language and emergent literacy data on 251 deaf children between three and five years of age. The researchers measured ASL receptive skill, fingerspelling ability, and letter knowledge (including the ability to say or sign letters, and the ability to write letters). These researchers found that young deaf children's ability to say/sign and write letters correlated with ASL receptive skill and fingerspelling ability (Allen, 2015; Allen et al. 2014), suggesting that these language skills, unsurprisingly, are related to the development of emergent literacy. These findings align with Whitehurst and Lonigan's (1998) assertion that emergent literacy consists of two major skill types – knowledge of letters and sounds (although sounds were not measured for participants in the EELS study), and knowledge of language and concepts. In his dissertation, McCann (2018) went a step further, and followed 72 deaf children between ages four and six longitudinally for two years, measuring letter knowledge and passage comprehension, alongside ASL proficiency. Results indicated that ASL comprehension was a significant predictor of both word identification ability and passage comprehension for the study participants. Interestingly, a case study of a deaf child with deaf parents found that these parents engaged in rich book sharing activities using ASL to explore the text (Bailes, Erting, Erting, & Thumann-Prezioso, 2009) – a practice that is likely to support emergent literacy development as the child grows older. Overall, holistic assessments of ASL skill and emergent literacy skill suggest an important relationship between each.

Two researchers have been primarily responsible for a body of research on the effects of an emergent literacy *intervention* conducted in ASL on skill development among deaf preschool-age children (Golos, 2010; Golos & Moses, 2011; Golos & Moses, 2015). In the first study, Golos (2010) created an educational video (similar to a program such as Sesame Street or Between the Lions) designed to promote emergent literacy skills (such as vocabulary acquisition and fingerspelling) and showed it to 25 deaf students between the ages of three and six. Participating children viewed the educational video created by the researcher in small groups. The video was 43 minutes in duration. Golos assessed the children before and after video viewing on target vocabulary, and coded student behaviors during video viewing. Findings revealed that students interacted during the video by signing and fingerspelling target vocabulary or making comments on the story being viewed. Additionally, the students grew from pre-test to post-test in their target vocabulary knowledge. In a follow-up

ASL Fluency and English Literacy **175**

study, Golos and Moses (2011) created an interactive guide for teachers to facilitate instruction during viewing of the same educational video. This guide included teacher-led activities such as making connections between ASL and English, fingerspelling activities that targeted key vocabulary, and supporting story comprehension (e.g., encouraging students to respond to questions or point to on-screen items identified by the characters). As in the first study, children took pre- and post-tests on target vocabulary knowledge, and their literacy behaviors during video viewing were coded. The researchers found that the children increased their vocabulary knowledge from pre- to post-test. In addition, the children engaged in more literacy behaviors (defined by the authors as signing new vocabulary terms, fingerspelling, or otherwise discussing the events of the video with their teachers or peers) than students in the 2010 study who viewed the video without teacher mediation (Golos & Moses, 2011). In a further extension of this line of research, Golos and Moses (2015) recreated the previous two studies with the same educational video in ASL, but added supplemental activities led by the classroom teacher after video viewing, rather than during viewing as had occurred in previous iterations (Golos & Moses, 2011). These supplemental activities focused on skills such as vocabulary (matching a fingerspelled word with a print word), vocabulary (selecting the correct word to complete a sentence), and reading comprehension (arranging events from the story in the correct sequence). Researcher observations suggested that students engaged in the emergent literacy activities targeted by the supplemental activities. To assess the specific ASL and emergent literacy skills that were the focus of the intervention, the researchers designed an assessment that included the target vocabulary as well as story grammar and sequencing. The participating students on average increased their scores on this measure, suggesting that this array of instructional tools in ASL (the educational video, teacher mediation strategies, and supplemental instructional modules) supported skill development.

Overall, these findings suggest that opportunities to engage in instruction in ASL seem to have a significant relationship with emergent literacy skills among young deaf students. Importantly, interventions that use ASL in a targeted way to support emergent literacy have promise for providing students with the opportunity to develop these skills. According to Cummins' (1979) hypothesis, the development of foundational language proficiency has the potential to contribute to later academic achievement. Ultimately, the goal of developing strong early ASL proficiency and emergent literacy is to support the reading and writing abilities of deaf students as they grow older.

Reading Comprehension. The ultimate goal of any reading activity is comprehension of the text. Reading comprehension is by definition a meaning-making activity. Because language use and comprehension are also meaning-making activities, there is a natural potential for connection between these skills. This connection is theoretically supported by Cummins' linguistic interdependence hypothesis. Hoffmeister and Caldwell-Harris (2014) built upon Cummins' work by proposing their own evidence-driven theoretical model of reading development for deaf children. According to their model, children begin their journey toward literacy in English by connecting vocabulary in print to signs in ASL (comprehensible input, Krashen, 1985). As they develop these connections, children begin to learn the nuances between the two languages (for instance, multiple-meaning words, idiomatic expressions; threshold hypothesis, Cummins, 1979). Finally, as complex language features are mastered, deaf children who learn English in this way can be considered proficient bilinguals.

Some studies exploring the relationship between ASL proficiency and reading comprehension used a researcher-designed, holistic measure of ASL proficiency (or proxy measure such as presence of a deaf parent or number of years educated in an ASL environment) and tested for a correlation with a standardized assessment of reading comprehension (e.g., DeLana et al. 2007; Hoffmeister, 2000; Strong & Prinz, 1997). For instance, Hoffmeister (2000) assessed 50 students between the ages of 8 and 16, 14 of whom had deaf parents. He identified students as having had either limited or intensive exposure to ASL. Analysis of these students' literacy abilities found a significant correlation between having intensive exposure to ASL and having improved reading comprehension. These results echoed findings from others who identified higher levels of ASL proficiency as measured by a researcher-designed assessment as significantly correlated with reading ability. In fact, ASL proficiency contributed to reading comprehension above and beyond the effects of having a deaf parent among middle school age students (Strong & Prinz, 1997). Researchers have also found a relationship between parent signing skill (a proxy for exposure to ASL) and reading outcomes (DeLana et al. 2007). One unique study obtained school-level data on ASL proficiency of students, ultimately using a dichotomous label of highly proficient or not highly proficient, to represent ASL proficiency. These researchers also found a significant relationship between ASL proficiency status and reading comprehension (as well as mathematics and knowledge regarding the English language) (Hratinski & Wilbur, 2016). Finally, a study conducted by a collaborative of international researchers compared deaf students learning different written languages (i.e., English, Turkish, Hebrew, and German). The researchers reported across all languages compared that deaf students with deaf parents (a proxy measure for ASL proficiency) outperformed both deaf children with hearing parents and hearing students with dyslexia in word reading (Clark et al., 2016). The authors suggested that their results lend support to the importance of access to a signed language at an early age as an important factor for later reading comprehension (ibid.).

Other studies used measures of ASL proficiency that focused on one or several linguistic subskills rather than using a global or holistic measure of

ASL Fluency and English Literacy   **177**

language proficiency. For instance, in one study that focused on older deaf learners, Scott and Hoffmeister (2017) examined whether proficiency in the academic register of English uniquely contributed to reading comprehension abilities among deaf learners. Although early statistical models exploring the relationship between reading comprehension and academic English suggested that a potential relationship between these two skills existed, final regression models found that ASL proficiency as measured by the American Sign Language Assessment Instrument (ASLAI; Hoffmeister et al., 2014) was the main predictor of reading comprehension over and above proficiency with academic English. Scores on the ASLAI subtest of antonym knowledge also predicted reading comprehension of a large population (n = 564) of deaf learners (Novogrodsky et al. 2014), suggesting an important relationship between ASL vocabulary and reading comprehension. In addition, McQuarrie and Abbott (2013) measured phonological awareness in ASL and found that this skill also significantly related with reading skills in English. Similarly, although not a measure of ASL proficiency per se, Haptonstall-Nyzaka and Schick (2007) found that providing instruction that used lexicalized fingerspelling (as compared to a condition that included no fingerspelling) appeared to support word learning, an important element of reading ability. These studies taken together suggest that vocabulary knowledge, language proficiency, phonological awareness, and fingerspelling comprehension may all be important contributors toward English literacy for deaf students who learn using ASL.

There has also been limited research on the use of ASL in classroom reading comprehension instruction. For example, researchers found that ASL was an effective medium for implementing dialogic reading instruction, with evidence that an elementary-aged student improved his ability to read and comprehend text after participating in dialogic reading activities conducted in ASL (Scott & Hansen, 2019). Similarly, a qualitative analysis of deaf adults in a literacy program also found that after participating in a bilingual, ASL focused English class, participants not only improved in their test scores but also had more positive attitudes and orientations toward reading (Enns, 2009). Though such research is nascent, these studies indicate positive effects of the application of ASL to reading instructional contexts.

In summary, there is growing evidence documenting the relationship between ASL proficiency and reading ability among deaf children who are educated using ASL or another natural-signed language. Following Krashen's (1985) input hypothesis, the provision of comprehensible input in ASL (alongside other scaffolds where appropriate and necessary) may be an important scaffold for accessing and eventually becoming fluent in the second language, English.

Writing. Writing is much less studied in deaf education research as compared to reading. However, writing is an essential skill, and to not properly explore writing development is to ignore half what is required to be considered literate.

178 Jessica Scott

When it comes to writing and its relationship with ASL, there is even less available research. There is evidence, however, that suggests a relationship exists between writing skills and ASL proficiency.

Strategic and Interactive Writing Instruction (SIWI) is a program that was developed by researchers that purposefully employs face-to-face language (both ASL and spoken English depending on the child's communication modality) as a tool for bridging to written language (Wolbers et al. 2011). A single case study exploring SIWI for improving writing quality used National Assessment of Educational Progress (NAEP) rubrics to assess student writing. Results suggested that using a face-to-face language (i.e., ASL or English) was an important component of an effective writing intervention (Wolbers et al., 2015). Similarly, a study with only deaf students who used ASL found that SIWI could even reduce the appearance of ASL-like features in writing (for instance, a noun appearing before an adjective, the appearance of topic-comment construction, or idiomatic phrases such as "time late" used to mean "it was late") (Wolbers et al., 2014).

Scott & Hoffmeister (2018) studied the relationship between one specific feature of academic writing, the use of superordinate precision, and ASL proficiency. Superordinate precision refers to the ability to categorize words precisely when writing definitions (Galloway & Uccelli, 2015). For instance, a writer who has underdeveloped superordinate precision in writing might describe winter as "a time when it snows and is very cold," whereas a writer with stronger superordinate precision in writing might describe winter as "one of the four seasons." When deaf students were evaluated on their ability to use superordinate precision when writing definitions for words, researchers found that ASL proficiency as measured by the ASLAI (Hoffmeister et al., 2014) was a significant predictor of producing definitions with superordinate precision, alongside their comprehension of academic English (Scott & Hoffmeister, 2018). This finding may be related to Singleton and colleagues' (2004) findings indicating that students who were more proficient in ASL had less formulaic writing and used more vocabulary tokens (which were also lower frequency words) during writing. Underlying language proficiency, regardless of modality, may be important for the development of skills in writing.

Although further research is necessary, existing literature demonstrates that there appears to be a relationship between these ASL proficiency and writing. Like emergent literacy, there is also evidence that instructional interventions, which use ASL purposefully to promote skill development can be successful in the area of writing. Also like emergent literacy, the existence of a relationship between ASL and writing corroborates Cummins' (1979) hypothesis and provides evidence that ASL is a unique contributor towards the developing of writing skill in English. These findings have important implications for classrooms educating deaf children.

ASL Fluency and English Literacy **179**

Practical Applications and Implications

The research evidence summarized in this chapter has important instructional implications for teachers who work with deaf students. These implications are presented below: Implications for emergent literacy, implications for reading instruction, and implications for writing instruction.

Emergent Literacy Implications. The importance of early language exposure and acquisition on the development of literacy is widely acknowledged (Rescorla, 2002; Scarborough, 2009). The identification of a relationship between ASL and early literacy skills extends this finding specifically among deaf children (Allen, 2015; Allen et al. 2014; McCann, 2018). The most apparent implication is for early interventionists to seek out opportunities for families of deaf children (and deaf children themselves) to acquire ASL as quickly as possible. Ideally, such learning opportunities might mean pairing hearing families with deaf mentors, in addition to offering formal ASL classes and providing opportunities to interact with deaf adults in social settings. Training and employing more deaf adults as early interventionists may be a way to support families, educate children, and provide ASL models in one fell swoop. Similarly, the evidence that reading aloud to a child is an important predictor of later literacy (e.g., Swanson et al., 2011) suggests that training parents on how to engage in shared book reading in ASL (Berke, 2013) may be another necessary element of early childhood deaf education.

There is also evidence that using educational multimedia alongside purposeful teacher instruction that utilizes ASL has promise for improving early literacy knowledge, as well as being an engaging avenue to present both stories as well as fluent ASL models (Golos, 2010; Golos & Moses, 2011; Golos & Moses, 2015). In recent years, there has been growth in multimedia in ASL that has been designed for young deaf children (e.g., HandsLand; the VL2 Storybook App), and early interventionists may consider directing families toward these resources. Classroom-based early intervention teachers, such as preschool teachers, may wish to incorporate educational multimedia into their regular classroom routine, alongside engaging play-based instruction.

Reading Instruction Implications. Unfortunately, there are fewer studies of the relationship between ASL and reading that include interventions or instructional tools. This is because much of the research on literacy in deaf education has focused upon establishing the existence and strength of the relationship between ASL and reading comprehension. However, there is related research that can be used to explore more practical applications in the classroom. For instance, a case study of students who were newcomers to the United States and enrolled in a bilingual ASL/English classroom environment found that a bilingual approach to learning appeared to benefit them. In fact, the authors wrote, "In order to gain access to English as it is used in classrooms and among Deaf signing Americans, deaf children must also acquire ASL" (Ramsey &

180 Jessica Scott

Padden, 1998, p. 21). The authors noted class discussions in ASL and using ASL during word writing (including fingerspelling and engaging in discussion about word meanings) as particularly useful practices that were evident in the ASL/ English bilingual classroom (Ramsey & Padden, 1998).

Researchers have found the use of ASL during text discussions to be a practice that may be important for reading skill development (Maxwell, 1984; Scott & Hansen, 2019). Specifically, teachers noted during interviews that using meta-cognitive strategies in ASL to engage with texts in English was necessary for teaching students how to engage with text (Mounty, Pucci, & Harmon, 2014). The importance of metacognitive strategies for supporting reading development among deaf learners has also been found through research with children – a single case study found the metacognitive strategy approach to be effective (though the participants in this study did not use ASL; Benedict, Rivera, & Antia, 2015). Researchers have also theoretically argued for the importance of using ASL to allow students to access English text as an instructional technique that engages language development as well as literacy (Andrews & Rusher, 2010; Bailes, 2001). Such an approach would have as its goal for students to engage in activities that support their development of ASL proficiency, and provide them with purposeful opportunities to learn analogue linguistic constructs that exist in English print (Andrews & Rusher, 2010). In fact, a dialogic reading approach – one that emphasizes active face-to-face discussion surrounding text – may be an effective practice for improving reading using ASL (Scott & Hansen, 2019). Building upon Krashen's (1985) input hypothesis, to provide students with op-portunities to engage in meaningful and accessible discourse in ASL around an English text would be the equivalent of providing comprehensible input. Comprehensible input in the form of ASL may scaffold understanding of English print, rendering it more accessible to developing readers.

Writing Instruction Implications. As with reading, there is limited research that systematically examines the use of ASL as an instructional tool to support English writing – with the research conducted with SIWI being a notable ex-ception. However, there are important implications to be drawn from SIWI and related research that could be useful practitioner tools for developing writing skills among bilingual deaf learners that are explored below.

Interestingly, one study of a self-editing tool that was designed for use with adolescent deaf writers who use sign language found that rather than the tool itself, it seemed to be interaction about the tool in ASL that helped support improvement in student writing (Appanah & Hoffman, 2014). The importance of interaction is reflected in the practices embraced by SIWI, which intentionally uses face-to-face language (ASL among signing deaf students) to navigate and support language development that is directly linked to writing practices (Wolbers et al. 2011). There is also documentation that in bilingual ASL/English classrooms, children used ASL when developing and discussing their own writing with peers, and these interactions appeared to be motivating to the students

ASL Fluency and English Literacy **181**

(Bailes, 2001). Overall, these findings indicate that allowing children to utilize ASL during the writing process may be important. The inclusion of ASL during writing could also include such practices as encouraging children to engage in prewriting activities using ASL, and providing opportunities for writing to be a shared (rather than solitary) process that involves face-to-face feedback from and discussion with others.

Conclusion: Setting Sail for New (research) Shores

Recent years have shown a significant increase in the amount and quality of research with bilingual deaf students, which has allowed us to better understand the role that ASL proficiency plays in the development of print literacy in English. As explored above, there is significant evidence that ASL proficiency is important for emergent literacy, reading comprehension, and writing (Allen, 2015; DeLana et al. 2007; Golos, 2010; Hoffmeister, 2000; Hoffmeister & Caldwell-Harris, 2014; Scott & Hoffmeister, 2017, 2018; Strong & Prinz, 1997; Wolbers et al., 2014; Wolbers et al., 2015). These studies are a strong start, but there are many new shores to explore to better understand the relationship between ASL and literacy, and importantly, how to apply research-generated knowledge to instructional practice in classrooms with deaf children.

Firstly, although there is emerging evidence regarding ASL proficiency and its relationship with English literacy for deaf students across a range of ages, to this author's knowledge there is currently no comprehensive study of the trajectory of ASL development and English reading and writing as it develops over time. Although we know that there are certain subskills of ASL proficiency that may predict English literacy (for instance, phonological awareness; McQuarrie & Abbott, 2013 or vocabulary, Novogrodsky et al. 2014), further exploration of these skills, as well as their manifestation at different developmental stages would be a useful contribution to the literature.

Theoretical pursuits that result in knowledge or understanding are, of course, valuable in and of themselves. However, in a practical field such as deaf education, the ultimate goal of such theoretical pursuits is arguably to impact the lives of deaf children. As such, an important step in our understanding of the relationship between ASL proficiency and English literacy is to test the best ways to leverage ASL during instruction to strategically and systematically support the development of English literacy. Although there is nascent research that specifically incorporates ASL into instruction or intervention (i.e., Scott & Hansen, 2019; Wolbers et al., 2015), such research is limited. A long-term goal of researchers in deaf education and literacy may even be to develop a comprehensive ASL/English literacy curriculum that teachers can use in bilingual classrooms and schools serving deaf children.

Finally, it is well-established in the field that a small number of deaf children are born to parents who are able to provide them with fluent and accessible language models in ASL (Mitchell & Karchmer, 2004). Given the evidence that ASL proficiency is linked to English literacy outcomes, and that most deaf children will not have the opportunity to learn ASL from birth from fluent parents, it is worth exploring the question of whether interventions designed to improve ASL proficiency among deaf children with hearing or non-signing parents could have distal impacts on English literacy. Such a study would require a longitudinal sample of children and would take many years, but could ultimately have great impacts on deaf education.

Dr. Hoffmeister's legacy on the trajectory of research in deaf education is undeniable. Specifically, in literacy his contributions toward our understanding of the relationship between ASL and literacy and their influence on the work of other scholars (this author included) will reverberate in the literacy research with deaf children for years to come. As our knowledge in the area of ASL and its relationship with English literacy continues to grow, and new scholars emerge to explore the contribution of ASL proficiency to English literacy, the literacy education of deaf children will only improve. As we better understand the role that ASL plays in English literacy processes, we can develop interventions and instructional approaches that utilize linguistic strengths to teach deaf children to navigate the world of English literacy.

References

Abu-Rabia, S. (2001). Testing the interdependence hypothesis among native adult bilingual Russian-English students. *Journal of Psycholinguistic Research*, *30*(4), 437–455.

Allen, T. E. (2015). ASL skills, fingerspelling ability, home communication context, and early alphabetic knowledge of preschool-aged deaf children. *Sign Language Studies*, *15*(3), 233–265. 10.1353/sls.2015.0006.

Allen, T. E., Letteri, A., Choi, S. H., & Dang, D. (2014). Early visual language exposure and emergent literacy in preschool deaf children: Findings from a national longitudinal study. *American Annals of the Deaf*, *159*(4), 346–358.

Andrews, J., & Rusher, M. (2010). Code-switching techniques: Evidence-based instructional practices for the ASL/English bilingual classroom. *American Annals of the Deaf*, *155*(4), 407–424.

Andrews, J. F., & Wang, Y. (2015). The qualitative similarity hypothesis: Research synthesis and future directions. *American Annals of the Deaf*, *159*(5), 468–483.

Appanah, T. M., & Hoffman, N. (2014). Using scaffolded self-editing to improve the writing of signing adolescent deaf students. *American Annals of the Deaf*, *159*(3), 269–283.

Bailes, C. N. (2001). Integrative ASL-English language arts: Bridging paths to literacy. *Sign Language Studies*, *1*(2), 147–174.

Bailes, C. N., Erting, C. J., Erting, L. C., & Thumann-Prezioso, C. (2009). Language and literacy acquisition through parental mediation in American Sign Language. *Sign Language Studies*, *9*(4), 417–456.

Benedict, K. M., Rivera, M. C., & Antia, S. D. (2015). Instruction in metacognitive

ASL Fluency and English Literacy **183**

strategies to increase deaf and hard-of-hearing students' reading comprehension. *Journal of Deaf Studies and Deaf Education, 20*(1), 1–15.

Berke, M. (2013). Reading books with young deaf children: Strategies for mediating between American Sign Language and English. *Journal of Deaf Studies and Deaf Education, 18*, 299–311.

Bournot-Trites, M., & Reeder, K. (2001). Interdependence revisited: Mathematics achievement in an intensified French immersion program. *The Canadian Modern Language Review, 58*(1), 27–43.

Clark, M. D., Hauser, P. C., Miller, P., Kargin, T., Rathmann, C., Guldenoglu, B., Kubus, O., Spurgeon, E., & Israel, E. (2016). The importance of early sign language acquisition for deaf readers. *Reading and Writing Quarterly, 32*(2), 127–151.

Cummins, J. (1979). Cognitive/Academic language proficiency, linguistic interdependence, the optimum age question and some other matters. Working Papers on Bilingualism, No. 19, *Toronto Institute for Studies in Education*. Toronto: Bilingual Education Project. Retrieved from ERIC database. (ED184334).

Cummins, J. (2006) The relationship between American Sign Language proficiency and English academic development: A review of the research [1]. Paper presented at the conference Challenges, Opportunities, and Choices in Educating Minority Group Students, Norway.

DeLana, M., Gentry, M. L., & Andrews, J. (2007). The efficacy of ASL/English bilingual education: Considering public schools. *American Annals of the Deaf, 152*(1), 73–87.

Easterbrooks, S. R. (2008). Knowledge and skills for teachers of individuals who are deaf or hard of hearing. *Communication Disorders Quarterly, 30*(1), 12–36.

Enns, C. (2009). Critical literacy: Deaf adults speak out. *Exceptionality Education International, 19*(2–3), 3–20.

Galloway, E. P., & Uccelli, P. (2015). Modeling the relationship between lexico-grammatical and discourse organization skills in middle grade writers: Insights into later productive language skills that support academic writing. *Reading and Writing, 28*(6), 797–828.

Gaustad, M. G., & Kelly, R. R. (2004). The relationship between reading achievement and morphological word analysis in deaf and hearing students matched for reading level. *Deaf Education, 9*(3), 269–285.

Golos, D. B. (2010). Literacy behaviors of deaf preschoolers during video viewing. *Sign Language Studies, 11*(1), 76–99.

Golos, D. B., & Moses, A. M. (2011). How teacher mediation during video viewing facilitates literacy behaviors. *Sign Language Studies, 12*(1), 98–118.

Golos, D. B., & Moses, A. M. (2015). Supplementing an educational video series with video-related classroom activities and materials. *Sign Language Studies, 15*(2), 103–125

Gregg, K. (1984). Krashen's monitor and Occam's razor. *Applied Linguistics, 5*, 79–100.

Haptonstall-Nyzaka, T. S., & Schick, B. (2007). The transition from fingerspelling to English print: Facilitating English decoding. *Journal of Deaf Studies and Deaf Education, 12*(2), 172–183. 10.1093/deafed/enm003.

Hermans, D., Ormel, E., & Knoors, H. (2010). On the relation between the signing and reading skills of deaf bilinguals. *International Journal of Bilingual Education and Bilingualism, 13*(2), 187–199.

Hoffmeister, R. (2000). A piece of the puzzle: The relationship between ASL and English literacy in deaf children. In C. Chamberlain, R. Mayberry & J. Morford (Eds.), *Language acquisition by eye* (pp. 143–163). Mahweh, NJ: Lawrence Erlbaum.

184 Jessica Scott

Hoffmeister, R. J., & Caldwell-Harris, C. L. (2014). Acquiring English as a second language via print: The task for deaf children. *Cognition, 132*, 229–242.

Hoffmeister, R., Fish, S., Henner, J., Benedict, R., Rosenburg, P., Conlin-Luippold, F., & Caldwell-Harris, C. (2014). *American Sign Language Assessment Instrument (ASLAI-revision 3)*. Boston, MA: Center for the Study of Communication and the Deaf, Boston University.

Hratinski, I., & Wilbur, R. B. (2016). Academic achievement of deaf and hard-of-hearing students in an ASL/English bilingual program. *Journal of Deaf Studies and Deaf Education, 21*(2), 156–170. 10.1093/deafed/env072.

Krashen, S. D. (1985). *The input hypothesis: Issues and implications.* Boston, MA: Addison-Wesley.

Loschky, L. (2008). Comprehensible input and second language acquisition: What is the relationship? *Studies in Second Language Acquisition, 16*(3), 303–323.

Maxwell, M. (1984). A deaf child's natural development of literacy. *Sign Language Studies, 44*, 191–224.

McCann, J. P. (2018). *The contribution of American Sign Language comprehension on measures of early literacy in deaf and hard-of-hearing children: A longitudinal study of four-, five-, and six-year-olds through early elementary school.* Washington, DC: (Unpublished doctoral dissertation). The George Washington University.

McQuarrie, L., & Abbott, M. (2013). Bilingual deaf students' phonological awareness in ASL and reading skills in English. *Sign Language Studies, 14*(1), 80–100.

Miller, E. M., Lederberg, A. R., & Easterbrooks, S. R. (2013). Phonological awareness: Explicit instruction for young deaf and hard-of-hearing children. *Journal of Deaf Studies and Deaf Education, 18*(2), 206–227.

Mitchell, R. E., & Karchmer, M. A. (2004). Chasing the mythical ten percent: Parental hearing status of deaf and hard of hearing students in the United States. *Sign Language Studies, 5*, 83–96. 10.1353/sls.2005.0004.

Morrow, L. M., Tracey, D. H., & Del Nero, J. R. (2011). Best practices in early literacy: Preschool, kindergarten, and first grade. In L. M. Morrow & L. B. Gambrell (Eds.), *Best practices in literacy instruction, Fourth Edition* (pp. 67–95). New York, NY: The Guilford Press.

Mounty, J. L., Pucci, C. T., & Harmon, K. C. (2014). How deaf American Sign Language/English bilingual children become proficient readers: An emic perspective. *Journal of Deaf Studies and Deaf Education, 19*(3), 333–346. 10.1093/deafed/ent050.

Novogrodsky, R., Caldwell-Harris, C., Fish, S., & Hoffmeister, R. J. (2014). The development of antonym knowledge in American Sign Language (ASL) and its relationship to reading comprehension in English. *Language Learning, 64*(4), 749–770. 10.1111/lang.12078.

Paul, P. V., & Lee, C. (2010). The qualitative similarity hypothesis. *American Annals of the Deaf, 154*(5), 456–462.

Pica, T., Doughty, C. J., & Young, R. (1986). Testing the interdependence hypothesis among native adult bilingual Russian-English students. *International Journal of Applied Linguistics, 72*(1), 1–25. 10.1075/itl.72.01pic.

Ramsey, C., & Padden, C. (1998). Natives and newcomers: Literacy education for deaf children. *Anthropology and Education Quarterly, 29*(1), 5–24.

Rescorla, L. (2002). Language and reading outcomes to age 9 in late-talking toddlers. *Journal of Speech, Language, and Hearing Research, 45*, 360–371.

Scarborough, H. S. (2009). Connecting early language and literacy to later reading (dis) abilities: Evidence, theory, and practice. In F. Fletcher-Campbell, J. Soler & G. Reid

ASL Fluency and English Literacy **185**

(Eds.), *Approaching difficulties in literacy development: Assessment, pedagogy, and programmes.* (pp. 23–38). Los Angeles, CA: Sage Publishing.

Scott, J. A., & Hansen, S. G. (2019). *Comprehending science writing: The promise of dialogic reading for supporting upper-elementary deaf students. Communication Disorders Quarterly, 41*(2), 100-109. 10.1177/1525740119838253.

Scott, J. A., & Hoffmeister, R. (2017). Factors predicting the reading comprehension of bilingual deaf and hard of hearing students. *Journal of Deaf Studies and Deaf Education, 22*(1), 59–71.

Scott, J. A., & Hoffmeister, R. H. (2018). Superordinate precision: An examination of academic writing among bilingual deaf and hard of hearing students. *Journal of Deaf Studies and Deaf Education, 23*(2), 173–182. 10.1093/deafed/enx052.

Singleton, J. L., Morgan, D., DiGello, E., Wiles, J., & Rivers, R. (2004). Vocabulary use by low, moderate, and high ASL-proficient writers compared to hearing ESL and monolingual speakers. *Journal of Deaf Studies and Deaf Education, 9*(1), 86–103.

Stokoe, W. C., Jr. 1970. *The study of sign language (Report No. AL002346).* Washington, DC: Center for Applied Linguistics Retrieved from ERIC database. (ED037719).

Strong, M., & Prinz, P. M. (1997). A study of the relationship between American Sign Language and English literacy. *Journal of Deaf Studies and Deaf Education, 2*(1), 37–46.

Swanson, E., Vaughn, S., Wanzek, J., Petscher, Y., Heckert, J., Cavanaugh, C., Kraft, G., & Tackett, K. (2011). A synthesis of read-aloud interventions on early reading outcomes among preschool through third graders at risk for reading difficulties. *Journal of Learning Disabilities, 44*(3), 258–275. 10.1177/0022219410378444.

Trussell, J. W., & Easterbrooks, S. R. (2015). Effects of morphographic instruction on the morphographic analysis skills of deaf and hard of hearing students. *Journal of Deaf Studies and Deaf Education, 20*(3), 299–241.

Trussell, J. W., Nordhaus, J., Brusehaber, A., & Amari, B. (2018). *Morphology instruction in the science classroom for students who are deaf: A multiple probe across content analysis. Journal of Deaf Studies and Deaf Education, 23*(3), 271–283.

Verhoeven, L. T. (1994). Transfer in bilingual development: The linguistic interdependence hypothesis revisited. *The Canadian Modern Language Review, 58*(1), 27–43. 10.3138/cmlr.58.1.27.

Wang, Y., Spychala, H., Harris, R. S., & Oetting, T. L. (2013). The effectiveness of a phonics-based early intervention for deaf and hard of hearing preschool children and its possible impact on reading skills in elementary school: A case study. *American Annals of the Deaf, 158*(2), 107–120.

Webb, M., Lederberg, A. R., Branum-Martin, L., & Connor, C. M. (2015). Evaluating the structure of early English literacy skills in deaf and hard of hearing children. *Journal of Deaf Studies and Deaf Education, 20*(4), 343–355. http://dx.doi.org/10.1093/deafed/env024.

Whitehurst, G. J., Zevenbergen, A. A., Crone, D. A., Schultz, M. D., Velting, O. N., & Fischel, J. E. (1999). Outcomes of an emergent literacy intervention from Head Start through second grade. *Journal of Educational Psychology, 91*(2), 261–272. http://dx.doi.org/10.1037/0022-0663.91.2.261.

Whitehurst, G. J., & Lonigan, C. J. (1998). Child development and emergent literacy. *Child Development, 69*(3), 848–872. 10.1111/j.1469-8624.1998.tb06247.x.

Whitehurst, G. J., Zevenbergen, A. A., Crone, D. A., Schultz, M. D., Velting, O. N., & Fischel, J. E. (1999). Outcomes of an emergent literacy intervention from Head Start through second grade. *Journal of Educational Psychology, 91*(2), 261–272. https://doi.org/10.1037/0022-0663.91.2.261.

Wolbers, K. A., Bowers, L. M., Dostal, H. M., & Graham, S. C. (2014). Deaf writers' application of American Sign Language knowledge to English. *International Journal of Bilingual Education and Bilingualism, 17*(4), 410–428. 10.1080/13670050.2013.816262.

Wolbers, K. A., Dostal, H. M., & Bowers, L. M. (2011). "I was born full deaf." Written language outcomes after 1 year of strategic and interactive writing instruction. *Journal of Deaf Studies and Deaf Education, 17*(1), 19–38. 10.1093/deafed/enr018.

Wolbers, K. A., Dostal, H. M., Graham, S., Cihak, D., Kilpatrick, J. R., & Saulsburry, R. (2015). The writing performance of elementary students receiving strategic and interactive writing instruction. *Journal of Deaf Studies and Deaf Education, 20*(4), 285–395. 10.1093/deafed/env022.

12

USING ASL TO NAVIGATE THE SEMANTIC CIRCUIT IN THE BILINGUAL MATHEMATICS CLASSROOM

Claudia M. Pagliaro and Christopher Kurz

If asked to think about communicating mathematics, most would conjure up something that looks like this: $2 + 3 = 5$, or this: $2x + 4xy + 3y$, or dare we propose this: $EV = \sum_{i=1}^{n} x_i P(x_i)$. However, mathematics is actually communicated via several representational systems, including mathematical notation (shown above), visual models, and language, collectively referred to as the "semiotic circuit." A person who can express a mathematical concept in each of the different representation systems is said to have a complete and functional understanding of that concept (Lesh, Post, & Behr, 1987; Pagliaro & Ansell, 2012). While the semiotic circuit presents a full expression of a mathematics concept, each system within has its own rules, its own intents or purposes, and unfortunately, its own challenges which can impact learning. This chapter will present a brief description of each representation system in the semiotic circuit as well as some inherent obstacles. The chapter will then show how the conceptual and linguistically accurate use of American Sign Language (ASL) provides bilingual Deaf students with a resource that supports the learning of mathematics and may reduce some challenges within each of the traditional representation systems. The chapter ends with suggestions for instruction.

The Semiotic Circuit

As mentioned above, the semiotic (i.e., meaning making) circuit consists of several representations systems, or ways, to convey or share mathematics including language (in various modes), mathematical notation, and images/models. While most people may think of mathematics in its notation form, mathematics is primarily learned (informally and formally) through language. Language is considered the primary source of the other representation systems (Chapman, 1993)

188 Claudia M. Pagliaro and Christopher Kurz

because it provides the context for mathematics. Informally, we use mathematics daily, even hourly. The words in the previous sentence, "daily" and "hourly" are examples as time is a mathematics concept. When communicating mathematics more formally, like in the classroom, we tend to use the mathematics register of a language, that is, a unique and specific set of content-based vocabulary, meanings, and structures; words in English like "polynomial" and phrases and sentences such as, "The expected value is equal to the weighted average of a finite number of finite outcomes." Not knowing the linguistic register for mathematics may hinder mathematics learning (Bedore, Peña, & Boerger, 2010). In fact, the relationship between mathematics and language has been studied for more than three decades with the majority of research showing a positive correlation between language proficiency and mathematics achievement.

The Language Representation System

Cognitive development including mathematics processing, problem solving, and 3-D perception is not only associated with language development but also holds a significant relationship with bilingualism. Bilinguals perform better than monolinguals on cognitive tests (Diaz, 1983; Hakuta 1986; Hakuta & Diaz, 1985; Henner, Pagliaro, & Hoffmeister, 2020; Jiminez, Garcia and Pearson, 1996; Menéndez, 2010) and in mathematics achievement (Clarkson, 1992). These findings supply theoretical and empirical support for the development of cognitive and linguistic knowledge and skills in a primary language and their transfer to a second language.

As Figure 12.1 indicates, the bilingual mathematics learner weaves an intricate web of associations between language (L1 and L2), mathematical notation, experience, and concepts, defining, representing, translating, and substantiating along the way. These associations – be they one-way or two-way – provide the learner with multiple pathways by which to understand, strengthen, and communicate mathematical concepts. The ability to use multiple representations and to translate within and between them, as mentioned above, indicates a robust and meaningful understanding of concepts (Lesh *et al.* 1987; Pagliaro & Ansell, 2012). It is also within that communication that errors and misconceptions in understanding may be revealed (Bresser, Melanese, & Sphar, 2008). Accordingly, a balanced bilingual who is provided appropriate and accurate input pedagogically, conceptually, and linguistically, should have little difficulty in forming a strong understanding of mathematics, particularly if language is used as a resource in the learning episode (Planas, 2014). However, if either language is weak, the linguistic/educational input faulty, or if the notation or visual system is misunderstood, the whole system will break down (Moschkovich, 2007; Ní Ríordáin & O'Donoghue, 2009). This is often the case with students who are non-native to the sole or main language of instruction (Wilkinson, 2018).

Using ASL to Navigate the Semantic Circuit **189**

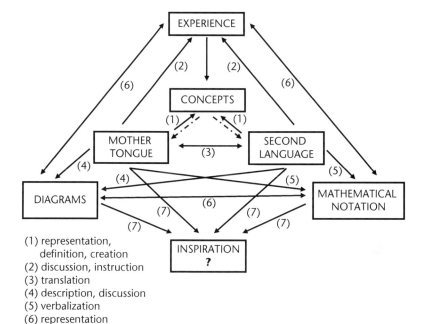

FIGURE 12.1 A model for considering the role of language in mathematical activity
Source: (Clark, 1975)

In the United States (and many other countries in the world), English dominates as the language of mathematics instruction, and many second-language students, including Deaf students, are challenged in this linguistic environment. Numerous studies involving these students show the resulting breakdown in learning when taught mathematics in English. In a study by Christodoulou (retrieved June 2017, http://www.psy.gla.ac.uk/~steve/courses/archive/CERE11-12-safari-archive/Nia/webarchive-index.html), students with limited English proficiency scored 29% lower than their native English-speaking peers in mathematics, a gap that widened when problems included or required more language (i.e., English), such as word problems (Alt, Arizmendi, & Beal, 2014; Bernarndo & Calleja, 2005; Bresser *et al.* 2008). Often the difficulty with English for these students arises from semantic, syntactic, and discourse differences between English and the first language (L1) (Christodoulou, 2017; Kidd, Madsen, & Lamb, 1993). Semantically, some mathematical terms in English hold multiple meanings, many of which have nothing to do with mathematics. The term

190 Claudia M. Pagliaro and Christopher Kurz

"base" in English, for example, can be the side of a triangle perpendicular to its height, the indication of the numeral system in use (in the United States, we use a base 10 counting system), a musical instrument, a foundation, a center of operations, or one of the four required touchpoints on a baseball diamond, just to name a few. Syntactically, English structure can be difficult for students with limited proficiency to decipher given phrases such as "three times half as many as." Morphological variations in words that significantly change meaning present another challenge. For example, the additional morpheme "ly" in "yearly" versus "year" greatly impacts the answer to a problem (as well as your bank account!) when there is a "yearly interest" vs. "a year's interest." Abbreviations as well can cause confusion (Why does the abbreviation "lb." represent "pound" when no "L" and no "B" is anywhere in the word?!). Within discourse too, a student with limited English proficiency may have difficulty following the interactions within the classroom, which are often conducted at a more rapid rate than the student can manage. If the language in these discussions is not clear, students are less likely to benefit from them (Bresser *et al.* 2008). It is incredibly important that "any classroom that may contain children whose dominant language is not [the language of instruction], needs to have a teacher who can analyze the dominant language of these children and create second-language mathematics descriptions that are meaningful based on their language's use of the mathematics concepts" (Schindler & Davison, 1985, pp. 27–28).

The Notation Representation System

Developed and refined through countless modifications and changes over hundreds of years, mathematical notation presents the relationships or patterns between units (Wilkinson, 2019). These now standardized special symbols and positions encode mathematical relations representing both participants and processes in the most precise and efficient manner (O'Halloran, 2015). Information dense and grammatically elaborate, and able to present the most intricate of mathematical nuances, the notation representation system is limited to mathematics and is not without its challenges to the mathematics learner. Despite its use of linguistic elements, notation symbols represent different concepts, multiple concepts and processes (i.e., operations), or undefined concepts. These symbols then combine according to unique grammatical arrangements (rules), which do not necessarily unfold linearly, may have encrypted meaning (e.g., order of operations), and are based on prior knowledge, not context (O'Halloran, 2015).

The Diagram/Model Representation System

The diagram or model representation system of mathematics is the notation system turned inside-out. Whereas the notation system communicates mathematics in abstract ways, the model system exposes a visual representation of implicit mathematical relationships, processes, and patterns (Wilkinson, 2019). Using established standards of portrayal and properties (e.g., points, lines, x and y axes, and 2-D and 3-D shapes), insights into mathematical actualities are visually evident. Still, challenges within this system on its own persists, mainly related to the amount and depth of information that can be displayed even in a small image, and the involvement of the other representation systems within it (i.e., symbolic and linguistic notation) (O'Halloran, 2015).

In studying mathematics learning with Deaf students and thinking about the visual, spatial, and manual properties of ASL, researchers and educators have come to believe that the use of conceptually and linguistically accurate, property-embedded signs in mathematics instruction may overlap the systems within the semiotic circuit and, thereby, assist Deaf learners in their understanding of mathematics.

The Affordance of ASL to Facilitate and Promote Comprehension of Mathematical Content

American Sign Language (ASL) is conceptual in that signs provide a unique representation based on meaning. The "table" at which you eat breakfast is not signed the same as the "table" that shows demographic data. Similarly, the English words "year" and "yearly" have distinctly different productions in ASL that are not easily overlooked. This conceptual basis directly relates to meaning and reduces the challenges often experienced in the majority language representation system (i.e., English) in which mathematics is taught. Thus, ASL in its use as a linguistic representation system can also be a resource to clarify and enhance overall conceptual understanding. Using phonological parameters (i.e., handshape, location, movement, palm orientation, and non-manual markers) associated with concept meaning, sign production, intensity, grammar, and syntax, ASL signs can provide the Deaf learner with not only a label for a mathematics concept but also a window to its properties that can help define it and connect it to related concepts. For example, to express the concepts of 2-D shapes (circle, square, etc.), ASL uses the 1-handshape, but for 3-D shapes such as sphere and cube, the sign is made using the 5-handshape recognizing the faces inherent to the latter constructs. Another example is with fractions. The definition of a proper fraction is a fraction with the greater number in the denominator. The definition of an improper fraction is its opposite: a fraction with the greater number in the numerator. The ASL signs for these two types of fractions reveal their opposing properties in terms of the magnitude of handshape (See Figure 12.2 for a depiction of these signs; See Kurz & Pagliaro (2020) for a more in-depth explanation.) Thus, the use of conceptually and linguistically accurate signs presents a mathematics register of ASL that may assist the Deaf learner in accurate cognitive organization of concepts.

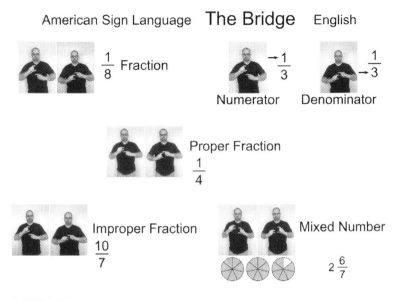

FIGURE 12.2

ASL's inherent visual, spatial, and manual aspects further circumvent some of the challenges presented in the typical representation systems within the semiotic circuit. The manual nature of ASL allows for simultaneous counting and/or tracking in problem solving, for example. In ASL, each hand can maintain a separate counting string, allowing counting up or down with both hands from different starting numbers, or counting up with one hand and down with the other hand (e.g., when adding 5 and 3, start with 5 and count up, on the one hand, while the other hand starts with 3 and count down to zero in a one for one fashion) reducing cognitive load in working memory (Pagliaro & Ansell, 2012). Additionally, the use of space as well as the rules of establishing location in ASL present the learner with a visual depiction of a mathematics concept or function (akin to the model or visual representation system) or present a notation "in the air" within this linguistic representation. These expressions can then be manipulated to further instruction, understanding, and/or problem-solving. For example, in a study by Pagliaro & Ansell (2012), Deaf children in lower elementary grades made use of space/location in ASL to set up groups of quantities, providing for themselves an additional manipulative or marker.

Suggestions for the Classroom

The semantic use of ASL within bilingual strategies provides Deaf students with a resource to understand mathematics that English alone cannot do. Still, Deaf learners must be assisted in transitioning from the level of ASL they typically use in casual conversations to the advanced mathematics register. Thus, it is critical that teachers not only understand the interaction of their students' proficiency in language (L1 and L2) with their mathematics understanding but also utilize instructional strategies that enhance and expand the relationship between the two. The following are some suggestions for the classroom.

First and foremost, nothing can be achieved unless teachers (or interpreters) of these bilingual Deaf learners themselves are proficient in the mathematics register of each language. Unless mindful of their own understanding of mathematics and related use of language within mathematics instruction, a teacher *cannot* assist students in their mathematics development, and in fact, may impair students' understanding and progression in this vital subject area. As Boulet (2007) explains, teachers will often mis-state a fraction in English as "a over b" instead of "a out of b" focusing not on the concept but on the written representation. Likewise, learners of ASL as a second language are likely to make nuance mistakes in their ASL delivery. These teachers may misrepresent a concept using incorrect number signs, for instance, using the number signs for the ordinal first, second, and third as placeholders in a race instead of the accurate first-place, second-place, and third-place signs, or express the tens place value position as an English-based plural (i.e., TEN+S). Thus, teachers for Deaf students need to be "bilingual in mathematics" (Schleppegrell, 2007). While fluency in ASL might help reduce such mistakes, we encourage teachers who are non-native ASL users to work with Deaf L1 signers for observation and feedback.

Second, Deaf students should be introduced to mathematical ideas in their primary language (i.e., ASL) with an optional/additional second language (i.e., English), and within context. Introducing new mathematics concepts via an accessible linguistic representation system within the context of stories, personal experiences or real-world situations, and comic strips, for example, can stimulate students' background information and/or prior experiences, allowing them to make associations and possibly decode for comprehension. This contextualized approach reinforces the importance of viewing comprehension which may lead to sign production as the new concept is discussed in the classroom. Language study and fluency in both ASL and English can commence when comprehension has been established and it is time for Deaf students to analyze new signs/words through the decontextualized lens using linguistic parameters. For example, using the fractions example outlined above, the Deaf student can more easily understand the English terms "proper fraction" and "improper fraction," noting the reference to two opposite types of fractions by the prefix "im." Using language, any language, as a tool to understand mathematics can support conceptual learning.

Third, theoretically grounded bilingual approaches have been shown to be a catalyst for improving outcomes relatively quickly, even among late L1 learners who experienced early language deprivation (Lange, Lane-Outlaw, Lange, & Sherwood, 2013). Deaf students of widely varied backgrounds demonstrated

194 Claudia M. Pagliaro and Christopher Kurz

performance gains in mathematics that brought them in line with hearing peers after only two years in a well-designed bilingual program. Lessons and activities should be designed so as to engage and support the student's use of both languages (in all modalities), in mathematics notation, and related models and images, i.e., that involves and requires Deaf learners to represent their understanding and traverse their learning within and across the semiotic circuit. One example is the use of bridging. For Deaf students, bridging involves translation within the linguistic representation [from one language (e.g., ASL) to another language (e.g., English)] and between representational systems. Teachers and/or students can make a "bridge poster" or binder where Deaf students can have access to the linguistic representation system (ASL and English) as well as the notation and the model systems. Encompassing the full semiotic circuit can support understanding of language and of mathematics. Figure 12.2 provides an example of such a poster.

In addition, while teaching and learning new mathematics vocabulary is essential, classroom interaction and discussion are needed to construct meaning. Both language and mathematics learning are social constructs that develop within contexts and through interaction (Krouse, 2017; Masochkovich, 2007). Encouraging discussions around mathematical topics and problem solving will allow the Deaf student to learn new vocabulary in contexts that link label to concept. Teachers are encouraged to codeswitch and "revoice" students' contributions so that they more closely match the academic register of the mathematics representation systems (Civil, 2012; Moschkovich, 2007; Planas & Morera, 2011; Schleppegrell, 2007). This practice calls attention to the mathematics register across languages (codeswitching) or within a language (revoicing) without disrupting instruction or discourse and can help clarify technical vocabulary and meaning for students.

Finally, especially within this discourse-based design, it is critical that teachers use and manage students' learning in each of the representation systems within the semiotic circuit (Boulet 2007, Wilkinson, 2018, 2019). Deaf learners should experience mathematics concepts in each of the representation systems, and teachers should model these systems accurately and appropriately, given their intended purposes (e.g., unless specifically referring to the notation, expression of an equation "out loud" should be in the language form, i.e., "the expected value (EV) given possible outcomes and the probabilities of those outcomes occurring.") The linguistic representation system can provide clarity in explanation, while the diagram/model representation system can offer a visual image that is particularly helpful for abstract concepts, and the notation representation system can communicate an easy, standard, and universal way to express and perform mathematical ideas and processes. Taken together, the semiotic circuit offers safe passage by which to navigate the Deaf learner's meaningful understanding and true communication of mathematics.

References

Alt, M., Arizmendi, G., & Beal, C. (2014). The relationship between mathematics and language: Academic implications for children with specific language impairment and English language learners. *Language, Speech, and Hearing Services in Schools, 45*(3), 220–233. 10.1044/2014_LSHSS-13-0003

Bedore, L, Peña, E, & Boerger, K. (2010). Ways to words: Learning a second language vocabulary. In M Schatz & L Wilkinson (Eds.), *The education of English language learners: Research to practice*. Guilford Press.

Bernarndo, A. B., & Calleja, M. O. (2005). The effects of stating problems in bilingual students' first and second languages on solving mathematical word problems. *Journal of Genetic Psychology, 166*(1), 117–128. 10.3200/GNTP.166.1.117-129

Boulet, G. (2007). How does language impact the learning of mathematics? Let me count the ways. *Journal of Teaching and Learning, 5*(1), 1–12. https://DOI.ORG/10.22329/JTL.V5I1.125.

Bresser, R., Melanese, K., & Sphar, C. (2008). *Supporting English language learners in math class, grades 3–5*. Math Solutions.

Chapman, A. (1993). Language and learning in school mathematics: A social semiotic perspective. *Issues In Educational Research, 3*(1), 35–46. http://www.iier.org.au/iier3/chapman.html.

Christodoulou, N. (downloaded in 5/26/2017) Language barriers in mathematical learning. http://www.psy.gla.ac.uk/~steve/courses/archive/CERE11-12-safari-archive/Nia/webarchive-index.html.

Civil, M. (2012). Opportunities to learn in mathematics education: Insights from research with "non-dominant" communities. In T. Y. Tso (Ed.), *Proceedings of the 36th Conference of the International Group for the Psychology of Mathematics Education* (Vol. 1, pp. 43–59). Taipei: PME.

Clark, R. (1975). *Some aspects of psycholinguistics*. In E. Jacobsen(Ed.), *Interactions between linguistics and mathematical education: Final report of the symposium sponsored by UNESCO, CEDO and ICMI, Nairobi, Kenya*, September 1-11 1974 (UNESCO Report No. ED-74/CONF.808).

Clarkson, P. C. (1992). Language and mathematics: A comparison of bilingual and monolingual students of mathematics. *Educational Studies in Mathematics, 23*, 417–429. https://doi.org/10.1007/BF00302443.

Diaz, R. (1983). Thought and two languages: The impact of bilingualism on cognitive development. *Review of Research in Education, 10*, 23–54. https://doi.org/10.3102/0091732X010001023.

Hakuta 1986Hakuta, K. (1986). *Cognitive development of bilingual children*. Center for Language Education and Research Educational Report Series, No. 3 UCLA.

Hakuta, K., & Diaz, R. (1985). The relationship between degree of bilingualism and cognitive ability: A critical discussion and some new longitudinal data. In K. Nelson (Ed.), *Children's Language (vol. 5*, pp. 319–344). Hillsdale, NJ: Lawrence Erlbaum Associates.

Henner, J., Pagliaro, C., & Hoffmeister, R. (2020). *Let us count the ways: Predicting mathematics achievement in signing deaf and hard of hearing children*Unpublished manuscript.

Jiminéz, R., García, G., & Pearson, P. (1996). The reading strategies of bilingual Latina/o students who are successful English readers: Opportunities and obstacles. *Reading Research Quarterly, 31*(1), 90–112.

Kidd, D., Madsen, A., & Lamb, C. (1993). Mathematics vocabulary: Performance of residential deaf students. *School Science and Mathematics*, *93*(8), 418–421.

Krause, C. M. (2017). DeafMath: Exploring the influence of sign language on mathematical conceptualization. In T. Dooley & G. Gueudet (Eds.), *Proceedings of the Tenth Congress of the European Society for Research in Mathematics Education* (pp. 1316–1323). Dublin University, The European Society for Research in Mathematics Education Inst. of Education.

Kurz, C., & Pagliaro, C. M. (2020). Using sign languages to teach mathematics to deaf students. In R. Rosen (Ed.), *Handbook of sign language pedagogy* (pp. 85–99). Routledge.

Lange, C., Lane-Outlaw, S., Lange, W., & Sherwood, D. (2013). American Sign Language/English bilingual model: A longitudinal study of academic growth. *Journal of Deaf Studies and Deaf Education*, *18*, 10.1093/deafed/ent027

Lesh, R., Post, T. R., & Behr, M. (1987). Representations and translations among representations in mathematics learning and problem solving. In C. Janiver (Ed.), *Problems of representations in the teaching and learning of mathematics* (pp. 33–40). Lawrence Erlbaum.

Menéndez, B. (2010). Cross-modal bilingualism: Language contact as evidence of linguistic transfer in sign bilingual education. *International Journal of Bilingual Education and Bilingualism*, *13*(2), 201–223. https://doi.org/10.1080/13670050903474101.

Moschkovich, J. (2007). Using two languages when learning mathematics. *Educational Studies in Mathematics*, *64*, 121–144. https://doi.org/10.1007/s10649-005-9005-1.

Ní Ríordáin, M., & O'Donoghue, J. (2009). The relationship between performance on mathematical word problems and language proficiency for students learning through the medium of Irish. *Educational Studies in Mathematics*, *71*(1), 43–64.

O'Halloran, K. L. (2015). The language of learning mathematics: A multimodal perspective. *Journal of Mathematical Behavior*, *40*, 63–74. https://doi.org/10.1016/j.jmathb.2014.09.002.

Pagliaro, C. M., & Ansell, E. (2012). Deaf and hard-of-hearing students' problem-solving strategies with signed arithmetic story problems. *American Annals of the Deaf*, *156*(5), 438–458.

Planas, N. (2014). One speaker, two languages: Learning opportunities in the mathematics classroom. *Educational Studies in Mathematics*, *87*, 51–66. https://doi.org/10.1007/s10649-014-9553-3.

Planas, N., & Morera, L. (2011). Revoicing in processes of collective mathematical argumentation among students. In M. Pytlak, E. Swoboda & T. Rowland (Eds.), *Proceedings of the 7th Congress of the European Society for Research in Mathematics Education* (pp. 1380–1389). Rzeszów: ERME.

Schindler, D. E., & Davison, D. M. (1985). Language, culture, and the mathematics concepts of American Indian learners. *Journal of American Indian Education*, *24*(3), 27–34.

Schleppegrell, M. J. (2007). The linguistic challenges of mathematics teaching and learning: A research review. *Reading and Writing Quarterly*, *23*(2), 139–159. https://doi.org/10.1080/10573560601158461.

Wilkinson, L. C. (2018). Teaching the language of mathematics: What the research tells us teachers need to know and do. *Journal of Mathematical Behavior*, *51*, 167–174. https://doi.org/10.1016/j.jmathb.2018.05.001.

Wilkinson, L. C. (2019). Learning language and mathematics: A perspective from *Linguistics and Education*. *Linguistics and Education*, *49*, 86–95. https://doi.org/10.1016/j.linged.2018.03.005.

PART III

Sailing into the Wind

Challenges of Signed Language Assessment

13

BUILDING THE ASL ASSESSMENT INSTRUMENT

Patrick J. Costello

In the 1760s, the Abbé de l'Épée took the groundbreaking step of undertaking to learn the sign language of Parisian Deaf people, with the aim of employing the sign language to offer them accessible education. Laurent Clerc was an alumnus of the Paris school for the Deaf which de l'Épee eventually founded. Thomas Gallaudet recruited Clerc to help establish the first school for the Deaf in the United States and to be its first teacher. Beginning in 1817, Clerc and Gallaudet together began to witness the birth of American Sign Language (ASL) at the school. ASL was used for academic instruction, but not taught as an academic subject. By the 1860s, academic instruction in ASL was already under threat from the oralist movement spearheaded by A. G. Bell. In the 1880s, ASL and other signed languages were banned in schools and programs serving Deaf children across the world, as a result of the Milan Convention. In response to the ban, in 1906, George W. Veditz employed the ground-breaking technology of moving picture film to spread his impassioned argument in favor of the value of Sign Language. But ASL had moved underground and was used only in some upper grades of Deaf schools and in the Deaf community. In 1965, William Stokoe, with Deaf colleagues Dorothy Casterline and Carl Croneberg, used linguistic analysis to make the ground-breaking claim that signed languages were true languages, with their own grammatical/syntactical rules.

So it was, that Hoffmeister's conception and development of the ASL Assessment Instrument (ASLAI) followed a long train of respect for, and advancement in thinking about, signed languages.

200 Patrick J. Costello

Historical Timeline

- 1970–1978: While at the University of Minnesota, Hoffmeister starts to collect ideas about the development of ASL in Deaf Children of Deaf Parents (DCDP).
- 1975: Hoffmeister establishes the first bilingual (ASL and English print) graduate program in the education of the Deaf at Temple University.
- 1979: Hoffmeister at Boston University changes an oral program to a bilingual program (implemented fall 1980) incorporating ASL and Deaf culture into the M.Ed. curriculum for teachers.
- 1982: Hoffmeister establishes the Center for the Study of Communication and the Deaf at Boston University and continues work on investigating ASL as a first language and English print as a second language in Deaf students.
- 1987: Hoffmeister begins work on the American Sign Language Assessment Instrument as part of a research project examining reading in Deaf children.
- 1988: Hoffmeister and team of Deaf and Hearing graduate students create the first version of the ASLAI using videoprint for frozen images of signs to create answer booklets; ASLAI on cassette tapes is used to begin collecting data at The Learning Center for the Deaf (TLC).
- 1988: TLC becomes a bilingual-bicultural school.
- 1996: Hoffmeister refines the initial ASLAI tasks and begins to collect data across the US with assistance from Ben Bahan and Marie Philip.
- 2000: Hoffmeister establishes the Center for Research and Training (CRT) at TLC, a research and training center to examine and assess bilingual programs collecting data on both ASL as a first language and English print as a second language.
- 2000: Hoffmeister & Fisher design and implement a computerized version of the ASLAI: first time five video windows showing ASL clips are used to construct a multiple-choice test in ASL.
- 2007: The expressive component of the ASLAI is discontinued; technology had not caught up to make an expressive ASL test workable.
- 2010: Hoffmeister and Caldwell Harris receive first IES grant specifically to enhance digitization of current tasks.
- 2014: Hoffmeister and Caldwell Harris publish first step in a bilingual model of Language development in ASL and English print.
- 2015: A computerized multiple-choice ASL language measure is used to collect data on over 1,500 Deaf students.
- 2015: ASL norms for Deaf Children age 4 to 18 are created based on 1,500 students.
- 2016: CRT establishes procedures to make the ASLAI available to schools and programs for the Deaf nationwide.
- 2017: US Schools for the Deaf begin using the ASLAI.
- 2018: Currently data has been collected on over 2,000 Deaf students nationwide.

- 2019: CRT: The ASLAI is currently available for use by schools and programs serving Deaf students in the United States.

(R. Hoffmeister, personal communication, October 1, 2019)

Beginnings (1970s–1996)

At the University of Minnesota, while collecting and analyzing data from infant and toddler Deaf children coupled with advances in video technology, Hoffmeister began thinking about how to create an assessment that would provide information on ASL development in Deaf children. It wasn't until 1987 that the ASLAI began to be officially formatted, initially as a research instrument in connection with a Department of Education grant (Hoffmeister et al., 1988–1991) to examine English and Reading in Deaf children. At the outset, and before it was called the ASLAI, Hoffmeister wanted an instrument that would measure the actual language capabilities of Deaf children (R. Hoffmeister, personal communication, October 1, 2019)

Picture-to-sign tests [such as the Peabody Picture Vocabulary Test] were popular at the time, but Hoffmeister noticed that Deaf students he tested sometimes responded to a different element of the picture than that which was intended as the prompt. Hoffmeister gives the example of the Peabody Picture Vocabulary Test picture of a train engine: the answer is intended to be "Engineer." Not responding to the exact target created a definite disadvantage for Deaf children, because their answer would be counted as incorrect. Janis Cole, Janey Greenwald Czubek, and Ben Bahan worked as part of the team with Hoffmeister, DeVilliers, and Blackwell to figure out how to create a video of ASL and present it to deaf students, narrowing down a question requiring a limited range of response options.

At approximately the same time – the late 1980s – Dr. Ted Supalla and his team were also working on developing an ASL test for research. The Boston University team asked to borrow Ted Supalla's American Sign Language Test Battery to assist in the generation of ideas to develop an educational test for Deaf students. Supalla was generous and sent Hoffmeister a copy of his tasks in 1987. This was incredibly fortunate for Hoffmeister as now there seemed to be a model on which to create, develop, and implement ideas on how to accurately measure ASL. As a result, the initial ideas for the video version of an ASL measure were born.

Supalla's ASL test, incorporating 15 categories, was in development at the University of Illinois for use in research. The work was led by Ted Supalla working with Sam Supalla and Jenny Singleton. The idea of measuring ASL in children incorporated thinking that both expressive and receptive tasks needed to be developed. Many of Supalla's tasks were expressive, and the Boston University (BU) team began looking at how expressive tasks could be developed,

202 Patrick J. Costello

implemented, and scored. The BU team asked permission to use two expressive components of the University of Illinois measure: the "Verbs of Motion Production Assessment" (VMPA), and "Verb Agreement Production" (VAP) alongside the fledgling ASLAI, which at the time comprised only receptive tasks. Data was collected on over 300 students in schools across the United States. The person-hours to both collect the data, then analyze and score the data were enormous. Obtaining agreement on correctness of "signs" was incredibly difficult and time consuming. Although Hoffmeister continued to collect data on over 1,000 students using his own expressive tasks, these tasks were discontinued in 2007 because of lack of funding.

Due to the enormous problems in scoring the expressive tasks, Hoffmeister and his team analyzed these two expressive tasks of the Supalla test (VMPA and VAP) and used the results of these tasks as a model to create receptive tasks. Two new receptive tasks were created: the Real Objects (RO) task and the Plurals (PLU) task. The RO task expanded the ideas from the expressive tasks and created a multiple-choice receptive task. Videos were taken of real objects depicting both static and movement scenes; for example, a picture of a car on a highway passing a stop sign. These were paired with four signed response choices. Lana Cook later recalled that Hoffmeister asked the test development team to follow the common "multiple-choice" system of one answer being correct, one or two that were close but incorrect, and one or two that were far off the mark (L. Cook, personal communication, May 7, 2020). The original RO task consisted of 45 items. The verb agreement task was used later as a model to develop a syntax task when the computerized version of the ASLAI became available in the 2000s.

The Plurals (PLU) task was developed to examine an area in ASL that is not discussed very much. Items in the PLU task presented questions that examined simple and more complex plurals. For example, a simple plural could be a repetition of a noun, while a more complex plural might be when two classifiers are represented one on each hand, such as the 3CL or the BCL to represent a car. If the 3CL or the BCL is produced on each hand, this depicts two vehicles. If these classifiers are used in sentences, as in a drag race (both hands representing B handshape, palm down next to each other) or to depict spatial arrangements of objects, plurality is an underlying meaning. This can then be extended using the 3CL to reference an individual group of objects or the group as a whole: EACH CAR IN A ROW vs. ALL THE CARS IN A ROW. These sentences have different movements that depict their meanings. This task not only looked at plurality in ASL but at how classifiers function in different sentences.

Hoffmeister's team then analyzed the data collected from Supalla's receptive tasks. With the support and cooperation of Warren Schwab, founder and Executive Director of The Learning Center for the Deaf (now called Marie Philip School, the K-12 education component of The Learning Center for the Deaf). Supalla's Sign Order Comprehension (SOC) task was used to collect data on over 200 TLC students. After analyzing the data, the SOC task was felt to be a good task as a research measure, but it did not provide the statistical separation for age needed to look at language development from year to year. A different task needed to be developed and designed to measure syntax in ASL.

From the beginning, the BU team examined what were considered to be measures of "language" in hearing students. Most language acquisition tests were for children aged 0–4 or 0–5 years. But language tasks for older students consisted of tasks requiring reading or matching pictures to printed words. Most of these language tasks were included in academic achievement measures, which traditionally were also used for Deaf children. After examining a large number of 'language' tasks for hearing students, three or four tasks common to all the test versions were identified. The most common were the following measures: vocabulary (extent and depth), synonyms, antonyms, analogies, and sentence correctness. As a result of this examination, parallel ASL tasks were created: ASL synonyms (SYN), ASL antonyms (ANT), ASL simple vocabulary (VOCS) (extent), and at a later time the ASL rare or infrequent vocabulary (VST) (depth) task was designed. These components became the initial set of receptive ASL tasks implemented as part of the original Hoffmeister, DeVilliers, and Blackwell grant and research study.

During the early development, in an attempt to parallel tests of English for hearing children, the focus was on the synonyms and antonyms tasks in ASL. Hoffmeister noticed that identifying synonyms and antonyms requires different thinking on the part of students than a simple naming task: it requires using metalinguistic thinking. Students had to understand and make decisions based on correct similarity and an understanding of opposites in meaning. The team, at that time, held lengthy discussion sessions. There were obvious candidate items like "hot/cold," "black/white," but after those, determining how two items were different becomes more complicated. Over time the team developed enough examples to populate the Synonyms and Antonyms subtests.

Equipment

While researching ASL acquisition in the 1970s, Hoffmeister began working with video technology, using an "open reel" portable video camera, which had two open reels on a deck the size of a large shoebox, which hung by a strap from the camera operator's shoulder. A camera connected by a set of cables to the recording deck was mounted on the shoulder. This new video camera and playback system allowed Hoffmeister to collect data on very young Deaf Children of Deaf Parents in their homes. Within ten years, the original cumbersome video camera and separate recorder were replaced by an integrated video camera with a video cassette that rested on the shoulder. The video and recording were integrated into a somewhat large camera. This made collecting live ASL much easier and encouraged Hoffmeister to continue to pursue the idea of creating a test of ASL development.

FIGURE 13.1 ASL Synonyms Stimulus & Response Example (© 1989 Hoffmeister, R. ASL Synonyms)

In the early 1990s, Hoffmeister was hired to work on a grant with Duffy Engineering (National Institutes of Health – Small Business Innovation Research, NIH-SBIR) to create speech-to-text support for Deaf people and reduce dependence on the teletype (TTY) relays being developed at the time (Duffy Engineering, 1987–1991). Hoffmeister was introduced to the capabilities of technology, especially the power of the computer for video. During this time Hoffmeister began thinking about a standard five-part array of videos/pictures becoming part of each question for the ASL testing.

These innovation and research grants also allowed for the development of improved digitized booklets. By this time, the team at BU had grown: now Ben Bahan, Janis Cole, Janey Greenwald, and Vassilis Kourbetis were joined by Marie Philip, Patrick Costello, Jimmy Challis (Gore), Lana Cook, and other graduate students in the Education of the Deaf graduate program. Janis Cole and Lana Cook recalled that the work on the ASLAI was an education in academic work for those graduate students as well. Cole remembered Hoffmeister passing around quantities of books and articles among the group members for them to read and give their thoughts on: "I really benefited from working with him, learned about research. He has the most amazing mind, and all over the map. We'd have meeting after meeting, wide-ranging discussions, developing subtests, what they would look like, how it would be administered, in very, very specific detail" (J. Cole, personal communication, May 3, 2020). Lana Cook recalls Hoffmeister's "huge heart": "He'd always take all the staff out for Chinese food and talk politics, linguistics, international/national level goings-on at different colleges and universities, who was writing what kind of research, what each

Building the ASL Assessment Instrument **205**

researcher was known for, and we'd learn from that" (L. Cook, personal communication, May 7, 2020). Hoffmeister emphasized that without this team and all the Deaf and Hearing graduate students who followed, the ASLAI would never have been developed.

Recording and editing for the ASLAI were initially done offsite, at Cambridge Community Television (CCTV) studios in Cambridge, MA. Hoffmeister recalls hours spent in the studio filming Cole, then with Greenwald, Bahan, and Cole, editing recordings of the signing of the ASL prompts and answer choices. The team recorded a large number of potential test questions and four-option answers, not knowing which signs would yield the most discriminant information that they wanted. The edited videos were then transferred to ½" cassette tapes.

A key piece of equipment had just been created at the time, called the "video printer," which the team rented from Crimson Camera, Cambridge, MA. The video printer was connected to the video cassette editor and captured pictures of selected individual frozen frames of ASL signs on a strip of special paper. Specific frozen frames of ASL signs were selected to present the most salient segments of a sign. These static 'video' pictures were hand-cut and affixed by the team in a multiple-choice format on answer sheets. These originals were photocopied and assembled into the ASLAI answer booklets (see Figure 13.1 for an example of an answer sheet with 'video' pictures).

Hoffmeister was eventually able to purchase a video editor for the project. At the time, he notes, the editor cost some US$15,000. This allowed editing work to be completed in the lab at CSCD.

The Goal of Group Testing

One goal of developing ASL tasks was to be able to present the test to multiple students at the same time: group testing. Presenting the same stimuli to groups of deaf children reduced the variation found when different signers presented translations of printed tests to Deaf children. The availability of ½" cassette video for presenting the receptive tasks stimuli offered this opportunity at last. One issue was that the items were presented sequentially, not simultaneously as can be done in print. The task items were presented on a large TV (30"): the students had a printed version depicting the frozen forms of the task items and were asked to mark the picture of the sign that they thought was either a synonym, antonym, or rare sign. This was the first time ASL was presented without signed variation, in a signed-question-to-signed-responses format. The booklet (see Figure 13.1) contained frozen signed images printed on a page, allowing testing of groups of Deaf children for the first time. Most previous assessments had required 1:1 administration. The ASL receptive tasks were piloted at The Learning Center (TLC).

In 1996, formal testing began at TLC with the enthusiastic support of Executive Director Mike Bello. The testing setup for the receptive tasks had a

206 Patrick J. Costello

Deaf tester with a VCR and television in the front of a classroom. A circle of students, each with an answer booklet, were required to look at the TV. All the students needed to view the screen at the same time – looking away meant rewinding to view the segment again. Hoffmeister recalls Janis Cole as being very good at controlling this process and engaging the students. Most importantly, the research assistants noticed that the students liked the test. This was the first time that Deaf students had full access to a test in their language that could help them in their education.

The group testing of children's ASL abilities permitted the collection of a large amount of data in a short period of time. It also reduced testing time so that schools could fit the testing into their schedules.

Improvements (1996–early 2000s)

Improvement of the ASLAI was not always a smooth process. Upgrading a vocabulary task once led to a memorable two-hour argument between Hoffmeister, Philip, and Costello about the "correct" sign for TRUCK. Hoffmeister recalled the fireworks and pointed the blame at the influence of English, which uses the one lexical item "truck" for a wide variety of vehicles. He noted that many of the different signs for TRUCK were rooted in the appearances/functions of various types of trucks (the steering wheel "horizontal" instead of tilted up; the connection of a "tractor" with a "trailer"; lights along the top of some trucks; the bricklike shape of some trucks) appropriately marked in ASL. This confirmed Hoffmeister's belief (1996) that Signed English, Manually Coded English (MCE) and the myriad artificial "signs" used by hearing teachers can only end in failure.

While developing potential test items for vocabulary tasks, Hoffmeister researched various English tests of language for elementary school students. These tests stratified vocabulary according to high-frequency vs. low- and very-low-frequency words. Hoffmeister then wondered how best to identify low- and very-low-frequency signs. These were not regional variants, but rather low-frequency synonyms for more common signs.

Hoffmeister and his team consisting of Cook, Philip, Cole, and Bahan began to discuss the issue of signed vocabulary. One problem was that there were no studies done of frequent and infrequent ASL vocabulary as there were for spoken language. The team initiated a discussion to identify signs that very few hearing people would have been exposed to or would know. As a result of many extended discussions, the team came up with approximately 40 signs. Hoffmeister categorized these signs as "rare" or infrequent signs. From this initial list, 14 signs were selected to be used as test items. These became the foundation of a new subtest, the vocabulary in sentences task (VST). A vocabulary item (single sign) was presented, then four sentences using this item were presented. The student had to choose which sentence used the vocabulary item correctly. The researchers found that this proved to be a challenging task for the students due to lack of exposure, even though they had the advantage of viewing the item in context.

Bay State Road

I remember a graduate school dinner break with Hoffmeister, on a bench on Bay State Road behind the BU School of Education. Hoffmeister was envisioning the future of the ASLAI. He was certain that the way forward was an interface that would allow data to be recorded directly into a database from the subject's answer selections during the test, without the need for print booklets and data entry – essentially, the five-part array he had begun to envision during the NIH-SBIR grant. At the turn of the millennium, the ASLAI began to move toward becoming a computer-based test. Lana Cook recalled, "Bob was always very eager to expand the ASLAI. He was frustrated with his own limited technical skills and would avidly recruit others to help set up databases and other technical aspects" (L. Cook, personal communication, May 7, 2020). Cole added, "Bob was excited about how computer testing could put the data directly into a database for research and analysis. It was a real learning curve … the research was the fascinating part. He was brilliant about research and figuring out what needed to be done. He would find people who were specialists in statistics and the numbers part, because that was not his area. But Hoffmeister understood the big picture, and he had the vision." (J. Cole, personal communication, May 3, 2020). Many graduate students have expressed similar sentiments and benefits about the experience of working with Hoffmeister.

References

Duffy Engineering. (1987–1991) *Telecommunications for the deaf.* Mashpee, MA. (National Institutes of Health – Small Business Innovation Research Grant).

Hoffmeister, R. (1989). *The American Sign Language assessment instrument.* [Measurement Instrument]. Boston University.

Hoffmeister, R., DeVilliers, P., & Blackwell, P. (1988–1991) *English acquisition in the deaf.* The Corliss Institute, Boston University, and Smith College (National Institute on Disability and Rehabilitation Research Grant).

Hoffmeister, R. (1996). What do deaf kids know about ASL even though they see MCE! *Proceedings from Deaf Studies IV: Visions of the past – Visions of the future*, pp. 273–308. Gallaudet University Press.

14

ASSESSING ASL VOCABULARY DEVELOPMENT

Rama Novogrodsky

Acquisition of vocabulary is a *natural* process that occurs when children are exposed to language input and the language mechanism is intact. Children with typical language and no impairment, acquire *more words* with age. A child's specific vocabulary depends on his/her experience and interests.[1] One core question in language assessment is how to measure vocabulary. Vocabulary tests must be linguistically and culturally fair, to avoid a bias that will over diagnose children only because they are exposed to a variety of language input that does not include the tested items. Furthermore, it is important to avoid under diagnosis because a test is too easy and does not identify children with language difficulties. The question of how to measure vocabulary is relevant for professionals (educators and clinicians such as teachers, speech and language therapists, and psychologists) and for researchers. The current chapter presents evidence from the American Sign Language Assessment Instrument (ASLAI), highlighting its ability to demonstrate an in depth view of a child's vocabulary.

Vocabulary Development in Sign Language

While sign language is the mother tongue of signing communities, 90–95% of deaf children are born to hearing families (Mitchell & Karchmer, 2004) and are not naturally exposed to sign language from birth. Ideally, children are exposed to sign language during 0–3 early intervention programs, but this is not always the case. Later, when they attend a school or a program for the deaf, sign language will be part of the intervention (in the United States, usually at four to six years of age). The delay in exposure to sign language affects its acquisition in all linguistic domains (for an example of the effect on the acquisition of ASL syntax, see Novogrodsky, Henner, Caldwell-Harris, & Hoffmeister, 2017). The lack of

Assessing ASL Vocabulary Development **209**

exposure to sign language is crucial for language development because it leaves many deaf children with no access to language in their critical period for language acquisition. For numerous deaf children, access to spoken language is limited due to the hearing loss (Novogrodsky, Meir, & Michael, 2018), resulting in language deprivation. Specifically, it is not the limitation of the deafness but rather the lack of accessible linguistic input. (Henner, Novogrodsky, Reis, & Hoffmeister, 2018b). Thus, assessment of sign language is important as it estimates the child's knowledge and ability to acquire language naturally, in his intact modality. To test the child's vocabulary, there are various direct assessment measures (these are measures based on testing the child directly by an examiner, e.g., naming an object or a picture) and indirect assessment measures (these measures are based on indirect information from caregivers of the child, e.g., parental questionnaires).

For example, the MacArthur-Bates Communicative Developmental Inventory parental questionnaire (Frank, Braginsky, Yurovsky, & Marchman, 2017) is a common vocabulary assessment tool at preschool age. It has been adapted for different sign languages: American Sign Language (ASL) (Anderson & Reilly, 2002; Caselli & Pyers, 2017), British Sign Language (Thompson, Vinson, Woll, & Vigliocco, 2013), Israeli sign language (Novogrodsky & Meir, 2020), Spanish Sign language (Rodríguez-Ortiz, et al. 2019), and Turkish Sign Language (Sümer, Grabitz, & Küntay, 2017). Parents know their children best and at preschool age, they experience more hours with them than any external examiner does. The studies cited above showed that as children grew, their scores on the tests improved, indicating larger sign language vocabularies. This was shown across different sign languages, similar to children who acquire spoken languages (Frank et al., 2017). The Communicative Developmental Inventory is an indirect valid measure based on an adult's reporting. It displays vocabulary size of a child, its growth over time (when using the test at different time periods), and the characteristics of early lexicon use. For example, studies showed that iconicity (e.g., Novogrodsky & Meir, 2020) and frequency (e.g., Caselli & Pyers, 2017) of signs supports the process of early vocabulary acquisition. However, in the case of hearing parents who learn the sign language in parallel with their children, their reports might be less precise.

While indirect measures are valid for preschoolers, by school age, direct testing is required. According to Hoffmeister (1994), knowing a sign for a concept comprises three levels: its direct definition, its use in context, and a metalinguistic knowledge of its relations to other signs/words. One challenge at school age is the diverse experiences and cultural backgrounds children have, which will affect their performance on any vocabulary test.

The ASLAI tests include various subtests that explore ASL vocabulary breadth and depth. Here we present three of these tests: Synonym (Novogrodsky, Fish, & Hoffmeister, 2014), Antonym (Novogrodsky, Caldwell-Harris, Fish, & Hoffmeister, 2014a), and Analogical Reasoning (Henner, Caldwell-Harris, Novogrodsky, & Hoffmeister, 2016; Henner, Novogrodsky, Caldwell-Harris, & Hoffmeister, 2018a).

The three subtests are video-based, receptive, and multiple-choice tasks. The items represent frequent and infrequent signs from different lexical categories. For example, the Antonym subtest (Novogrodsky, et al., 2014a) includes pairs of adjective antonyms and pairs of verb antonyms. The items also represent various semantic fields. For example, in the Analogical Reasoning subtest (Henner, et al., 2016) the Whole-Part and Part-Whole items test participants' abilities to understand and produce proportional relationships from different semantic areas (e.g., NOSE is to FACE, like TIRE is to [CAR], which is the correct response). Each item in the tests consists of a prompt, a target, and three false options.

At the breadth level, the Synonym (Novogrodsky, Fish, & Hoffmeister, 2014b), Antonym (Novogrodsky, et al., 2014a), and Analogical Reasoning (Henner, et al., 2018a) subtests measure quantity scores. However, and this is critical, these subtests allow exploring the child's depth vocabulary knowledge beyond the quantity score. Depth knowledge infers the number of meanings of a sign a child knows, different usages of a sign, and the relationships between signs (for more discussion of breadth and depth of vocabulary knowledge, see, Novogrodsky, et al., 2014a). For example, does the child understand that different signs have the same meaning (e.g., WORK and DO-WORK[2])? Is the child aware of opposite semantic relations between signs (e.g., VAGUE and CLEAR) and how many analogical relations between signs does she knows (e.g., causal relations, RAIN–WET: SUN–DRY).

Our research showed that native signers scored higher on these three subtests compared with nonnative signers (Novogrodsky, et al., 2014b; Novogrodsky, et al., 2014a; Henner, et al., 2018a), supporting the importance of sign language input at an early age. However, when exploring the effects of age, Antonym knowledge and language status (being a native signer versus a nonnative signer) on English reading comprehension, the only variable that explained reading comprehension was the Antonym score (Novogrodsky, et al., 2014a). Nonnative signers who scored high on the Antonym subtest, scored high on the Stanford Achievement test – Reading Comprehension test (Traxler, 2000). This finding suggests that it is not the language status that counts (whether the child is a native or a nonnative signer) but rather knowledge of the language. Children who knew more antonyms, representing depth vocabulary knowledge, scored higher in a reading task. This result supports the need for language and the importance of a signing environment with linguistic input for children who are native, and even more so for nonnative signers.

The studies also showed that native signers reached a ceiling at middle school in both Synonym and Antonym subtests. This finding does not mean that children do not learn more synonyms and antonyms after this age but rather that the test is sensitive to evaluate development in elementary and middle school. For nonnative signers who scored lower than native signers, both subtests were sensitive throughout school age, including high school, suggesting that children use their knowledge of relationships between signs to learn more signs when the language is accessible to them, even during high school.

Notably, the analysis of the Analogical Reasoning subtest showed how different linguistic knowledge is required for various analogical relationships. For example, while syntactic abilities were linked to analogical reasoning items of noun-verb and causal relations, vocabulary (and syntax) were linked to whole-part reasoning items (Henner, et al., 2018a). This dissociation emphasizes how understanding a child's profile in different parts of the subtest discovers his/her deep linguistic knowledge. Clinically, scoring low on one of the Analogical Reasoning parts of the test and not on others can indicate possible language difficulties beyond the score of the test itself. For example, low scores on noun-verb and causal relations subtests and high scores on the other analogical reasoning subtests might support difficulties in syntax beyond analogical reasoning.

Finally, the ASLAI can be used to assess language disorders in deaf children. In a retrospective study (Novogrodsky, et al., 2014c), two native signers were tested three times over a period of years on the Synonym and Antonym subtests. Their reading comprehension scores and academic profile scores, as rated by teachers, were compared with the language measures. Both children demonstrated progress in their performance over the years, but it was consistently lower than that of their mean age group. In addition, their low performance on the ASLAI subtests was in line with their low reading comprehension scores and low academic profile scores. These findings add to the growing literature regarding language disorders among people/children who use sign languages (Mason, et al., 2010) and specifically in ASL (Quinto-Pozos, Forber-Pratt, & Singleton, 2011).

The subtests of the ASLAI are useful assessment tools beyond a simple score per age. Some children come from diverse ASL backgrounds and might not match the norms (Henner, et al., 2018b). For example, they use another sign language at home and ASL at school, or they use ASL variation (Woodward, 1973) that is not similar to the ASL of the test. In these cases, exploring the child's performance qualitatively might be useful (Hou & Kusters, 2019)[3]. For example, a child might not match his age score even if he understands the concept of antonyms and most of the errors are semantic (see the next section for more information regarding error analysis). This means that the child does not know the exact signs for the Antonym subtest, but has the linguistic capacity of antonyms. Following the child's progress after a period of time might substantiate this assumption.

Similarities between Signed and Spoken Languages

In addition to evaluating ASL vocabulary, the ASLAI research allowed comparison of acquisition patterns between sign language and spoken language measures from standardized spoken tests. As discussed in the first section, similarly to spoken languages, signing children's scores on vocabulary measures improved with age (e.g. on Analogical Reasoning, Henner, et al., 2016). The current section discusses additional similarities between signed and spoken modalities.

We explored error types on the Synonym subtest in two studies and showed that children's errors shifted from being primarily phonological to primarily semantic in the same way as children using spoken languages (for signs, Novogrodsky, et al., 2014b; Novogrodsky, Fish, & Hoffmeister, 2013; for words, Felzen & Anisfeld, 1970). At the beginning of elementary school, when hearing children erred in receptive vocabulary tasks, they tended to choose words that rhymed with the prompt items. In middle school, they chose words that were semantically related to the prompt items, when they did not know the answer (Felzen & Anisfeld, 1970). Error patterns on the Synonym subtest (Novogrodsky et al., 2013) revealed that with increasing age, native signers tended to prefer semantic false options over phonological false options when choosing the incorrect answer.[4] Additionally, when children had two phonological false options in a question, they preferred the phonologically close one over a distant phonological false option, suggesting that they prefer neighbor signs over signs that do not belong to the neighboring phonological category; in line with findings of hearing children (Garlock, Walley, & Metsala, 2001). In another study that explored errors, the analysis revealed similar findings. Both native and nonnative signing children demonstrated a decrease in phonological false choices with increasing age (Novogrodsky, et al., 2014b).

Another similarity between signed and spoken languages is the age when synonyms emerge. Global scores on the Synonym subtest showed chance performance at age four to five years. However, item analysis revealed that at this age, similarly to children acquiring spoken languages (Doherty & Perner, 1998), native signers performed above chance on three items of the subtest. This finding suggests that children who acquire ASL are expected to understand the semantic concept of synonym signs by age five.

Finally, the comparison between scores on the Synonym and Antonym subtests showed that at young ages, children performed higher on the latter, representing ease of acquisition of signs with opposite meanings, as compared to signs with similar meanings (Novogrodsky, et al., 2014a). The gap between the two tasks supports the theoretical idea of the principle of lexical contrast in acquisition (Clark, 1978). The idea behind this principle is that at early ages of language acquisition, it is easier for children to learn new words/signs with meanings that are different from known words/signs. As they age, children learn that there are also words/signs with other related synonyms. Clinically, it suggests that a young child is expected to score higher on the Antonym task than on the Synonym Task.

The examples presented in this section support the assumption that ASL vocabulary development of native signers follows the typical developmental path of children acquiring spoken vocabulary. This has important clinical implications, when testing a specific child's ASL knowledge. A child is expected to show

Assessing ASL Vocabulary Development **213**

typical age scores at any tested age for the different subtests of the ASLAI; each subtest has its own age reference norm. If a child does not meet the test criteria, intervention is suggested, as with children who communicate in spoken languages. Further, the child is expected to show increased scores with age, which is an option if one uses the ASLAI, as it has age reference scores throughout school age. Qualitative analysis of the performance allows understanding the child's deep vocabulary knowledge. Characteristics of the errors (e.g., phonological versus semantic); items known by the child at an early age and the gaps between subtests might shed light on ASL progress and on typical versus atypical acquisition. While the score on a subtest can give us an estimation of a child's vocabulary, a broader language capacity is hidden behind this number.

The Importance of Early Exposure to Sign Language

The research presented here supports the importance of early sign language exposure. Likewise, the findings support that both quantity and quality input of sign language show positive effects on children's performance (e.g., Henner, et al., 2016). The gap between native and nonnative signers persisted throughout the school-age years and was not easily closed even after years of ASL exposure (e.g., Novogrodsky, et al., 2014a). This is strong evidence for the benefits of early sign language input, representing a quantity effect of input. Furthermore, age of entry to school for the deaf also had a significant effect (Henner, et al., 2016). This variable relates to systematic exposure to ASL, specifically for nonnative signers, supporting the unique benefit of the qualitative sign language input children receive at school. The findings showed that age of entry into an academic signing environment after six years of age (regardless whether native or nonnative signer) was associated with poorer performance on the Analogical Reasoning subtest at later ages (Henner, et al., 2016). However, this qualitative effect does not mean that nonnative signers cannot develop proficient ASL; our findings indicate the contrary. For example, both native and nonnative signers with high ASL scores showed strong academic achievements based on their reading comprehension scores (2014a) and teacher ratings (Novogrodsky, et al., 2017). Furthermore, children who entered schools for the deaf at younger ages and had more years of ASL experience, had higher scores on the Analogical Reasoning subtest. Importantly, half of the nonnative signers scored as well as the native signers did on the Analogical Reasoning subtest (Henner, et al., 2016), demonstrating the ongoing effects of ASL learning.

The findings from the studies of ASLAI vocabulary subtests suggest that early sign language is necessary but is not sufficient. Ongoing linguistic input is the only way to develop a proficient vocabulary.

To conclude, the current chapter presented three ASLAI subtests illustrating how they can be used to assess ASL skills beyond simple comparisons to the norms. This was demonstrated through different qualitative analyses of the subtests, by comparisons among the subtests and by discussing the similarities between ASL and spoken languages. Finally, the importance of early ASL and qualitative input during the school years are suggested as keys to enabling children to become proficient signers.

Acknowledgments

The current chapter is based on the collaborative work of the ASLAI team. The author thanks specifically, Sara Fish, Jon Henner, Cathy Caldwell-Harris, and Robert Hoffmeister. During the writing of this chapter, Rama Novogrodsky was funded by an ISF grant (number 1068/16).

Notes

1 Some children learn all the Pokémon's names (hundreds of names with their specific features), other children know hundreds of sport players' names.
2 Following convention, all English glosses of ASL signs are written in capital letters.
3 The effect of bilingualism on children's lexical scores and the need to consider it in language assessment of a bilingual child is shown also in spoken languages (e.g., Degani, Kreiser, & Novogrodsky, 2019).
4 For example, for the prompt sign STUMPED, the semantic false options was DIFFI-CULT and the phonological false options was NAB, differing in only one phonological parameter from the prompt sign (Novogrodsky, et al., 2014b).

References

Anderson, D., & Reilly, J. (2002). The MacArthur Communicative Development Inventory: Normative data for American Sign Language. *Journal of Deaf Studies and Deaf Education, 7*, 83–106.

Caselli, N. K., & Pyers, J. E. (2017). The road to language learning is not entirely iconic: Iconicity, neighborhood density, and frequency facilitate acquisition of sign language. *Psychological Science, 28*(7), 979–987.

Clark, E. V. (1972). On the child's acquisition of antonyms in two semantic fields. *Journal of Verbal Learning and Verbal Behavior, 11*, 750–758.

Degani, T., Kreiser, V., & Novogrodsky, R. (2019). The joint effects of bilingualism, DLD and item-frequency on children's lexical retrieval performance. *International Journal of Language and Communication Disorders, 54*(3), 485–498.

Doherty, M., & Perner, J. (1998). Metalinguistic awareness and theory of mind: Just two words for the same thing? *Cognitive Development, 13*, 279–305.

Felzen, E., & Anisfeld, M. (1970). Semantic and phonetic relations in the false recognition of words by third- and sixth-grade children. *Developmental Psychology, 3*, 163–168.

Frank, M. C., Braginsky, M., Yurovsky, D., & Marchman, V. A. (2017). Wordbank: An open repository for developmental vocabulary data. *Journal of Child Language, 44*(3), 677–694.

Garlock, V. M., Walley, A. C., & Metsala, J. L. (2001). Age-of-acquisition, word frequency, and neighborhood density effects on spoken word recognition by children and adults. *Journal of Memory and Language, 45*(3), 468–492.

Henner, J., Caldwell-Harris, C., Novogrodsky, R., & Hoffmeister, R. (2016). American Sign Language syntax and analogical reasoning skills are influenced by early acquisition and age of entry to signing schools for the Deaf. *Frontiers in Psychology*, 7, 1982.

Henner, J., Novogrodsky, R., Caldwell-Harris, C., & Hoffmeister, R. (2018a). The development of American Sign Language–based analogical reasoning in signing deaf children. *Journal of Speech, Language, and Hearing Research*, 62(1), 93–105.

Henner, J., Novogrodsky, R., Reis, J., & Hoffmeister, R. (2018b). Recent Issues in the use of signed language assessments for diagnosis of language related disabilities in signing deaf and hard of hearing children. *Journal of Deaf Studies and Deaf Education*, 23(4), 307–316.

Hoffmeister, R. J. (1994). *Metalinguistic skills in deaf children: Knowledge of synonyms and antonyms in ASL* (pp. 151–175). Washington, DC: Gallaudet University Press, *Post Milan: ASL and English Literacy Conference*.

Hou, L., & Kusters, A. M. J. (2019). *The Routledge handbook of linguistic ethnography* (pp. 340–355). Routledge.

Mason, K., Rowley, K., Marshall, C. R., Atkinson, J. R., Herman, R., Woll, B., & Morgan, G. (2010). Identifying specific language impairment in deaf children acquiring British Sign Language: Implications for theory and practice. *British Journal of Developmental Psychology*, 28(1), 33–49.

Mitchell, R. E., & Karchmer, M. A. (2004). Chasing the mythical ten percent: Parental hearing status of deaf and hard of hearing students in the United States. *Sign Language Studies*, 4, 138–163.

Novogrodsky, R., Caldwell-Harris, C., Fish, S., & Hoffmeister, R. J. (2014a). The development of antonym knowledge in American Sign Language (ASL) and its relationship to reading comprehension in English. *Language Learning*, 64(4), 749–770.

Novogrodsky, R., Fish, S., & Hoffmeister, R. (2013). Semantic and phonological knowledge of native signers of American Sign Language (ASL) in a synonym task. *LSA Meeting Extended Abstracts 2013*.

Novogrodsky, R., Fish, S., & Hoffmeister, R. (2014b). The acquisition of synonyms in American Sign Language (ASL): Toward a further understanding of the components of ASL vocabulary knowledge. *Sign Language Studies*, 14(2), 225–249.

Novogrodsky, R., Henner, J., Caldwell-Harris, C., & Hoffmeister, R. (2017). The development of sensitivity to grammatical violations in American Sign Language: native versus nonnative signers. *Language Learning*, 67(4), 791–818.

Novogrodsky, R., Hoffmeister, R., Fish, S., Benedict, R., Henner, J., Rosenburg, P., Conlin-Luippold, F., & Caldwell-Harris, C. (2014c). Two case studies of SLI in American Sign Language (ASL). A poster presented at a workshop of Specific Language Impairment, Experimental Psycholinguistics Conference (ERP), Madrid, Spain.

Novogrodsky, R., & Meir, N. (2020). Age, frequency and iconicity in early sign language acquisition: Evidence from the Israeli sign language MacArthur-Bates communicative developmental inventory. *Applied Psycholinguistics*.

Novogrodsky, R., Meir, N., & Michael, R. (2018). Morpho-syntactic abilities of toddlers with hearing-impairment and normal hearing: evidence from a sentence repetition task. *International Journal of Language and Communication Disorders*, 53(4), 811–824.

Quinto-Pozos, D., Forber-Pratt, A. J., & Singleton, J. L. (2011). Do developmental communication disorders exist in the signed modality? Perspectives from professionals. *Language, Speech, and Hearing Services in Schools*, 42, 423–443. https://doi.org/10.1044/0161-1461(2011/10-0071).

Rodríguez-Ortiz, I. R., Pérez, M., Valmaseda, M., Cantillo, C., Díez, M. A., Montero, I., & Saldaña, D. (2019). A Spanish Sign Language (LSE) Adaptation of the Communicative Development Inventories. *The Journal of Deaf Studies and Deaf Education*.

Sümer, B., Grabitz, C., & Küntay, A. (2017). Early produced signs are iconic: Evidence from Turkish Sign Language. In *the 39th Annual Conference of the Cognitive Science Society (CogSci 2017)* (pp. 3273–3278). Cognitive Science Society.

Traxler, C. B. (2000). The Stanford Achievement Test: National norming and performance standards for deaf and hard-of-hearing students. *Journal of Deaf Studies and Deaf Education, 5*, 337–348.

Thompson, R. L., Vinson, D. P., Woll, B., & Vigliocco, G. (2013). The road to language learning is iconic: Evidence from British Sign Language. *Psychological Science, 23(12)*, 1443–1448.

Woodward, J. C., Jr (1973). Some observations on sociolinguistic variation and American Sign Language. *Kansas Journal of Sociology, 9(2)*, 191–200.

15

ASSESSING ASL

Comprehension, Narrative, and Phonological Awareness

Lynn McQuarrie and Charlotte Enns

"A real voyage of discovery consists not of seeking new landscapes but of seeing through new eyes." ~ Marcel Proust

Formal methods of signed language assessment are fundamental to the provision of an equitable education for bilingual deaf children (Enns & Herman, 2011). Not only does valid assessment form a crucial aspect in effective language teaching and planning, the ability to successfully monitor students' language and academic progress can play a powerful role in the legitimization and public acceptance of bilingual programs. Although there are many assessments for evaluating the influence of spoken language skills on learning, there are few comparable assessments of deaf children's signed language ability for educational use (see Herman, 1998, Hoffmeister, 2000, Mann & Prinz, 2006, Singleton & Supalla, 2011). For assessments to be useful to educators, standardized norms for monitoring phonological acquisition and receptive and expressive signed language skills in young deaf children are needed. By identifying norms for language development, signed language development can be monitored to ensure that deaf children acquire language structures (e.g., vocabulary, syntax, and grammar) at rates comparable to those for hearing children. The work we report on in this chapter was initiated to fill this gap with the goal to develop effective tools for monitoring the normative process of American Sign Language (ASL) acquisition in deaf children. These assessments will help educators monitor whether the ASL acquisition of a given child is delayed, advanced, or developing normally.

In the past, the assessment of signed language abilities in deaf children was generally not considered necessary because it was deemed unrelated to their academic programming. In programs focusing on a monolingual approach, there was no recognition of signed languages as separate languages, even those incorporating sign systems of a spoken language (e.g., Signed English, Total Communication). So signed language assessments were either not done at all or were done using informal measures (Hoffmeister, Kuntze, & Fish, 2013). As educational programming shifted to incorporate a cultural perspective on Deaf people and bilingual programming in the 1980s, more emphasis was placed on assessing and monitoring children's signed language skills. However, the development of signed language abilities was seen primarily as a way of enhancing spoken and written language skills. For this reason, formal assessments typically consisted of simply adapting existing spoken language tests by administering them in signed language. Using translated tests is problematic because they are not developed for deaf children or signed languages, the norms based on spoken languages often do not apply to signed languages, and translated tests may not be assessing the same things in another language (Woll, 2016). For example, naming body parts is often used to assess preschool English vocabulary, but in ASL, simply pointing to the body part represents the name/sign, so the test item does not measure the same developmental construct and level of vocabulary acquisition. In general, the results of these translated assessments were not accurate and often did not focus on relevant or appropriate structures of signed languages.

It was only through the strong advocacy of pioneers, like Hoffmeister (2000), who believed in the legitimacy of signed languages and the benefits they could contribute to children's learning that tests specifically designed to assess children's abilities in signed languages were developed. There has been increased research interest over the past decade to create tests specifically developed and designed to assess signed languages and to fit with the visual learning needs of deaf children. As only a few of such signed language tests have been developed, the variety of assessments available is limited in comparison to tests for spoken language, particularly regarding different components of language (receptive, expressive, phonology, vocabulary, syntax, and discourse). Research regarding signed language assessment is only possible due to increased knowledge and data related to signed language acquisition (Baker & Woll, 2009) because identifying atypical development cannot occur until there is a solid understanding and definition of the typical developmental sequence. As a result, test development is not possible in signed languages where limited linguistic research is available. The connection between signed language acquisition research and the development of practical assessment tools continues to be strengthened and extended across signed languages in the creation of important experimental and formal measures. The increased accuracy of these measures contributes to determining a more complete picture of children's overall linguistic abilities to more effectively guide their literacy development and academic learning.

The purpose of administering a signed language assessment with deaf children varies and includes both educational and research objectives (Enns & Herman, 2011). Often, the purpose of assessment is to determine overall signed language proficiency, or the level of knowledge of particular aspects of signed language.

For educators, key purposes of assessment are to guide instruction and to monitor progress (Stiggins, 2002). Assessment should be comprehensive and address a range of language features, as well as the use of language in various contexts. Such assessment requires knowledge of signed language acquisition, so that assessment can focus on the components and structures of signed language that are most indicative of delays or disorders in development (Quinto-Pozos, Singleton, & Hauser, 2017). This can be accomplished through both formal and informal measures, as long as they accurately identify language strengths and difficulties (i.e., provide diagnostic information). Several different tests are often needed to provide a complete picture of a child's signed language abilities so that appropriate programming and instruction can be determined.

The following section outlines three ASL tests for assessing specific components of language including receptive and expressive ASL grammar knowledge and ASL phonological awareness. The tests are described separately, according to each of the language components, but test results must be considered in combination and compiled to form a complete picture of a child's language abilities.

Test Descriptions

ASL Receptive Skills Test

The *ASL Receptive Skills Test (ASL-RST)* (Enns, Zimmer, Boudreault, Rabu, & Broszeit, 2013) measures children's (ages 3–13 years) comprehension of ASL morphology and syntax. The test was adapted from the *British Sign Language Receptive Skills Test* (Herman, Holmes, & Woll, 1999) through a series of phases, including consultation with experts, development of new test items, videotaping of ASL stimuli, and re-drawing of picture responses. Two rounds of pilot testing were administered with native signing children (deaf children of deaf parents) to establish appropriate stimuli and distracter items and the accurate developmental ordering of test items. Following the first round of pilot testing (with 47 children in Canada and the United States), revisions were needed for 23 of the original 41 pilot test items, and four new items were added to assess understanding of the more complex structures of role shift and conditional clauses. The second round of pilot testing revealed that modifications to previous test items and the new test items made the test more challenging and more clearly distinguished children's skills at different ages. Analysis comparing age and raw score showed a significant correlation and high *r* value (r (34) = 0.821, p < .001). Final modifications included deleting three test items (considered redundant) and re-ordering test items to more appropriately reflect the developmental sequence of ASL acquisition (for more detailed information regarding the adaptation process, please see Enns & Herman, 2011).

The *ASL-RST* uses a vocabulary check (20 items) that precedes the main test of 42 items. The purpose of the vocabulary check is to ensure that the child

FIGURE 15.1   Example of ASL-RST Test Item

knows the signs used in the test, and therefore any incorrect responses can be attributed to not understanding the ASL morphology and syntax. The *ASL-RST* assesses eight grammatical structures: (1) number/distribution, (2) noun-verb distinction, (3) negation, (4) spatial verbs, (5) handling classifiers, (6) size-and-shape classifiers, (7) conditional clauses, and (8) role shift. The original test format (video of stimulus items and picture book of responses) was revised by digitizing the picture responses and incorporating them into the test USB (Figure 15.1). This eliminates the need for the picture book, and the child is not required to shift eye gaze between the computer screen and the picture book, thus reducing distractibility errors.

The child's raw score (out of a possible 42 items) is converted to a standard score (mean = 100; standard deviation = 15) to determine categorization into Above Average, Average, and Below Average according to same-age peers. The normative (standardization) sample is based on 203 children throughout Canada and the United States. Deaf children from hearing families were included in the standardization sample; however, only if they had been exposed to ASL by age 3 or younger (according to parental report or attendance in ASL preschool program). All 203 children were deaf and had a non-verbal IQ of 70 or above (or where formal testing was not available, were determined to be functioning within the average range intellectually by school personnel). There were 77 native signers and 126 nonnative signers (acquired <3 years old), 106 females and 97 males, and the ages ranged from 3 to 13 years. Testing took place in the children's schools and was administered by deaf and hearing researchers with fluent ASL skills. We recognize that our sample of 203 children may be limited in how accurately it represents the overall population of deaf children, and for this reason, future research will involve additional testing and data collection to expand our sample. However, statistical analyses of the standardization data revealed that the test is reliable (showed internal consistency) and is a valid measure of developmental changes in ASL comprehension.

ASL Expressive Skills Test

The *ASL Expressive Skills Test (ASL-EST)* (Enns, Zimmer, Broszeit, & Rabu, 2019) is an adaptation of the *British Sign Language Production Test* (Herman *et al.* 2004), which involves a narrative elicitation task through the use of a language-free story on video (Spider Story). Specifically, the child watches the video story and then spontaneously re-tells the story, including answering three comprehension questions. The child's responses are video recorded and analyzed according to specific scoring guidelines. Analysis and scoring focus on narrative content/structure (events in the story and story development), as well as ASL grammar, including spatial verbs, agreement verbs, aspect, manner, and role shift. *ASL-EST* testers must be trained (attend a mandatory training workshop) to ensure that they have the necessary skills to score the narratives accurately and consistently.

An important aspect of developing the *ASL-EST* was to create additional versions of the test, or parallel video-based stories that would elicit comparable narratives. Having alternate elicitation videos allows for re-testing students without them becoming familiar with the story over repeated viewings. Creating additional video stories also facilitated updating the original Spider Story, from the BSL test, to incorporate American cultural features and improve the video quality. The two new stories, "Home Alone" and "Tiffany's Breakfast", follow the basic narrative structure of the Spider Story. Each story consists of similar events (a series of back-and-forth interactions between protagonist and antagonist) but with slightly different settings, characters, and consequences. There are also parallels between the objects and actions in each of the stories that allow for opportunities to elicit the same kinds of grammatical structures (spatial verbs, agreement verbs, aspect, manner, and role shift). Pilot testing of the three stories/versions of the test was conducted with a sample (n = 47) of typically developing ASL signers aged 4–12 years. The results of pilot testing confirmed the effectiveness and reliability of the scoring guidelines, as well as equivalency across the three test versions.

The *ASL-EST* was standardized on a sample of 215 deaf children attending schools for the deaf in Canada and the United States between the ages of 3.5 years and 13.9 years. The sample was not exactly gender balanced, with 125 girls and 90 boys, but no statistical evidence for differences in test performance based on gender were found (ANOVA Sig = 0.933, greater than 0.05). Also, most of the children (n = 144) had at least one deaf parent, with the remaining 71 children having nondeaf parents. Again, no statistical evidence was found for differences in test performance between children with deaf parents or nondeaf parents (Asymp. Sig = 0.659, greater than 0.05). It is important to keep in mind that the sample was selective and only children with early exposure to ASL (before the age of 3 years) were included. The purpose of this selection was to have a normative sample that represents what achievements are possible when children have early and rich full access to language, or are acquiring ASL age-appropriately.

In order to check if the test was measuring what it was designed to measure (children's ASL abilities), scores (based on the categories of average, above average, below average) from the *ASL-EST* were compared with the same children's scores on the *ASL Receptive Skills Test* using a Pearson's correlation. A highly significant correlation (0.91, p < 0.01) was found, suggesting good concurrent test validity. Inter-scorer reliability was assessed by having 10% (30 videos) of the data independently scored by two different trained testers and comparing the results. Statistical analysis using Pearson's correlation resulted in a highly significant correlation of 0.87 (p < 0.01), indicating inter-scorer reliability was very good.

An investigation of the relationship between children's ages and total test scores revealed a weak linear relationship (R-Square Linear = 0.619). These findings were supported with both Pearson and Spearman's rho coefficients and the results were 0.787 and 0.767, respectively, which were slightly better (greater than 0.70). These statistical analyses point out the considerable variability that occurred in children's scores at each age level. For this reason, percentiles, rather than standard scores, are used when comparing individual scores to the norms. Percentiles are based on mean scores, and the range of scores around the mean, at each age level, for the Total score, and the sub-sections of Grammar, Role Shift, Questions, and Narrative. The younger children are grouped by one-year age ranges (4-, 5-, and 6-year olds), whereas the older children are grouped in two-year (7- to 8-year olds) or multi-year (9 years and older) ranges. The reason for this is because rapid language development occurs in these younger years, but development levels out as children get older. Also, grouping the ages together allows for larger numbers of participants in each group, which provides a more reliable basis for the means and percentiles. As noted previously, there was considerable variability within the groups, particularly for the younger ages; however, the *ASL-EST* is an effective measure for assessing and diagnosing the strengths and weaknesses of children's expressive ASL abilities.

American Sign Language Phonological Awareness Test

The American Sign Language Phonological Awareness Test (ASL-PAT) (McQuarrie & Cundy, 2019) is a computer-based test designed to assess children's (4–13 years) awareness of the phonological structure of ASL (i.e., the sublexical parameters of handshape [HS], location [L], and movement [M]). The ASL-PAT measures a child's ability to identify phonological similarity relations (i.e. discriminate minimal contrasts) in signs across three comparison conditions: signs with three (HS + L + M), two (HS + M, L + M, and HS + L), or one (HS, M, or L) shared parameters.

Test Construction. McQuarrie's (2005) receptive-based phonological similarity judgment task (picture matching-to-sample) was used as a prototype in developing a downward extension of the measure more suitable for 4- to 13-

year-old children. Test construction began in 2012 as part of a larger project on dual language literacy development. The aim was to develop a signed language phonological measure that was quick to administer for educators, yet sensitive enough to discriminate young children's phonological knowledge based on age, and to distinguish native and late-learners of ASL. A first draft of the ASL-PAT (24 test items) was developed within this project. To ensure validity in the development of the assessment, a large pool of potential test items was constructed and vetted by a team of Deaf native ASL users who were knowledgeable about child signed language development and were able to suggest representative and age-appropriate content. The items were then pilot-tested on a group of 12 deaf children (four children in each of the youngest age categories). The purpose of the pilot test was to evaluate the feasibility, usefulness, and usability of the test items, and to examine the effectiveness of the instructions, items, and item delivery method (see McQuarrie, Abbott, & Spady, 2012 for more information regarding test development and design). Building on the knowledge acquired in this phase of test development, a final version of the ASL-PAT was optimized by including 48 test items that best predict phonological awareness in ASL and are most sensitive to developmental differences in phonological awareness. A four-year norming study for the ASL-PAT is currently underway. Data is being collected from multiple schools with a high number of DHH students in Canada and United States. To date (year 3 of the study) 175 children have been tested; a subgroup of deaf children of deaf parents will be used to establish normative scores for each age group (Group 1: ages 4–4:11, Group 2: 5–5:11, etc.). At time of writing, we anticipate that a one-year extension to this project will be necessary due to school closures related to the COVID-19 pandemic.

Test Procedures. The testing procedure consists of five phases: (1) log in and background demographic questionnaire, (2) vocabulary check, (3) instruction video in ASL, (4) Part 1 practice trials and test block, and (5) Part 2: practice trials and test block. The testing takes about 15–20 minutes for each test-taker.

Log in/Questionnaire: An identification number is assigned to each user on log in. A brief questionnaire including background information (e.g., date of birth, gender, age of onset, age of exposure/acquisition, use of hearing technologies, and age of implantation) is completed online by the test administrator.

Vocabulary Check: The test begins with a vocabulary check in the form of a picture dictionary presented as a 5×5 grid picture display. Children are instructed to name each picture in ASL. If a child is uncertain or unable to generate a sign for a picture item, a video prompt of the sign is available by clicking on the picture. Prompted items are subsequently added to the end of the picture display and retested without the video prompt prior to beginning the test. It is essential that children associate the correct sign with each test pictures prior to taking the test; thus, if a child was unable to name all items, testing would be discontinued at this point.

Instruction Video: At the completion of the vocabulary check, participants watch an instructional video in ASL presented by a Deaf adult native signer. The instructions are child friendly, the parameters of sign formation (HS, M, L) are reviewed, and an example of what the test items look like and what the child is required to do is modeled. The instructions encourage the children to try their best.

Practice and Test Block: Each practice and test question screen consists of a signed cue (video), with three picture items below representing the target/phonological match and two distracter items (see Figure 15.2). Test-takers are required to select the picture that best matches the signed cue along the phonological parameter(s) tested. The test consists of two sections. Part 1 requires discriminating a single parameter match between cue and target (i.e. identifying signs made with the same HS, L, or M). Students complete three practice trial questions (one practice example for each parameter). The students are given feedback on the practice trials. Twenty-four test questions immediately follow this practice. No feedback is provided on test items. Part 2 requires discrimination along two or three shared parameters and includes four practice trials followed by 24 test items. Again, feedback is provided on the practice items, no feedback is provided on test items.

Scoring: An online database records accuracy (correct match – 1; incorrect match – 0) and error response choice for each test item. Overall test performance

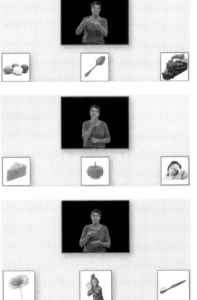

3 shared parameters: HS + M + L
- Signed Cue: SOON
- Picture Items: Eggs, Spoon, Train
- PA Target: TRAIN

2 shared parameters: HS + M; L + M; or HS + L
- Signed Cue: LIGHT
- Picture Items: Cheese, Pumpkin, Sick
- PA Target: PUMPKIN

1 shared parameter: HS, M, or L
- Signed Cue: MONEY
- Picture Items: Flower, Clown, Toothbrush
- PA Target: FLOWER

FIGURE 15.2 Example ASL-PAT Test Items

scores are determined by the number of correct responses out of 48. Reaction/response time data is also recorded. Similar to the ASLAI (Hoffmeister, 1999), multiple users can access the assessment at the same time, and all individual user responses are uploaded to a central database in real time. However, given the young age of our test-takers, we have maintained a standard practice of individual administration.

Upon completion of the norming study, the ASL-PAT will be available for teachers and clinicians to provide information on children's sign phonological development and to identify children who lack explicit sign phonological knowledge. Of note, previous versions of the ASL-PAT have been used in various research studies in which the predictive relation between ASL phonological awareness and written/spoken language skills in English was studied. Evidence of positive relationships between signed language phonological awareness and measures of English word recognition and reading comprehension were documented in bilingual deaf students aged 7–18 using the first version of the test (76 test items) (see McQuarrie & Abbott, 2013; see review in McQuarrie & Parrila, 2014). In addition, results from a school-based signed language phonological awareness intervention study (see McQuarrie & Enns 2015; 2018) document a clear functional relation between explicit instruction in ASL phonological awareness and increases in sign vocabulary and print vocabulary learning in young (ages 6–10) deaf dual language learners. Changes on the ASL-PAT (24 test items) administered at the beginning and end of the intervention confirmed these results. More recently, Keck & Wolgemuth (2020) report positive correlations between ASL phonological awareness skills (as measured by the ASL-PAT and English reading skills in deaf children (ages 4.7–13.7) who had early ASL exposure (i.e., deaf children with deaf parents, n = 27). Taken together, the evidence that knowledge transfer of signed language phonological awareness correlates with English reading skills suggests that assessing signed language phonological awareness can provide insights into young bilingual deaf children's readiness for learning to read. In addition, it will allow educators to establish targeted phonological learning objectives and plan effective sign phonological instructional interventions for bilingual deaf students.

Conclusion

Language assessment for the purpose of guiding instruction with deaf dual language learners needs to provide diagnostic information about the specific components of both spoken and signed language that contribute to learning. In the past, deaf children's dual language resources were often not acknowledged, and therefore, could not be leveraged for language and literacy instruction. As more research becomes available regarding bilingual and multilingual learners, there is also more evidence for the ways that a robust signed language foundation can facilitate spoken and written language abilities. In particular, signed language

226 Lynn McQuarrie and Charlotte Enns

skills (as L1) contribute to establishing background knowledge, concepts, and content and facilitate the development of strategies, like problem-solving and abstract thinking. These are the potential language resources that Hoffmeister (2000) recognized decades ago when he emphasized the importance of deaf children learning ASL for its own merit – not simply as a stepping stone or bridge to learning English – but for the explicit value of establishing fundamental cognitive structures and learning mechanisms that are needed for all higher-level thinking and academic development. Assessing the degree to which deaf children have acquired these concepts and strategies, sheds light on how best to scaffold their ongoing language and literacy learning processes.

Although there is an ongoing need for additional valid and reliable assessments of signed language abilities, there are currently a few tools available, as described in this chapter, that can assist educators and researchers in determining the strengths and gaps in children's ASL abilities that contribute to language and literacy development. For information on additional signed language assessment please refer to Enns *et al.* (2016).

The development of signed language assessments has led to an increased understanding of the influence of signed language skills on learning (Hoffmeister & Caldwell-Harris, 2014; Mayberry & Kluender, 2018). It has also led to more widespread recognition of the consequences on learning that result from variability and diversity in children's language repertoires (e.g., Lederberg *et al.* 2019; Quinto-Pozos *et al.* 2017). As noted by Swanwick (2016) "this new knowledge also highlights the need for more integrated approaches to assessment which recognize the fluctuating dominance of different languages in children's lives and different language proficiencies across different domains" (p. 15). Understanding and applying the knowledge gained from assessing all language abilities, including and in particular signed language skills, will help educators and researchers to see the learning potential of deaf children through new eyes.

References

Baker, A. E., & Woll, B. (2009). *Sign language acquisition.* Amsterdam: John Benjamins.

Enns, C., Haug, T., Herman, R., Hoffmeister, R., Mann, W., & McQuarrie, L. (2016). Exploring signed language assessment tools around the world. In M. Marschark, V. Lampropoulou & E. K. Skordilis (Eds.), *Diversity in deaf education* (pp. 171–218). New York, NY: Oxford University Press.

Enns, C., & Herman, R. (2011). Adapting the assessing British Sign Language development: Receptive skills test into American Sign Language. *Journal of Deaf Studies and Deaf Education, 16*, 362–374.

Enns, C., Zimmer, K., Boudreault, P., Rabu, S., & Broszeit, C. (2013). *American Sign Language Receptive Skills Test.* Winnipeg, MB: Northern Signs Research, Inc.

Enns, C., Zimmer, K., Broszeit, C., & Rabu, S. (2019). *American Sign Language Expressive Skills Test.* Winnipeg, MB: Northern Signs Research, Inc.

Herman, R. (1998). The need for an assessment of deaf children's signing skills. *Deafness and Education: Journal of the British Association of the Teachers of the Deaf, 22*(3), 3–8.

Herman, R., Grove, N., Holmes, S., Morgan, G., Sutherland, H., & Woll, B. (2004). *Assessing BSL development: Production test (narrative skills).* London, UK: City University Publication.

Herman, R., Holmes, S., & Woll, B. (1999). *Assessing BSL Development: Receptive Skills Test.* Coleford, UK: Forest Bookshop.

Hoffmeister, R. J. (1999). *American Sign Language assessment instrument (ASLAI). Unpublished test, Center for the Study of Communication & the Deaf.* Boston: Boston University.

Hoffmeister, R. J. (2000). A piece of the puzzle: ASL and reading comprehension in Deaf children. In C. Chamberlain, J. P. Morford & R. I. Mayberry (Eds.), *Language acquisition by eye* (pp. 143–163). Mahwah, NJ: Lawrence Erlbaum Associates.

Hoffmeister, R. J., & Caldwell-Harris, C. L. (2014). Acquiring English as a second language via print: The task for deaf children. *Cognition, 132*(2), 229–242.

Hoffmeister, R. J., Kuntze, M., & Fish, S. (2013). Assessing American Sign Language. In A. J. Kunnan (Ed.), *The Companion to Language Assessment (Vol. 4)* Assessment Around the World. Malden, MA: Wiley-Blackwell.

Keck, T., & Wolgemuth, K. (2020). American Sign Language phonological awareness and English reading abilities: Continuing to explore new relationships. *Sign Language Studies, 20*(2), 334–354.

Lederberg, A. R., Branum-Martin, L., Webb, M., Schick, B., Antia, S., Easterbrooks, S. R., & Connor, C. (2019). Modality and interrelations among language, reading, spoken phonological awareness, and fingerspelling. *Journal of Deaf Studies and Deaf Education, 24*(4), 1–16.

Mann, W., & Prinz, P. M. (2006). An investigation of the need for sign language assessment in deaf education. *American Annals of the Deaf, 151*(3), 356–370.

Mayberry, R. I., & Kluender, R. (2018). Rethinking the critical period for language: New insights into an old question from American Sign Language. *Bilingualism: Language and Cognition, 21*(5), 886–905.

McQuarrie, L. (2005). *American Sign Language Phonological Similarity Judgement Task.* Edmonton, Alberta: [Unpublished test] University of Alberta.

McQuarrie, L., & Abbott, M. (2013). Bilingual Deaf students' phonological awareness in ASL and reading skills in English. *Sign Language Studies, 14*(1), 80–100. 10.1353/sls. 2013.0028.

McQuarrie, L., Abbott, M., & Spady, S. (2012). *American Sign Language phonological awareness: Test development and design* (pp. 142–158). Honolulu, Hawaii##*10th Annual Hawaii International Conference on Education*

McQuarrie, L., & Cundy, L. (2019). *The American Sign Language Phonological Awareness Test (ASL-PAT).* Edmonton, AB: Sign2Read Literacy Initiatives Inc.

McQuarrie, L., & Enns, C. (2018). *Developing sign-symbol aptitude to support word reading acquisition.* Paper presented at the Workshop on Reading, Language and Deafness (WoRLD), Basque Centre on Cognition Brain and Language, San Sebastian, Spain.

McQuarrie, L., & Enns, C. (2015, July). *Bridging the gap: Investigating the effects of a signed language phonological awareness intervention on language and literacy outcomes in bilingual deaf children.* Paper presented at the 22nd International Congress on the Education of the Deaf (ICED), Athens, Greece.

McQuarrie, L., & Parrila, R. (2014). Literacy and linguistic development in bilingual deaf children: Implications of the 'and' for phonological processing. *American Annals of the Deaf, 159*(4), 372–384.

Proust, M., Scott-Moncrieff, C. K., Kilmartin, T., & Enright, D. J. (1992). *In search of lost time. (À la recherche du temps perdu #1–7).* London: Chatto & Windus.

Quinto-Pozos, D., Singleton, J., & Hauser, P. (2017). A case of specific language impairment in a deaf signer of American Sign Language. *Journal of Deaf Studies and Deaf Education, 22*(2), 204–218.

Singleton, J. L., & Supalla, S. J. (2011). Assessing children's proficiency in natural signed languages. In M. Marschark & P. E. Spencer (Eds.), *The Oxford handbook of deaf studies, language, and education, volume 1, second edition* (pp. 289–302). New York, NY: Oxford University Press.

Stiggins, R. J. (2002). Assessment Crisis: The absence of assessment for learning. *Phi Delta Kappan, 83*(10), 758–765.

Swanwick, R. A. (2016). Deaf children's bimodal bilingualism and education. *Language Teaching, 49*(1), 1–34.

Woll, B. (2016). *Assessing sign language acquisition.* Paper presented at the meeting of Assessment of Multimodal Multilingual Outcomes in Deaf and Hard-of-Hearing Children Stockholm, Sweden.

16

THE LEGACY OF ROBERT HOFFMEISTER

On the Importance of Supporting Deaf scholars

Jonathan Henner, Patrick Rosenberg, and Rachel Benedict

Introduction

A year after Dr. Henner had come to Boston for his graduate education, he found himself in a small room in The Learning Center, surrounded by laptops, wires, and dividers. The laptops were placed in the nooks between the dividers, with the goal that participants could use the laptops without seeing participants next to them. The wires connected all the laptops to a central hub computer, which controlled what was on each laptop's screen, and each laptop sent information to the central hub about buttons clicked or other interactions with them. When all of the laptops were running, they showed the American Sign Language Assessment Instrument (ASLAI) in the earliest stages of execution.

Participants would stream into the small room, several at a time, and take several receptive, non-production assessments that targeted their American Sign Language vocabulary knowledge. They would then call an assistant over to set up a production assessment built into each laptop. There were three production assessments. The receptive assessment results were sent to the hub. The production assessment data was saved to each laptop, and then transferred to USB memory sticks at the end of the testing day.

We, the ASLAI team composed of mostly deaf researchers, educators, and linguists, were testing the deployment of the first online adaptation of the ASLAI, then an almost 30-year old assessment. The ASLAI was previously pen-and-paper based, but the Boston University researchers had recently been awarded a multi-year Institute of Educational Sciences grant to move the battery online and expand it beyond the vocabulary assessments initially offered. Over the next couple of years, our work on the ASLAI brought us from that cramped little room to schools for the deaf all over the country, including Riverside, Honolulu,

230 Jonathan Henner et al.

Providence, and Jacksonville, and even to exotic-to-us places like London, Melbourne, and Zurich. Most importantly, we were able to learn about how to assess deaf children and use these skills to build our careers.

While some people would argue that the ASLAI is Dr. Hoffmeister's greatest legacy, what made it work during the years of building was the team behind it. Dr. Hoffmeister was unique among hearing scholars of Deaf Education in that his team was entirely deaf. He sought out and built pipelines for deaf scholars. The three of us who graduated with doctoral degrees, the two of us who graduated with master's and educational specialist degrees, the two administrative assistants, and the doctoral student who eventually found a satisfying career outside of academia were all invaluable to the project in different ways; and we were all deaf signers. Dr. Hoffmeister had a gift for recognizing the intrinsic talent that each of his deaf scholars brought to the table. As Robinson and Henner (2018) explain, deaf people in the academy are often only recognized as teachers of signed languages, and as ways for university systems to profit off signed language knowledge without giving back to deaf communities. Accordingly, Dr. Hoffmeister pushed for us to present at conferences, or publish, or work on the team according to our unique skills and talents.

The true legacy of Dr. Hoffmeister, therefore, is not the ASLAI battery, which is groundbreaking in its own right. Over the years the ASLAI has become one of the de-facto standards for computerized assessment batteries of signed language, and the data from it continues to revolutionize how we understand how US signing deaf children use languages. The publications created from the ASLAI dataset push researchers closer to Dr. Hoffmeister's stated dream of showing concrete connections between signed language abilities and academic achievement. Yet, the true legacy of Dr. Hoffmeister was and is his willingness to build pipelines for deaf scholarship. This chapter will focus on why a lack of deaf scholarship is problematic, and how non-deaf scholars can follow in Dr. Hoffmeister's legacy to support deaf scholarship.

The Need for Deaf Scholars in Education of the Deaf and Linguistics Research

For a variety of reasons, it is difficult to quantify the number of deaf people who have advanced degrees such as master's or doctorates. Any count requires first that people identify themselves as having the degree and second that they identify themselves as members of the deaf communities. But, for a generation of deaf people, the source of the number of deaf doctorates was located in the back of Jack Gannon's Deaf Heritage (1981). Many of us grew up reading the names and wondering if we would be one of them one day. These days, the number of deaf doctorates plus those with advanced graduate degrees would likely be numerous enough that the book itself would extend into the thousands of pages were it to contain a comprehensive list of all of us!

The Legacy of Robert Hoffmeister **231**

Regardless of how much the number of deaf people with advanced degrees has increased since 1981, the actual number is still small (although we cannot quantify the exact number as mentioned previously). The National Deaf Center (2019) reports that 6.6% of deaf people in the United States have at least a master's degree (compared to 12.5% of non-deaf people) and 0.6% have a doctoral, medical, or a juris doctorate degree (compared to 1.3% of non-deaf people). Additionally, while exact numbers are not available about the ranking of the degrees awarded, at least 3.9% of the degrees awarded to deaf people are in literature and languages, and 10.7% are in education. In total, the number of deaf people who have advanced degrees in either linguistics or education of the deaf are a small percentage of a small population. This is unfortunate because these are two of the fields that most need input from deaf people, and deaf people who are in positions where they have the credentials (e.g., a doctoral degree) to push back against misinformation and tropes about deaf people (e.g., that deafness causes behavioral challenges).

Since the early 1990s, various disability communities have rallied around the expression *Nothing about us without us*. Disability historian scholar Charlton (1998) mentions that he first heard it spoken in disability contexts in South Africa in 1993, from people who picked it up in Eastern Europe. However recent the phrase, the idea that disability justice cannot be done without disabled people involved is not recent. Ed Roberts, one of the founders of the modern twentieth-century disability rights movement, was fond of saying that "… when others speak for you, you lose" (Charlton, 1998, p. 3). Essentially, Roberts' point was that abled people have been dictating agency for disabled people to their detriment. Because abled people cannot conceptualize outside of their own understanding of the world, they make assumptions about what disabled people want based on their own ability (Butler & Bowlby, 1997). The results of narrow expectations of what disabled people want, based on abled assumptions, are often what Jackson (2019) calls *disability dongles,* or "… a well-intended, elegant, yet useless solution to a problem we never knew we had." Disability dongles can refer to mechanical wheelchairs that can climb stairs, when ramps would be the preferred accommodation (Jackson, 2019). When Dr. Henner went to the 17th international ACM SIGACCESS Conference on Computers and Accessibility back in 2015, one of the exhibits was technology that showed deaf people disembodied lips to promote lip-reading. The presenter admitted that there were no deaf people on his team, nor were there deaf consultants. He just assumed that deaf people wanted to read lips.

By and large, the signing American deaf communities have chosen to reject abled expectations of *hearing* and *speaking* where possible. The deaf community in the United States appears to have a longer history of activism and agitation, largely because of how tied deaf education was to language rights and justice. Towards the end of the nineteenth century, arguments between the manualism and oralist approach to deaf education had intensified, leaving deaf children

232 Jonathan Henner et al.

damaged in its wake. By 1896, Edward Miner Gallaudet was regularly receiving letters from parents that described the damage from oralist philosophies. One father wrote, "His teacher regarded him as the smartest boy in his class, and if my statement is of any value, from a general knowledge of his classmates, I think the teacher was right. Notwithstanding this, he is unable to understand anyone, or make himself understood outside his own home circle," (p. 2). Another mother explained about her daughter,

> She was put under the instruction, or rather guidance, or Prof. Bell to whom I am greatly indebted for the preservation of her voice, which now, at the age of seventeen, is remarkably good *for a deaf person* [emphasis our own]. And yet it is not perfectly intelligible to any but members of her own family or intimate friends. Neither can she read the lips of strangers with facility; and after ten years of the most expensive instruction in this country and in Europe, I am forced to the conclusion that your theory is correct: that the combined method is best. For these reasons chiefly: so much time is given to voice drill and lip-reading that the general education obtains but limited consideration. (p. 3)

The purpose of these quotes is to demonstrate that oralist approaches to education have always depended on convincing parents of deaf children that their methods will help the deaf children become more hearing, if not actually *passing for hearing.*

Indeed, by 1880, before hearing parents of deaf children were writing Edward Miner Gallaudet about the damage that oralism had done to their children, deaf people were realizing that they could not depend on hearing people to defend the manual language and deaf communities. The focus on "voice drill and lip-reading that the general education obtains but limited consideration" existed because hearing people prioritized speech over all kinds of knowledge. Like Harmon (2013) writes, "as much as possible *hearingness* [emphasis ours] is the goal" (p. 1). Rote learning of speech and listening was still the pedagogical approach for oral teaching of deaf children in the mid-twentieth century as explained by Jackie Roth to Andrew Solomon in a 1993 New York Times Magazine article, "We spent two weeks learning to say 'guillotine' and that was what we learned about the French Revolution." Even in the early twenty-first century, oral listening and speaking skills are a prime facet of pedagogies for the deaf and hard of hearing. During the COVID-19 pandemic, Warren (2020) described deaf students in the Memphis Oral School as entirely dependent on hearing prostheses because required masks covered the face, especially the lips. In oralist education, there can be no multi-modal approaches to communicating. Even relying on reading the lips evidences a failure against performative hearingness. The only acceptable experience for living in the world is communicating through the ears.

Dr. Hoffmeister used to tell us a story about the time he attended a conference where the presenter was a hearing researcher of deaf education. The researcher was experimenting with a new oral-based pedagogy structure and was proudly recounting the hundreds of words that the child participating in the study knew. Dr. Hoffmeister, then in the audience, during questioning, strolled up to the microphone in his long-legged, languid manner, in a T-shirt, sweatpants, and a Boston University cap on, and into the microphone, instead of questioning, mentioned that signing deaf kids at that age knew thousands of words instead of hundreds. Dr. Hoffmeister's goal in telling us this story was to remind us, his deaf graduate students, that every instance of audism in the field had to be pushed back against. No false statements about the abilities of deaf children and adults should be allowed to stand without question or comment, lest people accept them as verified and evidence based.

Pushing back against the hearings has a strong tradition in the deaf communities. Ladd (2003) called these 1,001 small victories. And in the late-nineteenth century, the signing deaf community in the United States was working on rejecting the oral movements. At the first National Deaf-Mute Convention (1880), which took place in Cincinnati Ohio, Theo Froehlich proclaimed:

> So far as I understand, the object of this Convention is to bring the deaf-mutes of the different sections of the United States in close contact and to deliberate on the needs of deaf-mutes as a class by themselves. As deaf-mutes among the other inhabitants of this country, we have interests peculiar to ourselves, and which can be taken care of by ourselves. (p. 36)

As Sampson (2020) exclaimed on Twitter after reading the quote from Froehlich, "for the deaf, by the deaf!". Sampson's enthusiasm shows how profound it is for deaf people to see deaf leadership. *Same same* (see Figure 16.1) is absolutely critical, and also points to the importance of not only showing white, male leadership in deaf communities, because *same same* extends to far more than deafness alone.

The Consequences of Not Having Deaf Scholarship in Linguistics and Education of the Deaf Research

The consequences of a lack of representation from the communities being taught or studied is a well-researched phenomenon with other marginalized communities (see citations in this section). Accordingly, the lack of deaf scholarship in linguistics and education has detrimental consequences for the validity of the research on deaf people and communities because non-deaf people interpret data using hearing and abled lenses. Although, we clarify that we cannot draw direct comparisons between all deaf communities and communities that have racial marginalization because white deaf people are still white, and deaf black, indigenous, and other people of color can be multiply marginalized based on race in addition to deafness. Our goal in sharing these examples is not to say that they are

FIGURE 16.1 Signing the concept of "same-same"

analogous but to spotlight adjacent examples which can help readers understand possible application to deafness.

For example, Milner and Howard (2004) point out that the depressed academic assessment results of black students cannot be attributed solely to socioeconomic status, but rather from a consistent environment of racism and a paucity of black leadership and mentoring that does not exist to enforce structural racism. black students mostly have white teachers who teach values and information rooted in structural racism. When black students do have black teachers, the black teachers are often in administration where they are forced to be disciplinarians. According to Milner and Howard, in these situations, black students experience black adults only punitively. When Dr. Henner was in elementary school, deaf members of the community were only included as recess parents. Their job was to police the actions of the deaf children in the playground. The recess parents did not play with the kids nor did they provide examples on how to mediate relationships with the hearing people who could not communicate with us. Instead, they only interacted with us when we were doing something contrary to the hearing expectations of play that were never adequately communicated to us.

Part of the issue raised by Milner and Howard (2004) is how teacher education programs can compound the issue of whiteness in pedagogy by training teachers of color to enact the policies of whiteness. Escamilla (2006) details that students of color in teacher preparation programs are told that students of color have deficits that must be addressed within the schooling system. The deficits, accordingly, are assigned to color rather than existing in a racist society. Racist beliefs, even internalized, tended to manifest in statements by the teachers such as "Spanish is easier to learn to write than English" (p. 2340) and by blaming Spanish for any perceived deficiencies in the students themselves. In later discussions, the researchers and the teachers realized that the errors they noticed in the bilingual students' writing were similar to the errors that any students that age would have made and could not be faulted by speaking Spanish and learning English. For some, it may seem odd that racism could be applied to Spanish, a major spoken language and one with a colonial history; however, in the United States at least, Spanish is racially marked as a *brown* language (Rosa, 2019). English, especially white, spoken English, is the accepted norm by which *deviance* is measured.

Annamma, Boelé, Moore, and Klingner (2013) explain that schools construct and enforce policies of normalcy which are modeled by the dominant culture in which the schools reside. In the United States, that is whiteness, hearingness, and English competency. Students who are not white, or who are not hearing, and do not demonstrate monolingual English competency according to the metrics are marked as broken and in need of remedial help. As such, students of color find themselves largely placed in specialized education for learning, behavior, and emotional disabilities (Annamma *et al.* 2013). This is also true of deaf students, and doubly true for deaf students of color.

The insufficiency of what ASL users call *same same* can create issues where teachers misinterpret the actions of their students because they use lenses established by their own culture, communities, and experiences. Schalge and Soga (2008) were asked to study why students were not attending ESL classes that they registered for in a Minnesota community center. Teachers blamed student absenteeism on external factors unrelated to the classes such as family issues, money problems, transportation, or cultural challenges. But when the students were asked, they did not speak to that. Instead, they talked about how the class was too easy for them, or that the instruction was not specific enough to help them communicate with people in the communities or in the workforce. Students mentioned that they felt that the teachers underestimated their intelligence and their abilities to learn English. Schalge and Soga indicated that teacher perspectives on student actions and abilities were influenced by racism and linguicism (Phillipson, 1992). Linguicism, as defined by Phillipson, is the belief that languages are hierarchical. In the States, English is believed by many to be the best language, which is reinforced by the sheer amount of English monolinguals and attachment to white nationalistic behavior (McIntosh & Mendoza-Denton, 2020).

Similarly, nondeaf researchers of deaf people attribute behaviors that deaf people exhibit while living in a hearing world to deafness, rather than to other factors. They claim that deafness causes these behaviors that they see as negative. For example, Antia, Jones, Luckner, Kreimeyer, and Reed (2011), in a five-year longitudinal study of the social skills of deaf students in inclusive classrooms, found that deaf students tended to rate themselves as having better social skills than the rating they received from their teachers. Antia et al. did not provide an in-depth discussion of why there were differences between teacher ratings of deaf children, and student ratings of themselves. They instead seemed to stress that the ratings from both the teachers and the students were pretty normal and any possible deviance could be attributed to communication challenges. However, these communications challenges were afforded to deafness instead an entirely inclusive language environment. Their suggestions for intervention focused on changing the students rather than changing the environment which could cause communication breakdowns. Marschark et al. (2017), in a description of the Antia et al. findings, wrote that deaf children were simply overconfident about their own social skills. To further emphasize the difference between deaf perceptions of themselves and nondeaf perceptions of deaf people, Marschark et al. referenced the results of another study by Borgna et al. (2010) that concluded that deaf college students tended to think that they learned more than they actually did, whereas nondeaf college students were better about knowing how much they learned. In response, Marschark et al. described deaf college students as "unskilled and unaware" (p. 23), which is a damning way to label a historically marginalized population.

Research focused on deafness rarely has deaf scholarship which can account for some of the very negative ways that deaf people are described in the literature (e.g., unskilled and unaware). Marschark et al. (2017) claimed that their work had some validity because the assessment used in collecting data had been modified from the original assessment to be used with deaf people by three interpreters (nondeaf) and one (nondeaf) audiologist. However, authority on deafness granted by proximity to deafness amounts to nothing. Proximity to deafness is not a substitute for deafness. Indeed, interpreters and audiologists are often vectors of oppression for deaf people. As Dr. Hoffmeister recognized, the way to change the field is to put more deaf people in leadership and researcher positions within the field. He did this by mentoring and creating pipelines.

Mentoring and Supporting Deaf Scholarship

Listman and Dingus-Eason (2018) explain that the lack of deaf scientists, researchers, and teachers can be explained by the presence of what they call *phonocentric hegemony*. Phonocentric hegemony describes the general expectation that scholars be able to "hear and communicate verbally in spoken English" (p. 280). Phonocentric hegemony explains, in part, why nondeaf academics tend to be relatively successful compared to their deaf colleagues in fields that focus on deafness, such as signed language linguistics, and deaf education. Robinson and Henner (2017) point to the fact that just like deaf people prefer *same same*, nondeaf people also want to engage with people who have their understanding of the sonorous-based world and can communicate with them easily. For these reasons, nondeaf people seek out nondeaf scholars, researchers, and professionals to talk about deafness. They do this through phone calls, or by amplifying nondeaf voices at the expense of deaf perspectives. Hearingness, and proximity to deafness, has become the leading criteria for expertise. And non-deaf scholars, researchers, and professionals augment their careers via the lived knowledge of the deaf people they are supposed to support and serve.

Scott (2020) writes that many privileged teachers working in marginalized communities have Superman-like identities. They want their students to "catch up, fill in blanks" and "save students from a corrupt world" (p. 71). However, Superman was never an equal with the people he purported to serve. Superman always had the power and was always more powerful than an average person. Just the same, nondeaf people always have more power, and are always more powerful than deaf people.

The first step to supporting deaf scholars is to give deaf scholars the space and opportunities to reclaim deaf knowledge and show deaf expertise. This means directing journalists to talk to deaf scholars, ensuring that edited books have chapters by deaf authors, and working to make sure that conferences about deafness have invited deaf speakers either as a keynote, or in a prominent speaker position. Many of our recent academic experiences were a result of nondeaf linguists and researchers of deaf education, in a position of allyship, giving us the opportunity to write chapters, or to be co-authors on articles. If nondeaf scholars can do so, they should also seek out deaf collaborators and promote them to receive opportunities that would otherwise be granted to nondeaf people. Part of working against phonocentric hegemonies means giving deaf scholars a seat at the table.

While we encourage nondeaf scholars to work to elevate deaf scholars, we caution them against using deaf scholars as tokens, or shields against criticism. Using deaf scholars to say that there is a deaf scholar at the table, without actually allowing deaf *scholarship* is worse than ignoring deaf scholars, because deaf scholars in these situations are used to prop up nondeaf scholarship and to defend the phonocentric hegemony. To summarize, it is not an allyship to have deaf co-authors if the deaf scholars are never in a position to assert their ideas, or if they are only co-authors and not leading the research. This does extend to nondeaf/deaf partnerships as it gives the impression that deaf scholars can never be in leadership positions over nondeaf people.

The experiences of deaf scholars in academia can be paralleled, but not perfectly explained by Martinez-Cola's (2020) description of how early career scholars of color are treated by white faculty. In Martinez-Cola's ontology, white faculty who mentor scholars of colors can be placed into three categories: (1) collectors, (2) nightlights, and (3) allies. Collectors, as explained by Martinez-Cola, are white faculty who collect mentees of color because they think they have to, and do not reflect on the systems of whiteness that they place their mentees in. Collectors, for example, lavish praise on themselves for supporting scholars of color, however, continue to perform both macro and microaggressions on their students of color. Nevertheless, Martinez-Cola stresses that Collectors are not necessarily bad people. They are just embodiments of the system. Nightlights, on the other hand, use their privilege to help scholars of color navigate the systems. They confront other white people when they recognize that scholars of color are being marginalized. And they ask questions publicly that help scholars of color recognize covert rules and curriculum that are often passed among white people and not typically shared with people of color. Allies, according to Martinez-Cola, "have done the work it takes to develop an appreciation and admiration for the experiences of students of color, and this work informs their mentoring relationship." (p. 36).

We can use Braun, Gormally, and Clark (2017) to extend Martinez-Cola, as Braun et al. examined specifically what deaf mentees looked for in non-deaf mentors. They developed a survey, the Deaf Mentoring Survey, to find out what affects the mentoring experience that deaf individuals have with mentors. They found that respondent answers could be divided into four main factors: (1) being a scientist, (2) Deaf community capital, (3) asking for accommodations, and (4) communication access. Basically, effective mentors should work in the field that the mentees want to work in, should have access to Deaf community cultural capital, should know how to manage being disabled in the world, and should be able to provide direct access to communication for their mentees. We should recognize, though, that a person can meet all four factors as designated by Braun et al. and still be a Collector under the Martinez-Cola ontology! Being an effective mentor for deaf scholars means recognizing complex factors that can influence the relationship between mentor and mentee. Dr. Hoffmeister, for example, sought funding to support deaf pipelines through higher education. He also established collaborations with other universities to ensure that deaf scholars from different institutions were in touch with each other. Dr. Hoffmeister's commitment to deaf scholarship is evident through many of the authors in this book who came up through his praxis.

Wrapping Up

Creating pipelines for deaf scholarship is challenging, given that there are few researchers, professionals, and advocates for deaf people who can do anything about institutional gatekeeping. However, supporters of deaf scholarship can continue to work to find ways to break down these institutional barriers. Some of this includes ensuring that scholarship about deaf communities and languages is always represented by deaf scholars. Dr. Hoffmeister's greatest gift to the linguistic and educational communities is a history of promoting deaf scholarship and ensuring that he trained members of the deaf communities in his values and advocacy.

References

Annamma, S. A., Boelé, A. L., Moore, B. A., & Klingner, J. (2013). Challenging the ideology of normal in schools. *International Journal of Inclusive Education*, *17*(12), 1278–1294. https://doi.org/10.1080/13603116.2013.802379.

Antia, S. D., Jones, P., Luckner, J., Kreimeyer, K. H., & Reed, S. (2011). Social outcomes of students who are deaf and hard of hearing in general education classrooms. *Exceptional Children*, *77*(4), 489–504. https://doi.org/10.1177/001440291107700407.

Borgna, G., Convertino, C., Marschark, M., Morrison, C., & Rizzolo, K. (2011). Enhancing deaf students' learning from sign language and text: Metacognition, modality, and the effectiveness of content scaffolding. *Journal of Deaf Studies and Deaf Education, 16*(1), 79–100. https://doi.org/10.1093/deafed/enq036.

Braun, D. C., Gormally, C., & Clark, M. D. (2017). The deaf mentoring survey: A community cultural wealth framework for measuring mentoring effectiveness with underrepresented students. *CBE—Life Sciences Education, 16*(1), ar10. https://doi.org/10.1187/cbe.15-07-0155.

Butler, R., & Bowlby, S. (1997). Bodies and Spaces: An Exploration of Disabled Peopleas Experiences of Public Space. *Environment and Planning D: Society and Space, 15(4), 411-433. https://doi.org/15*(4), 411–483.

Charlton, J. I. (1998). *Nothing about us without us without us: Disability, oppression and empowerment.* Berkeley and Los Angeles: University of California Press.

Escamilla, K. (2006). Semilingualism applied to the literacy behaviors of Spanish-speaking emerging bilinguals: Bi-illiteracy or emerging biliteracy? *Teachers College Record, 108*(11), 2329–2353. https://doi.org/10.1111/j.1467-9620.2006.00784.x.

Froelich, T. (1880, August). *First national convention of Deaf-Mutes,* Cincinnati, Ohio.

Gallaudet, E. M. (1896). *The combined system: Approved by friends of the orally taught.* Gallaudet College.

Gannon, J. (1981/2011). *Deaf heritage: A narrative history of deaf America.* Gallaudet University Press.

Garberoglio, C. L., Palmer, J. L., Cawthon, S., & Sales, A. (2019). *Deaf people and educational attainment in the United States: 2019.* U.S. Department of Education, Office of Special Education Programs, National Deaf Center on Postsecondary Outcomes.

Harmon, K. (2013). Growing up to become hearing: Dreams of passing in oral deaf education. In J. Brune & D. Wilson (Eds.), *Disability and passing: Blurring the lines of identity.* Temple University Press.

Jackson, T. I. L. (2019, April 22). A community response to a #DisabilityDongle. *Medium.* https://medium.com/@eejackson/a-community-response-to-a-disabilitydongle-d0a37703d7c2.

Ladd, P. 2003, *Understanding deaf culture: In search of deafhood.* Multilingual Matters.

Listman, J. D., & Dingus-Eason, J. (2018). How to be a deaf scientist: Building navigational capital. *Journal of Diversity in Higher Education, 11*(3), 279–294. https://doi.org/10.1037/dhe0000049.

Marschark, M., Kronenberger, W. G., Rosica, M., Borgna, G., Convertino, C., Durkin, A., Machmer, E., & Schmitz, K. L. (2017). Social maturity and executive function among deaf learners. *Journal of Deaf Studies and Deaf Education, 22*(1), 22–34. https://doi.org/10.1093/deafed/enw057.

Martinez-Cola, M. (2020). Collectors, nightlights, and allies, oh my! White mentors in the academy. *Understanding and Dismantling Privilege, 10*(1).

McIntosh, J. & Mendoza-Denton, N. (Eds.). (2020). *Language in the Trump era: Scandals and emergencies.* Cambridge University Press.

Milner, H. R., & Howard, T. C. (2004). Black teachers, black students, black communities, and brown: perspectives and insights from experts. *The Journal of Negro Education, 73*(3), 285. https://doi.org/10.2307/4129612.

Phillipson, R. (1992). ELT: The native speaker's burden? *ELT Journal, 46*(1), 12–18. https://doi.org/10.1093/elt/46.1.12.

Robinson, O. E., & Henner, J. (2017). The personal is political in the deaf mute howls: Deaf epistemology seeks disability justice. *Disability & Society*, April, 1–21. https://doi.org/10.1080/09687599.2017.1313723.

Robinson, O., & Henner, J. (2018). Authentic voices, authentic encounters: Cripping the university through American Sign Language. *Disability Studies Quarterly*, 23.

Rosa, J. (2019). *Looking like a language, sounding like a race: Raciolinguistic ideologies and the learning of Latinidad*. Oxford University Press.

Sampson, T. (2020, August 14). For the deaf by the deaf! https://twitter.com/TorytheLinguist/status/1294302399150972929.

Schalge, S. L., & Soga, K. (2008). "Then i stop coming to school": Understanding absenteeism in an adult english as a second language program. *Adult Basic Education and Literacy Journal*, 2(3), 12.

Scott, W. (2020). You think you know, but you have no idea: An autoethnography of the actualization of privilege. *Understanding and Dismantling Privilege*, 10, 1.

Solomon, A. (1994, August 28). Defiantly Deaf. *The New York Times*. https://www.nytimes.com/1994/08/28/magazine/defiantly-deaf.html.

Warren, A. (2020). Oral School for the Deaf reopening Aug. 11. *The Daily Memphian*. Retrieved August 20, 2020, from https://dailymemphian.com/article/15964/memphis-oral-school-deaf-reopening-covid-19-coronavirus.

INDEX

abuse, at residential schools 12
African-American students: at American School for the Deaf 6; at Gallaudet University 7; at National Deaf-Mute College 7; at residential schools 23; sign language use by 9, 23
alerting 61
Allies 237–38
Alphabetic Principle 142
American Annals of the Deaf 6
American School for the Deaf 12; age of students at 5; black students at 6; Clerc at 5; Gallaudet at 5; history of 4; monetary problems for 5
American Sign Language: academic recognition of 12; advantages of, for deaf children 81; Anchor Standards in 157–58; apps in 108; books and, combined use of 107; chaining of 83; claims regarding 152–53; conceptual nature of 191; discouragement of, in educational settings 37; early access to 108; emergent literacy and 173–75, 179; English literacy and 171–82; English taught using 82–83; exposure to, in residential schools 22–23, 28; fractions signed in 191–92; Grapheme System 142; high-achieving deaf readers use of 84–87; history of 199; home exposure to 106; interactions with 108; language acquisition through 102; linguistic properties of 12; mathematics

comprehension facilitated using 191–94; phonological awareness 108; print literacy and 181; proficiency in 171–72, 173–81; pronoun use in 38; as psycholinguistically accessible language 102; rare or infrequent vocabulary 203; reading aloud in 104, 107; reading and 81–82, 84–85, 107, 175–77, 179–80; sandwiching of 83; simple vocabulary 203; 3-D shapes signed in 191; transliteration 140; 2-D shapes signed in 191; verbs of motion in 50–52; visuo-spatial nature of 152; writing and 178, 180–81; written 82; written language learning through 103–4
American Sign Language acquisition: assessment of 217; by deaf children of deaf parents 17–19, 28; by deaf children of hearing parents 19–21; by hearing parents 28; identity development through 105–7; from peers 27–29; timeline for 17–18
American Sign Language assessment(s): American Sign Language Assessment Instrument *see* American Sign Language Assessment Instrument; American Sign Language Phonological Awareness Test 222–25; ASL Expressive Skills Test 221–22; ASL Receptive Skills Test 219–20, 222; group testing 205–6; importance of 217; methods of 217;

242 Index

picture-to-sign tests 201; research regarding 218

American Sign Language Assessment Instrument: Analogical Reasoning subtest 209–10; Antonyms subtest 203, 209–10, 212; description of 177–78; development of 199–203; editing for 205; equipment 203–5; expansion of 229–30; future of 207, 229–30; improvements in 206–7; language disorders assessed using 211; recording for 205; subtests 203, 209–11; Synonyms subtest 203–4, 209–10, 212; timeline of 200; vocabulary assessment 208–14; vocabulary in sentences task 206

American Sign Language glossing 82

American Sign Language Phonological Awareness Test 222–25

American Sign Language Test Battery 201

Americanization 8

Analogical Reasoning subtest, of American Sign Language Assessment Instrument 209–11

Antonyms subtest, of American Sign Language Assessment Instrument 203, 209–10, 212

apps, in American Sign Language 108

"arbitrariness" 35, 39

ASD *see* American School for the Deaf

ASL *see* American Sign Language

ASL Expressive Skills Test 221–22

ASL Receptive Skills Test 219–20, 222

ASLAI *see* American Sign Language Assessment Instrument

ASL-EST *see* ASL Expressive Skills Test

ASL-PAT *see* American Sign Language Phonological Awareness Test

ASL-RST *see* ASL Receptive Skills Test

attention: definition of 61; effortful nature of 62; spatial 61; sustained 61; visual spatial 61

auditory phonological coding 80

auditory scaffolding hypothesis 66, 68

auditory-neurocognitive model 68

Bahan, Ben 201, 204, 206

Battiste, Hume 7

Baughman, E. Austin 10

Bedrock Literacy Curriculum: components of 135; Cumulative Vocabulary Recognition Test 137; goal of 134; Handshape Holder technique 143, 145; independent writing instruction 135,

142–46; long-term memory 136–37; "Quick Writes" daily activity 143–46; reading instruction and comprehension 135, 138–42; spelling practice 135–38; vocabulary development 135–38; word lists in 136; writing instruction 135, 142–46

Beecher, Henry Ward 5

Beecher, Lyman 5

Bell, Alexander Graham 8–9, 199

bilingual education: American Sign Language in 82–83; in Greece 114; research on 114; skills learned from 127; value of 14

Bilingual Grammar Curriculum: access to 159–60; Anchor Standards 157–58; architecture of 157–58; design of 156–57; metaphors 154; objectives 160–69; overview of 150–51, 157; reasons for developing 155; Santa Fe/ New York City Template used in 153–54; task-analysis approach in 158

bilingual learning mode 78

Bilingual-Bicultural model of education 37

bilingualism 14

biopsychosocial systems theory 67

Bjorlee, Ignatius 10

black students: at American School for the Deaf 6; at Gallaudet University 7; at National Deaf-Mute College 7; at residential schools 23; sign language use by 9, 23

Boardman, Eliza 7

books, American Sign Language and 107

Booth, Edmund 8

Booth, Frank 8

Booth, Mary 8

Boston University 201–3

Bottom-Up reading model 138

bound morphemes 35

Braidwood Academy 3

Brazilian Sign Language 17

bridging 194

British sign language 209

British Sign Language Production Test 221

British Sign Language Receptive Skills Test 219

Brown, Roger 36–37

Buck, Daniel 3

Caldwell, John 3

California School for the Deaf 10

Carlisle School 8

Casterline, Dorothy 12, 199
Center for Research and Training 200–201
chaining 83
Challis, Jimmy 204
child labor 8
Childhood Development after Cochlear Implantation study 64
Chilocco Indian school 8
chunking 137–38
Civil Rights movement 12
Civil Service Exam 9
Civil War, residential schools during 6
Clarke School for the Deaf 12, 14
classrooms: family setting versus 26; learning in 24–27; mainstreaming in 22, 24–25, 114; observational studies in 25; primary language acquisition in 24–25; reading comprehension in 177; sign language interpreters in 25–26; see also preschool classrooms
Clerc, Laurent: at American School for the Deaf 5; Gallaudet and 3–4; marriage by 4, 7; at National Deaf-Mute College 7; religious instruction by 4; in sign language development 199; teaching by 4–5; in United States 4
cochlear implants: connectome disease hypothesis of 66–67; description of 28; studies of, with nondeaf children 64; sustained attention testing in children with 63
codeswitching 194
cognitive development 188; auditory access for 68; deafcentric approaches to 68–69
cognitive iconicity 40
cognitive linguists 39
Cogswell, Mason Fitch 3
Cole, Janis 201, 204, 206
Collectors 237–38
Columbia Institution for the Instruction of the Deaf, Dumb, and Blind 6
Communicative Developmental Inventory 209
communicative intent 75–76
comparative learning process 78
compensation hypothesis 61
comprehensible input 75
Connecticut Asylum for the Deaf-Mutes and Dumb 4
"connectome disease" 66–67
continuous performance test 62–63
Convention on the Rights of Persons with Disabilities 114

Cook, Lana 204, 206–7
Costello, Patrick 204
COVID-19 232
CPT see continuous performance test
critical thinking, in literacy development 101
Croneberg, Carl 12, 199
crosscultural language socialization 26
CRPD see Convention on the Rights of Persons with Disabilities
CRT see Center for Research and Training
cultural identity 105
cultural literacy 14
cultural transmission 106
Cumulative Vocabulary Recognition Test 137
CVRT see Cumulative Vocabulary Recognition Test
Czubek, Janey Greenwald 201, 204

Darwinism 7
Davis, Jefferson 6
DCDP see deaf children of deaf parents
DCHP see deaf children of hearing parents
deaf, as "connectome disease" 66–67
deaf characters: in media 107; in print 106
deaf children: American Sign Language advantages for 81; continuous performance test in 62–63; first exposure to ASL by 18, 20; hearing loss diagnosis in 19; homesigning systems for 21; language deprivation effects on 99, 102, 209; literacy development in 99–100; with no formal sign language input 21–22; in preschool classrooms 26; speech training for 80; sustained visual attention in 62–65; visual language acquisition by 13; visual spatial attention in 61
deaf children of deaf parents: English literacy in 133–34; motion events within verbs of motion studies 52–57; sign language acquisition in 17–21, 27–28, 56, 113; Test of English as a Foreign Language performance by 74
deaf children of hearing parents: American Sign Language proficiency interventions for 182; motion events within verbs of motion studies 52–57; sign language acquisition in 19–21, 208
deaf communities: activism in 231; formation of 22, 29; patriotism by 10
deaf connectome 67

244 Index

deaf drivers: discrimination against 10; licenses to 10
deaf education: advanced degrees in 230–31; audist approach to 106; changes in 91; deaf scholarship in 233–36; history of 3–14, 150; medical approach to 106; in nineteenth century 6; options for 23–24; research in 181–82; in twentieth century 7–9; *see also* education
Deaf Heritage 230
deaf lawyers 14
deaf organizations 11; *see also specific organization*
deaf parents, deaf children of *see* deaf children of deaf parents
deaf peers: in residential schools 24, 27; as role models 108; sign language acquisition from 27–28, 27–29
deaf people: with advanced degrees 230–33; compensation hypothesis in visual systems of 61; societal contributions by 14
Deaf President Now movement 13
deaf scholars: mentoring of 237; need for 230–33
deaf scholarship: lack of, in deaf education 233–36; supporting of 236–38
deaf schools: discrimination in 8; language acquisition and 22–24; National Deaf-Mute College 6–7; racism in 8; sex segregation in 22; *see also specific school*
deaf signing communities 17
deaf students: English literacy skills in 132; mainstreaming of 14, 23, 25, 29, 114; mathematics instruction for 192–94; reading levels of 73
deaf teachers: college training programs for 133; in early twentieth century 23; literacy instruction by 133; in residential schools 24; salary of 5; therapeutic language approach by 25–26; *see also* teacher(s)
deafcentric approaches to cognitive development 68–69
Developmental Psychology 74
diagram/model representation system, of mathematics 190–91
dialogic reading approach 180
Dictionary of American Sign Language 12
Digital Sign Language Library 116–19
disability dongles 231
disability rights movement 231

discrimination: of deaf drivers 10; in deaf schools 8; "hearing loss" as basis for 10; Rehabilitation Act of 1973 prohibition of 13
division-of-labor hypothesis 65–66
DPN movement *see* Deaf President Now movement
dual route theory 79
duality of patterning 35
Duffy Engineering 204

Early Education Longitudinal Study 174
early literacy framework 100
e-Books 122, 125–26
education: Bilingual-Bicultural model of 37; sign language discouragement in 37
educational media 108; *see also* deaf education
EELS *see* Early Education Longitudinal Study
embodied learning 76
emergent literacy: academic outcomes and 174; access to communication as key to 109; American Sign Language and 173–75, 179; description of 99–100; early language exposure and 179; literacy development and 101–2; in preschool classrooms 104; print and 104; proponents of 103–5
English as second language via print: American Sign Language for 81–83; bilingual learning mode 78; communicative intent 75–76; developing conversation about 89–91; difficulties of 76; embodied learning 76; foreign language learning curricula used in 90–91; heuristics of 84–89; immediate rewards 76; keywords used in 85, 87–88; mapping lexical signs 77; neglect of studies regarding 74; overview of 73–74; print-to-sign mapping task 88–89; semantic activation 79; simple translation breakdown 77–78; simple translation equivalents 77; social interaction for 74–76; spoken-word phonology not necessary for 79–81; theoretical and practical implications 79–83; without American Sign Language 83–84
English literacy: American Sign Language proficiency and 171–82; Bedrock Literacy Curriculum for *see* Bedrock Literacy Curriculum; deaf and hard of

Index **245**

hearing students skill in 132; in deaf
children of deaf parents 133–34; mass-
marketed materials for learning of 133
English morphology 90
enhanced subtitling 90
ESL-VP *see* English as second language via
print
executive functions: biopsychosocial
systems theory of 67; in cochlear implant
children 60; deficits in, language as
primary driver of 68; definition of 60;
development of 67; sustained attention
see sustained attention

families: gestures-based communication
system for 21; non-signing 22, 28
fingerspelling 23, 138
Finney, Charles Grandison 5
Finnish Sign Language 17
forced-choice sentence completion test 87
foreign language, reading used to
improve 74
Foster, Andrew 7
fractions 191–92
French Sign Language: Clerc's teaching of
4; residential schools and 22
Froehlich, Theo 233

Gallaudet, Thomas Hopkins: Clerc and
3–4; in France 3–4; historical
information about 3–4; ministry of 5;
Normal School 11; oralism and 232;
paternalism by 5; Second Great
Awakening and 5–6; in sign language
development 199
Gallaudet University: black students
at 7; deaf president of 13;
Pope at 11–12
Gannon, Jack 230
Gavagai problem 75
genetic tests 14
Georgia School for the Deaf 6
gestures-based communication system 21
Governor Baxter School for the Deaf 12
grammar 151–54
Grapheme System 142
graphemes 79
Great Depression 10–12
Greek Sign Language: curriculum for
teaching 115; description of 113; Digital
Sign Language Library 116–19;
e-Books 122, 125–26; as first language
115–28; lack of exposure to 113;

Manual Alphabet of 122; signing books
121–24; teaching materials for 115–28
Greek Sign Language Dictionary 119–21
GSL *see* Greek Sign Language

Hampton, Ida Wynette 7
Hands Land 108
Handshape Holder technique 143, 145
Hanson, Olof 9
Harris, Caldwell 200
Hartford 3–5
hearing, language and 68
hearing children, iconic spoken word
production by 42
hearing loss: average age of diagnosis 19;
discrimination based on 10
hearing parents: American Sign Language
acquisition by 28; deaf children of *see*
deaf children of hearing parents;
non-signing 22
hearingness 232, 235–36
Hoffmeister, R. 199–203, 205–7, 218,
229–30
home, American Sign Language exposure
in 106
homesigning 21
horizontal transmission 106
Hudson, Henry 3

iconic mappings 41–42
iconicity: age and 42–43; cognitive 40;
definition of 38; early research on
37–39; in first-language acquisition in
children 42; functioning of 40; as
"guessing" strategy 41; high 41; history
of 36–37; in homesigning 21; in
language learning 39–40, 42–43; low 41;
metaphor and 40; questions regarding
43; in sign language 18, 36–41; in sign
language acquisition 38; as "sound
symbolism" 40, 42; in spoken languages
40–41; structural mapping theory
of 40
IDEA *see* Individuals with Disabilities
Education Act
identity development: literacy
development and 105–7; teachers' role
in 106–7
immediate rewards 76
inattentional blindness 61
Indiana School for the Deaf 11
Individuals with Disabilities Education
Act 23–24

246 Index

Input Hypothesis 173, 177
Institu National de Jeunes Sourdes de
    Paris 4
insurance companies 10
internment camps 10
interpreters: in classrooms 25–26;
    studies of 25–26
"invented spelling" 142
Israeli Sign Language 39, 209
Japanese-American Children 10
Johnson, Lyndon Baines 12
Jordan, Irving King 13

Kentucky School for the Deaf 6
keywords 85, 87–88
Kourbetis, Vassilis 204

language: complexity of 156; conceptual
    frameworks and 156; hearing and 68;
    linear organization of 152; predicate in
    156; proficiency in 175; social
    interaction for learning of 74–76; subject
    in 156; see also spoken language; sign
    language; written language
language accessibility 102
language acquisition: American Sign
    Language for 102; critical period for
    102; description of 102; early research
    on 37–39; social learning for 74; whole
    object constraint in 75
language deprivation: in deaf children 99,
    102–3, 209; definition of 103;
    detrimental effects of 103, 109
language development: access to
    communication as key to 109; critical
    period for 102; description of 102–3,
    109; Input Hypothesis for 173, 177;
    interactive communication in 101; sign
    language exposure and 209
language disorders 211
Language Equality and Acquisition for
    Deaf Kids movement 14
language learning, iconicity in
    39–40, 42–43
language socialization: literature regarding
    27; peers in 27–28
language syllable reproduction 41
LEAD-K movement see Language Equality
    and Acquisition for Deaf Kids
    movement
learning: in classrooms 24–27; rote 232;
    sign language skills influence on 227
learning of second language: embodied

learning 76; immediate rewards and 76;
    social interaction for 74–76;
    see also English as second language
    via print
lexical signs, mapping 77
Lincoln, Abraham 7
linguicism 235
linguistic deprivation 103
linguistic interdependence hypothesis
    175–76
linguistic responsivity 26
Linguistic Society of America 36
linguistics 12
lipreading 9, 232
literacy: emergent see emergent literacy;
    English see English literacy; visually
    based 99–100
literacy development: Bedrock Literacy
    Curriculum for see Bedrock Literacy
    Curriculum context for 101; critical
    thinking in 101; in deaf children
    99–100; early language exposure effects
    on 179; emergent literacy and 101–2;
    identity development and 105–7;
    literature's role in 107–9; media's role in
    107–9; recommendations for facilitating
    105; sign language acquisition effects
    on 113
literacy identity 105
literature, in literacy development 107–9
Little Paper Family 11
long-term memory, word storage in
    136–37
LTM see long-term memory

MacArthur-Bates Communicative
    Developmental Inventory 209
mainstreaming 14, 23, 25, 29, 114
manualism 231
Manually Coded English 19, 25
mapping lexical signs 77
Maryland School for the Deaf 6, 10
mathematics: American Sign Language for
    comprehension of 191–94; bilingual
    learner of 188; diagram/model
    representation system of 190–91; in
    English instruction 189; fractions
    191–92; language representation system
    188–90; notation representation system
    190; representational systems for 187;
    semiotic circuit 187–88; 3-D shapes
    191; 2-D shapes 191
MCE see Manually Coded English

Index **247**

media: educational 108; literacy development role of 107–9
mentoring 236–38
metalinguistic awareness 105
metaphors 40, 154
Microsoft Power 150, 152, 4154
Milan Convention 199
minority languages, in schools 22
morphological awareness 90
motion events: acquisition of 51–52; deaf children's comprehension of 56; definition of 48; feature of 48–49; illustration of 49; in signed languages 49–52; studies of 52–57; theory of 48; in verbs of motion 51–57

NAD *see* National Association of the Deaf
NAEP *see* National Assessment of Educational Progress
National Assessment of Educational Progress 178
National Association of the Deaf 9, 11
National Center for Hearing Assessment and Management 24
National Deaf-Mute College: black students at 7; Clerc at 7; Deaf President Now movement 13; founding of 6–7; purpose of 7; women at 7
National Deaf-Mute Convention 233
National Fraternal Society of the Deaf 10–11
National Institute for the Deaf 12
Native Americans: children of 8; residential schools for 8
NCHAM *see* National Center for Hearing Assessment and Management
Nebraska School for the Deaf 8, 11
New Deal 11
New Jersey School for the Deaf 12
New York School for the Deaf: abuse at 12; description of 6; patriotism during World War I by 10
newspapers: decline during Great Depression 11; editors of 11–12; residential school printing of 9, 11
NFSD *see* National Fraternal Society of the Deaf
Nicaragua 28
Nightlights 237–38
Normal School 11
North Carolina School for the Deaf and Dumb and the Blind 6
notation representation system 190

NTID *see* National Institute for the Deaf

One-third Stories 91
Online Interactive Digital Sign Language Library 116–19
onomatopoeia 40
oralism: Bell's support for 8–9, 199; definition of 7; description of 231; Gallaudet and 232; in residential schools 23; sign language versus 8–9; in white schools 8–9
Palmer, Willie J. 6
parent-infant programs 14
paternalism 5
patriotism 10
Peabody Picture Vocabulary Test 201
Pearl Harbor 10
peers *see* deaf peers
Pennsylvania School for the Deaf 20
Peter's Picture 108
Philip, Marie 204, 206
phonocentric hegemony 236
phonological awareness: American Sign Language Phonological Awareness Test 222–25; description of 108
physical abuse 12
picture-to-sign tests 201
Pope, Alvin 11–12
Porter, George 11
practicing 154–55
predicate 156
preschool classrooms: deaf children in 26; emergent literacy in 104; vocabulary assessments in 209
primary language acquisition: in classrooms 24–25; from peers 27–28; in schools 24
print: deaf characters in 106; in emergent literacy 104; English as second language via *see* English as second language via print; preschool classroom exposure to 104
print-to-sign mapping task 88–89
probabilistic thinking 91
Progressivists 8
PSE 25
psycholinguistically accessible language 102
public education 8
Public Law 94-142 13

racism 8
reading 91–92; American Sign Language and 81–82, 84–85, 107, 175–77, 179–80; auditory activation and 79;

248 Index

child's understanding of 104; dialogic
approach to 180; foreign language
improvements through 74; high-
achieving deaf readers 84–87; learning a
language through 89–90; as learning a
new language 101; learning to read 101;
shared 105; strategies for 84–87; syntax
for 85, 88
reading aloud 104, 107, 140
reading comprehension 175–76
reading instruction: American Sign
Language and 175–77, 179–80; in
Bedrock Literacy Curriculum 135,
138–42; English phonological system
used for 134
Rehabilitation Act of 1973 13
residential schools: abuse at 12; African-
American students in 23; American Sign
Language exposure in 22–23; Bell's
support for 9; black students in 23;
during Civil War 6; classrooms of
24–25; deaf children of deaf parents in
27; in deaf community formation 22;
deaf peers in 24, 27; deaf teachers at 24;
description of 4–5; education in 23; in
Greece 114; identity development in
106; for Native Americans 8; native-
signing peers in 28; newspapers printed
at 9, 11; oralism in 23; pedagogical shifts
in 11; physical abuse at 12; primary
language acquisition in 24; resistance by
9; sexual abuse at 12; sign language in 6,
22, 24; teachers at 9, 24; *see also* school(s)
RIT *see* Rochester Institute of Technology
Roberts, Ed 231
Rochester Institute of Technology 12
Roosevelt, Franklin Delano 10–11
Roosevelt, Theodore 9
rote learning 232
Roth, Jackie 232

sandwiching 83
Santa Fe/New York City Template
153–54
scaffolding 91
school(s): normalcy models in 235;
practicing in 154–55; primary language
acquisition in 24; *see also* residential
schools
school newspapers: decline during Great
Depression 11; editors of 11–12;
printing of 9, 11
Second Great Awakening 5–6

semantic activation 79
semiotic circuit 187–88
sexual abuse 12
SF/NYC *see* Santa Fe/New York City
Template
shared reading 105
Sicard, Abbe Roch-Ambroise 4
Sign First 121
sign language(s): advantages of, for deaf
children 81; age of onset 18; black
students' use of 9; discouragement of
36–37; early exposure to 208–9,
213–14; in educational settings 37; first
exposure to 18, 20, 108, 208–9; as first
language 113–14; history of 199, 233;
iconicity in 18, 36–41; lack of exposure
to 113; learning benefits of 227;
Linguistic Society of America
recognition of 36; motion events in
49–52; oralism versus 8–9; recognition
of, as "full-fledged languages" 36; in
residential schools 6, 22, 24;
socioemotional growth affected by 113;
spoken language and 36, 39, 211–13,
218, 225–26; Stokoe's work with 12,
199; verbs of motion 49–52, 57; visuo-
spatial modality of 39; vocabulary
development in 208–11;
written language and 139;
see also American Sign Language;
Greek Sign Language
sign language acquisition: in deaf children
of deaf parents 17–21, 27–28, 56, 113; in
deaf children of hearing parents 19–21;
iconicity in 38; literacy development
benefits of 113; from peers 27–29;
research on 37–39, 218; spoken
language acquisition versus 36; timeline
for 17–18
sign language assessment: ASL Expressive
Skills Test 221–22; ASL Receptive Skills
Test 219–20, 222; comprehensiveness of
219; description of 217–18; purposes of
218–19, 225
sign language interpreters: in classrooms
25–26; studies of 25–26
Sign Order Comprehension task 202–3
Signed Stories 108
signing books 121–24
signwriting systems 82
Sigorney, Lydia 3
Simple View of Reading 101
Singleton, Jenny 201

SIWI *see* Strategic and Interactive Writing Instruction
social interaction, for learning of second language 74–76
social learning 74
Social Security Act 11
Solomon, Andrew 232
"sound symbolism" 40, 42
South African Sign Language 88
Spanish sign language 209
spatial attention 61
speech sounds 41
spelling: Bedrock Literacy Curriculum practice of 135–38; fingerspelling for 138
spoken language: executive functions and 68; iconicity in 40–41; linear organization of 152; sign language and 36, 39, 211–13, 218, 225–26; written language and 125
spoken language acquisition: identity development and 106; sign language acquisition versus 36; timeline for 17–18
St. John's School for the Deaf 12
Stokoe, William 12, 199
Strategic and Interactive Writing Instruction 178, 180
structural mapping theory 40
subtitling, enhanced 90
Supalla, Sam 201
Supalla, Ted 201–2
superordinate precision 178
sustained attention: in cochlear implant children 63–64; continuous performance test of 62; description of 61; as temporal attention 61
sustained visual attention: auditory scaffolding hypothesis regarding 66; biopsychosocial systems theory of 67; connectome disease hypothesis of 66–67; in deaf children 62–65; description of 61; division-of-labor hypothesis regarding 65–66
SVR *see* Simple View of Reading
Sweden 114
Synonyms subtest, of American Sign Language Assessment Instrument 203–4, 209–10, 212
syntax 85, 88

talk, vocabulary growth and 103
teacher(s): cultural influences on 235; identity development facilitation by 106–7; linguistic responsivity of 26; in preschool settings 26; at residential schools 9; as role models 106; therapeutic language approach by 25–26; training programs for 132; *see also* deaf teachers
teacher education programs 234
teletype 204
Terry, Nathaniel 3
Test of English as a Foreign Language 74
Texas School for the Deaf 9
text-based literacy approach 101
Thailand 28
The Learning Center for the Deaf 200, 202, 205
TLC *see* The Learning Center for the Deaf
TOEFL *see* Test of English as a Foreign Language
Top-Down reading model 139
transliteration 140
trilingualism 14
Turkish sign language 209

UDL *see* Universal Design for Learning
unbound morphemes 35
Universal Design for Learning 116

VAP *see* Verb Agreement Production
Veditz, George W. 199
Verb Agreement Production 202
verbs of location 53
verbs of motion: description of 48; in large-scale space 49–50; motion events within 51–57; in signed languages 49–52, 57; in small-scale space 49–50; studies of 52–57
Verbs of Motion Production Assessment 202
vertical transmission 106
"video printer" 205
vigilance 61–62
Virginia School for the Deaf 6
visual attention: compensation hypothesis of 61; sustaining of 62; temporal aspects of 61–62
visual basis for literacy model: description of 99; schematic diagram of 100
visual spatial attention 61
visually based literacy 99–100
VMPA *see* Verbs of Motion Production Assessment
vocabulary: acquisition of 208; American Sign Language Assessment Instrument assessment of 208–14; Bedrock Literacy

250 Index

Curriculum development of 135–38; development of, in sign language 208–11; growth of, talk effects on 103; long-term memory storage of 136–37
vocabulary assessment: description of 208; MacArthur-Bates Communicative Developmental Inventory for 209
vocabulary tests 208
VOLs *see* verbs of location
VOM *see* verbs of motion
Wadsworth, Daniel 3
War of 1812 4
whole child approach 99
whole object constraint 75
women, in National Deaf-Mute College 7
word(s): composition of 90; morphological awareness for learning 90
word learning: communicative intent in 75–76; comprehensible input in 75

word lists 136
Works Progress Administration program 11
World War I 10
World War II 10
writing: American Sign Language proficiency and 178, 180–81; dual route theory of 79; superordinate precision in 178
writing development 177–78
writing instruction: in Bedrock Literacy Curriculum 135, 142–46; Strategic and Interactive Writing Instruction 178
written language: American Sign Language for learning of 103–4; communicative access as means of learning 103; linear organization of 152; signed language and 139; spoken language and 125

Zinser, Elisabeth A. 13

Printed in the United States
By Bookmasters